A WELL REGULATED MILITIA

A WELL REGULATED MILITIA

THE BATTLE OVER GUN CONTROL

WILLIAM WEIR

Archon Books 1997

First published 1997 as an Archon Book,
an imprint of The Shoe String Press, Inc.,
North Haven, Connecticut 06473.

Library of Congress Cataloging-in-Publication Data
Weir, William, 1928–
  A well regulated militia: the battle over gun control/
by William Weir.
      p.   cm.
  Includes bibliographical references and index.
  ISBN 0-208-02423-9 (alk. paper)
  1. Gun control — United States.   2. Firearms — Law
and legislation — United States.   3. United States —
Constitutional law — Amendments--2nd.   I. Title.
HV7436.W45   1996
363.3'3'0973—dc20   96-16147
                                                              CIP

The paper in this publication meets the minimum
requirements of American National Standard for
Information Sciences—Permanence of Paper for
Printed Library Materials, ANSI Z39.48-1984. ⊚

Printed in the United States of America

AUTHOR'S NOTE

The author is a member of Handgun Control, Inc. He is also a member of the National Rifle Association. As readers of this book will quickly see, he finds some things to admire in each organization, but far, far more to deplore. Needless to say, he has not received any funding from either group or from any advocacy group involved in the gun control controversy. Any money that has changed hands between the author and HCI or the NRA has moved from his hands to theirs, mostly as membership fees. It has been worth it, however, to keep abreast of the garbage these groups are unloading on the American people.

For Alison, Joan, and Bill

■ CONTENTS

ACKNOWLEDGMENTS

This book could not have been written without the help of many, many people. A good number of those people would not agree with its conclusions. Even more would take issue with various parts of the book. All, however, were unfailingly friendly and helpful.

Among those particularly helpful were Shawn Taylor Zelman, communications coordinator for Handgun Control, Inc.; Jennifer Jackson of the Coalition to Stop Gun Violence; and the librarian at the NRA's Institute for Legislative Action (whose name I unfortunately did not get). Mary Jo Hoeksema, legislative assistant in the office of Congresswoman Rosa DeLauro, was quite helpful. So were staffers in the office of Sen. Howard Metzenbaum (whose names I regret I also failed to get), even though their boss had just announced his retirement, and they were looking for new jobs. Clerks at the Bureau of Justice Statistics and the Federal Bureau of Investigation were well informed and moved swiftly to send any information requested. The recordkeepers at both of these organizations are admirably thorough. As always, the staffs of the Connecticut library system were able to find about any book I wanted.

Many ordinary citizens from all walks of life helped, too. Among them were Kent and Janice Hadley of Divide, Pennsylvania; Mike Cohen of Guilford, Connecticut; and Bill Davis and Daniel Sheehan of the Romero Institute of Santa Barbara, California.

Special thanks must go to Jim Thorpe, late president of The Shoe String Press, who more or less inspired this book, and to his widow, Diantha, who, in spite of a sea of troubles, saw it through all the processes of publication.

Special thanks, too, are due my brother, George, not only because he provided and set up the computer system used to write this book, but for his information about Switzerland, its people, and its militia system. George spent several years counseling the insurance gnomes of Zurich about the world of bits and bytes.

My wife, Anne, took time from her busy schedule as a registrar of voters, a municipal commission chair, and board member of several organizations to read every chapter and make valuable comments.

Guilford, Connecticut
May 26, 1996

▌INTRODUCTION

Now that the Cold War is over, there seems to be general agreement that crime is one of the most pressing problems facing our country. When people speak of the crime problem, they usually include two slightly different but related issues—drug control and gun control.

About drug control, most Americans—unfortunately—think that what is needed is more of what we've been doing for the last 70 or so years. (Those interested in a different point of view should see my previous book, *In the Shadow of the Dope Fiend: America's War on Drugs*, Archon, 1995.)

There is no such agreement on gun control. Instead, we have two factions, the gun lobby and the anti-gun lobby, figuratively—and sometimes literally—screaming at each other at the top of their lungs. The "debate" between these factions is really no such thing. Each starts from articles of faith it believes to be self-evident but that are completely inconceivable to the other side.

The gun lobby, for example, idolizes the Second Amendment to the U.S. Constitution: "A well regulated Militia, being necessary to the security of a free State, the right of the people to keep and bear Arms shall not be infringed." The gun lobby holds that the amendment means that any restriction on gun ownership, even a short waiting period before buying a pistol, is as gross a violation of the Constitution as censoring newspapers. The anti-gun lobby, on the other hand, says the first clause of the amendment, which it accuses its opponents of ignoring, means only that the states can keep National Guard units.[1]

The anti-gun lobby believes that guns are intrinsically evil. The more guns to be found in a society, the more murders and suicides there will be, but guns in "civilian" hands are useless for defense.[2] (That there is an inherent contradiction in that belief seems not to have occurred to them.) The anti-gun lobby can present mountains of statistics to back up its belief. The gun lobby believes that the same guns the anti-gunners excoriate are the defenders of national and personal virtue. Guns are needed to prevent the development of domestic tyranny and to repulse foreign invaders. Guns are also necessary so that citizens can defend themselves in an increasingly crime-ridden world. (Although the existence of guns makes some crime possible.) The gun lobby, too, offers reams of statistics.

The gun lobby makes no distinctions about which guns are most suitable for the noble tasks mentioned above.[3] The anti-gun lobby, however, periodically singles out particular types of "devil guns" for special loathing. We'll discuss why a bit later.

There is a grain of truth in all the claims of the gun lobby and the anti-gun lobby. But it's a very small grain. The statistics each side presents are sometimes simply imaginary. More often, they are based on grotesquely flawed surveys and laughably biased studies. Both lobbies manage to get their "facts" publicized regularly in the news media. There are criminologists, sociologists, and lawyers trying to set the record straight, but the academic journals in which they publish don't reach 1 percent of the public that absorbs the lies each side gets into the daily papers and television news programs.

Each side in the "debate" stereotypes the other. To the anti-gunners, the gun lobby supporters are at best anachronisms. Anti-gun lobbyists have at various times characterized their opponents as thugs, violent and mentally unstable characters, and sexually inadequate males.[4] To the gunners, the anti-gunners are gun grabbers, liberal bleeding hearts, and, until recently, Communists. (Since the end of the Cold War, the Communists have become "jack-booted Fascists," but no more likable.)[5]

Osha Gray Davidson quotes Sarah Brady, chair of Handgun Control, Inc., the largest anti-gun lobby organization, on James Jay Baker, at one time the chief lobbyist for the National Rifle Association. She told Davidson she couldn't believe Baker was a "true believer" because he seemed so personable. Baker, however, said his personal beliefs are more "hard-line" than his employer's.[6] The irony of Brady's statement is that although she's also remarkably personable, she is every bit as true a believer as Baker. Each side not only tells the public that its opponents have horns, it expects to see them.

The trouble with all this is that the propaganda of fanatics makes a poor basis for public policy. And make no mistake, the leaders of each lobby are fanatics—well-tailored, polite, and charming fanatics. Gun-owner rights and gun elimination are their religions, and the strength of their beliefs may not be shaken by objective fact or logic.

The volume of their advocacy is deafening. If the public gets only those "facts" that the advocates present, the country faces several dangers. One has already begun—a serious polarization of the population.

In addition to the small groups of shouting advocates, you now have armed groups who call themselves militias and seem to be united only by opposition to gun control. These "militias" are, of course, a very small segment of the American people, most of whom still don't seem to care much about gun control one way or the other. Trying hard to change that indifference are powerful politicians, including the president of the United States and most of the news media, who are trying to sell gun control. Gun lobbyists tend to see a conspiracy here (many of the "militia" are convinced of it), but it really seems to be another manifestation of an old American tradition: when a problem appears, someone suggests a course of action that is cheap and easy (for the majority). Because the action is cheap and easy, it attracts support. Because it attracts support, politicians and other leaders jump on the bandwagon. This has been the history of movements as diverse as William Jennings Bryan's "free silver" crusade and Prohibition. The problem in this case is crime. As with Prohibition, the prescription has brought no relief. Further, as we'll see, applying more of the same medicine is likely to bring nothing but more pain.

Because the anti-gun lobby has demonstrated far better public relations sense than has the gun lobby, there are two other, and more serious, dangers. One is constitutional. The greatest danger in this category is not the potential loss of the citizen militia mentioned in the Second Amendment. The militia has been allowed—and, as we'll see, with the connivance of the NRA—to drift into near-oblivion. Its effectiveness in time of war has been seriously jeopardized. It is potentially far more effective militarily than its critics say, but it is by no means in a class with the militias of Switzerland and Israel.

The greatest danger is to the Constitution itself. There is a process for amending the Constitution, but it's easier to change interpretations of the wording. For example, although the Fourth Amendment says searches require a warrant issued "upon probable cause, supported by oath or affirmation, and particularly describing the place to be searched, and the persons or things to be seized," police can stop a car and search it if they have "probable cause" but no warrant. As there is no description of the persons or things to be seized, such a search is a fishing expedition.

Modifying the Constitution through interpretation is not, of course, a new activity. It goes back at least as far as the Louisiana Purchase in 1803. In this century, the interstate commerce clause has been stretched to lengths undreamed-of by James Madison and his fellow framers. But stretching is one thing, and contradicting an established meaning that, viewed in its historical context, is crystal-clear, is something else. That appears to be the fate of the Second Amendment. The amendment, aptly called "The Embarrassing Second Amendment" by Sanford Levinson in the *Yale Law Journal*, is not merely slighted but almost ignored in most standard commentaries on the Constitution.[7] That's because there is no way to justify the currently popular interpretation.

Of course, as Oliver Wendell Holmes told his fellow Supreme Court justices, "The Constitution is the Constitution, regardless of what we say it is." But as Mr. Dooley (Finley Peter Dunne's philosophical bartender) said, "The Court follows the election returns." If the Constitution can be contradicted by propaganda-induced interpretation, it's no longer the keystone of our liberties we learned it was in school.

The constitutional problems, although serious, are long-range. The other problems posed by ill-considered gun laws will affect us more quickly. And they could be so serious that the constitutional questions will seem merely academic. Briefly, unless we're careful, we could pass legislation that will legally disarm everyone but the criminal. Later in this book, you'll see why criminals will *always* have guns. You'll also see incontrovertible evidence that an armed citizenry does counter crime and does not significantly increase homicide. And you'll also see how gun prohibition, or merely handgun prohibition, would increase crime and create a major new criminal activity.

By now, the reader will have guessed that this book contains much that is critical of the anti-gun position. It is by no means a brief for the pro-gun side, though—neither its positions nor its tactics. Harlon Carter, the moving spirit of the modern NRA, was once asked while testifying before a congressional subcommittee if he would "allow those convicted violent felons, mentally deranged people, violently addicted to narcotics people to have guns, rather than to have the screening process for the honest people like yourselves?"

"That," Carter replied calmly, "is a price we pay for freedom."[8] And that, friends, is the voice of a fanatic.

Conflicting claims will be analyzed and compared with facts that have been drowned out by all the shouting. Finally, some suggestions for sensible gun policy will be presented.

First, though, let's take a look at the history of gun control. It has a long history—longer than most people realize. In a sense, it goes back farther than guns themselves. Understanding the history of the relationship between government and armed citizens in the Western World will also make clear just what that "well regulated militia" really is.

PART I

THE MILITIA—
WHAT'S THAT?

CHAPTER 1

AN OLD, OLD PROBLEM

WEAPONS CONTROL THROUGH THE AGES

To many people today, the effort to limit the availability of weapons to the general population is one more step in the continuous progress of humankind toward true civilization. Most people, whether they agree with that premise or not, see gun control as a problem of our times. It seems as characteristic of the 1990s as Prohibition was of the 1920s and the abolition of slavery was of the 1850s and 1860s.

Actually, the effort to control popular access to weapons has a long history. It's been a problem since long before there were guns. Rulers have always preferred that they—not their subjects—have the tools of power. Those tools may be chariots or castles or machine guns or main battle tanks. And at certain periods of history, it's been easy for an emperor or a handful of dukes and counts to hold all the power. An ancient Egyptian peasant could no more afford a light chariot, a brace of fast horses, and a superb composite bow than a modern factory worker could afford his own helicopter gunship. When the dominant weapons on an era's battlefields were expensive or complicated or required a team to operate them, civilian weapons control was simple. And life was easy for royalty and nobles.

But when the dominant weapons were cheap and easy to use and could be fielded in great quantity, the situation was quite different. When heavily armored cavalry dominated Europe in the Middle Ages, a comparatively few fighting men decided the fate of nations. Full armor was fabulously expensive, and the horses that could charge carrying an armored man even more so. Knights made up only a tiny minority of any nation. But the key weapon in evolving tactical systems was not

3

always expensive. In the middle nineteenth century, the rifle was the key weapon. It outranged the smoothbore artillery of the time and made cavalry charges obsolete. Rifles were cheap, and the more riflemen a nation could field, the stronger it was. In medieval times, governors tried to prevent the governed from arming themselves "beyond their station." In the middle of the last century, many governments put no such limits on their citizenry. If the citizens were familiar with arms, they would be better soldiers if called upon to defend their country. On the continent of Europe, governments often developed riflemen by drafting all young men and keeping them in reserve units for years after their regular military service. That discouraged revolution (although revolts happened anyway), but it wasn't cheap. Sometimes, in the inexpensive-weapon eras, governments would expect citizens to buy their own battlefield weapons, keep them at home, and practice with them regularly. That was the cheapest way to have an effective army ready for any emergency. A fully armed populace never made rulers comfortable. But if the rulers could not—and their enemies could—raise regiments of armor-cleaving halberdiers or masses of musketeers, they would have been a lot less comfortable.

ARMAMENTS AND GOVERNMENT

Not surprisingly, the way weapons are distributed in a nation has always had a strong effect on its government. In his *Politics*, Aristotle says that in early times, Greek government was aristocratic because warfare was dominated by horsemen. The mass of people, who couldn't afford horses, had no clout in government.[1] Greek city-states became democratic after the infantry phalanx was developed.[2] Individual prowess, as displayed by the Homeric heroes, was useless against a moving wall of armor bristling with spears. At first, kings led the citizen-soldiers. But a phalanx is not adapted to tactical surprises and brilliant maneuvers. Leadership played little part in phalangial tactics; the job was done by the individual spear-carriers. So kings, too, were phased out. Each citizen kept his armor, spear, and sword at home. Each was legally—and to a large extent, actually—the equal of the next.

The same system was used in early republican Rome. Citizens *had to* keep armor and weapons at home.[3] Later, the Second Punic War drove home the need for long-service armies, and the imperial expansion that began immediately afterward confirmed the need.[4] Armies became professional. Then leadership of an army became the main route to political power in Rome. Ambitious generals didn't want a lot of armed civilians messing up their plans. Serious armament—helmets, shields, corselets and the distinctive Roman throwing spear, the *pilum*—was issued by commanding generals and no longer available to mere citizens. The soldier's armor belonged to the army and was reissued for generations. Things stayed that way through most of the empire. Citizens could keep clubs and swords for personal protection. In the Gospels, the Apostle Peter used his sword to cut off the ear of one of Jesus' attackers in the Garden of Olives,[5] and on another occasion Jesus advised, "Let him who has no sword sell his tunic and buy one."[6]

THE RISE OF THE MILITIA

As the Western Roman Empire slowly dissolved into anarchy, each freeman armed himself with whatever he could afford, and every slave who had a chance armed himself, too (and so became free).[7] Every freeman, Roman or German, was a warrior. Rich Romans and barbarian war-band leaders sometimes armed followers who looked like promising warriors. Most men, though, provided their own battle equipment. Armies of the Dark Ages usually included everyone from mailed horsemen to unarmored peasants with clubs. Charles Martel and Charlemagne issued edicts requiring all men in the Frankish kingdom to appear at feudal musters bearing specific types of weapons and armor.[8]

The Frankish kingdom, pounded by barbarians on all sides and torn apart by powerful and ambitious nobles, eventually broke up in the ninth century. The idea of requiring every freeman to provide himself with decent weapons to defend the commonwealth did not die, however. In 1181, Henry II of England revived it. His Assize of Arms specified that each freeman having goods worth ten marks was to serve in a mail vest and iron skullcap and carry a spear. Those with less property would wear quilted armor instead of mail. All those who held the amount of land called a "knight's fee," whether they were knights or not, would have to show up with helmet, mail shirt, shield, and spear. Jews, being ineligible for the aristocracy, were ordered to surrender any metal armor they had, no matter what their wealth was.[9] Henry's assize, with different classes armed differently, was consistent with the aristocratic society of the time. It also meant, though, that all freemen, now called "the militia," shared in the defense of the realm.

The history of the English militia is important if we are to understand the Second Amendment. When the framers of the U.S. Constitution used the term "militia" they were referring to a concept centuries-old in the English-speaking world. France, Spain, and Portugal, three other countries that were to play a leading part in the colonization of the New World, also had viable militias in early medieval times. Those forces, though, were allowed to deteriorate as nobles, then kings, became increasingly powerful.

In 1242, Henry III issued a new Assize of Arms to update the militia. Henry also gave the militia a new responsibility. As well as defending against foreign invaders and insurrectionists, it was to aid in keeping the peace. Under the new assize, anyone with an annual income of 15 pounds or more had to come mounted as well as armed and armored. Those with incomes of between two and five pounds had to appear with bows and arrows.[10] That provision was to have a considerable influence on both the military history of Europe and the government of England. The longbow was hardly a new weapon; similar bows had been used in Europe since the late Stone Age. The tactics the English evolved for it, though, combined with their development of masses of highly skilled archers, turned the longbow into a weapon of great power.[11] Archery put England on a more democratic course than its continental neighbors. On the Continent, the peasantry was gradually disarmed to make life more comfortable for the nobility. For a while, the French tried to form a corps of archers to fight the English on their own terms. After the fourteenth-century peasant revolt, the *Jacquerie*, however, the terrified nobility forced the king to eliminate the archers.[12]

There was a militia in France, but it was poorly trained and even more poorly armed (not a matter of great importance, because the weapons were stored in armories except during war). While the nobility retained weapons and also the right to hunt, by 1726 the militia was, for all practical purposes, dead.[13] In 1475, an Englishman, Sir John Fortescue, writing about the French peasantry said, "Thai gon crokyd, and ben feble, not able to fight, nor to defend the realm; nor thai haue wepen, nor money to bie them wepen withall." There were no French fighting men, Fortescue charged, except the nobles. The French king, therefore, had to hire Scots, Spaniards, Germans, and other foreigners to fill his armies.[14]

Jean Bodin, a French political theorist of the seventeenth century, argued that a monarchy would court disaster if it armed the masses:

> The slave asks only to be unfettered; once removed from his shackles, he desires liberty; once freed, he asks the right of the bourgeois; from the bourgeois, he wishes to be made a magistrate; when he is in the highest rank of magistrates, he wants to be king; once king, he wants to be the only king; finally, he wants to be God.[15]

Bodin thought that the state should rely on the nobility for military power or, failing that, a professional army. Although the nobility had been consistent troublemakers, most recently in the War of the Fronde, Louis XIV did call out the nobles in 1674. A general who inspected the assembled vassals urged the king never to call them out again, as they were "a body incapable of action and more likely to stir up disorders than to remedy troubles."[16] France also decided not to rely on freelance mercenaries of the type that had ravaged Germany during the Thirty Years War. It opted for a professional army and prohibited arms ownership by commoners. Death was the penalty prescribed for anyone carrying unauthorized weapons.

In the meantime, the English militia continued to develop. Forty-three years after Henry III's Assize of Arms, Edward I further democratized English society by ordering *all men*, not just freemen, to have arms.[17] This decree, the Statute of Winchester, was to remain in effect until the late sixteenth century. The statute also set up night watches which would be staffed by the militia and ordered all men to pursue fleeing criminals.

In the sixteenth century, Queen Mary, Henry VIII's elder daughter, issued, with her husband, Philip II of Spain, a four-page militia statute, listing in great detail the equipment each man should have, depending on his wealth. Both bows and guns were mentioned.[18]

The most important duty of the militia was the defense of their home counties. Their officers were the gentry of their localities, and they were led by the county sheriff, or later, the lord lieutenant of the county. Some men were accepted into special units called "trained bands," where they were to get specialized military training. The most training the others got was shooting arrows at targets after church services on Sundays and holidays. Members of the militia could be called up by the king to serve outside their counties—but not outside the country—for periods of up to 40 days. When outside the county, they would be paid by the king. Otherwise, they were paid from county funds. Officials called commissioners of array, usually justices of the peace, chose the militiamen who would follow the king away from home. Members of the trained bands were theoretically needed to defend their counties, so they were not called. The trained bands became a haven for those who wanted to avoid fighting.[19]

The idea that an armed militia is a guardian of liberty became rooted in English political philosophy. Niccolò Machiavelli's writings, translated in the sixteenth and seventeenth centuries, were a strong influence. J.G.A. Pocock, a modern historian, asserts that "the rigorous equation of arms bearing with civic capacity is one of Machiavelli's most enduring legacies to later political thinkers."[20] Sir Walter Raleigh said a tyrant always tries "to unarm his people of weapons, money, and all means whereby they resist his power."[21] Another sixteenth century political thinker, Sir Thomas More, had both men and women in Utopia trained with weapons so they could defend their country and their homes.[22]

ROYAL REACTION

Some kings were uneasy with an armed populace. In 1328, Edward III forbade any person "great or small" from going armed in a public place.[23] That was in an era when every man wore a knife or dagger and almost every man carried a quarterstaff. A succession of court decisions watered down the statute so that only those who went armed in a way "terrifying to the good people of the land" were liable to punishment. In the Middle Ages, as today, there were also municipal attempts to restrict weapons in the hands of citizens. In the thirteenth century, for instance, the City of London prohibited any school "to teach the art of fence" within the city walls.[24]

Although English panegyrists from the fifteenth to the twentieth century have written about how their country was defended by "free-born Englishmen" from all walks of life, things weren't quite so democratic. All males between 16 and 60 belonged to the militia, true, but the trained bands were chosen from the more well-to-do. So was the *posse comitatus* ("power of the county"), the men called out by sheriffs to enforce the law. And the trained bands and the posses, rather than the militia at large, were what the monarchy relied on to keep internal order.[25] After the Reformation, Catholics were barred from bearing arms. There was an exception for Catholic gentlemen, who might possess "a sword, a case of pistols, and a gun."[26]

The Catholic Irish were totally disarmed. English officers of army units refused to train Irish Catholic soldiers in marksmanship because, as one officer put it, "within a week there would not be one living landlord left in Ireland."[27] After their rebellions in 1715 and 1745, the Scottish Highlanders, too, were totally disarmed. They were also forbidden to wear tartans or speak Gaelic, and the many Catholics among them were forbidden to practice their religion.[28] Life in the Highlands became so intolerable that many Scots fled the country. Thousands sailed to America. Many who couldn't afford that trip went to Ireland, which was something like jumping out of the fire into the frying pan.[29]

Before that, the absolutist Tudors tried to limit popular armament. Henry VIII, ostensibly to crack down on criminals, prohibited anyone with an income of less than 300 pounds a year from owning a handgun with a barrel less than a yard long or a crossbow. (In those days, and often in Britain today, "handgun" meant a gun that could be held by the hands to fire, as opposed to one, like a heavy machine gun, that must be fired on a mount. In the United States, it usually means a pistol.) As we'll see, the idea of limiting weapons to the wealthy is a recurrent one, variations of which are still appearing in the United States. When war with France threatened, Henry lowered the property qualifications so he could field more crossbows and guns. When peace came, the qualifications were reinstated. A new war with France threatened. Henry then revoked the order entirely and wished his "loving subjects practiced and exercised in the feat of shooting handguns and hackbuts."[30] The game laws, though, forbade owners of these weapons to hunt with them unless they had an income of at least 100 pounds.[31]

After Henry, his daughter, Mary, zeroed in on sidearms. "Divers naughty and insolent persons," she wrote, had been trying to make "quarrels, riots and frays. . . . and for the accomplishment of their naughty purposes and quarrels have caused swords and rapiers to be made to a much greater length than heretofore hath been accustomed or is decent to use and wear; and with said weapons do use and wear gauntlets and vambraces [arm guards] and bucklers with long pikes in them, contrary to the ancient usage of this realm."[32] Such naughty persons who carried anything but "their common swords, daggers, and bucklers" would lose their weapons and suffer fines and imprisonment.

The Stuarts, who followed the Tudors, were equally absolutist and tried to eliminate weapons in the hands of the people by passing a series of game laws.

Trouble between Parliament and the Stuart monarchs had been brewing for a long time. Actually, it had been brewing before the Tudors. The people, backed by the militia, had become increasingly independent, causing friction with whoever held the monarchy. The friction was not very evident under the Tudors. That dynasty benefited from the public revulsion at the bloodshed and turmoil of the Wars of the Roses that had brought it to power. The Tudors also had an innate sense of what was later called public relations. Getting along with their subjects had never been a Stuart strong point. The trouble was that both the Stuarts and the Tudors believed in their hearts (such as they were) in the divine right of kings, although the Tudors were able to win popular support by seeming to defend England against foreigners.

During the reign of Charles I, Parliament, which was controlled by the landed gentry, claimed that it had the right to regulate the militia.

"By God, not for an hour!" the king roared.[33] Judging from the history of the militia, he was probably right. The rural magnates who officered the militia, however, were closer to the people than the king was. So were the urban capitalists who led the London militia.[34] The Londoners asserted their independence, and a royal army gathered and marched on London. The royalists were met by 20,000 London militiamen. They backed down. The English Civil War began, and Charles I lost his head.

The Protectorate, under the "Protector," Oliver Cromwell, made people look back nostalgically to the monarchy. Cromwell burdened the English people with more regulations than they had ever had before, and he enforced them with a standing army. After Cromwell died, Parliament and the army, then the army alone, were the real rulers of England. They intruded in English life even more than Cromwell. In 1659, for instance, all householders in the country were required to submit lists of all lodgers, and all weapons and ammunition, in their houses.[35] Weapons were seized from "any Popish Recusant, or other person that hath been in arms against the Parliament, or that have adhered to the enemies thereof, or any other person whom the Commissioners shall judge dangerous to the Peace of the Commonwealth."[36]

When Charles II was restored to the monarchy in 1660, he took measures to prevent another revolt. He first ordered all gunsmiths to report all sales of guns. Then he banned the importation of guns. The Militia Act of 1662 confirmed the king's sole control of the militia. It also authorized the king's agents "to search for and seize all arms in the custody or possession of any person or persons who the said lieutenants or any two or more of their deputies shall judge dangerous to the peace of the kingdom."[37]

That didn't establish enough royal control. Despite orders, the militia refused to attack Dissenters. Militiamen deserted in droves. Sir Henry Capel, a member of Parliament, told his fellow MPs, "Our security is the militia: that will defend us and never conquer us."[38]

The culmination of Stuart disarmament efforts was the Game Act of 1671. The act barred 95 percent of the population from hunting and prohibited nonhunters from owning guns.[39] To make the law effective, daytime searches of the homes of suspects were allowed. Gamekeepers on large estates had the power to make the searches. If weapons were found, the culprit could be brought before a justice of the peace—usually one of the local gentry—who could confiscate his weapons. Historian Joyce Malcolm points out that this was probably an attempt by the gentry to regain control of "the power of the sword" the king controlled through the Militia Act.[40] James II, however, used it in an attempt to disarm his opponents.

If the law had been enforced effectively, this "game law" would have deprived England of its militia. That was the idea. Sir William Blackstone, the famous commentator on English law, later wrote that "the prevention of popular insurrections and resistance to government by disarming the bulk of the people, is a reason oftener meant than avowed by the makers of the forest and game laws."[41]

After passage of Charles's Game Act, the militia declined to turn their guns over to the royal officers. And the royal officers—probably wisely—refused to conduct many searches. Charles's brother, James II, noted that "a great many persons not qualified by law" were still keeping guns in their houses. He ordered a "strict search to be made for such muskets or guns and to seize them and safely keep them till further order."[42] But in 1686, a year after James took the throne, and after a certain Sir John Knight was arrested for carrying weapons, a judicial decision held that the people had the right to "ride armed for their security."[43]

With the militia actively hostile, James attempted to kill it through neglect. He simply refused to call any militia musters. At the same time, he enlisted a volunteer force of Royalists, then raised a standing army.

THE BILL OF RIGHTS

Eventually, James's enemies invited William of Orange to replace him.[44] James gathered an army to oppose the Dutchman, but it deserted without losing a life. The parliamentary leaders had already arranged with William that his would be a limited monarchy. William was no democrat, but he knew a good deal when he saw it, so he signed the 1689 Bill of Rights granting his Protestant subjects the right to keep arms for their defense and for militia duty. Malcolm points out that militia service through most of English history was considered an onerous civic duty. When the authorities began confiscating their weapons, however, Englishmen suddenly saw weapons ownership as a cherished right. But even in the "Bill of Rights," there was a catch-22. The Protestants were allowed to have weapons "suitable to their conditions and as allowed by law."[45] The modern Mexican Constitution has a similar provision, which has resulted in just about every type of gun being illegal for just about every Mexican citizen to possess. In England, the law tended to recognize only "gentlemen" as being suitable to own guns.[46]

According to Thomas Macaulay, historian and essayist, Britain's Parliament grew stronger, while continental parliaments declined, because the British monarchy's power depended on the militia—the general population—which Parliament represented. The militia, Macaulay said, provided the people with "the power of the sword. . . . The legal check [on the monarchy] was secondary and auxiliary to what the community held in its own hands."[47]

Earlier, Blackstone called the right to bear arms "the fifth auxiliary right of the subject." He explained that "in cases of national oppression, the nation has very justifiably risen as one man, to vindicate the original contract subsisting between the king and his people."[48]

Macaulay and Blackstone viewed the history of their country through rather rosy glasses. There was no doubt, though, that the English were far better armed than any of their European contemporaries (except the Swiss) and that they had a much more limited monarchy than any in Europe (again excluding the republican Swiss, who had no monarch). It is not unreasonable to suppose that the second condition was at least partially a result of the first.

These events in England were followed closely in the British colonies in North America. The Americans knew that, in spite of all the talk about the natural right to bear arms, that right had been denied outright by the monarch and had at other times been vitiated by game laws and other restrictions. It might also be denied at any time in the future by Parliament, as it had by the Parliament of early Restoration times. Britain had no written constitution, so the will of Parliament was supreme. When they later rejected English rule—and much of English law—the Americans decided against leaving the protection of their rights to the whim of the government in power.[49] They included those rights in a Bill of Rights. The American Bill of Rights was not, like its English namesake, an act of the legislature. It took the form of amendments to the national Constitution, the most basic law of the land. In the United States, the Constitution, not the legislature, is sovereign.

CHAPTER 2

THE MILITIA IN AMERICA

SEA CHANGE

When the first English colonists came to America, they brought their institutions with them, but they quickly adapted them to the conditions they found in the New World. One of those institutions was the militia.

In England, a man's place in the militia was determined, like so many other things, by heredity. The gentry were the officers; the small land holders and hired hands, the enlisted men. The American colonies had a serious shortfall of gentry. No one who enjoyed the good life in England was attracted to life in a virgin forest filled with wild beasts and wild men. There was a short-lived attempt to create an American gentry. The first 105 settlers in Jamestown included 54 who were labeled gentlemen and were expected to be the musket-bearers who would protect the other colonists.[1] There were two drawbacks: (1) the colony couldn't afford to have half its number carrying muskets but doing no other work; (2) in the event of Indian attack, it couldn't afford to have the other half unarmed. The notion that only gentlemen could carry guns quickly vanished. So did the idea that only gentlemen could officer the militia. As a result, the militia—all the men in a colony—elected their officers.

John Smith, a soldier of fortune whose enemies also characterized him as a rogue and a renegade, became captain of the Jamestown militia because he knew more about fighting than any other man in the colony. For a while, he was virtually a military dictator. Miles Standish of Plymouth—"Captain Shrimp" to the other colonists—enjoyed similar prestige. To a stranger, the diminutive Standish, who loved bright red cloaks and became tongue-tied in the presence of a pretty woman, might have seemed a ridiculous figure. But the men of Plymouth elected him captain because he was both brave and devious. He was not afraid to face any number of savage warriors, but he was not above giving troublesome chiefs a roast of pork and stabbing them in the back when they started to eat it.[2]

WAR WITHOUT END

In England, the militia began to decline after the Glorious Revolution. For centuries, England had been in a state of intermittent civil war. After the crowning of William and Mary, however, most English fighting was done abroad. The major exceptions were the Scottish uprisings of 1715 and 1745. Aside from them, there was nothing but a few local riots. The English militia, consequently, had almost nothing to do.

Things were different in America. Warfare with the Indians was endemic from the beginning of the first English colony at Roanoke (now part of North Carolina) in 1585 until the massacre of some 300 Sioux at Wounded Knee, December 29, 1890. Roanoke, known as the "Lost Colony," was probably annihilated by the Indians. In addition to the Indians, there was fighting with England's European rivals, the Spanish, the Dutch, and the French—especially the French. For more than a century, France and England struggled for northern North America. For most of that period, most of the struggling on the English side was done by the colonists, not regular troops from England.

The earliest English colonies were almost military outposts. In 1623, Virginia law required "that men shall not go to work in the ground without their arms and a centinell upon them."[3] The "centinell," under the Martial Laws of Virginia, "shall shoulder his piece, both ends of his match being alight, and his piece charged and primed, and bullets in his mouth, there to stand with careful and waking eye untill such time as his Corporall shall relieve him."[4] The primary weapon in those days was the matchlock musket, which used a slow-burning cord, called a match, to ignite the powder. Targeteers, soldiers armed with sword and shield, were required to also have either a wheel-lock or a flintlock pistol.[5] The wheel-lock, invented about a century after the matchlock, ignited the powder with a shower of sparks caused by the contact of iron pyrites with a spinning steel wheel. Its ignition was faster and more reliable than the flintlock's, but it broke down easily and was expensive. In spite of those disadvantages, quite a few wheel-locks got to America.[6] The colonists wanted the best arms they could get.

Gun ownership was not limited to members of the militia. A Connecticut law, for example, required that all citizens, not just "listed" soldiers of the militia, "always be provided with and have in continual readiness, a well-fixed firelock . . . or other good fire-arms . . . a good sword, or cutlass . . . one pound of powder, four pounds of bullets fit for his gun, and twelve flints."[7]

Every outlying plantation had its commander, usually the owner, who was responsible for its defense. Virginia law specified "that the commander of every plantation take care there be sufficient powder and ammunition within the plantation."[8] In Plymouth in 1632, the colonial legislature decreed "it is further ordered that every freeman or other inhabitant of this colony provide for himself and each under him a sufficient musket and serviceable peece for war and bandeleros [bandoliers] and . . . two pounds of powder and ten pounds of bullets."[9]

The colonists not only had to have guns, they had to carry them. Newport, in what became Rhode Island, had a law requiring that "noe man shall go two miles from the Towne unarmed, eyther with Gunn or Sword; and that none shall come to any public Meeting without his weapon."[10]

As time went on, the colonies became less like military camps, but the militia laws were not ignored. They became more specific.

In 1645, the General Court of the Massachusetts Bay Colony decreed: "It being requisite that all inhabitants within this jurisdiction should endeavor after such armes as may be most useful for their own and the countryes defense, it is therefore ordered that no pieces shalbe allowed for serviceable, in our trained bands, but such as are ether full musket boare, or bastard musket at the least [roughly 12 or 16 gauge], and that none should be under three foote 9 inches, nor any above foure foote 3 inches in length, and that every man have a priming wyre, a worme, and scourer, fit for the boare of his muskett, which we find not required in any former order."[11]

The militia laws did not ban weapons not deemed "serviceable." "Serviceable" weapons, however, were required for drill and regular militia duty. Other guns were often owned for such purposes as hunting. One of the most popular types was the "long fowler," a heavy gun with a barrel up to seven-and-a-half feet long. "Let your piece be long in the barrell; and fear not the weight of it," Edward Winslow of Plymouth advised prospective colonists, "for most of our shooting is from stands."[12] The long fowler was used for long-range shots at ducks and geese traveling the north–south flyways. In time of war, though, it, like all other guns, was pressed into service. Its range and power made it particularly useful for defending forts.

Hunting in America was completely different from hunting in Europe. Here, all game belonged to everyone, not a few favored landowners. Hunting game was a necessity of life in the early colonies. It later became a thriving commercial enterprise. In 1770, more than 800,000 pounds of dressed deer skins were exported from America. Their value was 57,738 pounds sterling.[13] Every American man was a hunter.

One visitor wrote, "There is not a Man born in America that does not understand the Use of firearms and that well. . . . It is almost the First thing they Purchase and take to all the New Settlements and in the Cities you can scarcely find a Lad of 12 years That [does not] go a Gunning."[14] Another said that when a boy became 12, "he then became a fort soldier, and had his port-hole assigned to him. Hunting squirrels, turkeys, and raccoons, soon made him expert in the use of his gun."[15]

NEW WEAPONS, NEW TACTICS, NEW OUTLOOK

By the middle of the seventeenth century, the matchlock had almost disappeared from the American colonies. It was replaced with what contemporaries called firelocks—weapons modern collectors call the snaphaunce, the English lock, the dog lock, the Scandinavian lock, the miquelet lock, or the "true" flintlock, the latest development of the firelock. In England, the matchlock was still standard military equipment as late as 1689. Constant war had forced the Americans to get the latest and best weapons.

Tactics changed, too. In the seventeenth century, the musket and the pike were the main infantry weapons in Europe. In America, though, the Indians didn't form lines and meet pike charge with pike charge. And carrying a 12 to 18-foot spear in dense woods was more than a minor annoyance. The pike quickly disappeared. In Europe, battles were decided by a combination of arms. Infantry held ground and resisted cavalry charges with pike and musket. Cavalry was effective against scattered or disorganized infantry or foot soldiers who were not standing on their feet to level their pikes and load their muskets. Artillery could mow down masses of standing infantry but was almost useless against infantry scattered or taking cover. Consequently, European generals used cavalry to force the enemy's infantry to stand up in formation, then used their artillery to blast the enemy formations. When the enemy infantry was sufficiently blasted, the cavalry and infantry could drive them from the field. Of course, an attack seldom went so smoothly because the enemy's cavalry, artillery, and infantry would be trying to use the same tactics. But that was the idea.

The idea didn't work in America. Artillery was scarce. Moving a cannon through roadless swamps and forests was no easier than dragging a pike through the same terrain. Cavalry was just as scarce. There were a few troopers in early colonial times, but they almost never fought mounted. Horsemen were effective on treeless plains, but there were practically no treeless plains in the eastern third of the continent. By the end of the eighteenth century, roads had improved enough to make artillery practical. Enough land was then under cultivation, especially in the South, to permit a modest revival of cavalry.

In Europe, in the seventeenth century, there was no key weapon. Two inexpensive weapons, the musket and the pike, had to be combined with expensive arms—cavalry and artillery. In America, the musket, supplemented by the sword, and later the bayonet, was supreme. Consequently, the individual armed citizen was supreme. This quirk of military logistics did nothing to hinder the growth of popular government in the American colonies.

THE MILITIA AT WAR

General Charles James Oglethorpe founded Georgia in 1733. Oglethorpe was a humanitarian who hoped to rescue debtors, convicts, and European refugees. To the Spanish, though, he was a thief. They considered Georgia to be part of their colony of Florida. King Philip V ordered his forces to drive the British from Georgia. When the Spanish occupied a fort Oglethorpe had built, the Scottish general invaded Florida. He had 200 men from his Highland regiment, several hundred Indian allies, and 125 South Carolina militia. He attacked St. Augustine, and the Spanish beat him off with heavy losses. As generations of regular officers were later to do, Oglethorpe blamed the militia. The militia blamed Oglethorpe.

All colonial fighting in the New World was not confined to what later became the United States. The English sent expeditions based on their colonies to the West Indies, South America, and Canada. Colonial militia were involved in these campaigns, too.

While Oglethorpe was fighting the Spanish in North America, a British fleet with 3,000 colonial militia attacked the Spanish fortress of Cartagena, in what is now Colombia. That attack fared no better than Oglethorpe's, and then yellow fever wiped out most of the attackers. As usual, regulars and colonials blamed each other.[16] As the regulars were in command, the colonials seem to have had a better case. Oglethorpe salvaged most of his reputation when he ambushed and routed a Spanish invasion force, ending overt hostilities on the southern border.

The militia troops in these, and in later campaigns that involved considerable travel, were really members of volunteer units raised from the militia. The militia proper were home defense troops. They rarely operated more than a day's march from home. Even with that limitation, though, they were able to cause considerable difficulty for colonial enemies like the French and the Indians. And during the Revolution, as we'll see, they neutralized Britain's greatest advantage—sea mobility.

In the north, regulars and militia clashed again over how to capture a fortress. In 1745, a large force of New England militia and a much smaller force of British regulars landed on Cape Breton Island to capture the French fortress of Louisbourg. The expedition was the brainchild of William Shirley, governor of Massachusetts, but the force was commanded, of course, by British regulars. The English commander ordered a direct assault on the fortress. The New Englanders, commanded by William Pepperell, a merchant of Kittery, Maine, thought otherwise.

The French had spent millions fortifying Louisbourg, and the militiamen, not drilled to blind obedience like regulars, saw that an assault would be mass suicide. They refused. The British commander was shocked, but since almost all his infantry were militia, there was nothing he could do. He complained that they "have the highest notions of the Rights, and Libertys, of Englishmen, and indeed are almost levelers, they must know when, how, and of what service they are going upon, and to be Treated in a manner that few Military Bred Gentlemen would condescend to."[17]

The militia knew that the British fleet had command of the sea, and there was no way supplies could reach the fortress by land. There was no need for bloody haste. They captured outlying batteries, chased French cannonballs and fired them back, went fishing when they felt like it, and treated the siege as a big picnic.[18] The disheartened French commander surrendered in six weeks. The victory is commemorated in the name of Louisburg Square on Boston's Beacon Hill and in the name generations of French-Canadians applied to all residents of the thirteen English colonies—*Les Bastonnais*, "the Bostonians."

In 1754, the war Americans call the French and Indian War began in western Pennsylvania when Virginia militia under Major George Washington clashed with French regulars. Washington was forced to retreat, but he returned the next year with a large force of colonial militia and British regulars commanded by British Maj. Gen. Edward Braddock. The force was ambushed and routed near Fort Duquesne. Braddock's handling of the army has long been blamed for the disaster. Equal credit, though, should be given to the skill and bravery of four French junior officers—Captains Daniel de Beaujeu, Jean Dumas, and François de Ligneris, and Lt. Charles de Langlade—who led the vastly outnumbered French and Indian ambushers.[19]

In the war that followed, the militia played a key part. As usual, the regulars criticized them roundly, but with the exception of James Wolfe, hardly covered themselves with glory. In 1758, New England militia under Col. John Bradstreet captured Fort Frontenac, the major supply depot at the head of Lake Ontario, and cut off supplies to Fort Duquesne. Later that year, George Washington and his Virginians joined the Pennsylvania militia, the Royal Americans (a British regular regiment created in America and composed of Americans), other militia units, and a few companies of the Seventy-Seventh Highlanders in a column commanded by Brig. Gen. John Forbes. Forbes's troops took Fort Duquesne and pushed the French out of most of what later became the United States. They did that a year before Wolfe took Quebec.

When the peace was signed, Charles Gravier, Compte de Vergennes, prophetically cautioned his British counterparts:

Delivered from a neighbor they have always feared, your other colonies will soon discover they stand no longer in need of your protection. You will call on them to contribute to supporting the burden which they have helped bring on you, and they will answer by shaking off all dependence.[20]

THE MILITIA IN THE REVOLUTION

The British eventually saw Vergennes's prophecy coming to pass. Lt. Gen. Thomas Gage, military commander in North America and governor of the rebellious colony of Massachusetts, learned that dissidents were storing guns, ammunition, and supplies in Concord, a little west of Boston. A picked force of British "flank companies"—light infantry and grenadiers—marched out to Concord. On the way, at Lexington, they met American militiamen drawn up on the town common. The militia were "minutemen"—chosen younger men, trained to respond instantly to any alarm. Major John Pitcairn, commanding the light infantry in the van of the British column, demanded that the minutemen lay down their arms and disperse. The militia were reluctant to fire on the King's troops. They started to disperse, but they didn't lay down their arms. There was firing, and the minutemen ran away, leaving eight dead.

The first shot in Lexington is often called "the shot heard around the world" from a later hymn by Ralph Waldo Emerson. Perhaps. But if that's all that happened, it would have been a shot quickly forgotten. There's no record that the British even wondered why the minutemen were waiting for them on Lexington Common. And their actions proved that they had no idea of what that boded for the future. The minutemen had been warned of the British approach by mounted couriers (one of them the Patriot spymaster, Paul Revere).[21] With any thought, Pitcairn and his commander, Lt. Col. Francis Smith, should have known that the Patriots in Concord had also been warned, and that they would have time to move the supplies stored there and make other preparations for resistance.

By the time the British arrived, some 400 militiamen had reported to Col. James Barrett, the local commander. They moved the most important supplies, stored in Barrett's house. The British knew about Barrett's house. The location of the supplies had been pinpointed by General Gage's spy, a soldier named John Howe, who posed as a Patriot gunsmith and had been shown all the rebel secrets. Pitcairn dispatched four companies of light infantry to the militia colonel's house. They found nothing.[22] Another company marched to the North Bridge, where they saw a crowd of armed farmers looking down on them from a hill.

Gage had ordered his men not to fire on the local people unless it was necessary. The commander of the company on North Bridge panicked, however. When the militia formed a column of twos and began marching diagonally down the hillside toward the bridge, Capt. Walter Laurie ordered the light infantry to form up for street fighting. In the drill for street fighting, soldiers formed a column four abreast. The first rank fired and ran to the rear, reloading as they ran. The second rank fired as the first was retreating, then the third. The idea was to sweep a narrow eighteenth-century street with continuous fire. The trouble was that they weren't on a narrow street. Concord was composed of scattered houses and open fields. The King's troops, with a firing line of four men, opened up on the armed farmers, who had a firing line of 200 men.

The light infantry fired two volleys. On the second, two militia members, Capt. Isaac Davis and a drummer boy named Abner Hosmer, were killed.

"Fire, fellow soldiers!" a militia officer yelled. A ripping, ragged volley exploded from the hillside. Twelve British light infantrymen went down, and the rest fled.

It wasn't particularly good shooting. The militia knew that what they were doing was treason, and they were nervous. The shooting was good enough to panic the British, though. They reported to Smith that thousands of rebels were approaching. Smith rounded up his 750 men and started for Boston. As they marched, more and more rebels converged on Concord. The troops fired at a group of militia they thought looked threatening. The militia fired back. And they kept on firing. They followed the British, and they lined the road ahead of them. Most were members of organized militia companies. Some, however, did not fit even the wide parameters for Massachusetts militia service—all males between 16 and 60, except ministers.

One group of rebels intercepted the ammunition wagons Gage had dispatched to resupply his men. The British convoy included 13 men under an officer. The rebels were all men on the "alarm list," those so old they were asked to fight only as a last resort, led by a black man named David Lamson. The British were not impressed by the old coots who tried to stop them. The teamsters whipped their horses to break through. The ancient warriors killed the lead horses in their traces to stop the wagons, and shot the officer and both sergeants. The rest of the British ran for their lives, threw away their muskets, and surrendered to an old woman, asking her to take them where they'd be safe. She took them to the local militia commander.[23]

Hezekiah Wyman may not have been old enough to make the alarm list—that day was his fifty-fifth birthday—but his wife told him he was too old to fight. Wyman didn't think so. He didn't bother to look for a militia company. He just climbed on his horse and proceeded to fight a war of his own. Witnesses noticed him particularly. He was tall and gaunt, with long gray hair. He rode a white horse and carried an old fowling piece. He would ride past the British column at a safe distance, stop, dismount, and rest his ancient weapon across the saddle of the horse. When the Redcoats got within range, he'd fire. Then he'd remount and ride to another sniping position.[24]

Wyman and members of Lamson's company were youngsters compared with

Samuel Whittemore, an old soldier of 78. Too crippled to run, Whittemore took a musket, two pistols, and a saber and hid behind a stone wall, 150 yards from the road. When the British column came close, Whittemore got off five shots so fast and so accurately the British thought he was a number of rebels. They sent a detachment to flush him out. Whittemore killed one of the attackers and wounded two more before he was severely wounded and left for dead. He didn't die. He lived to be 96.[25]

The British were saved by a relief force Gage sent out. They scrambled across Charlestown Neck and into Boston. Day after day, more militia appeared outside of Boston. The British were besieged.

The besieging army was a motley mass of militia, without any uniforms and almost without any organization. Colonels and generals from all over New England threw their weight around. Although General Artemus Ward of Massachusetts was nominally in charge, there was no unified command. General Israel Putnam of Connecticut and Colonel William Prescott of Massachusetts proposed fortifying Bunker Hill, overlooking Charlestown Neck, to forestall a British attempt to break out. Once on Bunker Hill, they decided to move forward and fortify Breed's Hill, a bit closer to Boston.

The next day, the British, commanded by Sir William Howe, landed at Charlestown and moved against Breed's Hill. Howe planned a flanking movement, using his favorite arm, the light infantry, to overrun makeshift rebel defenses along the Mystic River and take the Yankees in the rear. Three volleys in quick succession by John Stark's New Hampshire militia, who had remained hidden until the last second, broke the light infantry charge and ruined Howe's plan. Then the rebels in the hilltop fort and breastworks smashed the main British force with rapid musketry. A British officer later reported, "An incessant stream of fire poured from the rebel lines. It seemed a continuous sheet of fire for near 30 minutes."[26] All the men around Howe were shot down. The survivors ran down the slope. Howe reorganized them and started back up almost immediately. It was a bloodbath. Howe's boots later showed that he had literally waded through blood. A third charge, this time in column, with wide intervals between each file, finally gained the fort.

The victory was useless. The rebels still blocked Charlestown Neck. The British lost 1,054 killed or wounded compared with the rebels' 449.[27] Gage, Howe, and the other British officers never thought the raw American militia could stand up to the King's regulars. But they did. When they were finally forced from the hill, their retreat "was no flight," according to "Gentleman Johnny" Burgoyne, the British general who watched the action. "It was even covered with bravery and military skill."[28] William Howe, who led all three charges and seemed to have a charmed life, was deeply affected. Before "Bunker Hill," Sir Billy was considered the most daring and innovative general in the army. He left his audacity on the slopes of Breed's Hill. When he replaced Gage, he failed to take the initiative. When the rebels fortified Dorchester Heights, he evacuated Boston by sea and went to Halifax. If he had gone immediately to New York, as he did later, the rebels would have been in trouble.

One of the Americans killed on Breed's Hill was Dr. Joseph Warren, head of the Massachusetts Committee of Safety, the effective government of the colony. Massachusetts Patriot leaders petitioned the Continental Congress, then sitting in Philadelphia, to adopt the army and appoint a commanding general. The Congress appointed George Washington commanding general and voted to raise ten companies of riflemen from the frontier districts of Virginia, Maryland, and Pennsylvania. Many modern writers assume that all frontier riflemen were militia. These riflemen were not militia; they were the first Continentals.

The riflemen wore hunting shirts of buckskin or, when they could afford it, linsey-woolsey. Their weapon was the Pennsylvania rifle, a long, graceful weapon developed from the rifles Swiss and German settlers had brought to Pennsylvania from Europe. The rifle was extremely accurate. A good marksman could hit an enemy in the head at 200 yards. The same marksman with a smoothbore musket would be lucky to hit any part of a man at 80 yards. The rifle, however, was slow to load and, being stocked to the muzzle, would not take a bayonet.[29] The militia musket would take a bayonet, but few militiamen had bayonets, although colonial militia laws required bayonets to be kept at home. Even without a bayonet, Washington and most other regular officers preferred the musket to the rifle. A good musketeer could get off four shots while the rifleman was firing one.[30] At one point, General "Mad Anthony" Wayne said he never wanted to see another rifle, at least one without a bayonet. And even then, he'd prefer a musket.

The riflemen, themselves a rather motley crew, were shocked by the militia army outside of Boston.

"Such sermons," wrote Jesse Lukens, a rifleman from the South, "such Negroes, such Colonels, such Boys & such Great Great Grandfathers."[31] When Washington arrived, he tried to incorporate as many New England militiamen into the regular army as possible. The results were disappointing. The militia had no hesitation about fighting the Redcoats when they appeared in their neighborhoods, but they didn't like the idea of marching all over the country for even as long as a year, the standard length of enlistment then.

Congress and Washington never got as many Continentals as they wanted, but Continentals were only one source of Revolutionary manpower. There were also regular state troops—the Pennsylvania line, the Virginia line, etc. And there were the militia, who seldom fought unless the enemy was threatening their homes.

George Washington was no fan of the militia. He complained that their "want of discipline and refusal, of almost any kind of restraint and Government have produced . . . an entire disregard of that order and subordination necessary to the well doing of an army."[32]

MILITIA AND MYTHS

There are many myths about the Revolutionary War, and modern historians take pains to debunk them. One story is that Washington exploited the British fear of rifle-armed militia by dressing his regulars in hunting shirts. Actually, Washington had so much contempt for the militia and thought so little of riflemen, either regular or militia, it's doubtful he expected the British to fear them. Many regulars wore hunting shirts because they didn't have uniforms until around 1779. The hunting shirt was a practical garment widely used by civilians for all outdoor activities.

A popular target for debunkers is the notion that the rifle won the war. It didn't, of course. Most troops, Continentals, state troops, and militia carried muskets. But the rifle was a far more valuable weapon than is usually allowed. At Saratoga, riflemen under Col. Daniel Morgan repeatedly drove back British advance columns. Then a rifle-armed regular killed Acting Brig. Gen. Simon Fraser and ended all British chances to avoid disaster at that decisive battle. Militia, too, are greatly underrated, mostly because of statements by officers like Washington and Wayne. Militia riflemen wiped out Patrick Ferguson's Tory command at King's Mountain in North Carolina. George Rogers Clark led Virginia militia into the northwest frontier and secured what later became Indiana and Illinois. Other militia riflemen set the stage for Daniel Morgan to annihilate Tarleton's Legion at the Cowpens. Morgan understood the limitations of militia. He told his riflemen to fire two well-aimed shots at the British and then retire. That was all that was needed to disorganize the British line and prepare the American counterattack.

In debunking the idea that the Americans hid behind trees and stone walls to shoot down the lines of British infantry, some historians tend to go overboard. They assert that the Americans never used such vile tactics. But on many occasions they did, especially the militia. So, occasionally, did the British. Riflemen, in particular, almost always fired from the prone position or from the branches of a tree.[33]

The debunkers further assert that what turned the tide of the war was the Prussian drillmaster, Baron von Steuben, who taught the raw Continentals how to fight in the European manner. The man who called himself Baron Friedrich Wilhelm Ludolf Gerhard Augustin von Steuben was certainly a great asset to the Continental Army. But he wasn't a baron; he wasn't on Friedrich the Great's staff, and he wasn't a "von." He was a former Prussian captain retired on half pay.[34] He was an important asset, however. Before Steuben, both American regulars and militia, although they usually fought in the European manner, followed several different types of drill. Steuben wrote a simplified drill book and taught the troops to fight in lines of two ranks instead of the usual three, thus increasing fire effect and maneuverability. Nevertheless, the fact is that the Continental Army lost as many battles post-Steuben as pre-Steuben. Steuben worship probably stems in part from the reluctance of military professionals to believe that anyone but one of their own can win wars.

A NATIONAL WAR

Members of the oft-denigrated militia deserve as much credit for the ultimate victory as any other players in the Revolution. One of the British advantages in the war was mobility. There were few and poor roads, but the British traveled by water.[35] Wherever they landed, however, there were militia there to meet them. "Gentleman Johnny" Burgoyne, who certainly knew from experience, said, "Wherever the King's forces point, militia in the amount of three or four thousand people assemble in 24 hours; they bring with them their subsistence, etc., and the alarm over, they return to their farms."[36]

After the disastrous Saratoga campaign, British generals were afraid to travel far from the sea. In that British attempt to split the colonies along the Hudson River, the New York militia stopped St. Leger's troops, who were coming to support Burgoyne, and the New Hampshire, Vermont, and Massachusetts militia wiped out two German forces Burgoyne had sent to gather supplies and raise the Tories. Finally, swarms of armed men crowded into Gates's Continental army. They had been aroused by the murder of a young woman—a Tory, incidentally—by Burgoyne's Indians. In the final battle, the British were simply overwhelmed.

The year after Saratoga, the British War Office forbade any more expeditions to the interior.[37]

The British never realized that they were fighting a national war. In eighteenth-century Europe, civilians kept out of the way of armies. Consequently, British officers cared little about the feelings of the civilians around them. They never understood how much their "boys will be boys" attitude toward the frequent rapes of young Boston women turned the population against them. In 1776, New Jersey men kept out of Howe's and Cornwallis's way when they marched through the state. But after a year of looting by British and Hessians, the New Jersey militia came to life.

At the beginning of the war, there were enough Tories in the South to ignite a full-scale civil war. But the savagery of the British and their Tory and Indian allies turned most of the population against them. Lord Charles Cornwallis, an able leader faced with a series of incompetent Continental generals, for a while looked as if he might win the war. Then the militia wiped out Cornwallis's flank guard under Patrick Ferguson.[38] Cornwallis himself came up against the team of Nathanael Greene and Daniel Morgan. Morgan destroyed Tarleton's Legion, a mixed force of cavalry and infantry that had been devastating the South.[39] Cornwallis repeatedly beat Greene, but always suffered heavier losses than the American. Greene led him a merry chase through a hostile area where the British were unable to live off the country or even find help for their wounded.

Cornwallis resupplied his army at sea and turned north into Virginia. It was a replay of the Carolinas campaign, with the British winning all the battles but unable to subdue a hostile militia. Cornwallis again marched to the sea, at Yorktown. But instead of a British fleet to succor him, there was a French fleet to hem him in. Washington performed a masterful bit of deception that had Sir Henry Clinton, the current British commander in North America, preparing for an attack on New York while Washington and Rochambeau closed in on Yorktown.

A few weeks later, a British drummer climbed up one of the ramparts around Yorktown and beat a slow roll on his drum. He continued beating until the bullets ceased whizzing by him, indicating that the Americans and French recognized that Cornwallis was asking for terms. Cornwallis sent out Brig. Gen. Charles O'Hara to surrender, claiming that he was ill. His ego was sorely bruised. Washington would not deign to meet a subordinate and sent Brig. Gen. Benjamin Lincoln to take the surrender. The surrendered British marched out of Yorktown. Burgoyne's bandmaster had his troops play a popular music hall tune:

What happy golden days were those
When I was in my prime!
The lasses took delight in me,
I was so neat and fine;
I roved about from fair to fair,
Likewise from town to town,
Until I married me a wife
And the world turned upside down.[40]

And it had. In London, Lord North, the British prime minister, threw up his hands and cried, "O God! It is all over!" There was still some fighting in the west, where George Rogers Clark and his western Virginia militiamen smashed a final attack by Tories and Indians. But for all practical purposes, the war was over; independence was assured. That would never have happened without the militia.

The men who would write the constitution for the new republic understood that.

CHAPTER 3

"... THAT EVERY MAN BE ARMED ..."

ONE OR MANY?

As soon as the American people won their independence, they found themselves facing some tough questions: just what would this entity called the United States of America be—an association of closely allied but independent states, or a single country? If a single country, would most of the power be held by the central government or by the state governments? How could the American people be sure that a tyrant wouldn't take control of the country and abolish the freedom they had fought for? Educated people at that time were steeped in the history of Greece and Rome. They didn't want their new republic to suffer the fate of the Roman Republic.

Powerful and patriotic politicians arrayed themselves on each side. Patrick Henry, the Virginia firebrand who is credited with saying "Give me liberty or give me death!" feared that a strong central government would inevitably result in tyranny.[1] Thomas Jefferson, another (like Henry) wartime governor of Virginia, was only a little more moderate. Their fellow Virginian, George Washington, wanted a strong central government. Washington's military aide in the Revolution, Alexander Hamilton, wanted a *very* strong central government, with the state governors appointed by the president.

THE PROBLEMS OF CONFEDERATION

Under the Articles of Confederation, which governed the association of the thirteen colonies during the recent war, the Continental Congress had no power to levy taxes. It used the requisition system by which the British Parliament had raised revenues from the colonies before it opted for "taxation without representation." It would "requisition" money from each colony, and the colonial assemblies would then vote taxes to raise the money. As Benjamin Franklin pointed out in articles published in England on the eve of the Revolution, the colonies always came through and often exceeded the amount requisitioned.[2] But they had the power to turn down the request. In the postwar period, the former colonies were refusing Congressional requisitions.

There were also serious squabbles among the newly independent states, occasionally involving armed force. Connecticut and Massachusetts, citing royal grants of land from "sea to sea," claimed large areas in the unorganized northwest. Virginia, the largest state, claimed practically the entire west. New Hampshire and New York each claimed the land between the Connecticut and Hudson rivers—land the inhabitants claimed to be the independent republic of Vermont. New York and Pennsylvania went to the brink of war over Pennsylvania's desire for access to Lake Erie.

All the land claims were eventually settled, but these and other interstate quarrels demonstrated the chaos that could occur under the Articles of Confederation. Then rebellion broke out among the small farmers of Massachusetts, oppressed by unjust taxes and high-handed sheriffs.[3] The Massachusetts government asked the Continental Congress for aid in putting down Shays' Rebellion, but no aid came. The state called up some of its militia, formed a standing army, and put down the rebellion. But Daniel Shays and his followers had demonstrated another weakness in the Confederation.

CONSTITUTIONAL CONVENTION

Trade disagreements prompted five states—Maryland, Virginia, New York, Delaware, and Pennsylvania to meet at Annapolis to iron out their differences. Alexander Hamilton and another young man, James Madison of Virginia, persuaded the other delegates to recommend a convention of all thirteen states "to devise such further provisions as shall appear to them necessary to render the constitution of the federal government adequate to the exigencies of the Union."[4]

The convention met in Philadelphia in 1787 and drafted the U.S. Constitution, the longest-lived such document in the history of the world. The chief architect was Madison, a Federalist and a bitter foe of the Anti-Federalist, Patrick Henry. New York sent Hamilton to the convention, but neutralized him by sending two Anti-Federalists with him. The fight over the Constitution lasted three-and-a-half months, and when it was over nobody was completely satisfied. Hamilton said it was a "weak and worthless fabric," and Madison thought that, with luck, the Constitution might prove workable for a generation.[5] Both men, though, led the fight for ratification in their home states.

''OUR ULTIMATE SAFETY''

The opponents of the new Constitution were particularly worried because there was a provision for a standing army. A standing army had been viewed with extreme disfavor since Cromwell's time. The Revolutionary War, against the King's standing army, had not made the concept any more tolerable. Such an army, under the control of the federal government, could suppress the liberty of individual states. It could ultimately—and this, not some abstract theory of states' rights, is what worried people like Henry—suppress the liberty of each individual citizen. "It squints towards monarchy," Patrick Henry said of the Constitution.[6] The Anti-Federalists saw the militia—the individual citizens, armed with their own weapons—as a counterweight to the standing army. George Mason, author of the Virginia constitution, feared that the federal government might take measures to make the militia disappear:

> An instance within the memory of some of this House, will show us how our militia may be destroyed. Forty years ago, when the resolution of enslaving America was formed in Great Britain, the British Parliament was advised by an artful man, who was governor of Pennsylvania, to disarm the people—that was the most effectual way to enslave them—but they should not do it openly; but to weaken them and let them sink gradually, by totally disusing and neglecting the militia.[7]

On the need for the militia, the Federalists and the Anti-Federalists agreed. As Noah Webster, who wrote more than dictionaries, put it, "Before a standing army can rule, the people must be disarmed; as they are in almost every kingdom of Europe. The supreme power in America cannot enforce unjust laws by the sword; because the whole body of the people are armed."[8] Hamilton and John Jay, another Federalist, began writing letters signed "Publius" to the newspapers. Illness made Jay leave the project, but Hamilton convinced Madison to join. The letters were later collected and published as a book, *The Federalist* or *The Federalist Papers*. In them, both Madison and Hamilton tried to convince the Anti-Federalists that a standing army would be no danger *because* the country has a militia. In the 46th Federalist paper, Madison tried to show how impossible it would be for a standing army in the United States at that time to overcome the militia:

> The highest number to which, according to the best computation, a standing army can be carried in one country, does not exceed one hundredth part of the whole number of souls; or one twenty-fifth part of the number able to bear arms. This proportion would not yield, in the United States, an army of more than twenty-five or thirty thousand men. To these would be opposed a militia amounting to near half a million citizens with arms in their hands, officered by men chosen from among themselves, fighting for their common liberties, and united and conducted by governments [the

states] possessing their affections and confidence. It may well be doubted whether a militia thus circumstanced could ever be conquered by such a proportion of regular troops. Those who are best acquainted with the late successful resistance of this country against the British arms, will be most inclined to deny the possibility of it.[9]

Madison goes on to point out "the advantage of being armed, which the Americans possess over the people of almost every other nation," and charges that the governments of the kingdoms of Europe "are afraid to trust the people with arms."[10]

By the "militia," Madison obviously meant all male adult citizens. This was the force that had recently played such a prominent part in the Revolution. No one, Federalist or Anti-Federalist, knew of any other meaning for militia. In Federalist paper 28, Hamilton speaks of the uses of the militia. "If there should be a slight commotion in a small part of a State, the militia of the residue would be adequate to its suppression; and the natural presumption is that they would be ready to do their duty."[11] Notice that Hamilton refers to "the militia *of the residue*." If there were a disturbance in part of the state, the disturbing would have to be done by the militia—the armed citizens—of the area.

In 1794, Hamilton's theory was put to the test. The farmers in western Pennsylvania revolted against a new tax on whiskey. Congress called for the militia of nearby states to suppress the rebellion. Militiamen from Maryland and Virginia joined the Pennsylvania militia from areas not affected in putting down the rebellion. Hamilton, acting commander of the army as well as secretary of the treasury, led the government forces, while "Mad Anthony" Wayne and most of the small regular army were campaigning against the Indians in Ohio.

The founders of the country had just finished a successful revolution. They believed that revolts were almost inevitable. But if the majority of the people revolted, they thought, their cause would be justified. And the founders wanted to make sure that if the majority did try to overthrow the government, they would have the means to do so. "If the representatives of the people betray their constituents, there is then no resource left but in the exertion of that original right of self-defence which is paramount to all positive forms of government," wrote Hamilton.[12]

The Anti-Federalists were still not convinced. They feared that unless the rights of the people were spelled out in the Constitution, the federal government might usurp them. They wanted a Bill of Rights similar to those many of the states had already adopted in their constitutions.

Patrick Henry was particularly vehement on the need for the traditional militia. "The militia, sir, is our ultimate safety," the Virginian said. "We can have

no security without it. The great object is that every man be armed. . . . [E]very-
one who is able may have a gun."[13]

THE BILL OF RIGHTS

Anti-Federalists in many states called for a provision in the new constitution
guaranteeing the right of citizens to keep and bear arms. Pennsylvania legislators
proposed an article reading: "That the people have a right to bear arms for the
defense of themselves and their own state, or the United States, or for killing
game."[14] In Massachusetts, Sam Adams proposed "that the said Constitution
never be construed to infringe [on] the just liberty of the press and the rights of
conscience; or to prevent the people of the United States who are peaceable
citizens from keeping their own arms."[15] The Massachusetts constitutional convention recommended this amendment to Congress along with its notice of ratification. Delegates from New Hampshire, New York, and Virginia made similar
recommendations. The required nine states ratified the Constitution, but on the
condition that Congress would add amendments protecting individual liberty and
restricting federal power. Among those demanding a Bill of Rights were two
future presidents, John Adams and Thomas Jefferson, who rarely agreed on anything.

Madison thought a bill of rights unnecessary, but he changed his mind. The
enmity of Patrick Henry had kept him from a seat in the Senate, and his Congressional district was so gerrymandered that he had a difficult time being elected.
When he got to Congress, though, he began pushing his colleagues to adopt
amendments protecting the rights of the people.[16] Finally, he proposed twelve
amendments to the Constitution. If approved by Congress, they would be submitted to the states for ratification. (Congress eventually approved all twelve proposed amendments, but two of them—one, concerning the size of the House of
Representatives, and another, forbidding representatives and senators from raising their own salaries—were not ratified. If all had been ratified, the amendment
we call the second would have been the third.[17])

Madison had planned to have each amendment inserted after the part of the
Constitution to which it pertained.[18] He wanted the Second Amendment (the right
to bear arms) and the First Amendment (freedom of speech, religion, press, and
assembly) in Article I, Section 9, the part guaranteeing individual rights, such
as habeas corpus. If he had intended the Second Amendment to be a curb on the
federal government's power to interfere with state militias, he would have put it
in Article I, Section 8, which granted Congress the power to call up the militia
in national emergencies.

Congress, instead, placed all the proposed amendments at the end of the
Constitution, a procedure that has been followed ever since. Both houses made

a number of changes in Madison's original text, which read: "The right of the people to keep and bear arms shall not be infringed; a well armed and well regulated Militia being the best security of a free country: but no person religiously scrupulous of bearing arms, shall be compelled to render military service in person."

The House committee reviewing the amendment changed Madison's wording without changing his meaning. The amendment now read: "A well regulated Militia, composed of the body of the people, being the best security of a free State, the right of the people to keep and bear arms shall not be infringed, but no person religiously scrupulous shall be compelled to bear arms."

The full House focused debate on the conscientious objector issue. It changed the committee's wording back to Madison's, from being "compelled to bear arms" to being "compelled to render military service in person."[19]

The Senate then streamlined the wording and dropped all reference to conscientious objectors. It rejected a suggestion that "for the common defense" be inserted after "bear arms." The Senate, therefore, rejected the notion that the right to bear arms was a "collective right," rather than a right of individual citizens.[20] In 1689, the English Parliament similarly rejected drafts that limited the right to bear arms to situations where it was "necessary for the Publick safety" or "for their common defense."[21] That fact destroys the argument that as the American Bill of Rights is a direct outgrowth of the English one (which is itself a specious notion), it merely guarantees a collective right, which today's anti-gun lobbyists erroneously claim the English Bill of Rights did.[22]

The version of the Bill of Rights submitted to the states is the Second Amendment we have now: "A well regulated Militia, being necessary to the security of a free State, the right of the people to keep and bear arms shall not be infringed."

Aside from the dispute over conscientious objectors, there was little controversy over the amendment. The only commentary on it was in an article on the proposed Bill of Rights written by Tench Coxe, a Pennsylvania editor and friend of James Madison. Coxe explained the need for the Second Amendment in the *Philadelphia Federal Gazette* and the *Philadelphia Evening Post* of June 18, 1789, in an article that was later reprinted in Boston and New York papers.

"As civil rulers," he wrote, "not having their duty to the people before them, may attempt to tyrannize, and as the military forces which must occasionally be raised to defend our country, might pervert their power to the injury of fellow citizens, the people are confirmed . . . in their right to keep and bear their private arms."[23] He added:

The powers of the sword are in the hands of the yeomanry of America from 16 to 60. The militia of these free commonwealths, entitled and accustomed to their arms, when compared with any possible army, must be tremendous and irresistible. Who are the militia? Are they not ourselves? . . . Congress have no power to disarm the militia. Their swords and every other terrible implement of the soldier, are the birth-right of an American. . . . [T]he unlimited power of the sword is not in the hands of either the federal or state governments, but, where I trust in God it shall ever remain, in the hands of the people.[24]

Madison wrote to Coxe thanking him for the article, stating that the Bill of Rights "is . . . already indebted to the cooperation of your pen."[25]

In an 1803 revised copy of Blackstone's Commentaries that included American law, St. George Tucker, an American legal scholar, wrote of the Second Amendment:

This may be regarded as the true palladium of liberty. The right of self defense is the first law of nature; in most governments it has been the study of rulers to confine this right within the narrowest limits possible. Wherever standing armies are kept up, and the right of the people to keep and bear arms is, under any color or pretext whatsoever, prohibited, liberty, if not already annihilated, is on the brink of destruction.[26]

THE MEANING OF MILITIA

Soon after the passage of the National Firearms Act of 1934, a man named Jack Miller was charged with acquiring a sawed-off shotgun without paying the tax required by the act. The trial court dismissed the charge without taking any evidence. The government appealed. Jack Miller was too poor to afford a lawyer, so the appeal was made on the government's brief alone. In *United States v. Miller* (1939), The U.S. Supreme Court criticized the trial court for not examining evidence as to whether or not a sawed-off shotgun was a weapon that would be useful for the militia, and ordered a new trial. By that time, however, Miller had disappeared, and the case was never settled.

In its decision, the Court stated: "The Constitution as originally adopted granted the Congress power to 'provide for calling forth the Militia'. . . . [T]he Militia comprised all males physically capable of acting in concert for the common defense. . . . [O]rdinarily when called for service, these men were expected to appear bearing arms supplied by themselves and of the kind in common use at the time."[27]

The meaning of "militia" has changed in two centuries, but not nearly as much as many people think. When the Bill of Rights was written, "militia" meant all male citizens between 16 and 60. Under the current United States Code, "The militia of the United States consists of all able-bodied males at least 17 years of age and . . . under 45 years of age."[28]

From the history of the militia in England and America, and from the history of the Second Amendment, the amendment's meaning is obvious: Because the militia—all male citizens between 16 and 60—have weapons, they are the greatest bulwark against foreign invasion or domestic usurpation. Therefore they shall not be disarmed.

Whether the militia actually possess the military power in the 1990s that they had in the 1780s is another question. The question we are considering is not the founders' ability to foresee conditions two centuries later, but what they actually wrote.

They certainly were not protecting the rights of the states to keep National Guard units. The National Guard as we know it did not appear until the beginning of the twentieth century. And, as we'll see, the amendment is completely inapplicable to it because the Guard's weapons are owned by the *federal government*. Nor were they protecting the right of the states to keep any kind of troops with state-supplied weapons. The amendment refers to "the right of the *people* to keep and bear arms." Anywhere "the people" is used in the Bill of Rights it means the people, not the states. For example: in the First Amendment, "the right of the people peaceably to assemble . . ."; in the Fourth Amendment, "the right of the people to be secure in their persons . . ."; in the Ninth Amendment, "The enumeration in the Constitution, of certain rights, shall not be construed to deny or disparage others retained by the people;" in the Tenth Amendment, "The powers not delegated to the United States by the Constitution, nor prohibited by it to the States, are reserved to the States respectively, or to the people."

The Tenth Amendment makes it clear that the men who wrote the Bill of Rights did not think "the people" and "the states" were identical.

Somehow, though, the idea that the writers of the Bill of Rights meant just such nonsense has achieved popularity. The credit for that belongs to those professional enemies of plain English, the lawyers.

CHAPTER 4

SECOND THOUGHTS ABOUT THE SECOND AMENDMENT

The War of 1812 was still raging when Kentucky passed the first weapons control law. It was certainly not intended to disarm the militia. The Kentucky militia, in particular, was extremely active during the war. It participated in the attempts to invade Canada and again proved what every militia but the Swiss have repeatedly demonstrated: militia are useless for anything but defending their homes.[1] At the end of the war (actually after the peace treaty had been signed), Kentucky's citizen-soldiers also participated in the most resounding victory any militia ever scored against regular troops—the Battle of New Orleans.[2]

The lawmakers of Kentucky had no problem with citizens carrying muskets or, more usually, rifles. They worried about concealed weapons. In 1813, when they passed their pioneering weapons control law, Kentucky was a frontier state. And the "wild West" of the early nineteenth century was far wilder than the California goldfields and the Great Plains became in mid and late century. There were no effective police, and few courtrooms and jails. There were plenty of disputes, though. Land claims, card games, and just plain cussedness led to fights. The nature of the frontier was such that it attracted the most aggressive and ruthless of the citizens of the eastern seaboard. Also, most of the new Westerners had been Southerners, and Southerners had somehow arrived at the conclusion that they were all aristocrats and that hypersensitivity to slights was aristocratic behavior. Men carried sword canes, hid daggers under their coattails, and kept small pistols in their pockets. And they were not slow to use them.

The Kentucky law was aimed at concealed weapons. No one saw any conflict with the Second Amendment. As a matter of fact, most of

35

the few people who considered the question at all believed amendments to the U.S. Constitution did not apply to state laws. (And the U.S. Supreme Court, in *Barron v. Baltimore*, later in the first half of the century ruled that it did not.) That was a moot point, because most state constitutions also protected the right of the people to keep and bear arms. Those that didn't, like Connecticut's, provided for the calling up of a militia composed of all males of military age, all of whom were expected to have their own weapons. The Kentucky legislators, though, did not consider "dirk knives," pocket pistols, and sword canes to be particularly useful militia weapons. They based their decision on a developing legal doctrine called "the police power of the state." The doctrine appears to be based on the Tenth Amendment to the U.S. Constitution: "The powers not delegated to the United States by the Constitution, nor prohibited by it to the States, are reserved to the States respectively, or to the people"—on that, and on a desire to curb an epidemic of personal violence. Louisiana passed a similar law at the same time.

The neighboring frontier state of Indiana thought Kentucky's idea was a good one and adopted a similar law in 1819. The laws, unfortunately, did not curb violence. Violence spread, and the tools of violence continued to be developed.

In 1822, the Kentucky Court of Appeals, the state's highest court, voided the 1813 law. It found the law in conflict with the Kentucky Constitution, which stated "that the right of the citizens to bear arms in defense of themselves and the state shall not be questioned."[3] The Louisiana high court upheld the law because it did not affect the right of a citizen to carry weapons but only concealed weapons.

Around 1830, Henry Deringer of Philadelphia developed his famous pocket pistol. It sold in tremendous numbers in the West. In a few years it was carried by men in all parts of the country and from all walks of life. Senators and stevedores, gamblers and grocers all carried one of Deringer's products or one of the host of imitations it inspired. About the same time the Deringer pocket pistol was born, James Bowie acquired the huge single-edge knife that bears his name. Bowie's use of the knife made him nationally famous. The Bowie knife spread as fast as the derringer (uncapitalized and with a change of spelling that quickly became the generic name for all small, large-bore pistols). The Bowie knife settled barroom brawls and formal duels. It was named as the weapon to be used in at least one duel between two congressmen.[4] From Washington to San Francisco, the Bowie knife and the derringer became standard equipment for quarrelsome and tetchy men. The highest per capita possession of both weapons, though, was in the Old Southwest. That area, too, was the home of the "push dagger," a distinctively American weapon with a handle set at right angles to the blade for easier concealment. The push dagger, hung upside down under the armpit in a sheath with a spring retainer, was many a gambler's best friend. The southwestern frontier states of Arkansas and Georgia passed concealed weapons laws in 1837. However, the Georgia law, which banned the private *possession* of pistols, was declared unconstitutional because, according to the Georgia Supreme Court,

> The right of the whole people, old and young, men, women and boys, and not the militia only, to keep and bear arms of every description, and not such merely as are used by the militia, shall not be infringed . . . in the slightest degree; and all this for the important end to be obtained, the rearing up and qualifying of a well-regulated militia, so vitally necessary to a free state.[5]

In 1838, Virginia, which included what is now West Virginia, passed a weapons law. By 1850, every western state had passed laws barring the carrying of concealed weapons. After the Civil War, the states of the far West, where most settlements were small and had many miles of empty space between them, often left weapons regulation up to local authorities. That led to banning weapons within the city limits and having travelers check their weapons on entering a town and taking them back as they were leaving. Sometimes the travelers checked their weapons. More often, both strangers and residents carried revolvers hidden in their pockets. Photos of such rip-roaring cow towns as Dodge City taken in the 1870s and 1880s show no holsters and cartridge belts being worn. But most of the men were carrying guns.

In the Northeast, at that time, there were no weapons laws. Eastern clothing manufacturers in the period sewed holsters into the right hip pocket of every pair of pants they made. Of course, the customer would be carrying a gun.

KEEPING ''THOSE PEOPLE'' IN THEIR PLACE—THE SOUTH

The end of the Civil War had two effects on gun distribution in the United States.

First, it vastly increased the number of guns available and so greatly reduced their price. War-surplus rifles and revolvers could be bought for less than it cost to make them. Many soldiers, such as the Confederates who had surrendered to Grant, were allowed to take their sidearms home. The manufacturing industry, greatly stimulated by the war, began churning out thousands of small, cheap revolvers. These soon earned the name of "suicide specials" because, critics said, they were so inaccurate that were good for nothing but committing suicide.

Second, a large number of people—the former slaves—previously disarmed, were now able to keep and carry guns. Before the Civil War, all African-Americans, even those who had been freed, were forbidden to vote or own firearms. After the war, former slaves and all other blacks were legally emancipated. Not only could they vote, they could buy and carry guns. And guns were now cheap enough for a poor tenant farmer to afford.

Southern white traditionalists responded with the Ku Klux Klan. Through beatings, arson, and murder in southern communities and political manipulation in Washington, the white supremacists gradually regained their position of dominance. This was not accomplished solely by a bunch of poor rednecks wearing sheets. The Klansmen had a lot of help from high places. Like the U.S. Supreme Court.

After the election of 1872, two separate groups claimed that they were the state government of Louisiana. One was Unionist, the other Segregationist. In the town of Colfax, armed African-Americans, supporting the Unionist county government, occupied the courthouse. A mob of armed whites, led by a man named William Cruikshank, burned the courthouse and killed those who tried to escape the flames. Cruikshank and other leaders of the mob were arrested for violating the federal law that made it a criminal offense to deny any person his rights under the Constitution. The government charged that Cruikshank and his followers denied the African-Americans their rights peaceably to assemble and to keep and bear arms. The case eventually went to the U.S. Supreme Court.

The Supreme Court ruled in 1876 that the law under which Cruikshank was convicted was unconstitutional. It agreed that the Fourteenth Amendment gave Congress the right to prevent interference with rights granted by the Constitution. But the right peaceably to assemble and the right to keep and bear arms, it held, were pre-existing rights—beyond the power of the Constitution to grant or to deny. They were natural human rights "found wherever civilization exists." But although these rights, in the Court's reasoning, were superior to even the Constitution, there was no suggestion that Cruikshank had committed a crime by denying them to fellow citizens.

The Court further said that the Fourteenth Amendment only allowed Congress to legislate against *state* interference with civil rights, not against private conspiracies.[6] *United States v. Cruikshank* effectively killed the Fourteenth Amendment until the 1920s.

With the Segs back in control of southern state governments, blacks were rapidly disarmed. Klan raiding parties forcibly searched African-American homes for weapons without raising an eyebrow among the local authorities. In 1870, Tennessee passed a law forbidding the sale of any handgun except "the Army and Navy model"—the most expensive type, well beyond the means of most blacks and poor whites.[7] King Henry VIII's idea of limiting weapons to the affluent had not died. Arkansas copied Tennessee's law in 1881. Alabama in 1893 and Texas in 1907 took another tack to keep pistols out of the hands of the poor. They enacted extremely heavy business and transaction taxes on handgun sales. In 1906, Mississippi passed the first law registering gun dealers. All retailers had to retain records of who bought any guns or ammunition. Local authorities then illegally confiscated any weapons owned by African-Americans and other undesirables, such as union organizers. The rest of the Deep South states just went right on enforcing their illegal bans on gun ownership by blacks.

KEEPING ''THOSE PEOPLE'' IN THEIR PLACE—THE NORTH

The North began to worry about white undesirables at about the time of the Civil War. In New York, the draft riots of 1863 caused major alarm. Irish immigrants, most of them recently arrived, resented being drafted to fight a war they had no interest in—especially since the well-to-do could buy their way out of the draft with a $300 payment. The Irish burned property and lynched a number of African-Americans before troops put the riot down with rifle and artillery fire. The Irish, poor and illiterate, were already a disruptive element. All the big gangs in the big city had a predominantly Irish membership, and most of the petty criminals were also Irish. And the Irish had begun acquiring pistols.

The Irish immigrants were soon joined by other aliens. First came Germans and Scandinavians, especially the former, then Jews and Italians. Finally there were Greeks, Poles, Russians, and other Eastern Europeans with "unpronounceable names," most of whom were suspected of being anarchists. As civil rights lawyer Don B. Kates, Jr., put it, describing the immigrants' reception, "Of the three" [Jews, Catholics—like the Irish, Italians and many of the Germans—and anarchists], "Jews were the least suspect ideologically, being considered no more than usurious Christ-killers and perhaps congenitally criminal as well."[8] Catholics seemed much worse. Generations of Americans had been brought up on tales of the Inquisition and of how Catholics blindly obeyed everything their priests told them. These immigrants were a threat to democracy as well as being, like the Jews, congenitally criminal. Then there were the Eastern Europeans—generally believed to be anarchists and assassins who wanted to violently overthrow the government.

The flood of immigrants combined with labor unrest to spark the case that produced the second Supreme Court Second Amendment ruling.

A certain German immigrant, Herman Presser, organized a drill company for other German immigrants called *Lehr und Wehr Verein* "Learning and Weapons Club." It was similar to scores of other "volunteer" military companies that had been formed in various parts of the country since the 1830s. Volunteer units had begun to replace the militia in the Civil War. As the militia could not be sent out of the country, volunteer units, like Teddy Roosevelt's famous "Rough Riders," did much of the country's amateur soldiering right up to World War I. There were two differences between Lehr und Wehr and the other volunteer groups. The first was that Lehr und Wehr was composed of immigrants who spoke a foreign language. The second was that in 1870, Illinois passed a law aimed at controlling private paramilitary groups. The reason for the law was that after a number of strikes had been brutally suppressed by private guards, police, and elite volunteer troops, workers had begun organizing armed groups for their own protection.

In 1879, Lehr und Wehr paraded in Chicago, with Presser, wearing a sword, leading the group. He was arrested for violating the law barring unlicensed drilling while armed and fined $10. Presser took the case to the U.S. Supreme Court.

The Court's decision was that the Second Amendment did not protect independent paramilitary companies from state regulation. Further, the Second Amendment did not limit state governments, because none of ten amendments comprising the Bill of Rights did. That decision was later overruled in *DeJonge v. Oregon* which held that the First Amendment, and by implication, the rest of the Bill of Rights, did apply to the states. This 1886 decision was made ten years after the Court in the Cruikshank case said that the Fourteenth Amendment *did* allow Congress to legislate against state governments interfering with civil rights.

The Court, however, did go on to say something that has since confounded the militia-means-National-Guard school of thought:

> It is undoubtedly true that all citizens capable of bearing arms constitute the reserved military force or reserve militia of the United States as well as the States; and, in view of this prerogative of the General Government, as well as of its general powers, the States cannot, even laying the constitutional provisions in question out of view, prohibit the people from keeping and bearing arms, so as to deprive the United States of their rightful resource for maintaining the public security, and disable the people from performing their duty to the general government.[9]

To follow the Court's reasoning just a bit further, if the people's duty to the federal government requires them to have arms, and the states cannot prohibit them from keeping and bearing arms, the militia is not merely something to guarantee the independence of *state* governments. That confounds still another argument of the gun control lobby today.

Kristen Rand, an attorney for the Violence Policy Center of Washington, D.C., one of the more rabid anti-gun lobby groups, puts a rather strange spin on this decision. She says it means that "the Second Amendment functions only as a check on the power of the federal government—preventing it from interfering with the state's ability to maintain a militia." But the portion of the Court's decision quoted above says precisely the opposite: *the states may not disable the militia because to do so would deprive the federal government of a needed resource.*

Rand concludes, "States, therefore, are not prohibited by the Second Amendment from controlling private ownership of handguns in any way they see fit"[?!].[10]

Most people know that there are often numerous differing opinions of what a Supreme Court decision means. By now, though, it should be apparent to the reader that the opinions of the U.S. Supreme Court itself are not as unchanging as the North Star. There's more on this to come. But first, let's go back to all those nasty immigrants.

New York City in 1877 passed an ordinance requiring permits to carry pistols,[11] but permits were given to almost anyone who applied. Even then, the law was not strictly enforced. Gangsters, in particular, habitually carried guns without permits. Other citizens carried pistols, legally or illegally, to protect themselves from the gangsters. In 1892, the *New York Tribune* estimated that "a very fair percentage" of New Yorkers usually went armed.[12] Around the turn of the century, New York newspapers began to campaign against carrying firearms. Judges, magistrates, police officials, and prosecutors got on the bandwagon. State Senator Timothy D. Sullivan introduced a bill for state licensing of pistol carrying and also of pistol purchase and pistol possession. Licensing possession of pistols was a radical new step—the biggest since Georgia attempted to prohibit possession in 1837. Like the Kentucky law of 1813, the proposed New York law was based on the police power of the state. Sullivan pushed his bill with the kind of oratory that has since become familiar in the gun-control debate.

"If this bill passes," Sullivan said, "it will do more to carry out the commandment 'Thou shalt not kill' than all the talk of all the ministers and priests in the state for the next ten years."[13]

In 1911, the bill passed the Senate 37 to 5, and the House 123 to 7. Charles E. Van Loan, an early supporter of the bill, wrote, "New York State is the pioneer in a movement to make the pistol a dangerous thing to have in one's pocket. The results of this campaign will begin to appear when the Coroner issues his statistics for 1912, and the results will be worth watching."[14]

The coroner issued his report for 1912 on January 26, 1913. In 1910, the year before the Sullivan Law passed, there had been 108 homicides by firearms. A year after the Sullivan Law, the coroner's report showed that there had been 113.[15] Over the decades, the Sullivan Law as applied in New York City has grown progressively stricter, and the murders have grown steadily more numerous. By 1987, the initial application for a pistol permit in New York City cost $100, plus $19 for fingerprinting. If the application is denied (as almost all are), the fees are not refundable. The permit must be renewed every two years, for another $100 fee. As a result, most of the pistols in New York City are illegal. Theoretically, there should be almost no pistols there. But the murders and other shootings go on and on.

Since its passage, the Sullivan Law has had numerous imitators, in states as distant as Hawaii and Missouri. Basically, the New York law is a "discretionary" licensing system, with police officials deciding quite arbitrarily who may get a permit and who may not.[16] Its application in New York City is considerably more restrictive than in the rest of the state. According to Don Kates, "New York City permits are issued only to the very wealthy, the politically powerful, and the socially elite. Permits are also issued to: private guard services employed by the very wealthy, the banks, and the great corporations; to ward heelers and political influence peddlers; and (on payment of a suitable sum) to reputable 'soldiers' of the Mafia."[17] Former New York mayor John Lindsay, an ardent supporter of disarming the public, had a pistol permit. So did the late Arthur Ochs Sulzberger, the publisher of the *New York Times*, a paper that campaigns for ever more restrictive gun laws. Other permit holders included Dr. Joyce Brothers, who's said that no one needs a handgun and that men who have them may be suspected of sexual dysfunction; the late Nelson Rockefeller, a stout upholder of the Sullivan Law; and his brothers David and Winthrop.[18]

The last big-city mayor assassinated was Anton Cermak of Chicago, in 1934, and his assassin was really aiming at Franklin D. Roosevelt. But Lindsay was not alone in holding a permit. Just about every member of the U.S. Conference of Mayors, which campaigns incessantly for stricter gun control, has either a carry permit, armed bodyguards, or both. While some small town newspaper editors were killed in California during gold rush days, or in Oklahoma, during land rush days, the last nationally known publisher shot was Elijah Lovejoy, editor and publisher of the abolitionist *The Observer* in 1857.[19] And probably no pop television psychologists have been murdered. But people are being murdered every day in poor areas of New York. And few of them can legally own a gun.

At the time of its passage, there was no doubt in New York whom the Sullivan Law was targeting. As historian Lee Kennett writes:

> [There] was the clear inference that the new measure would strike hardest at the foreign-born element who were seemingly responsible for most of the violence in the city. It had long been held that pistols were found "chiefly in the pockets of ignorant and quarrelsome immigrants of law breaking propensities" [quoted from a newspaper editorial]. The Italian population seemed particularly addicted to criminality (the *Tribune's* annual index frequently crosslisted the entries "crime" and "Italians"). As early as 1903 the authorities had begun to cancel pistol permits in the Italian sections of the city. This was followed by a state law in 1905, which made it illegal for aliens to possess firearms "in any public place." This provision was retained in the Sullivan Law.[20]

The first person convicted under the Sullivan Law was an Italian immigrant, Marino Rossi, who lived in New Jersey and was passing through New York on his way to work in Connecticut. He carried a pistol because he had been threatened by criminals. While sentencing Rossi to a year in Sing Sing prison, the judge told him, "It is unfortunate that this [carrying guns] is the custom of you and your kind, and that fact, combined with your irascible nature, furnishes much of the criminal business of this country."[21] In the first three years of the Sullivan Law, 70 percent of those arrested had Italian surnames.

Fear of foreigners was the driving force behind gun control legislation not only in New York but in much of the country. In 1924, a California court, upholding a statute that banned gun ownership by foreigners, said:

> Native citizens are justly presumed to be imbued with a natural allegiance to their government which unnaturalized foreigners do not possess. The former inherit a knowledge and reverence for our institutions, while the latter as a class do not understand our customs or laws, or enter into the spirit of our social organization.[22]

Only born Americans, in other words, understand that murder, rape, and robbery are wrong.

THE LAWYERS AND THE LAW

For many years, the general public has been told by the news media that the right to keep and bear arms mentioned in the Second Amendment is a collective right; that it gives the states the right to maintain militias (sometimes described as the right to have National Guard units); that it has nothing to do with individual possession of guns. The courts, say much of the press, have decided this again and again. Typical is an Associated Press dispatch published December 12, 1993 (and published without even a feeble "news peg"): "Federal courts have offered little comfort to gun control foes who argue that a proposal to license gun owners nationwide threatens the constitutional right to bear arms," reads the lead. It goes on to quote Dennis Henigan of Handgun Control, Inc., who said, "All this talk about gun control violating the Second Amendment is just an NRA-created myth. I regard the Second Amendment as essentially irrelevant to the private ownership of firearms."

And, adds the AP, "So far, the weight of legal authority leans toward Henigan's view."[23]

Some lower courts have certainly leaned toward Henigan's view. But in the United States, the real weight of legal authority comes from the U.S. Supreme Court. And, as we've seen so far, that emphatically has not leaned toward Henigan's view.

The earliest U.S. Supreme Court case to mention the right to keep and bear arms is the infamous Dred Scott decision in 1856. The Court held that even free

African-Americans could not be citizens because that "would give to them the full liberty of speech in public and in private, upon all subjects in which its [a slave state's] citizens might speak; to hold public meetings upon political affairs, and to keep and carry arms wherever they went."[24]

In *United States v. Cruikshank* (1876), the Supreme Court held that the right to keep and bear arms is a natural human right, "found wherever civilization exists."[25]

In *Presser v. Illinois* (1886), the Court ruled that "all citizens capable of bearing arms" constitute the militia. And, it added, the militia is so important to the security of the United States that individual states cannot destroy it by disarming citizens.[26]

In *United States v. Miller* (1939), the Court again affirmed that the militia consists of all males capable of bearing arms and that when called up they "were expected to appear bearing arms supplied by themselves and of the kind in common use at the time." Further, in *Miller*, the Court approvingly quotes *Constitutional Limitations* by Thomas Cooley, a nineteenth-century legal scholar, who said of the Second Amendment:

> The right is general—it may be supposed from the phraseology of this provision that the right to keep and bear arms was only guaranteed to the militia; but this would be an interpretation not warranted by the intent. . . . [I]f the right were limited to those enrolled, the purpose of this guaranty might be defeated altogether by the action or neglect to act of the government it was meant to hold in check. The meaning of the provision undoubtedly is that the people from whom the militia must be taken shall have the right to keep and bear arms, and they need no permission or regulation of law for the purpose.[27]

In *Lewis v. United States* (1980), a case Violence Policy Center attorney Kristen Rand cites as the most important from a gun control standpoint, the Court merely upheld as being constitutional the part of the Gun Control Act of 1968 prohibiting convicted felons from owning guns. Rand cites it because "in its analysis, the Court applied a 'rational basis' standard" instead of the "more rigorous 'strict scrutiny' standard." She quotes the Court: "These legislative restrictions on the use of firearms do not trench upon any constitutionally protected liberties."[28] By "these legislative restrictions" the Court meant banning felons from having guns—which no rational person could seriously say "trenched upon constitutionally protected liberties" any more than confining felons in prison does.

Then there's *United States v. Verdugo-Urquidez* (1990). David B. Kopel, a former New York assistant district attorney and a widely quoted commentator on firearms law, said:

> The Supreme Court's most recent statement on the Second Amendment was that the "right of the people to keep and bear arms" and the "right of the people peaceably to assemble" protect the same class of people as "the right of the people to be secure in their persons, houses, papers and effects against unreasonable searches and seizures." In all cases, the Court said, the "right of the people" refers to individual American citizens. (And therefore a Mexican citizen in Mexico City could not complain that he was unreasonably searched by American drug agents.)[29]

Finally, there is federal statute (Title 10, United States Code, paragraph 311[a]) that says the militia consists of all males over 17 and under 45.

The U.S. Supreme Court has seldom ruled on the Second Amendment. It usually refuses to hear Second Amendment cases. It's not hard to see why. For much of the twentieth century, crime has been major news. At any period since 1925, the public has been convinced that the crime rate was increasing. Sometimes it was. Sometimes it was decreasing. It's been (with the exception of violent juvenile crime) remarkably stable for the last few years. But crime sells newspapers and attracts television audiences. And many people think that if guns could be eliminated, crime would disappear. Both are most unlikely situations, as we'll see, but that sentiment makes it hard to defend the right of citizens to own guns.

Another thing that makes the Second "the embarrassing amendment" is that it's based on the need for a militia. In the eighteenth and early nineteenth centuries, the militia was a most potent defensive arm. But this is the twentieth century. Governments have nuclear bombs and shells, airplanes and helicopters, tanks and monstrous artillery, not to mention rockets, flamethrowers, and poison gas. Citizens have rifles, most of them hand-operated, shotguns, and handguns. What good is the militia today?

Moreover, the government, with the compliance of the citizenry, has let the militia slowly disintegrate for more than a century.

CHAPTER 5

WHERE HAVE ALL THE MILITIAMEN GONE?

NOT QUITE SEMPER PARATUS

Even in colonial times, the militia was never all that it should have been. Laws governing the possession of weapons were laxly enforced. Each militiaman at the beginning of the Revolution should have owned a musket and a bayonet. At the Bunker Hill fight, though, few of the colonial militia had any kind of cutting or stabbing weapon. Muskets were useful for hunting. Bayonets might have been used as spits, but shish kebab did not appear on many colonial menus. If all the militiamen had followed the law, the Redcoats would have had to pay an even higher price for Breed's Hill. Sometimes even muskets were lacking. Before the Revolution, the colonial committees of safety frantically let contracts for muskets to every gunsmith extant. Because of the reputation of Pennsylvania gunsmiths, that colony had to pass a law forbidding the export of muskets so it could arm its own militia.[1] During the Whiskey Rebellion, only a few years after the Revolution, Alexander Hamilton had to give the Virginia militia 1,500 federal muskets.[2]

George Washington, as we've seen, was a frequent and bitter critic of the militia during the Revolution. Nevertheless, as president, in a note to Hamilton on May 2, 1783, he said: "Altho' a *large* standing Army in time of Peace hath ever been considered dangerous to the liberties of a Country, yet a few Troops, under certain circumstances, are not only safe, but indispensably necessary. Fortunately for us, our relative situation requires but few." He recommended an army of no more than 2,631 men. If danger threatened, there would be a "well-organized" militia. "The militia of this country," Washington said elsewhere, "must be considered as the palladium of our security and the first effective resort in case of hostility."[3]

Had the general changed his view on the utility of the militia? No, he had changed his view on what the militia should be. In another letter to Hamilton, rediscovered in 1930, Washington explained what he meant by a "well-organized" militia. It would be something like the system existing in Switzerland (and which still exists):

> It may be laid down as a primary position, and the basis of our system, that every Citizen who enjoys the protection of a free Government, owes not only a proportion of his property, but even of his personal services to the defense of it, and consequently the Citizens of America (with a few legal and political exceptions) from 18 to 50 years of Age should be borne on the Militia Rolls, provided with uniform Arms, and [be] so far accustomed to the use of them, that the Total strength of the Country might be called forth at a Short Notice on any very interesting Emergency.[4]

Washington took one recommendation from the Massachusetts "minuteman" system. He would have the younger men, up to 25 years of age, "always to be held in readiness for service."

In 1790, Henry Knox, Washington's wartime chief of artillery, presented a proposal for a militia system much like Washington's. Knox would include all men between 18 and 60. Those 18 to 20 would be enrolled in light infantry companies and given 30 days of training every year. Later, they would be enrolled in "the main body" and subject to only four muster days a year. At age 45, they would become inactive, subject to call only in the direst emergency.

Knox's proposal was introduced as a bill in Congress. What emerged was the Militia Act of 1792, which provided for something quite different from what Washington and Knox were thinking about. Under the act, each man between 18 and 60 would provide his own weapon and ammunition (24 rounds for a musketeer and 20 for a rifleman), including two spare flints.[5] (The act remained on the books until after the Spanish-American War, which occurred long after flintlocks and any other kind of muzzle-loader had become obsolete.) No one called to national service would be obliged to spend more than three months of a year in the service after reaching "the point of rendezvous." Men would be called out in rotation, and no one would serve "more than in due rotation with every other able-bodied man of the same rank." The three-month term limit quickly proved to be a serious handicap. During the Mexican War, Zachary Taylor had some 10,000 militiamen called up from Texas and Louisiana leave his army on the Mexican border when their term of service expired. Further, the militia, under the Constitution, could be called out only "to suppress insurrections and repel invasions." That made them useless for foreign wars.

THE VOLUNTEERS

These handicaps made national authorities turn more and more toward the volunteer units. Volunteer units had begun forming around the first quarter of the nineteenth century. They were composed of men attracted to the military life—marching, bands, uniforms, etc.—but who did not want to (or could not, the regular army being held to minuscule size) leave civilian life. The volunteers not only armed themselves, they provided their own uniforms—often copied from those of French, Algerian, Turkish, or other foreign soldiers. Like all other males of military age, they were part of the militia. Unlike the militia proper, though, they were willing to serve out of the country. Part of one volunteer regiment, the Louisiana Grays, went to the Alamo, in the Republic of Texas, and died there in 1836.[6]

When the Civil War began, both sides were loaded with colorfully dressed volunteer regiments. There were the usual problems with short enlistments, but eventually all troops were enlisted for the duration. The volunteer regiments tended to blend into the blue and gray masses as the war went on, and most of the volunteering became individual. Both sides had conscription, but the draft functioned mainly as a means to encourage volunteering.

The Union army's enormous increase in size led to a new concept, "the Volunteer Army," which was distinct from the regular army. All regular officers held ranks in the Volunteer Army, usually much higher than their regular ranks. George Armstrong Custer, for example, was a major general in the Volunteer Army while he was a captain in the regular army. After the war, the Volunteer Army was disbanded, and regular officers resumed their regular ranks. In World War I and later wars, when conscription was a major factor in raising troops, what was called the volunteer army in the Civil War became "the Army of the United States" to distinguish it from the regular United States Army.

The best-known unit in the Spanish-American War was the Rough Riders, a highly publicized cavalry regiment organized by Theodore Roosevelt and Leonard Wood. Roosevelt had enough political clout to get his troopers armed with Krag-Jorgensen bolt-action repeating carbines, which otherwise were limited to regular army personnel. The Rough Riders got credit for capturing San Juan Hill in Cuba, a feat actually performed by the African-American troopers of the Tenth Cavalry.

In general, the volunteer system worked quite well in the Spanish-American War. One volunteer unit, however, New York's elite Seventh Regiment, refused to put itself under federal authority. The Seventh Regiment is connected with two important changes in the U.S. military structure. The first involved a name. When the Marquis de Lafayette had visited the United States in 1824, the Seventh had adopted the name "the National Guard" after the French reserve corps Lafayette had commanded. The second was caused by the Seventh's actions in

1898. Congress changed the militia law and that led, as we'll see, to the creation of a new military force in the country.

The volunteer system was not totally abandoned after the Spanish War. When the United States entered World War I, the Army Signal Corps consisted of a handful of officers and fewer enlisted men. To remedy the situation, the U.S. telephone companies organized a volunteer battalion to provide telephone service at the front. By that time, though, volunteer military units were very much the exception.[7]

THE NATIONAL GUARD

The Civil War, like any major war, was followed by a reaction against things military. Volunteer units experienced a rebirth in the 1870s, however. The United States was undergoing a tremendous spurt of industrial growth, and the growing pains were violent. State governors tried to keep order (which usually meant protecting the moneyed interests) with the militia. The militia, though, often came from the same people who were striking the mines and factories. Some of the workers began forming armed paramilitary units, like the Lehr und Wehr Verein, for protection against the company guards and police. For help, the governors turned to certain fashionable volunteer units. One was the New York Seventh Regiment, the "National Guard." An article in *Harper's* in 1879 spoke glowingly of elite volunteer units:

> Especially the 7th Regiment of New York, with unusual resources for the selection of strong, patriotic, and wealthy young men of military tastes . . . and supported by a rich and appreciative community has been able, . . . in the perfection of its equipment and accomplishments, in the importance of its services, and lately in the completion of its magnificent armory at a cost of over $500,000 at private expense, to show what the citizen soldier may do for his country.[8]

The difference between the National Guard and the Lehr und Wehr was, of course, that the former were "patriotic and wealthy young men," who were only too willing to keep the poor in their place, and the latter were not only factory workers but immigrants who didn't speak good American. The National Guard was extolled; the Lehr und Wehr was suppressed.

The National Guard, the Seventh Regiment, was already famous when the *Harper's* article appeared. That same year, delegates from 19 states met in New York to establish the National Guard Association. Their aim was to duplicate New York's Seventh Regiment across the country. These units would provide the states with the means whereby their "laws may be enforced, social order maintained, and [protection afforded] against the sudden violence of popular faction."[9]

For several decades after that, from Pennsylvania to Colorado, National Guard units maintained social order at factories and mines with Gatling guns and Browning machine guns, making the history of American labor about the most violent in the world.

But no matter how well the "wealthy and patriotic young men" of the Seventh protected property and maintained social order during labor troubles, the unit's refusal in 1898 to put itself under "West Point martinets" did not please the federal government. Most of the men volunteered individually, but the proud state regiment refused to be called into the federal army. In 1903, the Dick Act was passed to prevent that from ever happening again. The Dick Act repealed the Militia Act of 1792 and recognized the National Guard as the "organized militia." All men between 17 and 45 remained "the unorganized militia," but the Dick Act emphasized a voluntary organization of state troops—precisely the sort of organization that, after a standing army, Patrick Henry and his faction most feared in the infancy of the republic.[10]

Richard Henry Lee, another Virginia Anti-Federalist of that period, had warned:

[T]he yeomanry of the country . . . possess arms, and they are too strong a body of men to be openly offended (but) they may in twenty or thirty years be, by means imperceptible by them, totally deprived of that boasted weight and strength. This may be done in great measure by Congress, if disposed to do it, by modeling the militia. Should one-fifth or one-eighth part of the men capable of bearing arms be made into a select militia, as has been proposed . . . and all the others put upon a plan which will render them of no importance, the former will answer all the purposes of an army, while the latter will be defenseless.[11]

Under the Dick Act, the federal government would arm the National Guard, provide other equipment and uniforms—all the same as the regular army's—and provide instructors for training. The Guard would remain state troops, but it could be called to federal service when needed.

THE STATE OF THE STATE MILITIA

Although the law recognizes the National Guard as the "organized militia," it is not militia in the traditional sense. The traditional militia provided its own weapons and served, usually without uniforms, under officers it elected. In spite of all the varying interpretations of the Second Amendment, *all* commentators agree that it was adopted to guarantee the existence of the traditional militia. The right to keep and bear arms is irrelevant to the National Guard. It's irrelevant even if you argue that the "right of the people to keep and bear arms" refers only to the states and not to the people. The *federal government*, under federal law, owns the weapons of the National Guard. It could be as logically argued that the Second Amendment guarantees the country the right to have an army.

So we still have the unorganized militia, thanks to the Second Amendment and Title 10, United States Code paragraph 311(a).

How militarily effective that militia may be is something else. We no longer make even the pretense of training all men of military age. The command structure of the militia is not only nonexistent, it's a joke. The only remnants of it are the honorary state colonel commissions, the best-known of which are the Kentucky colonels' commissions (like that of Colonel Sanders of fried chicken fame), handed out to favorite sons. There's no state or local law regulating the type of weapons militiamen must keep at home. About half of U.S. households don't have a gun of any kind. And now, U.S. citizens are forbidden to have the most effective military small arms—automatic weapons, rockets, hand and rifle grenades, mortars, and most of the other portable weapons used in modern warfare.

This prohibition began with the National Firearms Act of 1934, which was based to a large extent on a model bill crafted by the National Rifle Association of America.[12] The NFA features what was then believed to be a prohibitive tax ($200) on the transfer of any automatic weapon or unusually short rifle or shotgun. It was aimed at sawed-off shotguns, frequently used gangster weapons, and submachine guns, weapons less frequently used but more highly publicized. Gangsters probably bought a lot of shotguns and sawed off their barrels. They didn't buy that many submachine guns. The Thompson, the only SMG available in the United States, cost $225, a fortune in those days. John Dillinger got his tommy guns by holding up police stations. Clyde Barrow got both Thompsons and Browning Automatic Rifles by robbing National Guard armories.[13]

NRA Executive Vice President Milton Rekord testified in favor of a national version of his organization's model bill. He said, "We believe that the machine gun, submachine gun, sawed-off shotgun, and dangerous and deadly weapons could all be included in any kind of bill, and no matter how drastic, we would support it."[14] No NRA members, he said, had such weapons.

But in the end, the NRA did oppose the National Firearms Act. The reason: it included a registration of all pistols. When the pistol registration was dropped, the NRA dropped its opposition, and the bill passed. The Gun Control Act of 1968 strengthened the NFA. It added antitank rifles to the list of "destructive devices," such as grenades, rockets, flamethrowers, and bombs of any kind. In 1986, the NRA-sponsored McClure-Volkmer Act further removed automatic weapons from individual citizens. A last-minute amendment, which NRA executive J. Warren Cassidy defended, forbade the manufacture of machine guns (which includes SMGs) for sale to civilians other than police, and the sale of any new machine guns to private citizens.

The Director of Civilian Marksmanship program, which works largely through the NRA, has been drastically cut, but the government for a long time has provided surplus ammunition to licensed rifle clubs. The clubs, though, can use only hand-operated or semiautomatic guns. Almost all military small arms today are fully automatic. It is impossible to learn how to control a submachine gun, an automatic rifle, or a light machine gun in automatic fire by firing single shots. So today's militia is not only denied the hardware of modern war, it's denied the training to use it.

FOREIGN MILITIAS

Because most of its members can neither own nor use automatic small arms, the U.S. militia is less well equipped than the militias of many foreign countries. In Sweden, for example, submachine gun shooting is the most popular form of target practice.[15] Rifles are also plentiful in Sweden, and the ammunition companies, such as Norma Projektilfabrik, provide reloaded ammunition at very low prices.

The classic case of a "well regulated" foreign militia is, of course, the Swiss. The Swiss militia has an unbroken history going back to the Middle Ages, when Swiss pikemen and halberdiers destroyed the armored cavalry of the Hapsburgs and the Duke of Burgundy. The Swiss militiamen were so successful that their cantons hired them out to foreign princes. Swiss citizen-soldiers served in foreign armies because they thought it was their patriotic duty to earn money for their cantons. The Swiss militia is the only one that has proven itself effective when it is not directly defending its home.[16] The canton, incidentally, is the *Schweitzer's* real fatherland. Loyalty to the canton comes before loyalty to the Swiss Confederation.

Switzerland is the country most frequently cited by gun control opponents as a close-to-ideal society, because every man holding an enlisted rank in the militia keeps a machine gun—a true assault rifle—in his home. Every officer keeps a pistol. All Swiss men from 21 to 50 (55 for officers) are members of the militia. When they retire, they are given rifles or pistols, which are not registered. There is hardly any violent crime. The homicide rate, 1.8 per 100,000, is higher than that of England and Wales (.6 per 100,000) but lower than most of the world's, including Scotland's (3.3 per 100,000).[17]

The United Kingdom is the anti-gun lobby's favorite foreign country because, supposedly, private citizens don't have guns and there is hardly any violent crime.[18] The picture each side presents of its favorite foreign society is quite distorted. The U.K.'s violent crime rate, for instance, is considerably higher than the anti-gun lobby would have you believe, and it's rising rapidly. It is much higher now than it was before World War I, when there were no gun controls. As for Switzerland, it is perhaps the most socially stratified country in Europe.[19] Everyone knows his place. Although Swiss secondary education is of very high quality and Swiss colleges are virtually free, few Swiss attend college. For most people, a college education is simply not compatible with their place in life. All members of the Swiss militia start as privates, but those with a college education quickly become officers. Switzerland has a very low homicide rate, true, but it also has a very high suicide rate. (And surprisingly, in that heavily armed society, only about 23 percent of suicides are committed with guns. In the much less suicidal United States, about 59 percent of suicides use guns. Although the anti-gun lobby blames the number of American suicides on the number of guns available, there are obviously other factors at work.) The social stratification and lack of individuality in Switzerland makes possible a militia system Americans would probably never accept.

Anti-gun lobby spokesmen love to point out that all privately owned pistols in Switzerland have to be licensed. That's not exactly true.[20] A Swiss must have a permit, issued by his home canton, to buy a handgun of military size (caliber 6mm or larger). But permits are issued to anyone who is not a felon, insane, or otherwise unfit. In spite of Handgun Control, Inc.'s statement to the contrary,[21] the pistols are not registered. (Lies are so common in the gun control "debate" they're practically the norm.) More than half of the cantons require no permit to carry pistols. There is no difference in the crime rates in cantons that do and those that don't. Rifles, even semiautomatics, require no purchase permit. In Switzerland, as in the United States, retail dealers must keep records of guns sold. But unlike the United States, there is no need to record the sale of hunting guns, and no records are reported to the government. Further, individual citizens can buy submachine guns, heavy machine guns, and even artillery pieces with almost no red tape. These weapons are registered.[22]

Switzerland has very little crime, but it isn't because the Swiss lack guns. One anti-gun lobby pamphlet quotes a spokesman at the Swiss consulate as saying that few Swiss own pistols, "because there is very little crime in Switzerland and nobody feels the need to keep a pistol for protection." It's hard to escape the conclusion that the consulate official was diplomatically telling his questioner what the questioner wanted to hear. Probably few Swiss do feel the need to keep a pistol for protection. If you want protection in your home, an assault rifle (which most Swiss have) will do a bang-up job.[23] But target shooting with pistols is a most important sport in Switzerland, and the pistol collectors are avid. The Swiss have had two changes of service pistols in recent years. Older retired officers in the Swiss militia have the exquisite Swiss Luger. Widows of these older officers complain that when their husbands' obituaries appear, they are besieged by collectors wanting to buy the dead men's Lugers.[24]

The Swiss militiamen get plenty of training. They can use the government-issued ammunition for their assault rifles only in official training sessions, but commercial small arms ammunition of all kinds, including the service cartridges, is cheap and widely available. Service ammunition is sold at cost by the government. A much higher percentage of Swiss than Americans participate in target matches. There are 3,000 shooting ranges in that nation of six million people. Nor is their training only with small arms. At their annual training sessions, Swiss citizen-soldiers practice using artillery, rockets, tanks, and aircraft.

Once, in the middle nineteenth century, someone mentioned to Prince Klemens von Metternich of Austria, then the strongman of Europe, that Switzerland had no army.

"No," Metternich replied, "Switzerland is an army."[25]

Several centuries earlier, Niccolò Machiavelli had observed, "The Swiss are fully armed, and fully free."[26]

That is common knowledge in Europe. Because of it, the Swiss militia has not been put to the test in many, many years.

A militia that has been tested frequently is the Israeli. Virtually every Israeli man and woman serves time in the armed forces. After active service, each becomes a member of the reserve, subject to periodic retraining. The reservist keeps an issue weapon, usually a Galil assault rifle, at home. Every time the reservist wears the uniform, even if on the way from work to training, he carries the weapon. Permits to carry privately possessed handguns and submachine guns are easy to get for Israeli citizens, according to criminologist Abraham N. Tennenbaum.[27] And in spite of 1994's sensational "mosque massacre" in Hebron, murder is rare. The 4.5 million people in Israel generate only 40 to 60 murders a year.[28]

The armed citizenry of Israel provides a defense against terrorists as well as enemy armies. In April 1984, three terrorists began firing automatic weapons at a crowd in a Jerusalem café. They killed one diner before pistol-toting Israeli civilians killed two of the terrorists and wounded the third. The surviving terrorist said he and his companions planned to machine gun several crowded spots, then try to escape before the police arrived. He said they didn't realize Israeli citizens carried guns.[29] That may be the reason later terrorists have relied on car bombs and long-range rockets—attacks that can't be frustrated by pistol-packing citizens.

Israel's record in the Near East wars should be sufficient proof that its militia system works. Some critics, though, simply disparage the Arab armies the Jewish state has faced. They claim militia facing first-class armies would not be so effective. Some of them with a little historical knowledge point to the poor record of the *franc-tireurs* in the Franco-Prussian War.

The *franc-tireurs*, however, were hardly a typical militia. These irregulars included some Frenchmen who had never held a rifle before and a motley array of foreign adventurers, including a band of South American gauchos who came with lassos as well as guns, and a band of Italians led by Garibaldi who were dedicated to world revolution. Few of them had, like true militia, roots in the area where they fought.[30] More typical militia of about the same period were the Afrikaner burghers who fought the British in the First Boer War (1881) and the Second Boer War (1899–1902).

The South African Republic, known to the British as the Transvaal, had no regular army. When danger threatened, men in each area organized groups called commandos, each composed of up to several hundred men. They would then elect commandants to lead the commandos and lesser officers, such as cornets and corporals. For a big operation, a group of commandos would elect a commandant general. Each man in the commando would bring one or more horses, a rifle, and ammunition. The First Boer War ended with an Afrikaner victory, with the militia having beaten the British in every battle. The climax was the Battle of Majuba Hill, when an outnumbered force of Afrikaner farmers attacked British troops on top of a mountain and routed them. In the Second Boer War, the Orange Free State joined the South African Republic. The British eventually won that war, but only after they had flooded South Africa with many more soldiers than there were Afrikaner men, women, and children in the two republics; burned farms; slaughtered farm animals and confined hundreds of thousands of Afrikaner women and children in concentration camps, where huge numbers of them died.[31]

THE EFFECTIVENESS OF U.S. MILITIA TODAY

There is a rather small movement today to repeal the Second Amendment. It is composed primarily of people who believe the amendment is obsolete and that private ownership of firearms is a danger to society. Although their position is certainly open to criticism, these people at least are honest. They recognize that the Second Amendment means just what it says, and they are willing to go through the repeal process and leave the question of gun control up to the American people. (Most of the anti-gun lobby are afraid to be that open.) Of the two points in the repealers' position, the first—that an armed citizenry is obsolete for military purposes—is less tenable today than it was a few years ago.

After the Second World War, when fear of nuclear war was on everybody's mind, it was easy to dismiss the whole notion of militia. Tanks and infantry seemed outmoded to people convinced that devastation would come from the sky. Then we got into a messy and bloody ground war in Korea, and tanks and infantry were suddenly important again. But militia armed with rifles and homemade bombs? Oh, come on. Then we had another spot of trouble in Vietnam. Now nobody is ready to deny the effectiveness of well-managed guerrilla warfare. How effective a guerrilla force the U.S. militia could field is, of course, unknown. But with the very widespread ownership of guns in this country, and the fact that many gun owners are fairly skilled in their use, guerrillas here might be pretty effective. They'd certainly begin with better resources than those in Vietnam. Guerrillas could mean serious trouble for any invader who is not prepared to nuke the country into oblivion. In a civil war, when neither side wants to annihilate its own people, guerrillas are most effective.

The second point in the repealers' argument—that private ownership of firearms is a threat to public safety—is even weaker, as we'll see. It is, though, the main bone of contention in the gun control "debate." We'll examine that issue in the next two sections: first, the way the fight is being conducted in the U.S. Congress and in village councils; and second, how the propaganda from each side compares with reality.

But before turning to the struggle itself, let's look more closely at the importance of that "well regulated militia."

CHAPTER 6

DIGRESSION NO. 1: WEAPONS AND WARFARE

MILITIA IN TODAY'S WORLD

Because there is such a disparity between the weaponry available to any national government and that available to the individual militiaman, a little analysis is in order. Would the individual citizen, the militiaman—or even crowds of militiamen—have the slightest chance against government forces in armed conflict?

At the present time, militia could not be used, as the framers of the Constitution intended, in conventional warfare. The only practical use for lightly armed militia would be guerrilla warfare.

Fighting guerrillas, as both Vietnam and Afghanistan recently proved, is not the strong suit of modern armies. In most cases, the higher the tech, the lower its usefulness against guerrillas. Nuclear weapons, for example, are counterproductive. They not only utterly destroy huge areas, but, if used often enough, they can make a whole country uninhabitable, even for the nuke-users. The neutron bomb kills people without destroying property, but it kills people wholesale. It is useful only to somebody who wants to rule a desert. "Electronic warfare" is another "highest tech" area. Most of it is concerned with either detecting enemy aircraft and missiles, or foiling the enemy's detection efforts. Advances in chemistry and engineering have produced binary shells and bombs, which are more powerful than earlier versions. That power is useless, though, if it can't be applied to the guerrillas. Here are the weapons available to any first-class modern government:

STRATEGIC BOMBARDMENT: MISSILES AND BOMBERS

Strategic bombardment is devastating against fixed positions—very fixed positions. Guerrillas seldom try to hold fixed positions.

THE PATRIOT, NIKE ZEUS, AND OTHER
ANTI-MISSILE MISSILES

See above. No militia force would have the weapons these things are supposed to shoot down.

TAC AIR: HELICOPTER TRANSPORTS, GUNSHIPS,
FIGHTER-BOMBERS

These are a much more serious threat. However, experience in Vietnam did not show tactical airpower to be quite as devastating as Air Force officers would like to think. There have been innumerable instances where planes or helicopters have ignored guerrillas firing at the forces they're supporting from a line of trees and bombed and strafed the village behind them.[1] The airmen did not do that from a diabolical urge to destroy villages. They simply didn't see anything except the village. If there was firing on the ground, it must have been coming from the village. At the siege of Khe Sahn, the North Vietnamese completely fooled Air Force observers and bombers with make-believe trenches that would have been utterly useless for ground troops.[2]

In the last few years, every air force has been striving mightily to develop ways to neutralize increasingly sophisticated antiaircraft weapons. High-altitude antiaircraft rockets have made traditional high-altitude (40,000 feet or so) bombing so risky as to approach the suicidal—at least theoretically.[3] The new approach is to fly low, to avoid radar detection, and to fly fast. Thanks to electronic navigational aids, warplanes today can fly lower and faster than pilots a few years ago would have believed possible. But if the pilots can't see the targets, it doesn't do any good. And with even the best sensors, it's not easy to see men hidden in the trees as you skim the treetops at 1,400 miles per hour.

One of the prime objectives of any guerrilla force would be to secure the enemy's man-portable, ground-to-air missiles, like the Stinger, which was developed to counter low-flying planes. If the guerrillas were successful, the government's tac air would be even less effective.

TANKS AND ARMORED PERSONNEL CARRIERS

Armored fighting vehicles are a tremendous psychological weapon even in areas where they are not otherwise effective. And they've proven effective in some very unlikely territory. They were a prime street-fighting weapon in World War II and later. That's especially true when their enemies, like the Hungarian rebels in Budapest in 1956, rely on such ridiculously outmoded weapons as Molotov cocktails. On the other hand, German infantry with *Panzerfausts* and Russians with antitank grenades were able to make cities very unhealthy for tanks. Cities provide too many concealed firing positions for troops with powerful, but short-range weapons.

Tank armor has greatly improved, of course. In World War II, the "shaped charge," which creates a jet of hot gas able to burn through armor, made possible the bazooka, the Panzerfaust and a wide variety of antitank weapons. Today, we have reactive armor, which explodes to counter the shaped charge jet. It can make the first hit from an antitank grenade or rocket ineffective.[4] The second hit, though, would be an entirely different story. Then, too, reactive armor has a reaction on its own vehicle. Some relatively thin-skinned armored personnel carriers have crumpled like discarded candy wrappers from the explosions of their own reactive armor.[5] In spite of all the advances in armor, tanks are still vulnerable in cities, as the Chechens demonstrated to the Russian armored forces in Grozny. On January 3, 1995, Interfax, the Russian news agency, quoted a wounded Russian officer, Aleksandr Bondarev, as saying 17 of the 20 tanks in his unit had been burned with their crews.[6]

Tanks have always been vulnerable to explosions from above or below. Land mines, especially remote controlled mines, have always been a prime antitank weapon. Because they're easy to make, guerrillas have been particularly fond of them. They are especially effective when the tank has a limited number of directions to take. Tanks in cities are channeled that way. So are tanks in mountains, and in forests. There are plenty of cities, mountains and forests in the United States.

When the North Koreans used Russian T-34 tanks in Korea, newspapers and magazines in the United States fulminated against the American experts who said Korea is not tank country. The North Koreans would have disagreed with those editorials. By the end of the year, after less than six months of fighting, almost all their tanks had been destroyed.[7] It worked both ways. I remember counting 16 burned-out hulks of American tanks in the valley of Mundung-ni. They had been sent up that narrow valley by some fool who thought Korea *was* tank country, after all.

Most people who've seen movies of tanks pushing down relatively slender trees think forests present no obstacle. They're wrong. After a tank has pushed down a number of trees, they pile up, and if the vehicle keeps going in the same direction, the tankers soon find their treads out of contact with the ground. Sitting in an immobile tank in combat is a good way to keep from growing old. Tanks can make their way through woods, but they can't do it quickly. It takes good judgment of the ground and careful steering. And even then, the vehicle can be hung up, especially in hilly woods like those that cover most of the eastern states.

ARTILLERY

Artillery is devastating in classic warfare. It's just short of useless in hit-and-run guerrilla warfare. Guerrillas don't usually present the kind of densely populated target that makes artillery fire worthwhile. Nor do they have the sort of powerful, relatively immobile weapons, like field pieces and heavy machine guns, that artillery is expected to counter. There have been tremendous advances in artillery ammunition. Guns can fire several types of anti-armor projectiles. There are shells that can be guided by laser beams, and there are binary shells that are far more powerful than anything seen in wars to date. But plain, old-fashioned shells are more than sufficient to do in an unarmored guerrilla. You have to get it near enough to him to hurt him, though. Laser beams are fine for pinpointing tanks, but a tank is much easier to locate than a dug-in foot soldier.

Furthermore, artillery, even self-propelled artillery, is more road-bound than tanks in good guerrilla country. Air-transportable artillery can be quickly flown by helicopter to about any firing point. But once there, it stays there. Guerrillas don't.

Mortars, a form of artillery, are much more useful than their heavier cousins, because they can be carried anywhere an infantryman can go. Wise guerrillas work at not being good targets for mortars. In a war without flanks, as most guerrilla warfare is, guerrilla snipers hunt mortarmen and try to capture their weapons.

Recoilless tripod-mounted or shoulder-fired artillery pieces are as mobile as mortars but are used for direct fire.[8] Mortars typically are hidden behind a hill and fire over it to hit the enemy. Recoilless guns fire at targets they can see. They fire cannister (masses of steel balls) or beehive (clusters of darts) rounds as well as high explosive and antitank rounds. Cannister or beehive rounds make the gun into an enormous shotgun that has a devastating effect on bunched enemy troops. Otherwise, recoilless guns have about the same advantages and disadvantages as mortars in guerrilla warfare. One glaring disadvantage mortars don't have but recoilless guns do is a tremendous backblast on firing. That makes them a target for all enemy troops in the vicinity. It's a characteristic they share with . . .

. . . ROCKET LAUNCHERS

Rocket launchers, like the well-known Russian RPG-7, are useful against either walls or tanks. Guerrillas don't use tanks, and the RPG-7 and similar devices are very short-range weapons.[9] Use of the longer-range, wire-guided antitank rockets against guerrillas is unlikely. Guerrillas don't present much of a target; the rocketeer on many of these weapons is vulnerable to sniper fire because he has to keep the target in sight while he guides the missile. And government forces probably wouldn't use these weapons where they might be captured. They'd have little use against guerrillas, but they could be devastating in the hands of guerrillas.

MOTION DETECTORS AND NIGHT-VISION DEVICES

Motion detectors, based on vibration sensors or infrared rays, could be useful in guarding fixed positions.[10] One guerrilla tactic against such devices is to drive the defenders crazy with numerous feints, often using animals to set off the detectors. If the guerrillas have infrared-detecting glasses, they can also locate and knock out the infrared motion detectors.

Night-vision devices, really light intensifiers, are more useful for government forces. The image they produce, though, is monochrome, which makes camouflage easy. Still, a soldier who sees a "bush" moving is not likely to ignore what he sees. Heat sensors, which see the infrared waves emitted by a warm engine or a human body, are another threat to guerrillas attacking a position at night. The attackers would have to approach with all the care they would take in daylight. The advantage these sensors confer is mostly to troops in position. They have some use for troops on night patrols in limited areas. They are less practical for troops on the move, even though modern tanks are equipped with a variety of sensors.

SMALL ARMS

Heavy, high-tech weapons, then, are mostly useful against heavy, high-tech enemies. In guerrilla warfare, the decisive weapons are small arms—pistols, rifles, machine guns, and grenades—hand-thrown or fired from a gun.

Pistols are little used in conventional warfare. Pistols are the least powerful firearm used in war and the most difficult to shoot accurately. Typically, officers carry them as a last-ditch defense. In guerrilla warfare, pistols are used more frequently. Because they can be easily concealed, guerrillas may use them for surprise attacks, especially in urban settings. The government troops surprised may also have to rely on pistols because they may not have time to reach other weapons.

Rifles fall into three categories: repeaters, semiautomatics (sometimes called self-loaders, especially in Britain), and automatics. Automatics are usually selective-fire, meaning they are capable of either semiautomatic or automatic fire. Some single-shots were used by guerrillas in World War II, but they are unlikely to ever see military use again.[11]

Most modern national armies use selective-fire assault rifles. Assault rifles use cartridges much less powerful than the rifle cartridges of World War II.[12] The reason is that repeated recoil shocks make rifles with powerful cartridges uncontrollable in full automatic fire from the shoulder. Recoil increases with the power of the cartridge and decreases with the weight of the rifle. Rifles weighing more than about 10 pounds become a burden in combat and decrease the amount of ammunition the troops can carry. Something had to give, and it was the power of the cartridge. For comparison, the cartridge of the current U.S. assault rifle, the 5.56 x 45mm NATO (also called .223 Remington), has a muzzle energy of 1,282 foot pounds. The old .30-06 military cartridge had 2,739 foot pounds— more than twice as much power—and most civilian versions (available to militia, of course) are even more powerful.[13] (More information about the assault rifle appears in the chapter 17, "Devil Guns.")

Because of its lower-power cartridge, the assault rifle has much less range and penetration than the previous standard infantry rifle, either manually loaded, like the Springfield M-1903, or semiautomatic, like the Garand M-1. That's not a severe disadvantage, for in conventional warfare, troops move forward in armored personnel carriers under cover of fire from tanks and artillery. When they dismount, they are well within the effective range of their assault rifles. And because those assault rifles are capable of automatic fire, they can shower the enemy positions with bullets. That makes the enemy troops keep their heads down, while attacking forces advance on their positions.

Forced to fire at long range, the assault rifle is not so good. For a while, the U.S. Army relied on the old M-14, which uses a full-power cartridge, the 7.62mm NATO round. Now both the army and the U.S. Marine Corps use a militarized Remington bolt-action rifle that can take either the 7.62 NATO or the .300 Winchester Magnum, a *very* powerful cartridge.

The assault rifle's ability to penetrate trees, walls, and other objects enemies might use for cover is also unimpressive. The 5.56 x 45mm cartridge of the U.S. M-16 assault rifle will penetrate 10 one-inch pine boards.[14] The .30-06 cartridge of the World War II M-1 rifle would pierce *70* pine boards.[15] An enemy hiding behind a thick tree has good cover from an M-16's fire. From an M-1's, he doesn't.

The great advantage of an assault rifle is its rapidity of fire. An M-16 fires at a cyclic rate of between 700 and 900 rounds per minute.[16] That does not mean that it actually fires that many cartridges in a minute. The M-16, for instance, normally has a 20- or 30-round detachable magazine. If a soldier switched it to full automatic and kept his finger on the trigger, he'd empty the 20-round magazine in less than two seconds, the 30-rounder in less than three. Then he'd have to take the magazine out and insert another. Do that a few times, and the barrel becomes red-hot and the rifling erodes, giving the rifle the accuracy of a 1775 Brown Bess musket.[17] In actual practice, the rate for an assault rifle in combat is around 150 rounds a minute. That's still an improvement over the rate possible with a semiautomatic or a hand-operated repeater. But not as big an improvement as you might think. In 1866, the *single-shot* Peabody rifle fired 17 aimed and 35 unaimed shots a minute in U.S. Army tests.[18] Big-bore match competitors using bolt-action repeaters fire 10 carefully aimed rounds in less than a minute, including the time it takes to strip a five-round clip into the magazine.[19] Match rules are not very exacting when it comes to time limits: the time periods are long enough to let anyone get off the full number of shots without trouble. A well trained man with a Springfield bolt-action rifle can get off 25 to 30 aimed shots in a minute. With the British SMLE bolt action, he can fire even faster. With a semiautomatic like the M-1, a moderately trained man can exceed 30 aimed shots a minute. A very well trained man can reach 50 or 60 aimed shots a minute. Unaimed, but pointed, the semiautomatic can fire at a *rate* of more than 300 rounds a minute, but the need to replace magazines or clips cuts that time drastically. This sort of burst fire is occasionally useful at short ranges. The principal limit to speed of aimed fire with a semiautomatic is recoil. Each shot jars the gun off target, and the shooter must line up his sights again. Semiautomatic and manually loaded rifles heat up the same way automatics do (although more slowly, because the rate of fire is less). Heat can limit the rate of fire from them as well as from the automatics.

On paper, then, it looks as if automatics are not even five times more effective than semiautomatics. Actually, they're a good deal less effective than that. There are some situations where automatic fire is helpful, though. For instance, if you suspect an enemy presence in a clump of brush, it's easy to fire an automatic burst into the brush to see if there's a reaction. It's harder to organize five semiautomatic riflemen to volley into the same place. Automatics provide what squad tacticians call a "base of fire." That involves hosing down an area where enemy troops are hiding so your other riflemen can shoot them as they try to move away.

The automatic assault rifle is also excellent for close-quarters fighting. It can be used the same way as the submachine gun, an automatic weapon firing pistol cartridges. Because the assault rifle has more range and penetration than the submachine gun, the SMG is obsolete in most modern armies.

The automatic assault rifle has definite advantages. It also has some disadvantages. Accuracy, for instance. The M-16 is extremely accurate for an assault rifle. Fired semiautomatically, it can compare with a semiautomatic or a hand-loaded rifle. But if a good shot fires at a difficult target when the gun is on automatic, the first shot is likely to hit the target while the rest of the burst lands somewhere else. That wastes ammunition. To avoid waste, many assault rifles have three kinds of fire—single shots, automatic, and two- or three-round bursts. Some assault rifles are capable of only semiautomatic fire and short bursts. NO assault rifle, however, is limited to semiautomatic fire alone. Using three-round bursts, a good shot is still likely to hit a difficult target with the first shot and miss with the other two. But a poor shot whose first bullet misses may get a lucky hit with one of the other two. To look at it another way, if an assault rifle with a 20-round magazine is set to fire three-round bursts, its user really has only seven shots. In contrast, the old M-1 Garand had eight shots, each far more powerful as well as more accurate than any in the assault rifle.

In 1969, Capt. Henry Lum of the U.S. Army tested the accuracy of an M-16 rifle in semiautomatic and automatic fire. He set up man-size silhouette targets at 25 and 12.5 meters, ranges that seem ridiculously close for a trained rifleman but may have been common in the Vietnam jungle. He fired a number of 20-round magazines at them, shifting from one target to another after each shot fired semiautomatically and after each automatic burst. Firing semiautomatically at the 25-meter targets, he fired at an average of 19.8 targets with each magazine and scored 19.2 hits. The average time it took to hit all the targets semiautomatically was 22.1 seconds per magazine. Firing automatic two-round bursts at the same targets, Lum took an average of 14.8 seconds to hit an average of 8.5 targets per magazine. At 12.5-meters, Lum engaged 19.7 targets in 14.6 seconds and scored 18.5 hits firing semiautomatically. Firing automatically at that range, he cut his time by less than two seconds, finishing a magazine in 12.7 seconds while engaging 9.5 targets and scoring 17 hits.[20] Lum's test demonstrates that the effectiveness of automatic over semiautomatic fire is far less than it appears to be on paper, even at extremely short range. Semiautomatic fire appears to be often *more* effective.

To sum up, the assault rifle is inferior to an ordinary high-power rifle in range and penetration. At short ranges, though, it may be superior in some situations unless it's used against an enemy behind heavy cover, like thick trees or brick walls. It also gives its user a psychological advantage: people worry more about bursts of fire than single bullets.

Machine guns have the same psychological advantage to a greater degree. In general, they are far more powerful than assault rifles. The new U.S. squad automatic, the Belgian-designed "Minimi," is a machine gun using the same cartridge as the M-16.[21] The other machine guns, though, use the 7.62 NATO round. Either type of gun is more accurate than the assault rifle in automatic fire. The machine gun is fired from a rest, a bipod or a tripod, which makes holding it on target easier—much easier if the rest is a tripod. The disadvantage of the machine gun is weight. At just over 14 pounds, the Minimi is one of the lightest. Most of them weigh more than 20 pounds, or two or three times as much as an assault rifle. The gun also consumes ammunition rapidly, which means that additional troops carrying ammunition should accompany each gunner.

In World Wars I and II, there were water-cooled machine guns that would fire as long as the water jacket was kept full and the ammunition belts kept coming.[22] Today's machine guns are air-cooled. When the barrel gets too hot, the gunners replace it with a cool one. Even so, they can't keep up the volume of fire of the old guns. But they are far more mobile.

Machine guns definitely overmatch any guns militia are likely to have. Guns like the U.S. Minimi squad automatic, though, have the same limited range and power as the assault rifles. And the larger guns are less mobile and more likely to draw fire.

Grenades: Many military analysts are wondering if hand grenades are worth their weight in conventional warfare.[23] They are still useful in guerrilla war. There's nothing like an exploding grenade in an enemy guardhouse or police station to announce a surprise raid. Rifle grenades, or improvised "shotgun grenades," can play an important antitank role in guerrilla forces.[24] The regular armies' grenade launchers—guns that fire small grenades previously impossible distances—can also be most effective against guerrillas. Automatic grenade launchers, which look like big machine guns, could be extremely effective against guerrillas.[25] They have less range than machine guns but twice the range of hand-held grenade launchers. Their disadvantages are size and relative immobility, as well as the weight of the ammunition.

Shotguns: Since World War I, shotguns have been increasingly used in war. They were widely used by American forces in the jungles of the Pacific. There was little use for them in the mountain war fought in Korea, but they got a lot of use in Vietnam. They are very deadly at ranges of less than 30 yards.[26] And they are widely available to civilians.

MILITIA VERSUS REGULARS

Militia obviously could not beat regular forces in conventional battles. But militia have high-power rifles that could let them snipe at enemy regulars while remaining out of range of most regular fire. The value of marksmanship has been somewhat downgraded in regular armies, but it is of prime importance for guerrillas with slow-firing, long-range rifles.

Explosives are easy to steal and not difficult to make.[27] Guerrillas can fashion a variety of land mines and bombs from them. Guerrillas can stage surprise raids using concealed grenades, pistols, and shortened shotguns. If they can outnumber the regulars, the fire of semiautomatic and hand-operated rifles could match that of the regulars' automatics, especially if the guerrillas surprise the regulars.[28] Because of the nature of guerrillas and regulars, surprise is most often on the guerrillas' side.

The greatest military weakness of the American militia is lack of organization. The militia of the American Revolution had organization and a hierarchy of officers. The Viet Cong in the beginning lacked weapons but had a strong organization. The American militia has no organization whatever. It has even less than the Afrikaner militia of turn-of-the-century South Africa. The Afrikaners formed commandos and elected their officers, true, but a commando could vary in size from a couple of dozen men to a couple of hundred. Its sub-units, led by cornets and corporals, varied as widely. If an Afrikaner rifleman didn't like his superior officer, he would follow another one. He obeyed only orders he agreed with. But in two wars, the Afrikaner demonstrated to the British Empire that he was no contemptible warrior. It is possible that sufficiently motivated—after a foreign invasion, for example—Americans could evolve a rudimentary organization like that of South Africa. They have the weapons to make it work. There would, however, have to be sufficient motivation. In a democracy, in contrast to the oligarchies and military despotisms in third world countries or the aristocracies that plagued Europe in the past, there's little chance of an armed uprising. It's easier to vote the rascals out than to blast them out. A successful revolution must have the support of the majority of the people, and if opponents of the regime are in the majority, they'll win at the next election.

The NRA's fantasists dream of a *levée en masse* of armed citizens overthrowing a tyrannical government or overwhelming an enemy army. Such an attempt would be mass suicide. Determined militia guerrillas, supported by the mass of the people, could, however, make an occupying military force devoutly wish it were occupied with some other problem.

PART II
GUN FIGHT

CHAPTER 7

THE SEEDS OF DISCORD

THE GREAT SATAN

In testimony before Congress James Brady called it "the evil empire."[1] The anti-gun lobby views it the way the Ayatollah Khomeini viewed the United States. But back in 1871, the National Rifle Association of America didn't seem so sinister.

In that year, a pair of Civil War veterans, William C. Church and George W. Wingate, founded the organization to promote rifle practice. They had been appalled by the quality of marksmanship Union soldiers displayed. Church, editor of a military newspaper, had written: "The National Guard is again too slow in getting about this reform. Private enterprise must take up the matter and push it into life."[2] Wingate, a captain in New York's National Guard, agreed. The two got a charter for an organization to promote marksmanship from the state of New York and state aid in establishing a rifle range on Long Island. For a while, the NRA prospered. Its range at Creedmoor was the site of a series of international rifle matches between the U.S., Irish, and British teams. Though rifle shooting is seldom considered a spectator sport, thousands took the railroad from New York City to Creedmoor to watch the matches. The first match, against the Irish team, was especially exciting. The U.S. won the match on the last shot fired by the last U.S. competitor.

The good times lasted only until 1880. As the decade began, New York Governor Alonzo Cornell was looking for a way to economize. Cornell was no fan of the National Guard or of any other volunteer military unit. That was not an unreasonable position considering the role volunteer units had played (mostly in other states) in putting down strikes. Cornell's main objection, as he told Wingate, was, "There will be no war in my time or in the time of my children."[3]

"The only need for a National Guard is to show itself at parades and ceremonies," he continued. "I see no reason for them to learn to shoot if their only function will be to march a little through the streets."[4] Wingate tried to argue that the citizen-soldiers should know how to use the guns they carried. Cornell countered that the state should take away their rifles and sell them. "It would be more practical and far less expensive to arm them with clubs, which require no instruction for their use."[5] Cornell could not take the rifles away, of course, because the state didn't own them. The federal government didn't own them, either. Federal ownership of National Guard weapons—and, indeed, the National Guard as we know it—was still in the future. The volunteers owned their rifles. What Cornell could do, though, was eliminate any state expenditures to promote rifle practice, which meant any aid to the NRA. In spite of its name, the NRA was not really a national organization. It was heavily dependent on the state of New York. The NRA sold the Creedmoor range and moved to New Jersey, where it vegetated for several years.

Spanish-American War fever revived it. Rifle shooting became a popular sport, and the NRA took the lead in promoting matches and helping ranges open. For many years, its main activity was target shooting and helping local groups set up clubs and rifle ranges, as well as providing expert instruction in marksmanship and gun safety. After World War II, it expanded into hunting with the aim of showing returning veterans that acceptable hunting technique differed from what they had learned in the service. Hunters, for example, do not lay down barrages of bullets to bag game.

In the early part of the century, the NRA was not considered a lobby, although it maintained close connections with the government, particularly the War Department. It got army help in running the annual National Matches at Camp Perry, Ohio, and in getting the Director of Civilian Marksmanship program established. The DCM presented marksmanship awards to junior shooters, and loaned rifles and donated ammunition to NRA-affiliated rifle clubs. When the army had surplus weapons, the DCM sold them at cost or less to adult NRA members.

When New York passed its Sullivan Law in 1911, the NRA merely criticized the law in its national magazine, *Arms and the Man*:

> A warning should be sounded to legislators against passing laws which . . . seem to make it impossible for a criminal to get a pistol if the same laws would make it very difficult for an honest man and a good citizen to obtain them. Such laws have the effect of arming the bad man and disarming the good one.[6]

It was not until a national movement to restrict firearms ownership got underway in the 1930s that the NRA got involved in anything resembling lobbying as it is commonly understood.

Even then, its lobbying did not involve donations to politicians or political parties. The NRA technique then was to ask its members to communicate with their congressmen and, especially, to ask their gun-owning friends to do likewise. The friends were important, because NRA members are a tiny minority of gun owners and always have been. Today, there are around three to three-and-a-half million NRA members,[7] but some 20 million hunters and 70 million gun owners.[8] The NRA asked its members to oppose the National Firearms Act because it would register pistols. The resulting barrage of letters and telegrams killed the pistol-registration provision and has killed many legislative initiatives since. Although the NRA now has a formal lobbying organization, the Institute for Legislative Action (ILA), that does make political contributions, communications from gun owners are still its most potent weapon. On August 19, 1994, the Associated Press revealed the "shocking" information that the NRA had made $621,000 in political donations in 1994 before the vote on the 1994 Crime Bill.[9] By comparison, political action committees opposed to a stronger Clean Water Act contributed more than $56 million to congressional candidates between January 1987 and December 1993, according to the Public Interest Research Group, an environmentally oriented "watchdog" group with branches in each state.[10] According to the Federal Election Commission, in 1995, political action committees reported raising $192.6 million and spending $148.6 million, $67.6 million for federal candidates. Corporate PACs contributed almost $29 million to candidates and retained more than $43 million to make further contributions. For labor PACs, the figures are $11 million and $43 million.[11] Anyone who thinks the NRA could buy the whole Congress for $621,000 should consider that the *average* senator spends $4.5 *million* in a campaign and that candidates for the 435 House seats spent a total of $406 million in 1994.[12] The NRA's money for political contributions does not come from the firearms industry, as anti-gun lobbyist charge. (According to Josh Sugarmann, "the National Rifle Association has evolved into the unofficial trade association for the firearms industry.")[13] The money comes from those 3 million members. In recent years, the association, especially its ILA branch, has been dunning its membership almost continuously for donations to finance legislative action.

The NRA does get money from the arms industry for advertising in its magazines. That amounts to about 8 percent of the NRA budget,[14] but, by law, that money can't be used for lobbying. Further, major segments of the firearms industry have differed sharply with the NRA's stand on gun control. At the 1991 SHOT (Shooting, Hunting, Outdoor Trade) show, activist gun owners were urging a boycott of Ruger and Mossberg—major American gun makers.[15] The protesters deemed the management of the two companies insufficiently "hard-line." In 1968, Smith and Wesson and six other major firearms makers endorsed a proposal for a national Sullivan-type law.[16] That was a direct attack on the NRA position. Many in the organization urged a boycott of Smith and Wesson, too. But a boycott was impractical. S & W's bread and butter is not sales to individual Americans but orders from police agencies and foreign governments. There are so many of those that orders are backed up.

In spite of these facts, the anti-gun lobby has managed to portray the NRA as a regiment of troglodytes spreading around money from the enormous firearms industry (which actually accounts for about .03 percent of total U.S. industry).[17] In this way, the anti-gun lobby claims, the NRA has managed to defeat "sensible gun laws for the last century." (The phrase is Sarah Brady's, found on the dust jacket of Osha Gray Davidson's *Under Fire: The NRA and the Battle for Gun Control.* We'll see shortly what kind of gun laws Brady considers sensible.) The *Washington Post*, in particular, can be relied upon to credit any NRA legislative victory to the association's "paid army of House members."[18] The charge, that those who vote with the NRA have been bribed, is pure slander. If congressmen weren't public figures, it would also be legally libelous.

Osha Gray Davidson, no gun lobby sympathizer, interviewed Dennis Burke, an aide to Senator Dennis DeConcini, a pro-gun control senator from Arizona.

"You always hear these arguments," Burke said. "It's the NRA money; these guys are bought. I don't think these guys care about the contributions they get from the NRA. They care about the piles of mail, these nasty phone calls, and people picketing their state offices. They get no real pounding if they vote *with* the NRA. The pundits and the Op-Eds may nail them, but so what?"[19]

Somehow, it escapes many people—but not politicians—that what elects of-fice-holders is votes, not money. Money can help to get votes, but there's a long list of now-forgotten politicians who went down to defeat after outspending their opponents by wide margins. The NRA's power comes from including a large block of voters who are hypersensitive to what they consider attempts to infringe on their right to own and use guns. Their hypersensitivity comes from decades— but hardly a century—of propaganda by the NRA.

That NRA propaganda may have been instrumental in stirring up some of its membership and other gun owners, but it has also caused the gun lobby a lot of trouble. The NRA party line frequently suffers from rhetorical overkill. Here's a sample from Harlon Carter, former executive vice president of the association:

> Gun prohibition is the inevitable harbinger of oppression. It can only be pursued by "no-knock" laws under which jackbooted minions of gov-ernment invade the homes of citizens; by "stop-and-frisk" laws under which the person of citizens can be searched on the streets at the whim and suspicion of authority.[20]

This might be considered overkill even if a gun-prohibition law were under discussion. But no such law was being considered. About the only national gun law in prospect when Carter spoke was the imposition of a short waiting period before the purchase of a pistol.

By its hysterical protests against such measures as a seven-day waiting period, the NRA has made itself and its members look ridiculous. As the fight over gun control gets hotter, the NRA has been getting increasingly shrill. In the spring of 1994, it set some kind of record for stupidity by sending all its members printed and addressed postcards with the identical message. Members were expected to sign their names to these cards and mail them to three television anchors and a newspaper.

The message itself is easier to quote than to describe. Here's the one addressed to ABC News's Sam Donaldson, "c/o Roone Arledge, President of ABC News" (all cards to working news people are sent care of their CEOs):

Dear Sam Donaldson:

> *I want to make a few things clear to you.*
> 1. *Criminals are not being punished and citizens will always need the Constitutional right to defend themselves against domestic tyranny.*
> 2. *Gun control only makes it harder for law-abiding citizens to protect themselves.*
> 3. *If you want to stop crime, talk about locking up criminals—not banning guns!*

> *AND QUIT ATTACKING MY CONSTITUTIONAL RIGHT TO KEEP AND BEAR ARMS! IF THIS CONSTITUTIONAL RIGHT IS ABOLISHED, THE RIGHT TO FREE SPEECH AND THE RIGHT OF A FREE PRESS IS SURE TO FOLLOW!*

> *Sincerely,*
> ....
> *[member's name and address]*[21]

Such a mailing can have only one result. It will greatly reinforce the stereotype of NRA members as brainless yahoos with neither manners nor ideas of their own. The message itself is simplistic in the extreme. (1) As the United States has the second highest rate of incarceration in the world, *some* criminals must be undergoing punishment. And what punishing criminals has to do with domestic tyranny is not explained. (2) Some forms of what some people call gun control could certainly make it harder for law-abiding people to protect themselves. But some forms could make it easier. (3) Talking about locking up criminals is unlikely to stop crime. Even locking them up in record numbers hasn't stopped crime. Banning guns won't stop it either, not even if all guns could be eliminated. And as we'll see, they can't be.

Ham-handed attempts at public relations like this have allowed various politicians to build the NRA into a boogeyman. In many parts of the country, running against the NRA is as good a vote-getter as running against crime and drugs. In New Jersey, Governor Jim Florio's popularity was at an all-time low in 1991. It seemed to gun owners the perfect opportunity to repeal New Jersey's Draconian firearms law. The repeal bill looked like a sure thing before Florio began campaigning. He did not discuss the merits of the existing law. He just ran against the NRA. And won. And he retained enough popularity by election time to almost—but not quite—get reelected.

When the national 1994 crime bill got in trouble, President Bill Clinton played the NRA card. The bill contained a ban on 19 types of what the press called "assault weapons." A minority of congressmen opposed the bill on those grounds. Coming from rural areas where gun control was as welcome as a pig in a mosque, these congressmen did not hide their views. More opponents said they were against the bill because they thought many of its crime-prevention measures were a waste of money, or because the penalties it provided were not harsh enough. Black legislators opposed it because later versions of the bill dropped a provision aimed at ending racial discrimination in applying the death penalty. Some Republicans opposed it just because they believed Clinton had tried to ram the bill through without consulting with the minority party. After the House blocked a vote on the bill 225 to 210, however, Clinton blamed the setback entirely on the NRA.

"Yesterday, 225 members of Congress participated in a procedural trick orchestrated by the National Rifle Association," the president said the morning after his defeat.[22] Three days later, he held a press conference in the White House Rose Garden with relatives of three well-known murder victims. They were Marc Klaas, whose daughter, Polly, had been kidnapped at knife-point and later strangled; Steven Sposato, whose wife, Jody, was killed when a gunman shot up a San Francisco law office; and Janice Payne, whose 9-year-old son was killed days after he had written to Clinton about his fear of crime.

In his statement to the press, Sposato, like Clinton, blamed the NRA—not only for the defeat of the bill but for the death of his wife. "The fact is," he said, "the NRA doesn't give a damn that my wife, Jody, is dead. The fact is, the NRA doesn't give a damn that my daughter, Meghan, will grow up never knowing her mother."[23]

It was old-fashioned tear-jerker politics, but it worked. A week later, the bill passed the House 235 to 195. The next week, it looked as if the crime bill's opponents in the Senate might send it back to committee on a point of order. All they needed were 40 votes. Clinton continued fighting "the evil empire." The bill avoided being sent back by one vote—61 to 39. It passed 61 to 38.

While the president was presenting crime victims to the press, the president's people were desperately trying to work out a compromise with the Republicans. They had to agree to cuts in the crime prevention programs and to harsher penalties for some crimes. But the gun ban remained intact. That might indicate that the rifle association didn't have quite the hidden, sinister power that the president attributed to it. Nevertheless, running against the NRA is still good politics.

The NRA's propaganda has resulted in increasing acceptance of the stereotype that its members, and all gun owners, are "gun nuts," "bullies,"[24] and as Garry Wills put it, a "sordid race of gunsels."[25] That, combined with the organization's increasing politicization by aligning itself with the most conservative elements of the Republican party (more on this later), has made restricting firearms a prime liberal cause. It has become that in spite of the fact that all of the chairs of Handgun Control, Inc., the strongest voice in the anti-gun lobby—Ed Welles, Pete Shields, and Sarah Brady—have been conservative Republicans.

THE LIBERAL PANACEA: PROHIBITION

A liberal, according to one dictionary definition, is someone "favorable to progress or reform, as in religious or political affairs."[26] Of course, one person's progress may be another's reaction. But a conservative, according to the same dictionary is "disposed to preserve existing conditions, institutions, etc., and to agree with gradual, rather than abrupt change." [27]

Sometimes abrupt change has been good, sometimes bad. The Nineteenth Amendment, allowing women to vote was, beyond argument, a good change. The Eighteenth, prohibiting the manufacture, importation, transportation, and sale of intoxicating liquor, was not. It was also an example of the most common kind of abrupt change in American life. For some reason, it seems easier to prohibit something in existence than to come up with a new and unprecedented idea. In a way, Abolition was a kind of prohibition: it forbade slavery. Far more important, though, it granted full freedom and citizenship to members of an oppressed race.

Slavery gone, the liberals turned back to a problem that had engaged many of them before ending slavery became the all-consuming cause—the evils caused by liquor. Drunkenness was responsible for thousands of accidental deaths and more than a few murders. Liquor impoverished families and promoted disease. Corrupt politicians bought votes with drinks, and they themselves had been bribed by the financial interests that were robbing the good people of the country. Saloons were dens of gamblers and prostitutes that a good woman could not enter even if she wanted to.

So all the liberals of the late nineteenth century—those seeking a healthier America, those fighting crime, those opposed to corruption, even those who wanted votes for women—joined the Prohibition movement. Prohibition proved to be a failure, of course. One reason was that while slavery was an evil in itself, liquor was merely a contributor to other evils. Millions of people didn't see anything immoral about taking a drink. Another reason for Prohibition's failure was that you couldn't covertly operate a plantation with slave labor, but you certainly could covertly sell and consume forbidden substances.

Prohibition made crime hugely profitable, which created a quantum leap in political corruption and also gave birth to bloody "wars" among competing gangs. It made possible national criminal syndicates, which branched out into other types of crime. And it didn't stop drunkenness and the evils intoxication caused.[28]

The failure of Prohibition left many people disappointed and disillusioned. The hard-core prohibitionists, though, shifted to another prohibition without breaking stride. They strengthened laws against heroin, cocaine, and other drugs, and added marijuana to the list of forbidden fruits. Drugs, every liberal knew, led to crime. Getting rid of crime was the most, or one of the most, important items on the liberal agenda both before and after World War II.

Today, it is beginning to dawn on some liberals that the "War on Drugs" was lost years ago. Continuing the same futile gestures will only make the situation worse. Something else must be tried. For some, that means changing the restrictions on drugs so that drug smugglers will be forced out of business while drug consumption will be reduced.[29] Others, though, see the solution as still another kind of prohibition. Eliminate the tools of crime—guns—and criminals will be greatly restricted. Or so the theory has it.

Once again, the approach is the same as it was with liquor and still is with other drugs: pass a law and the evil will go away. And once again, the new prohibitionists see their opponents as benighted, crooked, brutal, and homicidal.

CRIME, THE NEW CRUSADE

Prohibition not only gave crime its biggest boost, it made crime and criminals national celebrities. Dion O'Bannion, crime lord of Chicago's North End, was a close chum of Charles MacArthur, a Chicago reporter who later became co-author of *The Front Page*, one of America's best-known plays, and who married Helen Hayes, the celebrated actress. O'Bannion's chief rival, "Scarface" Al Capone, was a welcome guest at some of Chicago's finest homes.[30]

Crime became big news in the 1920s. The liquor lords made so much money from their illicit trade that they were able to bribe officials wholesale. That made it possible for them to operate almost openly. The most brazen defiance of the law was common. When Hymie Weiss of the Northside Gang led a "funeral procession" that fired more than 1,000 submachine gun bullets into Capone's headquarters, that couldn't help making the front page of every newspaper in America. And when Capone henchmen lined the Northside Gang up against a wall and mowed them down with submachine guns, that, too, was big news.

The Thompson submachine gun, the product of retired Brig. Gen. John Taliaferro Thompson's determination to create a "trench broom" for the army, became identified with gangsters.[31] So was another, less new and spectacular weapon, the sawed-off shotgun. Both weapons were hard to conceal, but the big gangs in the Prohibition era didn't worry much about concealment. There was some public concern about their misdeeds, but as long as the gangsters killed each other, most people read about their crimes with a kind of amusement. The economy was booming; it was the age of hype in sports, entertainment, and crime; life was not a cabaret but a carnival.

Then the Depression began, and Prohibition ended. The ex-bootleggers began lowering their profiles. A new type of criminal captured the headlines—the automobile bandit.[32] The modus operandi of the typical bandit gang was to drive up to the place to be robbed, dash inside brandishing submachine guns and shotguns, scoop up all available cash, and race away in fast cars before the police knew what had happened. They used artillery as heavy as any bootlegging gang's, often heavier. Clyde Barrow's favorite weapon was the Browning automatic rifle, a machine gun four feet long, weighing 16 pounds unloaded.[33] Concealment was no problem, because the gangs always operated from cars.

Charles Arthur "Pretty Boy" Floyd, Bonnie and Clyde, the Barker Gang, "Machine Gun" Kelly, John Dillinger, and George "Babyface" Nelson replaced Capone and his associates as criminal celebrities. They didn't dine with socialites, though. In the Midwest, where they operated, these cultural descendants of Jesse James and the Dalton Gang inspired vigilante bands. Many people, though, had a sneaking admiration for anyone who robbed the bankers who were foreclosing on homes and farms.

Admiration for criminals was something the new administration could not tolerate. President Franklin D. Roosevelt saw crime as a "national malaise." His attorney general, Homer S. Cummings, called for a "war on crime."[34] Cummings found a general to lead the forces of law and order, J. Edgar Hoover, director of what was then called the Bureau of Investigation. Crime had always been mostly a state problem, but Cummings saw a way to enlarge the national government's role in law enforcement. It was based on the interstate commerce clause of the U.S. Constitution. If a criminal crossed a state line in the commission of a crime, it could be a federal crime. That was the basis of the "Lindbergh Law" passed in the last administration to make kidnapping a federal crime. Herbert Hoover and his advisors were never sure, even after passage of the Lindbergh Law, that the federal government should be involved in cops-and-robbers affairs. Roosevelt, Cummings, and J. Edgar Hoover, though, all saw law enforcement as another new area the New Deal could take on to lead the country out of its malaise.

Congress remained uncertain, however. Then, on June 17, 1933, local police and federal agents were escorting bank robber Frank "Jelly" Nash from Union

Station in Kansas City, Missouri, to a car that would take him to Leavenworth federal penitentiary. As the lawmen and their prisoner prepared to leave, Verne Miller, a sheriff-turned-badman, pointed a Thompson at the group. Two other gunmen were with Miller. There was a great deal of shooting, and the gunmen got away, leaving four lawmen dead and two wounded. Also dead was Nash, the prisoner. Exactly what happened has never been established. One story is that when Nash saw Miller and the submachine gun, he tried to get away, and Otto Reed, the police chief of McAlester, Oklahoma, shot him in the back of the head—the opening shot of the fusillade that left Reed dead seconds later.[35] Hoover's story was that Miller and his two associates killed all five men, including Nash. Miller was positively identified as one of the gunmen, but identification of the other two was extremely shaky. Nevertheless, the government firmly asserted that the other two were Pretty Boy Floyd and his partner, Adam "Eddie" Richetti. Floyd at the time was America's best-known bank robber.

The Union Station Massacre, as it was known locally, or the Kansas City Massacre, as it was called in newspapers from coast to coast, gave Cummings's war on crime a jump start. The next month, Hoover's Bureau of Investigation merged with two more Justice Department agencies to become the Federal Bureau of Investigation, commanded by J. Edgar Hoover. FBI agents got arrest power and the authority to carry guns. FBI agents began chasing bank robbers, and FBI headquarters began publicizing their exploits. There was probably more crime, even more bank robbery, in the 1920s, but the public in the 1930s was more aware of it.

THE NATIONAL FIREARMS ACT

One result of this awareness was the beginning of a movement to restrict the use and ownership of firearms.[36] The National Rifle Association and the U.S. Revolver Association responded to the pressure by drawing up model firearms statutes and urging states to adopt them. The firearms law passed by Congress for Washington, D.C., was largely an NRA effort. It provided for a 48-hour waiting period before buying a pistol, required permits to carry concealed weapons, added penalties for use of a gun in a crime, and forbade sale of pistols to those convicted of a violent crime, minors, drug addicts, and those "not of sound mind." It also forbade the sale and possession of submachine guns, silencers, and short-barreled shotguns within the District.

Cummings presented a similar bill to Congress. It did not forbid the possession of machine guns or sawed-off shotguns and rifles. The Second Amendment, in those days, was still respected, and it was believed that such a prohibition by the federal government would be unconstitutional. What the proposed National Firearms Bill did was impose a $200 tax on each transfer of one of the "gangster weapons." It also provided for handgun licenses and registration. The license fee for handguns was $1. It has been alleged that the $1 fee was the sticking point for the NRA. Actually, it was the provision for registration, which has always been considered by the NRA a preliminary to confiscation. (And as we'll see, registration has no other practical use but as an aid to confiscation.) In his amusing, and often right-on-target book, *The Saturday Night Special*, Robert Sherrill misses the mark on the NRA and the National Firearms Act.

> Unfortunately, there was the National Rifle Association, that ubiquitous organization that pops up inevitably to oppose gun controls and whose response to logic is much like stomach acidity's response to sauerkraut. The NRA did not want its heavily-armed members to run the risk of a five-year jail rap, so at its insistence "pistols and revolvers" was knocked out of the language of the bill.[37]

The "five-year jail rap" was, of course, copied from the additional penalty provision of the NRA's own model bill. Sherrill, though, is less confused than Josh Sugarmann in discussing the machine gun provision. Sherrill points out that the original version imposed the $200 tax on "any firearm which shoots automatically or *semiautomatically* [emphasis added] more than 12 shots without reloading."[38] Sugarmann says that description would have defined a machine gun under the act. Actually, the meaning of "machine gun" had been well established since the late nineteenth century. There is no way a weapon that fires only one shot for each pull of the trigger can be a machine gun. What the act did do is define certain types of guns—machine guns, sawed-off shotguns, etc.—as "firearms," but not other guns. That's zany enough. (In Britain, about the same time, rifles and pistols, but not shotguns, were legally firearms.)[39]

Another definition of a machine gun, according to Sugarmann, would have been "any weapon which shoots . . . automatically or semiautomatically more than one shot, without manual reloading, by a single function of the trigger."[40] That, says Sugarmann, would have limited untaxed guns to single-shot weapons. Rejection of that definition, Sugarmann calls a "missed opportunity" because, he thinks, it would have eliminated all guns but single-shot rifles, pistols and shotguns—the next best thing to eliminating all guns.[41] But the proposed definition would not have limited untaxed guns to single-shot weapons. All repeating rifles except semiautomatics require manual reloading before each shot. Further, no weapon can shoot more than one shot semiautomatically with a single pull of the trigger. If a gun fires more than one shot with a single pull of the trigger, it's an automatic, by definition. (All shotguns routinely shoot more than one *projectile* with a single pull of the trigger, but that's something else.) The definition was rejected simply because it made no sense.

The fight over the National Firearms Bill gave the NRA the first opportunity to flex its muscles. Letters and telegrams poured into congressional offices, and the regulations concerning pistols were dropped. The provisions against machine guns, sawed-off shotguns and rifles, and silencers, and trick guns, like pen guns or cane guns, remained. It has been frequently said—even by someone like Sen. Edward Kennedy, who should know better—that the NFA took the machine gun out of the American crime scene. It's true that use of the big, noisy tommy gun fell off for a while after Prohibition and the era of the automobile bandits ended. After crossing state lines to avoid prosecution became a federal crime and states developed efficient state police forces with radio cars, the Dillingers went the way of the Capones. In the new era, the noisy and unconcealable Thompson was more than a little inconvenient.

The submachine gun has not disappeared, however. In 1954, in Senator Kennedy's hometown, Boston, a hired assassin named Elmer Burke used a submachine gun in an attempt to kill Joseph "Specks" O'Keefe, one of the men who committed the decade's most publicized crime, the 1950 Brink's robbery.[42] In 1973, Ohio police officials estimated that there were 9,000 submachine guns in their state, only 3,000 of which were registered under the NFA.[43] During a one-month amnesty period, federal officials collected 68,000 submachine guns, most of them from World War II. Sherrill lists a number of incidents involving submachine guns in the late sixties and early seventies: American Indian Movement militants showed off a Russian SMG on television; in 1966, mafioso Salvatore Bonnano was wounded by submachine gun fire; the next year, three more mafiosi were killed the same way; in 1973, two youths held 20 people hostage with a submachine gun; the same year, a bank robber named Albert Lee Nussbaum used a submachine gun to hold up eight banks for a total of $248,541 and kill a prison guard.[44] In 1979, two Colombian drug dealers used a submachine gun to kill a pair of rivals and shoot up a Miami shopping center.[45] In 1984, right-wing extremists used a submachine gun to murder Denver talk show host Alan Berg. In 1994, two young men in Los Angeles were sentenced to prison for bank robbery by proxy. They supplied machine guns to kids ranging in age from 13 to 15 and taught them how to rob banks (and took the lion's share of the loot).[46] So much for the effectiveness of laws banning guns.

But submachine guns and other exotic weaponry had nothing to do with the next big push for gun control. The offending weapon was a plain, old-fashioned bolt-action rifle.

CHAPTER 8

TIME
OF
TROUBLES

DALLAS

On November 22, 1963, a sunny, pleasant day in Dallas, Texas, a very strange former marine named Lee Oswald carried a rifle into the place where he worked, the Texas School Book Depository. What happened after that has been a matter of debate for more than a generation and will probably be the subject of books for the next hundred years. Two things are certain, however: (1) Lee Oswald was involved, whether alone or as part of a conspiracy, in an attempt to kill President John F. Kennedy; and (2) Kennedy was shot and killed.

The United States went into a state of shock unequaled since the attack on Pearl Harbor. Amid the universal mourning, there were expressions of outrage at the violence of life in the United States. Sen. J. William Fulbright blamed America's heritage of "puritan self-righteousness and vigilante justice" for the assassination. The clear implication was that assassination was a peculiarly American crime. Columnist James Reston also blamed the killing on the violence of American life, unusual among the civilized nations of the world. Other, less noted voices, claimed that American were far more prone to assassinate their leaders than other people. Even the scholarly authors of the staff report to the National Commission on the Causes and Prevention of Violence seemed to lose their scholarly detachment. According to James F. Kirkham, Sheldon G. Levy, and William J. Crotty, "Although a precise ranking of countries is impossible, we can say with confidence that the United States falls well within the category of those nations that experience a high level of assassination."[1] Forgotten, apparently, were the assassinations in pre-war Japan, where literally scores of politicians were murdered in less than two decades.[2] Also forgotten were the assassinations in Europe west of Russia, a territory of about half the area of the United States and twice the population. In the twentieth century, this area has seen the assassinations of King Alexander and Queen Draga of Serbia; Archduke Franz Ferdinand and Countess Sophie of Austria-Hungary; Jemal Pasha of Turkey (in the USSR); Michael Collins, Chairman of the Irish Free State Provisional Government; President Gabriel Narutowicz of Poland; King Alexander of Yugoslavia (in Marseille); Kevin O'Higgins, acting president of the Irish Free State; Chancellor Engelbert Dollfuss of Austria; Benito Mussolini and Claretta Petacci of Italy; British Lord Louis Mountbatten (in Ireland); and Prime Minister Olof Palme of Sweden. All of the male victims were either heads of state, heads of government, or both, except Franz Ferdinand, an heir apparent; Mountbatten, uncle of the Queen of England; and Jemal Pasha, a former member of the "Young Turks" junta. The women were their wives, except Petacci, who was Mussolini's mistress. In the same period, two U.S. presidents were murdered—but no wives. One of the presidents, William McKinley, was killed in 1901. His assassination barely made the twentieth century. It made the century, in fact, by almost the same margin as the assassination of Empress Elizabeth of Austria-Hungary, murdered in 1898, missed it. A few years after the Kennedy assassination, there were *four* attempts to assassinate one French political leader, President Charles de Gaulle.

The Kennedy assassination caused a major change in public attitudes toward gun control in America. Before the assassination, gun control was almost a nonissue. At least it was to the general public. Gun owners had *started* to become sensitive to it since the National Firearms Act. Only two Gallup polls between the 1930s and 1959 asked even a single question about gun control.[3] After the assassination, the first instance of what would be a recurring phenomenon took place. There was an outcry for more restrictions on the ownership of pistols. Calls for legislation to license handgun owners, register handguns, or ban handguns have since been almost a knee-jerk reaction to every sensational murder. The fact that Kennedy was killed by a rifle made no difference. It didn't make any difference that earlier in the year, Medgar Evers, a civil rights leader, was also killed by a rifle. Ordinary rifles and shotguns had achieved a kind of immunity to legislation in the United States. Most hunters use these guns as their primary weapons. To many people, infringement of hunting is un-American. To hear politicians assure the public that the latest gun legislation will not affect arms "used for legitimate sporting purposes," you might think the Second Amendment was written to protect wildfowlers and deerslayers. Pistols are different. Many people who don't own guns see them as evil things, useful only for crime and suicide.

In January 1963, before either the Kennedy or Evers slayings, Sen. Thomas Dodd of Connecticut had begun hearings on a bill to restrict the mail-order sale of pistols. Why Dodd introduced the bill and how he campaigned for it is an interesting example of the politics of gun control as played on Capitol Hill.

WASHINGTON

Thomas Dodd stood for law and order. He had served for about a year in the FBI, spent time as a federal prosecutor of civil rights offenses in the South, and was a key member of the prosecution team at the Nuremberg war crimes trials following World War II. Elected to the House of Representatives in 1952, he got on the wave of McCarthyism sweeping the country and rode it into the Senate in 1958.

As a senator, he accused the *New York Times*, the *Providence Journal*, the *St. Louis Post-Dispatch* and the *Washington Post* of being part of a "Red network" of Communist-front newspapers trying to smear him. It wasn't hard to smear Dodd. Speaker of the House Tip O'Neill had once called him "the second nastiest drunk in town."[4] Dodd's penchant for living beyond his means led many to doubt his probity. And he appeared to be paranoid. He believed Attorney General Robert Kennedy was bugging his phone and conspiring with other liberals to frame him.[5]

The Red scare began to abate after Dodd reached the Senate. He needed a new issue to keep his name before the public. The gun issue presented an irresistible opportunity. It was a very new issue: the controversy over gun control was at such a low volume it was almost inaudible, but some well-chosen words in the Senate could change that. Dodd could pose as a champion of gun control—a position compatible with his law-and-order image. And at the same time, he could do himself a little good. Dodd talked tough about gun control—tough enough that some of the more paranoid members of the NRA began to think of him as the Devil incarnate. Talking tough also aroused the interests of American gun manufacturers.

Dodd's home state is also the home of some of the biggest names in the American firearms industry. Colt, Winchester, Remington, Marlin, Mossberg, Ruger, and High Standard all had plants there. They had large numbers of employees, and all of their employees had friends. They could make trouble for a politician who crossed them. But they might not make enough trouble to keep him from being reelected. In any case, they believed that it's easier to catch flies with honey than with vinegar. Dodd got many contributions from the gun makers. Carl Perian, staff director of Dodd's Juvenile Delinquency Subcommittee, told Robert Sherrill that a representative of a gun manufacturer "once told him— rubbing his fingers in the classic sign for money—'We've got Dodd in our pocket.' "[6] Dodd, though, told his staff that the "gun issue is good to keep alive."[7]

Hearings on Dodd's proposed bill went on and on. According to James Boyd, a Dodd staffer, "Dodd never really devoted any personal effort to the gun problem. He didn't give it day-to-day leadership. Once or twice a year, he would run the problem through his subcommittee for an executive session in which the legislation would be mashed this way and that, with no results. Nor would he hold a public hearing unless he wanted some publicity. Once or twice a year he would make a statement on the floor of the Senate, but very pro forma."[8] Those statements, however, were enough to excite gun owners and keep gun makers from relaxing. As long as he could keep the gun bill dangling before the public, Dodd didn't need a new issue.

Even if he had pushed through a bill banning mail-order sales of handguns, Dodd would not have seriously discomfited the gun manufacturers of Connecticut. Far from it. Through the 1950s and early 1960s, these makers of new guns were hard-pressed by competition from imported war-surplus guns. The manufacturers and their allies tried to characterize these former military weapons as "junk," "unsafe," and "not suitable for sporting purposes." For example, in his 1950 book, *The Practical Book of American Guns*, Capt. John Houston Craige dismissed war surplus guns as "first class decorations on the premises of clubhouses of the American Legion, the Veterans of Foreign Wars, and organizations of ex-GI's provided they are carefully disabled."

But gun buyers knew better. National governments have enormous resources, and no nation is going to equip its troops with unsafe weapons. Rifles and pistols accepted for military service have to prove their durability and efficiency in tests far more rigorous than any used by a private manufacturer. Some of the foreign rifles were undeniably homely. The Japanese Arisaka 6.5mm carbine looked junky. Craige called it "the worst of all." But it had a chrome-plated bore to minimize corrosion and a hinged magazine floorplate to allow the rifle to be unloaded quickly and safely. Only the most expensive domestic sporting rifles had that feature. Further, tests showed that the Arisaka was harder to blow up than the best American and German bolt-action rifles.[9] The Italian Mannlicher-Carcano rifle got a bad press. One was supposed to have blown up. That one case was highly publicized. Not publicized at all were many cases of domestic sporting rifles that blew up, one of which I saw. Most Mannlicher-Carcanos performed as well as could be expected—including the one Lee Harvey Oswald used to shoot John F. Kennedy.

The foreign guns were not only good, they were cheap. They sold for as little as one-tenth of the retail price of new domestic guns. Most of the sales were from mail-order houses. The manufacturers wouldn't have minded even if Dodd's bill banned mail-order sales of rifles, as well as pistols. But Dodd didn't think he could get away with that. Actually, he didn't seem too anxious to get any legislation accomplished.

The Kennedy assassination gave Dodd the opportunity to make more noise—and get more publicity—than ever on the gun control issue, but he did no more to push legislation through, although he did add long guns to the ban. Perian told Sherrill about one committee session he did not attend. "One of Senator Tydings' staffers who was there later told me, 'If you ever wanted a blueprint of how to defeat a piece of legislation, you would have to see your chairman in action at this meeting.' "[10]

In 1968, Martin Luther King, Jr., was assassinated, and a new wave of rioting broke out in large cities. Two-and-a-half months later, Robert Kennedy was assassinated. Dodd knew he'd have to do something. After King was killed by rifle fire, Dodd told Perian to put together a bill, "but leave rifles and shotguns out of it."[11] After Robert Kennedy was killed by a cheap .22 caliber handgun, President Lyndon Johnson demanded that the ban on mail-order gun sales be extended to long guns.[12] Such are the ways of Washington.

The result was the Gun Control Act of 1968. The act not only banned the interstate sale of handguns and long guns, it banned the importation of military surplus weapons and cheap handguns, often called "Saturday night specials." U.S. gun manufacturers could not have been more pleased, although the NRA—supposedly an arm of the gun industry—was livid with rage.

Banning the importation of "Saturday night specials," or SNSs as journalists have nicknamed them, was not a high priority for the domestic gun industry. The cheap handguns provided little competition for the domestic product. Most U.S. pistols were better made of better materials and far more expensive. Sirhan Sirhan used an American-made gun that might be called a SNS to kill Robert Kennedy, but there was no effort to ban domestic Saturday night specials. And no one even considered banning Remington pump guns like the rifle that had killed Martin Luther King. The impulse to ban the SNS came from outside the gun industry. One cause was probably the urban riots of the late 1960s. The SNS was the weapon of poor people. Nobody who could afford something better would touch one. Robert Sherrill notes, "Inasmuch as the assassination of John Kennedy failed to elicit any gun legislation from Congress, and inasmuch as the legislation finally passed in 1968 had nothing to do with the assassinations of King and Robert Kennedy, it seems reasonable to assume that the law was directed at that other threat of the 1960s, more omnipresent than the political assassin—namely, the black rioter."[13]

Fear of a violent underclass certainly was a factor. It's been a factor in all gun control measures since Henry VIII instituted a means test for those who wanted to own a gun. It was a major cause of gun control laws in the post-Civil War South and in turn-of-the-century New York. But it wasn't a generalized fear that inspired stories about how the SNS was the "gun of choice" for criminals and other nonsense we'll examine in chapter 17, "Devil Guns." That disinformation came from the second player in the battle over gun control—the anti-gun lobby. At the beginning of the Saturday night special controversy, the anti-gun crew was an inchoate force, rather than a lobby. A few intellectuals and writers were expressing opinions and feeding on each others' ideas. They would soon coalesce into a genuine lobby, with several national organizations.

NEW KIDS ON THE BLOCK

In 1974, a University of Chicago student named Mark Borinsky was held up and robbed on the street.[14] According to the official history of Handgun Control, Inc., Borinsky was so incensed by this assault with a handgun that he went to Washington looking for a chance to work with an organization lobbying for gun control. He found none, so he founded one. It was called the National Council to Control Handguns and had a headquarters staff of three. The staffers recruited members by contacting people on their holiday card lists. Borinsky didn't have time to run an organization, so he got a retired CIA agent named Ed Welles to be chairman. Soon after that, they were joined by Nelson T. "Pete" Shields, a Du Pont executive.[15] The people at HCI today don't talk much about Welles. Perhaps that's because he wasn't a victim, like their corporate heroes, Mark Borinsky, Pete Shields, and Sarah Brady.

Shields became interested in handgun control after his son, Nick, was killed in 1974 by a gunman the newspapers called the Zebra Killer. (The killer actually was a team of three African Americans who were killing white people at random in San Francisco.) Shields brooded over his son's death and the gun violence in the United States. Then he joined Borinsky and Welles. Two years later, in 1976, Shields retired from Du Pont so he could devote all his time to the gun control effort. He became executive director of the NCCH. In 1978, he became chairperson. The organization grew rapidly. In 1976, it had 5,000 members and a budget of $75,000. Two years later, it had 36,000 members and $600,000. Today, renamed Handgun Control, Inc. (HCI), the group has 400,000 members, although for several years its stationery had carried the logo "One million strong . . . working to keep handguns out of the wrong hands." Participants in the gun control debate tend to exaggerate a bit.

In 1981, Shields published a book, *Guns Don't Die—People Do*, which was at once touching (concerning his tragedy and those of others), misleading (concerning U.S. handgun deaths and foreign gun laws), and vituperative (concerning the NRA). The book was a success, and HCI's growth took another jump. In 1983, Shields founded the Center to Prevent Handgun Violence. The Center concentrates on education; legal action, such as supporting gun laws; and working with entertainment media. Handgun Control itself concentrates on lobbying.

The same year Shields's book appeared, a maniac named John Hinckley, Jr., tried to kill President Ronald Reagan. Hinckley had a small, cheap .22 caliber revolver loaded with exploding bullets. He approached the presidential party as Reagan was leaving a hotel after delivering a lunchtime address. Hinckley squatted as he had seen gunfighters do on television, drew the revolver, held it in both hands, and fired as fast as he could. As might be expected from his technique, his marksmanship was abominable. He hit about everyone but Reagan. The bullet that struck the president had first ricocheted off a car. Unfortunately, the bullet didn't explode when it hit the car; fortunately, it didn't explode when it hit Reagan, either. The most seriously injured was the president's press secretary, James Brady. The bullet struck him in the head and did explode. It just missed being fatal. It left Brady mostly paralyzed and with some mental functions, such as memory, impaired. In 1985, when she felt her husband had recovered enough to let her take a job, Sarah Brady joined the board of HCI. She became chairperson in 1989. Brady has more public relations talent than the leader of any other lobbying group in the gun control struggle. It's reflected in HCI's growth. In 1985, Handgun Control had 125,000 members. Since Brady's been on the board, it has gained more than 275,000 members.

Like Handgun Control, Inc., the Coalition to Stop Gun Violence (CSGV) got started in 1974. And like HCI, the Coalition started with another name, the National Coalition to Ban Handguns. The Board of Church and Society of the Methodist Church established it after negotiating with a number of religious, labor, and civic organizations that had already taken anti-gun stands. The National Coalition was exactly what its name says—a coalition of a number of existing groups. It started with about 30. At last count, there were 44, with Michael Beard, the Coalition's longtime director, coordinating their lobbying.

One of the groups in the original coalition was the National Council to Control Handguns. When its membership began to mushroom, the NCCH left the NCBH and later changed its name to Handgun Control, Inc. Today, spokespersons for both groups are quick to point out their doctrinal differences.

"We are for generally banning all handguns, with a few exceptions, like the police and the military," said Jennifer Jackson of the Coalition to Stop Gun Violence. "They [HCI] are for measures, such as licensing and registration, that we don't think are really effective."[16]

Shawn Taylor Zelman, communications coordinator for HCI, summarized her organization's activities: "Handgun Control lobbies on the federal, state, and local levels for stricter gun control regulation. That's our main function." The organization's aims, she said, are contained in a proposed bill HCI calls "Brady II."

"It's comprehensive legislation to overhaul the gun industry," Zelman said. "It features licensing owners and registering of secondary transfers. It looks to passing a [national] one-gun-a-month bill like the State of Virginia did. And mandatory safety training." Of the Coalition to Stop Gun Violence, she said, "They have a different legislative agenda. They work to ban handguns."[17]

At the time of the separation, however, the differences were much less distinct. In an interview published in *The New Yorker* in 1976, Shields said, "The first problem is to slow down the number of handguns being produced and sold in this country. The second problem is to get handguns registered. The final problem is to make possession of all handguns and all handgun ammunition—except for the military, police, licensed security guards, licensed sporting clubs, and licensed gun collectors—totally illegal."[18] By 1981, however, Shields had modified his position. In fact, he devoted a chapter of his book to what he called the "centrist position" in the gun control controversy. "This is the most difficult position because it satisfies the ideals of neither side," he wrote. "Yet if we continue to allow the debate to continue along purely idealistic, i.e., extreme, lines, I don't believe we will ever achieve handgun control nationally."[19]

There seems to be little love lost between the two anti-gun groups. Zelman said of the Coalition, "They don't really lobby that much. They're never seen on Capitol Hill." Actually, some of the Coalition's member organizations are extremely effective lobbyists in state capitals. Kim Harrison, lobbyist for the United Churches of Christ, for instance, is generally considered the most effective anti-gun lobbyist in Connecticut.

The Coalition to Stop Gun Violence changed its name from the National Coalition to Ban Handguns after its director of communications, Josh Sugermann, wrote *Assault Weapons and Accessories in America* in 1988. In this report, Sugermann concluded that the movement to ban handguns had bogged down, but "Assault weapons—just like armor-piercing bullets, machine guns, and plastic firearms—are a *new* topic. The weapons' menacing looks, coupled with the public's confusion over fully automatic machine guns versus semi-automatic assault weapons—anything that looks like a machine gun is assumed to be a machine gun—can only increase the chance of public support for restrictions on these weapons."[20]

The National Coalition to Ban Handguns voted to work for banning "assault weapons," too, and changed its name accordingly. It probably didn't go far enough for Sugarmann, though. He founded his own organization, the Violence Policy Center. VPC is more of a research group than a mass movement. It maintains fairly cordial relations with the CSGV, but in his book *NRA*, Sugarmann blasts HCI as being a mirror image of the NRA.

"Ironically, despite the genuine hatred that each organization feels for the other," he writes, "HCI and the NRA share a similar view of the nature of gun violence. Neither sees the handgun itself as inherently the problem, but views violence as stemming from the weapons being in the 'wrong' hands."[21]

The three national anti-gun groups leaped eagerly into the fray. "This is your first chance to tell the NRA to go to hell!" proclaimed the outside of an HCI fund-raising letter. Very soon, they were to lock horns with a new NRA—one quite different from the old sportsmen's association.

THE CINCINNATI REVOLT

Discontent had been growing in the rifle association since the debate on the 1968 Gun Control bill. It started when Maj. Gen. Franklin Orth, executive vice president of the NRA—the most powerful post in the association—said of the bill, "We do not think that any sane American, who calls himself an American, can object to placing into this bill the instrument which killed the president of the United States."[22]

The NRA members couldn't fire Orth, but they did keep him muzzled for the rest of his term. For the hard-liners, who made up the majority of the life, or voting, members, things didn't get better when Orth stepped down. Attacks on the NRA had increased in Congress, and Sen. Edward Kennedy was leading an effort to stop subsidizing the national shooting matches. The leadership decided to buy land in New Mexico and build a new range. That was bad enough: it took money from the NRA's Institute for Legislative Action, the lobbying arm. But the leaders also wanted to devote the land to camping, hiking, wilderness survival training, and conservation education. It would be called the National Outdoor Center. Hard-liners, learning that their association would be spending money for bird-watching as well as shooting, were horrified. Then they learned that the organization would move its headquarters from Washington to Colorado Springs, not far from the outdoor center. Lobbying would be de-emphasized with a vengeance.

The "Old Guard," as the hard-liners called the leadership, were not unaware of the grumbling. In November 1976, they made a preemptive strike. They fired 74 employees, most of them hard-liners, ostensibly in preparation for the move to Colorado.[23]

At the next NRA convention, May 21, 1977, the hard-liners struck back. The Old Guard was ousted, and Harlon Carter, a hard-liner's hard-liner, assumed leadership of the century-old organization. With the anti-gun lobby organized and public sentiment apparently becoming increasingly favorable to more gun control, Carter's task looked as hopeless as that of King Canute, the Middle Ages monarch who commanded the tide to reverse itself.

Carter had two aims: (1) to improve the NRA's image, which had been demonized by the anti-gun lobby; (2) not to yield another inch in the direction of gun control.

The first task was tough enough. A large part of the public, and an even larger part of opinion makers like media executives and columnists, was convinced that the organization was composed of "bumper sticker cretins," if not a "sordid race of gunsels." Carter initiated a series of magazine ads, "I'm the NRA," in which a wide variety of wholesome types—celebrities and unknowns, children and adults, black and white, male and female—explain why they are members and what benefits they find. Several magazines, including *Better Homes and Gardens*, *Modern Maturity*, *McCall's*, and *Audubon*, rejected the ads outright. *Reader's Digest* and *Southern Living* refused any ad showing a person holding a handgun, even when the person happened to be a law enforcement officer.[24] The NRA also tried to get commercials and documentaries on network television and was rejected each time.

Carter's second aim, no compromise on gun control, contributed greatly to the decibels, hysteria, and nonsense quotient of the current gun control "debate." But it also led to some interesting battles.

CHAPTER 9

HARLON "CANUTE" VERSUS THE TIDE

SWIMMING AGAINST THE TIDE

Harlon Carter's top priority was nullifying the Gun Control Act of 1968. He found a kindred soul in Rep. Harold L. Volkmer of Missouri, who entered the House in 1977, just a few months before the Cincinnati Revolt. Volkmer began drafting a bill to roll back some key features of GCA 68 in January 1978. The trouble was that all gun control bills had to pass through the House Judiciary Committee, whose chairman, Peter Rodino, was as pro-control as Volkmer was anti-control. Rodino simply would not let any bill he disagreed with leave his committee. Some congressmen began calling the House Judiciary Committee the "legislative mortuary."[1]

In the other wing of the Capitol, Sen. James McClure of Idaho took up the fight against GCA 68. Opposition to the gun control act was about all McClure and Volkmer had in common. McClure was a Republican; Volkmer, a Democrat. McClure was quiet and well liked; Volkmer, sarcastic and abrasive. For the next several years, however, they were a well matched team.

Not that they got anywhere. If Volkmer had Rodino, McClure had Kennedy. Sen. Edward Kennedy chaired the Senate Judiciary Committee, and he was almost as hard-line a gun control supporter as Rodino.

THE DISAPPEARING QUORUM

Kennedy and Rodino were both Democrats and were both fixtures in their committees as long as their party had the majority in both houses. But in 1981, Republicans took control in the Senate as a result of the Reagan landslide. No longer committee chairman, Ted Kennedy had to show his legislative talents. Although often derided as "the prettiest Kennedy" and as a senator who could deliver a speech superbly, as long as someone else had written it, Kennedy was a master of legislative maneuver. His particular forte was the little-known art of bill blocking. There are dozens of ways to stop a bill while appearing to support it. One way is to load it down with unreasonable amendments so that nobody will vote for it when it reaches the Senate or House floor. Kennedy preferred to kill bills in committee. His favorite ploy when no longer chairman was "the disappearing quorum."

At the committee hearings, the senior senator from Massachusetts would appear lugging an enormous briefing book. According to Jerry Tinker, a Kennedy aide, the senator would look around at the other committee members and ask, "Do you know what all the implications are for all the 50 states?" Then he'd open the briefing book, containing all of the 20,000 or so laws concerning guns, and start reading. Kennedy would drone on, occasionally looking up, and committee members would decide that they had more pressing business. Finally, Kennedy would look around and innocently note that there was no quorum. The chairman would have to adjourn the meeting.[2]

In 1982, Kennedy added an amendment to McClure's bill that would mandate a 14-day waiting period before the sale of a handgun. That was just in case the bill made it to the Senate floor. But it didn't. By 1984, though, the tide was turning. The Republicans still controlled the Senate, and McClure had picked up strong support.

THE GUN OWNERS' PROTECTION ACT

McClure's bill was given the usual self-serving title—in this case, "The Gun Owners' Protection Act" but only the gun lobby used that title. Everyone else called it the McClure-Volkmer Bill. Its major features were:

1. dropping the ban on selling guns across state lines;

2. allowing persons convicted of nonviolent felonies, such as tax evasion, to own firearms;

3. relieving dealers of the obligation to record the sale of every box of cartridges;

4. prohibiting the government from banning the importation of guns found "suitable for sporting purposes."

5. requiring agents of the Bureau of Alcohol, Tobacco, and Firearms (BATF) to have reasonable cause to inspect a dealer's records and to give dealers prior notification before inspection;

6. allowing dealers to transfer guns from their business inventories to their private collections.

The last point sounds innocuous. Actually, it would open a major loophole in the law. Guns sold from private collections didn't have to be recorded.

This time, Kennedy could not put the Senate Judiciary Committee off from voting on the bill. It rejected his waiting period amendment 11–3, then shot down another amendment that would have banned the interstate sale of handguns. Kennedy offered a compromise: if the committee would ban the interstate sale of Saturday night specials, he would drop his objections to the interstate sale of other types of weapons. It took the committee a while to agree to even this small concession. Bob Dole and Strom Thurmond, both powerful members of the committee, at first seemed agreeable, but the NRA demanded no compromise. They backed away. Nevertheless, the bill was voted out of committee.

And that's as far as it got. The fact that the bill got to the Senate floor, however, excited both the gun and anti-gun lobbies. Both cranked up their PR machinery.

THE BATTLE OF THE LOBBYISTS

The anti-gunners made statements and mailed news releases calling McClure-Volkmer an "outrageous piece of legislation" because of "the easy availability of handguns and the resulting handgun deaths."[3] (Actually, guns were less available than ever before, both because of GCA 68 and because many retail outlets had discontinued selling guns.) The anti-gunners did well in the press, but not well enough to cancel the effects of the NRA's big gun—letters to its members. Those letters generated letters *from* the NRA members and fellow gun owners that poured into congressional offices.

Observers are often puzzled at the vehemence of opponents of gun control, while most supporters of these measure could charitably be called lukewarm. One reason is that the opponents have something to lose. Guns are expensive. Some shotguns retail for as much as $27,000, some for $55,000; target rifles can cost $5,000, and a good deer rifle may cost between $500 and $1,500. Even the common .45 caliber pistol retails for more than $600, while its German counterpart, the P-38, costs nearly $1,000. Further, many, if not most, gun owners have more than one gun.[4] They become incensed at the thought that people who have nothing to lose are trying to take away something they own or forbid them from selling something they own. And all because of the deeds of a few sleazy criminals. On the other hand, most people who tell the pollsters they favor stricter gun controls don't even know what gun controls are now in force. They aren't concerned enough about the subject to write to a congressman.

SHOWDOWN ON CAPITOL HILL

On January 3, 1985, the first day of the 99th Congress, McClure introduced his bill again. Bob Dole, Senate majority leader, used the power of his office to put it directly on the Senate calendar. There would be no preliminary public hearing on the bill. It would go directly to the floor. Dole scheduled the bill for June 17. Kennedy's office learned of the date on June 13 and immediately called Handgun Control, Inc. HCI blitzed the senators with literature blasting McClure-Volkmer and tried to line up senators to filibuster when the bill got to the floor. McClure, Dole, and Orrin Hatch, who were pushing the bill, met with Kennedy and Howard Metzenbaum, who never saw a gun control bill he didn't like. Also present were representatives of the NRA and HCI. After four days, most of the gun controllers agreed not to filibuster if the anti-controllers would delay debate two weeks and accept certain amendments. Metzenbaum was the last to agree. The bill went to the floor July 9 with 52 cosponsors—a majority of the Senate. It passed 79–15.

The next step was for the bill to go to the House, where the Democrats had a majority and anti-gunners held the leadership positions. The most anti of those anti-gunners was Peter Rodino. The New Jersey congressman was eagerly waiting to add McClure-Volkmer to the long list of bills that died in his committee.

"That bill will be dead on arrival," Rodino said.[5]

Rodino soon regretted his comment. Other representatives, many of whose own bills had suffered the fate Rodino predicted for McClure-Volkmer, resented his arrogance. The stage was set for Harold Volkmer to use another parliamentary maneuver. If a majority of representatives petition that a bill be discharged from committee, it has to go to the floor. Rodino, a veteran of the House, had done many favors over the years. He now called in his IOUs. In the meantime, to prepare for the worst, he and Rep. William Hughes wrote a substitute bill. If it looked as if Volkmer would get the signatures he needed, Rodino would report out the substitute.

It looked as if Volkmer would get his signatures. Rodino rammed his bill through the committee when Volkmer was still shy one signature. Volkmer got the signature he needed the next day. The House Rules Committee had to decide what to do. Rodino's bill was reported out first, but Volkmer's had the majority of the House behind it. The rules committee ruled that Volkmer would be allowed to substitute his bill for the Hughes-Rodino bill. Volkmer's bill would be debated, and if the House so voted, it would replace the Hughes-Rodino bill.

On March 20, when debate was about to begin on McClure-Volkmer, Speaker Tip O'Neill ruled that the representatives were worn out from the 10-hour debate they had just finished and postponed debate on McClure-Volkmer until April 9. The delay, of course, was to give opposition time to work out a new strategy, and for the anti-gun lobby to twist more arms.

When debate finally began, William Hughes, Rodino's collaborator, offered one amendment after another to Volkmer's bill. All were defeated. When it looked as if the House would finally get a chance to vote on the bill, O'Neill observed that if they continued, they'd have to pay overtime to the Capitol staff. He adjourned debate until the next day.

The delay apparently gave the opposition time to regroup. Hughes offered another amendment, to ban the interstate sale of handguns. It passed, 233–184. The House this day was meeting as a "committee of the whole," which allows it to act when only 100 members are present. O'Neill had stepped down and appointed Rep. Charles Rangel of New York chairman. Rangel, like O'Neill, made no bones about his anti-gun sentiments. Just before time allotted for debate under the rules ended, Hughes stood up and said, "Mr. Chairman, I offer an amendment to the amendment to the amendment offered as a substitute for the committee amendment in the nature of a substitute."[6] In other words, he was offering one last amendment. It was to ban the manufacture and sale of new machine guns to anyone except the police and the military.

Rangel called for a voice vote. A chorus of voices answered both "aye" and "no." Rangel declared the ayes had it. He continued as if he had not heard the calls for a recorded vote. Eric Sterling, majority counsel for Hughes's crime subcommittee, admitted later that he couldn't be sure there were no calls for a recorded vote. "It was not the *most* flagrant abuse of the power of the chair that I've seen on the floor." he said. He added, "But it wasn't the fairest way it could have been handled, either."[7]

Rangel then called for a voice vote on the main question: should the Hughes-Rodino bill be replaced by the McClure-Volkmer Bill? This time, he declared that the noes had it. That would have killed the McClure-Volkmer bill. Volkmer jumped up and in a voice that could not be ignored demanded that a recorded vote be taken. Rangel could not have denied the request without starting a riot. Volkmer won 292–130—not exactly a close vote.

McClure-Volkmer then passed the House and went to the Senate again, which passed the version passed by the House. No matter how the anti-gun lobby tried to emphasize the ban on interstate sale of handguns and the ban on machine guns, McClure-Volkmer was a major victory for the gun lobby. The machine gun ban didn't bother the NRA very much. J. Warren Cassidy, head of the NRA's Institute for Legislative Action and soon to be executive vice president, rejected complaints by the owners of full-automatic guns. Didn't they understand, he wanted to know, "that in an organization that has fewer than 100,000 machine gun owners in a total of almost 3 million, something has to give?"[8]

Harlon Carter had retired before the passage of McClure-Volkmer, but he had the satisfaction of knowing that he had accomplished what the anti-gun lobby considered impossible. He had turned back the tide of gun control that seemed to be sweeping the country.

There was a price, however. Relations between the police and the NRA had begun to sour.

CHAPTER 10

GREEN APPLES, PLASTIC PISTOLS, AND PARALLEL PARANOIA

THE END OF A FRIENDSHIP?

Osha Gray Davidson, an anti-gun lobby supporter, and Josh Sugarmann, one of the more extreme leaders of the anti-gunners, agree that the NRA shot itself in the foot, if not a more vital place, after the passage of McClure-Volkmer. It accomplished this marvelous (from the anti-gun point of view) deed through its relations with the police.

According to the theory propounded by Davidson and Sugarmann, the NRA had always been close to the nation's cops. It gave them help in constructing shooting ranges. It trained firearms instructors. And it ran shooting matches, open only to police officers, which featured types of shooting useful in police work. The police and the rifle association were buddies. Then the NRA alienated the cops. The first blow was the NRA's support of McClure-Volkmer, which the police (or at least, the police chiefs) strongly opposed. Even worse, the association drove the police wild through its support of "cop-killer" bullets and undetectable plastic pistols.[1]

The theory is interesting, but real life is a little more complicated.

First, the NRA has never been as close to the police as it has been to the military. Harlon Carter was a former Border Patrol officer and head of the Border Patrol. Before Carter and the Cincinnati Revolt, though, a long string of generals had headed the association. The NRA has always slavishly defended the current Pentagon thinking, whether it concerned the short-lived and inappropriate M-14 rifle or the ridiculous tests that "proved" that the low-velocity, round-nosed .38 special cartridge had more "stopping power" than the .45 ACP service cartridge.[2]

From its beginning, the NRA has been in bed with the military (and reaped many rewards because of the relationship).[3] Its relationship with the police has been much more businesslike. Cops carry guns; cops need technical assistance on guns. The NRA is happy to give technical assistance because that enhances its own position. (And, incidentally, it still does give technical assistance, run police pistol matches, etc., even after its supposed break with the police.) Many cops like guns. The NRA, with features ranging from pistol matches to Director of Civilian Marksmanship (DCM) sales, is a garden of delights for gun lovers. But some cops don't care much for guns.

In other words, the NRA has a community of interest with some individual cops, but not others. It has always had working relationships with departments that need some kind of technical help. The gun industry, another—but quite different—part of the gun lobby, has always been close to the police. Cops are a huge market for its products. Things aren't the same between cops and gun owners. In many ways, gun owners and the nation's police chiefs are natural enemies.

If nobody but cops had guns, cops would feel safer. It's that simple. Of course, a lot of thinking cops know that no law will ever keep guns out of the hands of criminals, and more than a few recognize that an armed citizenry is a deterrent to crime. But there are probably at least as many who believe most gun owners don't know how to use their weapons and can't be trusted to have them. In New York and many other cities, the police resist giving citizens the use of even such nonlethal weapons as Mace. Cops like to think that only they can protect us. That is not a new development. Relations between gun owners, organized or unorganized, and the police have always been wary. And there are a lot more gun owners, organized and unorganized, than there are cops. It really should have been no surprise when, according to Davidson:

> As senators filed into the chamber on the day of the vote [on McClure-Volkmer] they had to pass uniformed policemen standing at attention before each chamber entrance—a silent reminder to "do the right thing" for the men and women in blue. Behan [Baltimore County police chief Cornelius "Neil" Behan] was shocked when the bill passed by a wide margin.[4]

COP-KILLER BULLETS

"Bullet-proof" vests go back at least as far as Wyatt Earp.[5] "Bullet-proof" is in quotation marks because nothing that can be worn by a human is totally bullet-proof. A maker of armored limousines years ago told me all his armor is "bullet-resistant." There always may be somebody out there with a bigger, faster, harder bullet that will penetrate anything that can be reasonably built into a car. And a car, of course, can carry much heavier armor than a person.

Early armor vests were made of steel. They were heavy, stiff, and quite un-comfortable. During World War II, air crews were issued "flak vests" made of aluminum plates. They were more flexible, but still heavy, appropriate only for a fighting man who didn't have to move. In 1952, during the Korean War, the U.S. Army began issuing armor vests to the infantry. The vests were made of nylon and were lighter and more flexible than the Air Force model. Still, they were bulky and weighed several pounds. They were nothing you could wear under a shirt. They were intended to stop fragments from exploding mortar and artillery shells. They could stop pistol bullets, too, but pistols are seldom used in military combat.

One soldier, on receiving his vest, handed another man his carbine and said, "Shoot me. I'm bullet-proof."

More sensible companions persuaded the soldier to take off his vest and hang it on the much-blasted remains of a tree. He fired his carbine at the vest. The bullet penetrated the front of the vest, the tree, and the back of the vest. Where it stopped, nobody knew.[6]

In the late 1970s, several companies began making ultra-light vests out of Kevlar, a "miracle fiber" from Du Pont. They were far lighter and less bulky than the army nylon vests. They could be worn under a shirt. But they still wouldn't stop a carbine bullet. (And the M-1 carbine is definitely a weakling among center-fire rifles.) The vests would stop such relatively low-velocity pistol bullets as typical .22, .32, .38, 9mm, and .45 slugs. They became extremely popular with police departments.

The vest manufacturers have estimated that between 1975, when they were first distributed, and 1980, the armor vests had saved the lives of some 400 officers.[7] This is a gross exaggeration. In 1978, according to the Bureau of Criminal Justice Statistics, 93 officers were killed in the line of duty; in 1979, 106; in 1980, 104. Since 1980, the number has declined, and since 1982, when there were 92 deaths, it has declined sharply. The average number of deaths between 1983 and 1992 was 71.3. In 1994, the latest year for which complete figures are available, there were 76 deaths, 75 from gunshot wounds.[8] Figures earlier than 1978 are not available. Before 1981, so few police officers were wearing body armor that the Bureau of Justice Statistics has no information on them. A high estimate of officers killed in 1975, 1976, and 1977 would be 100. That would mean an average of 100.6 officers were killed in each of the six years. It's barely possible the vests saved some 30 lives a year since 1982, but 400 lives in the first six years—an average of 66.7 a year—is most unlikely. Of the 62 officers killed in 1992, the latest year for statistics on the effectiveness of armor vests, 18 *were* wearing body armor,[9] although, as we'll see, none of them was killed by one of the so-called cop-killer bullets.

Those figures, incidentally, prompt another thought. There were more than

604,000 police officers in the United States in 1993. Only 70 of them were killed. That's a little more than 10 per hundred thousand. In other words, it's safer to be a cop than to be an ordinary citizen—man, woman, or child—in many parts of the country. If you're a citizen of the District of Columbia, you're over seven times more likely to be murdered than the average cop.[10] A cop is also safer than any citizen of Louisiana, Mississippi, New York, California, Maryland, Texas, Alabama, Georgia, Illinois, Arkansas, North Carolina, Missouri, Nevada, South Carolina, Tennessee, or Arkansas.[11] Citizens of many cities must cope with much higher homicide rates than the average cop. Compare the rate of police officers killed with these rates: Atlanta, 50.4 per hundred thousand; Baltimore, 48.2; Birmingham, 45.0; Detroit, 56.8; New Orleans, 80.3; St. Louis, 69.0; and, of course, Washington, D.C., where handguns are totally illegal, 78.5.[12] Of course, there are also many places where it's safer to be an ordinary citizen than the average cop. Overall, though, the 1993 murder rate for police officers (about 10 per hundred thousand) is just a hair higher than it is for all citizens—men, women, and children—for the whole United States (9.5 per hundred thousand), according to the U.S. Department of Justice.[13]

Remember these figures the next time you hear some policeman telling how the cop puts "his life on the line" every time he goes out. The cop's a lot safer than a lot of us.

One of the reasons he's safer, of course, is that he's liable to be wearing an armor vest. So, it turns out, are other people in hazardous work, such as stick-up men, gangsters, and drug dealers. Armor vests are a lot more likely to be seen in bad company than, say, "assault rifles." According to police in Bridgeport, Connecticut, almost all members of a particularly murderous drug gang, the Clear Top Mobsters, alias the Green Top Posse, had armor vests.[14]

Armor vests were not on the minds of Dr. Paul Kopsch, Daniel Turcus, Jr., and Donald Ward when they invented what came to be called the "cop-killer" bullet. Kopsch was a county coroner; his two partners were cops. They wanted to develop a bullet that would enable police with .38 special caliber revolvers to penetrate automobile bodies even when their bullets met car bodies at acute angles.[15] The typical "police service" .38 special cartridge had a round-nosed lead bullet. Lead is a soft metal that doesn't penetrate hard surfaces well. Kopsch and his partners tried bronze, softer than steel but much harder than lead. Bronze was soft enough to take the rifling in a revolver barrel, but so hard it wouldn't deform on striking an auto body.[16] It worked pretty well, but Kopsch, Turcus, and Ward wanted something better. They thought the bullet would punch through steel better if it were lubricated. But what lubricant could you put on a sizzling hot, spinning bullet? They tried Teflon. To give the bullet a distinctive look, they ordered apple-green Teflon. Penetration improved 20 percent.

Soon the little green apples were rolling off the assembly line and being stuffed into .38 special cases and shipped to police departments. They worked well. They worked too well. The Teflon-coated bronze bullets penetrated cars, penetrated the law-breakers in the cars, and penetrated the other side of the cars. Then they bounced around off walls and sidewalks and put everybody in the vicinity in grave danger.

As soon as the police departments realized what the "KTW" bullets would do, they stopped ordering them. Production slowed and stopped, leaving few of the little green apples in police hands, and far fewer in nonpolice hands. The whole fiasco would have been forgotten if somebody at NBC News hadn't heard about the KTW bullet. In 1981, NBC aired a news segment showing how the bullets (now unavailable) could penetrate lightweight armor vests. Instantly the bullet, designed for specialized police use, became the "cop-killer" bullet.

The nation's police, most of whom had never heard of the KTW bullet, went ballistic. (Collective paranoia among the police is never far from the surface.) Something had to be done. That thugs and gangsters, as well as police officers, were wearing armor vests was forgotten. And unknown to most of the criers-in-alarm was the fact that many other bullets, too, could perforate the lightweight vests. In fact, almost any bullet fired from a center-fire rifle would do so.

NRA officials are at least as paranoid as police chiefs. Neal Knox, then the association's chief lobbyist, responded to the uproar, proclaiming "There's no such thing as a good bullet or a bad bullet."[17] The NRA flatly refused to support any ban on any kind of bullet. Michael Beard of the National Coalition to Ban Handguns wrote to Harlon Carter to see if the NCBH and the NRA could work together on banning armor-piercing bullets. The NRA refused to cooperate. The association had adopted Carter's "potato chip" theory of gun control, which the NRA chief introduced in testimony before Congress back in 1975:

> [I]t's kind of like that old Bert Lahr commercial that used to be on television. He used to eat a potato chip and say, "I bet you can't eat just one." And I have no doubt that if it's a good thing to be in favor of a 14-day waiting period, next year the ATF [the Bureau of Alcohol, Tobacco and Firearms] is going to be back and say, "We cannot do it in 14 days. We will have to take 90." Frankly, I can see where that leads, knowing how bureaucracies work. It's a little nibble first, and I bet you can't eat just one."[18]

Carter believed that any kind of gun or ammunition regulation would be a step down the "slippery slope," from which there is no return. Although with the passage of McClure-Volkmer, the NRA proved that the slope isn't *that* slippery, it hasn't changed its philosophy.

Beard was as piously hypocritical as the NRA was intransigent. He said he was "astounded that the NRA, which claims to be a friend of law enforcement officers, wants to stop a bill aimed at saving the lives of those who protect our own."[19] At the time he spoke, there was no record of *even one* police officer being killed with a KTW bullet. Further, the bullets were almost entirely out of circulation.

Rep. Mario Biaggi of New York took up the cudgels. Biaggi had progressed from a much-decorated New York cop to a flamboyant congressman. A few years later, he would be sent to prison for extortion.

"These bullets are not used for legitimate purposes," Biaggi said, "but they have been used by criminals to shoot and kill police officers."[20] Actually, they had been used by police officers to shoot and kill criminals. When Biaggi spoke, there was still no record of a KTW bullet puncturing a cop's armor vest and killing him. A couple of cops—one a visiting Canadian—who had been killed with KTWs were found, but neither was wearing an armor vest. One of the two had been shot in the head, which made an armor vest irrelevant anyway.[21] Looking further, control advocates learned that a security guard had been shot with an armor-piercing bullet that went through his armor vest but did not kill him.[22] All of these shootings occurred long before the KTW went out of production.

Biaggi introduced his bill. The NRA said the bill as written would ban many common types of sporting ammunition. Biaggi, the anti-gun lobby, and almost all of the press laughed at that.

"They'll say anything," said Baltimore County police chief Neil Behan, one of those who sent cops to stand outside the Senate chamber during the McClure-Volkmer vote. "It ain't so."[23]

But it was.

"This is a case where the NRA was right," said Eric Sterling, an assistant counsel to the House Crime Subcommittee during the controversy. He helped write parts of the bill. But he later said, "The bill *was* too broad."[24]

Rudolph Giuliani, at that time associate U.S. attorney general and never a coddler of criminals, agreed. "We cannot justify legislation banning all ammunition capable of penetrating the type of soft body armor worn by law enforcement officers."[25]

Robert Powis of the Treasury Department told Congress, "Many sporting rifle cartridges would end up being restricted by this bill. This is a factual statement. It is not something we dreamed up. . . . [The bill] does not just ban true armor-piercing ammunition, it bans a considerable amount of sporting ammunition which is available in much greater quantity."[26]

But the anti-gun lobby went on howling for the NRA's scalp. HCI put an ad in police magazines headlined "HELP STOP THE COP-KILLERS." The facts about armor vests and armor-piercing bullets were not military secrets. There was plenty of time for everyone to learn the facts (although no one would ever get the facts from the newspaper articles on the subject). For the anti-gun lobby to continue this hysterical and fallacious campaign was simply dishonest—a cynical exploitation of the ignorance of the general public.

Eventually, the Reagan Administration took a hand. Leaders on both sides of the controversy were told that the Treasury Department (parent organization of the BATF) had investigated the matter and drafted a bill. It banned the manufacture and importation of bullets made solely of certain metals—tungsten alloys, iron, steel, bronze, beryllium copper, brass or depleted uranium—if the bullets would penetrate a standard police armor vest when fired from a handgun with a five-inch barrel. It was most unlikely that anyone would even attempt to make a bullet composed solely of tungsten alloy, cast iron, high-carbon steel, or depleted uranium. Such a bullet would not take the rifling, rendering the gun wildly inaccurate. And if it were the correct bore diameter, it would flatten the rifling with the first shot if it didn't blow up the gun.

If all sides did not publicly agree on the bill, the administration said, it would drop all support for a bill on the subject.

That pretty much ended the controversy, although there were squawks from congressmen who weren't invited to the White House conference. Three new bills appeared, but none of them got anywhere. The next year, the administration bill was introduced and passed in the House and Senate by wide margins. The green-apple fight was over. If the NRA had not been so worried about potato chips, it could have ended a lot earlier.

PLASTIC PISTOLS

If the evidence that KTW bullets were cop-killers was flimsy, evidence for the existence of plastic pistols was nonexistent. There are not and never have been any all-plastic pistols. Still, the controversy over these nonexistent weapons was as disrupting and polarizing as the fight over "cop-killer" bullets.

The controversy started with some syndicated newspaper columns by Jack Anderson. In January 1986, Anderson wrote that a new Austrian pistol, the Glock 17, could pass through airport security checks because it was mostly plastic. According to Anderson, a Pentagon security expert disassembled the gun and carried it through the X-ray machine and metal detector at an airport. What's more, Anderson said, "Libyan dictator Muammar Qaddafi [is] dickering to buy 100 to 300 of the Glock 17 pistols on the black market."[27]

Police and other officials were sure that Libyan terrorists would use the 9mm Glocks to carry out an orgy of skyjackings in the air and assassinations in the United States. Anderson kept the pot boiling. In another column, he quoted a cable sent to the secretary of state by the U.S. ambassador in West Germany. It was "a rough translation" of a German government report on the Glock. The translation included these statements: "The tests showed that the completely assembled weapon is extremely hard to recognize on the X-ray screen. Disassembled, the weapon was X-rayed together with a camera in a camera bag. In this condition only the barrel could be detected as a thick black line. The plastic parts could not be detected."[28]

The translation was either extremely rough or the German tests were. The equipment and personnel at the checkpoint used by the Pentagon official probably weren't too sharp, either.

The fact is that the Glock contains 19 ounces of steel. That's a greater weight of steel than many small pistols contain. It's greater than the *total* weight of such popular pistols as the Smith and Wesson Chief's Special Airweight, although much of that revolver's 13½-ounce weight is the less magnetic (and less detectable) aluminum.

American experts seriously disputed the alleged German report. John Battema, vice president of the Astrophysics Research Corp., wrote:

Fully assembled, the Glock 17 looks exactly like any other automatic pistol when viewed on the television monitor of our Linescan airport X-Ray security machine. Further, it causes our Mark 100 Metal Detector to alarm at the normal setting just as any other pistol does. When the Glock 17 is broken down into its three basic components (metal barrel, metal ammunition clip and plastic frame) all three components are still visible and identifiable on the television monitor of the X-Ray system by a trained security operator. In all tests, the Glock 17 was X-Rayed while inside a standard briefcase with a normal amount of paper (approximately 1' thick) and other items usually found in a briefcase. Even the plastic frame shows as clearly as a toy plastic gun which, incidentally, is one of the most common items identified by airport security personell [sic]. . . . In my estimation, it would be as difficult to pass a Glock 17 through an X-Ray security checkpoint as it would be to pass any other real pistol through the same checkpoint.[29]

Nevertheless, police groups, egged on by the anti-gun lobby, demanded legislation to ban plastic guns. Even though there were *no* plastic guns, the NRA opposed the legislation.

"Make no mistake about it," wrote NRA lobbyist James Jay Baker, " 'plastic' guns represent a clear and present danger to the security of the American people. The danger, however, is not posed by foreign terrorists brandishing non-metal firearms aboard jet airliners. No, the threat is much nearer to home. Some politicians are playing on the fear of terrorism to mask their anti-gun agendas."[30]

There was going to be a replay of the "cop-killer" bullet caper. The NRA was still thinking of potato chips. What followed was a long wrangle between the NRA on one side and the police organizations and the anti-gun lobby on the other over banning guns that didn't exist.

At the end of 1987, Howard Metzenbaum, the high priest of senatorial gun controllers, said he would introduce a bill that would ban all pistols containing less than 8.5 ounces of steel. The NRA went into a tizzy and sent an "emergency alert" to all of its members.

At first glance, that looked like a typical NRA overreaction. Very few pistols weigh less than 8.5 ounces. But there may have been some reason for the alarm—especially if you look at the bill called Brady II, also sponsored by Metzenbaum. Brady II would outlaw all magazines with a capacity of more than six rounds. That doesn't sound so harsh. It's not really a restriction on guns, just magazine size, and how many cartridges do you need in a magazine? But very few semiautomatic pistols now made have magazines that hold fewer than than six rounds. Meeting that standard would mean junking almost all pistol magazines and redesigning and manufacturing new magazines before the pistols could be used at all. Further, the bill also bans any magazines that could be converted to a larger capacity. It wouldn't be hard to make such magazines for most rifles. But because most pistol magazines fit into hollow handles, they have to be as long as the handles. It's hard to see how a practical nonconvertible magazine could be designed for most existing pistols. If Brady II were passed as proposed, almost all semiautomatic pistols and many revolvers would be illegal. There are some other cute features of Brady II we'll examine later. In short, Metzenbaum was a subtle senator. These days, many pistols are not all steel. Aluminum alloy is a common component. If pistols had to contain 8.5 ounces of *steel*, quite a few would be banned.

The police groups immediately began demanding that all pistols contain at least 8.5 ounces of steel. The NRA demanded just as loudly than there be no ban. Finally, as with the "cop-killer" bullets, the administration came up with a compromise. All guns would have to have a *detectability standard* of 3.7 ounces of stainless steel. The police got a detectability standard, which was ostensibly what they were looking for. The NRA got off the steel standard. And as usual with compromises, both sides were unhappy.

As with the "cop-killer" bullets, it was much ado about nothing. Eric Sterling, at that time counsel to the House Crime Subcommittee, reviewed the case with Osha Gray Davidson.

"There are no plastic guns," he said. "There never were. The Glock was made the fall guy for this thing. This airport security stuff—there was a lot of bullshit floating around here. Did Muammar Qaddafi have a bunch of those guns that he ordered? Was there a KGB plastic gun?" Sterling just laughed.[31]

WHOSE COP ARE YOU?

All of the above shenanigans were supposed to have caused a split between the NRA and the police. But Neil Behan, the Baltimore County police chief, was never a friend of the NRA. He certainly was not a friend of gun owners. Behan was a veteran of 31 years in the New York Police Department, where the culture is aggressively opposed to citizens owning guns. When it looked as if McClure-Volkmer might pass, he organized something called the Law Enforcement Steering Committee with representatives from a number of police groups. The LESC was to be a cops' lobby.

The NRA then gave Behan a big boost. It did that by not merely disagreeing with police officials who supported gun control but by viciously attacking them, even trying to have them fired. Many cops, incensed by the NRA's tactics, joined the anti-gun side of the fray. And Handgun Control, Inc. added fuel to the fire by running ads featuring police leaders who differed with the rifle association. Neil Behan was one. He later said:

When I got into this I was rather naive. It never occurred to me that when I was looking at the 20,000 deaths per year—that anyone would sustain an argument for more handguns. As a result I didn't know they [the NRA] were the enemy. Pretty soon I found out. When McClure-Volkmer heated up they began calling the elected officials around here asking for my removal. Here I'm exercising my First Amendment rights and they're trying to kill me for doing that. They're still after my head, trying to influence politicians to get rid of me.[32]

Another cop who agreed to work with HCI was Jerald Vaughn, executive director of the International Association of Chiefs of Police (IACP) from 1985 to 1988. In February 1985, during the McClure-Volkmer debate, Vaughn had written to G. Ray Arnett, then executive director of the NRA:

Your tactics have included taking the liberty of imporperly [sic] acting as a spokesman for law enforcement in this country. You have misrepresented our position, you have attempted to discredit and undermine the leadership of our professional law enforcement associations and have blatantly insulted our intelligence by implying that we are dupes of the anti-gun lobby. You have disorted [sic] facts to suit your purposes and have attempted to suppress free and open debate on perhaps the most critical public safety issue to come about in recent memory.[33]

That letter, and Vaughn's open support of HCI, earned him, he said, "a certain amount of hate mail and controversy. The tactics, the vindictiveness, the resources mustered against anyone who speaks out against them . . . no other group [can] even compare with the NRA."[34]

Vaughn took on the NRA about the same time he took his seat as director of the IACP. Joseph D. McNamara, then chief of the San Jose, California, police, was no old friend of the NRA, either. Like Behan, he was a product of the NYPD and a consistent supporter of gun control measures, including the banning of private ownership of handguns. He was, and still is, a dedicated anti-gun activist who appeared in a number of HCI ads and publicity pieces.

The NRA was not content with disagreeing with McNamara on the issues. It ran an ad in *Time, Newsweek,* and *USA Today* accusing McNamara of favoring the legalization of drugs. The accusation was untrue. What McNamara had said, on the Oprah Winfrey show, was, "It's time to consider this [the "war on drugs"] in an unemotional way. We must find a way to take the profit out of drugs."[35] Considering how the so-called war on drugs has tremendously increased crime, including homicide, and probably increased addiction as well, that's a reasonable statement.[36] McNamara was not willing to go further than that, however. He added, "That does not necessarily mean I'm for legalization. In fact, I'm opposed to it."[37]

The NRA didn't confine its attacks to enemies. Joe Casey, chief of the Nashville, Tennessee, police, believes, and always has, in the right of citizens to own guns, including pistols. But he supported a seven-day waiting period before the sale of a handgun.

The NRA sent a four-page letter to all its members in Tennessee headlined "HELP STOP NASHVILLE POLICE CHIEF'S LIES NOW." The Nashville mayor was bombarded with letters and phone calls asking for Casey's removal. Casey stayed on the job, though. And as Casey was then president of the IACP, the police organization sent a letter to all the country's police chiefs. It concluded:

When Joe Casey is attacked, the IACP is attacked and, therefore, *you* are attacked. You must act to protect your citizenry, your department and yourself. . . . Police executives must stand united. Work with your fellow chiefs and don't let the NRA victimize you. If you see a problem developing, contact IACP headquarters and your state association. We don't run away when thugs try to claim turf in our communities, and we shouldn't be intimidated by political extortionists like the NRA.[38]

Ever since then, the IACP and its state organizations have supported every gun control initiative to appear.

The NRA leadership was bothered by the open hostility of the police organizations. Many of its own members are political conservatives who think "Support your local police" is one of the Ten Commandments. The organization made some efforts to regain the confidence of the cops. One of the more contemptible was an article in *The American Rifleman* by retired executive director and former Border Patrol chief Harlon Carter denouncing civilian review boards. The letter earned him a rebuke from another hero of the Border Patrol, former firearms instructor and pistol champion W. T. Toney, Jr. In a letter to the NRA magazine, Bill Toney wrote:

> Aside from its many inaccuracies, your May article branding police civilian review boards a police peril seems to ignore a very important and fundamental principle. We of the criminal justice profession work for the "civilians" of this country. It is not the other way around.
>
> The Law Enforcement Code of Ethics, formally recognized since about 1955, begins, "As a law enforcement officer, my fundamental duty is to serve mankind. . . ." There is not a word about mankind serving public officials who are unwilling to submit their actions to public scrutiny.[39]

Of course, in any group that includes more than 600,000 people, there is no uniformity of opinion. The woods are not full of cops who think their chiefs are wonderful. Many police officers did not agree with the leaders of their organizations on gun control. Some of them formed their own organizations. One was a subordinate of Joe McNamara's in San Jose named Leroy Pyle. Pyle organized Law Enforcement for the Preservation of the Second Amendment, which later changed its name to Law Enforcement Alliance of America, Inc. and moved to New Jersey. LEAA later moved its headquarters from New Jersey to northern Virginia, to be in a better position for lobbying.

Bigger than the LEAA (Pyle's club, not the Law Enforcement Assistance Administration) are the many organizations founded by Gerald Arenberg, a 40-year veteran of law enforcement. They include groups like the National Association of Chiefs of Police, the American Federation of Police, and the American Law Enforcement Association, Inc. Their combined budgets come to more than $3 million a year.[40]

It's probable that Behan's LESC is more in tune with mainstream police opinions than either Pyle's or Arenberg's groups. But aside from NRA executives and law enforcement politicians, who cares?

The NRA's bullying tactics caused it more important losses far from Washington.

LOCAL SKIRMISHES

In 1981, Geoffrey LaGioia of Morton Grove, Illinois, applied for a business permit to open a police supply store. LaGioia planned to sell the usual array of police paraphernalia—flashlights, belts, holsters, guns, nightsticks, etc.—but he also planned to reload cartridges so the police could have cheap ammunition for practice. He had rented a store and bought automatic reloading equipment, an alarm system, and a walk-in safe. He expected no problems.

"I had researched everything at the library," he said. "There were no laws against opening a gun store."[41]

When he met the chief of police, however, the chief told LaGioia he didn't want to see a gun store in "his town." There were already two gun stores in Morton Grove. LaGioia thinks the chief didn't want to see competition with a friend operating a police supply store in a nearby town. LaGioia called the NRA. They were somewhat less than helpful. They told him, "The Constitution says you have the right to *bear* arms, not to *sell* them."[42]

LaGioia vowed to fight the ban.

That disturbed Neal Cashman, a village trustee. Cashman didn't like guns, period. He later said LaGioia's store would be a short distance from the junior high school, and "We didn't want the kids looking in the window, dreaming of guns."[43] Cashman called the village attorney to see if there was any way the village trustees could stop LaGioia. The attorney said they could pass a law banning the sale of handguns in the village. If they wanted to, he added, they could even ban the *possession* of handguns in the village.

At the next meeting of the village trustees, Cashman proposed a ban on handgun sales. The measure passed. Then he proposed a ban on possession of handguns. There would be no grandfathering, as there is in Washington, D.C. Current owners would have to turn in their handguns or face a $500 fine. In other words, all handguns would be confiscated. That was a bit much for the rest of the trustees. They scheduled a public hearing on the measure.

Now the NRA got interested. According to Osha Gray Davidson, "The lobby bussed scores of gun supporters from rural areas into Morton Grove [a suburb of Chicago] to make their presence felt at the June 8 hearing."[44] Whether they were bussed or not, NRA members from out of town were there in abundance, complete with hunting caps, camouflage outfits, and combat boots—everything but rifles and shotguns. Some village trustees weren't sure about that last part. Greg Youstra, a gun owner who was expected to vote against the ban, said the rural gun fans were 50 deep around the village hall. "I was afraid I was going to get shot," he said.[45] He voted for the ban.

The NRA was using the same tactic as the Law Enforcement Steering Committee—intimidation. And at the Morton Grove Village Hall as at the U.S. Senate chamber, it backfired. Public officials, whether in Washington or in the smallest town, resent attempts to push them around. They react negatively. Somehow, though, the NRA seems not to have gotten the word. Whenever there's a public hearing on gun control anywhere in the country, scores of men dressed as if they were planning to shoot bear instead of participate in local government crowd into the hearing room. Frequently, many come from out of the jurisdiction. And when it's all over, they wonder why the results were so unsatisfactory.

So Morton Grove became the first locality in the country to make handguns utterly illegal and require the confiscation of any existing pistols. Its example was quickly followed by two other Chicago suburbs, Oak Park and Evanston. Michael Beard of the NCBH was elated. He wrote to all the coalition's member groups asking them to duplicate "the miracle of Morton Grove."

Not much miraculous happened outside the Chicago area, though. Kennesaw, Georgia, reacted to Morton Grove by passing an ordinance requiring every head of a household to keep a gun and ammunition available. Like the Chicago suburbs, though, Kennesaw has taken no steps to enforce its law.

San Francisco passed a law forbidding possession of pistols, but it was quickly declared illegal. In California, state law preempts local gun laws. State preemption laws became a major NRA goal. A rash of such laws were passed in reaction to Morton Grove's action.

The effect of handgun prohibition in Morton Grove and other towns on the crime rate? Apparently none. At least no decrease. Some categories increased. The effect on the crime rate in Kennesaw as a result of that town's law? Residential burglaries dropped. (More on this later.)

Reduction of crime is the ostensible reason for gun control laws (as we'll see, there are also other reasons), although nobody has ever been able to show any drop in the crime rate because of them. Nevertheless, the politicians keep trying.

CHAPTER 11

POLITICIANS VERSUS CRIME

THE YEAR OF CRIME

According to somebody, 1993 was the Year of the Woman. Well, maybe. But there's no doubt that—as far as politicians were concerned, anyhow—1994 was the Year of Crime. Never have so many would-be elected officials proclaimed so vigorously that they don't like crime. That people running for office opposed crime was hardly surprising. No one's ever heard a politician say he was in favor of crime, not even when he was committing it. What was surprising was the strength of their protests and the unanimity of their statements. Everyone's opponent was "soft" on crime. The worst thing a candidate could say about his opponent was that the other guy hadn't supported the ban on "assault weapons." Each candidate had the same solution for the crime problem: build more prisons, lock up more people, and keep them in longer—except for the increasing number to be executed.

Less often mentioned—because the "assault weapon" ban was supposed to "make our streets safe"—was banning more guns. Rep. Charles Schumer of New York, however, wanted to do just that. Schumer was the godfather of the Brady law, which requires a waiting period before buying a handgun, and the 1994 crime law. He was also an enthusiastic supporter of the amendment banning "assault weapons," added to the crime bill by Sen. Dianne Feinstein. But just before the election, less than five months after the crime bill became law, Schumer was again calling for more gun bans.[1] That might indicate that Schumer didn't really believe his own rhetoric about the Brady law and the "assault weapon" ban. Maybe he knew the waiting period and ban on rare but ugly weapons wouldn't do much to fight crime. Or maybe he thought the crime rate had taken a monstrous and unexpected jump in the last few months. After all, to hear any of the 1994 campaign speeches, you'd think the whole country was drowning in the "rising tide of crime."

The politicians talk that way because the public opinion polls say voters believe that increasing violent crime is the country's greatest problem. And the voters think that because they see more crime news on television and in the newspapers than ever before.

It was disconcerting to learn around mid-year that the tide of crime wasn't rising. It wasn't ebbing much, either, but it was hardly the *tsunami* the pols, the polls, the papers, and the public thought it was. According to the FBI's *Crime in America*, better known as the Uniform Crime Reports, the rate of violent crime was lower in 1993 than in 1992, which was lower than 1991.[2] In New York City, Police Commissioner William J. Bratton not only said violent crime had been declining steadily since 1991, he said that in some neighborhoods it was down 25 percent.[3] In neighboring Connecticut, violent crime had dropped 14 percent since 1990.[4]

The good news about the decline in crime was quickly drowned out by the political rhetoric of congressional campaigning. Later, when elections were over, officials from the president to local police chiefs began congratulating themselves on how they had dammed the tide of violence. In New York, the question of who should get the credit for that city's felony shortfall led to a dispute between Mayor Rudolph Giuliani and Commissioner Bratton, and the commissioner moved to the private sector.

Rejoicing over the decline of crime seems to be tapering off as this book is being written in 1996. That's true even though in May of 1996, the FBI reported that violent crime had declined for the *fourth* straight year.[5] This, of course, is a year of presidential as well as congressional elections. President Clinton, to show his "toughness," has ridden over the objections of civil libertarians to get his terrorism bill passed. He also let a spokesman say that a federal judge who made a politically unpopular decision might be asked to resign. Senate Majority Leader Robert Dole, to show he's even tougher, stated that if he were president, all potential federal judges would have to be cleared by a panel of prosecutors and crime victims. Congressman Charles Schumer won't even admit that there has been a drop in crime. In a letter to HCI members dated April 12, 1996, Schumer began with:

> As surely as you're reading this letter, right now, somewhere in America an innocent child is bleeding to death on a "safe" suburban sidewalk, caught in the crossfire of a drive-by shooting.
>
> Somewhere in America a police officer is about to be gunned down in the line of duty.

Innocent children rarely get gunned down in drive-by shootings in supposedly safe suburban neighborhoods, even without a "crossfire." Those who do make the national news. That reflects not only the scarcity of such shootings in "nice" residential areas, but the prevalent indifference to the deaths of kids in poor urban neighborhoods. In all of 1996, up to Schumer's letter, no such shooting occurred. And we've already seen how frequently police have been killed in the line of duty even when the crime rate was considerably higher than it is now.

In spite of the politicians, though, the crime rate is definitely lower than it was a few years ago.

Looking at murder and non-negligent manslaughter, the most violent of violent crimes, the record is even better. Murder and intentional manslaughter hit a peak in 1980 and have never been that high since. As a matter of fact, the 1992 rate (9.3 per hundred thousand) is less than the 1973 rate (9.4) and the 1993 rate (9.5) is just a whisper higher. As a matter of fact, the current rate is just slightly higher than the 1972 rate (9.0).[6]

There is a crime problem, of course. Although the rate of violent crime has dipped in the last few years, it's far higher than it was years ago. In 1992, for instance, there were 757.5 violent crimes per 100,000 persons. In 1972, there were 401.0. The overall murder and intentional manslaughter rate, however, has remained stable for the last couple of decades, although murder by and of persons under 19 has been increasing steadily. Some experts say demographics is responsible for the current stability of the crime rate, especially the homicide rate. Most violent crime and homicide is committed by boys and young men between 15 and 25. That age group is a slightly smaller part of the population than it was in the early 1980s. In a few years, though, the children of yesteryear's baby boomers will cause the youth population to rise again. And, say the experts, the murder rate will rise with it.

Murder is the crime that inspires calls for gun control. Guns figure in 69.6 percent of the murders in the United States.[7] Guns figure in only about 42 percent of robberies and less than 10 percent of rapes.[8]

All the above crime figures are from the FBI's Uniform Crime Reports. The UCR is compiled from arrest records. It's long been known to police and criminologists, however, that there are many crimes committed that never get reported to the police. In general, these are minor crimes that the victim doesn't think worth reporting. Others, such as assaults by relatives, may not be reported because of family ties. The most serious crime often unreported is rape. It often goes unreported because of victim embarrassment.

LIES, DAMN LIES, AND STATISTICS

To learn more about these unreported crimes, the Bureau of Justice Statistics conducts "victimization interviews" with samples of persons over 12 years of age. Statistics from these interviews are often quite different from the UCR's. For one thing, they lack the objectivity of a compilation of arrest records. Interviewers have found that victims do remember and talk about unreported crimes. But at times the respondents have also forgotten crimes that *were* reported to the police.[9]

Statistics based on the recollections of victims show a surprisingly stable crime rate between 1973 and 1992. In fact, the number of crimes against the person recorded in the period—while the population was growing—has decreased. The number of crimes went from 20,322,000 to 18,832,000. The number of violent crimes did increase—from 5,351,000 to 6,621,000—but although that's an increase of almost 24 percent, the *rate* of violent crimes per hundred thousand *declined* slightly—from 32.6 to 32.1.[10] The stability shown by the victimization survey does not appear in statistics from the UCR. In the UCR figures, violent crime went from 875,910 in 1973 to 1,932,270 in 1992.[11] And the numbers from the victimization survey are much larger. That's probably because the victims remembered such results as black eyes and bloody noses that didn't prompt a call to the cops.

In the 1993 victimization survey, the BJS redesigned the survey. "The actual methodology and collection of the data is different for '93 than it was for '92," a Bureau spokeswoman said.[12] The methodology must have been very different. The results were carried in an Associated Press dispatch October 30, 1994, proclaiming that violent crime had increased 5.6 percent since 1993, a rather startling change from previous survey results.[13] In the news story, there was no mention of the change of survey methodology. The 1994 survey obviously included crimes that hadn't been covered in 1992. For instance, the new report said that all crime in 1993 was up 1.7 percent over 1992. As all crimes were said to number 43,600,000 in 1993, that would mean that all crime numbered 42,858,800 in 1992. But the 1992 survey gives the number as 33,649,340. The disparity is even greater in the violent crime category. The new report says there were 10,900,000 instances of violent crime in 1993, up 5.6 percent from 1992. If that were so, there must have been 10,289,600 instances in 1992. But the 1992 survey says there were 6,621,000. Even with restructuring, comparing the 1993 survey results with 1992 would seem to require, in the absence of data, some statistical legerdemain. The total effect is to make it look as if violent crime is increasing more than it is.

A call to the Bureau of Justice Statistics shed no light on how comparisons between the new survey results and those of previous surveys could be made. The newspaper stories simply ignored the fact that the latest survey used a new methodology. They just reported an increase in violent crime where the FBI found a decrease. Almost a year later, the BJS issued a report explaining the new methodology. It included "additional cues to help survey participants recall incidents; questions encouraging respondents to report victimizations that they themselves may not define as crimes; more direct questions on rape, sexual assault and other sexual crimes; new material to measure victimizations by non-strangers, including domestic violence."[14]

The Bureau cautions, "Comparisons of estimates of crime based on previous survey procedures with estimates from the data in the redesigned survey are not recommended. The improvements noted above and other fundamental changes introduced by the redesign make comparisons inappropriate."[15]

Special techniques are being developed to allow valid comparisons to be made, the Bureau reported. "Statisticians who are experts on this particular survey will be able to compare victimization trends under the old and new methods. Techniques to extend historial trends with estimates from the new methods *will be developed*"[16] [emphasis added].

Granting that comparisons cannot be made with previous survey results, the BJS nevertheless found that, looking at the whole picture a year after its news release, "annual data collected with the redesigned questionnaire indicate that year-to-year trends continue relatively unchanged: little change in violent crime and a slight decline in property crime."[17] And again, "Among the major crime categories, there were no statistically significant differences in the numbers of victimizations between the two years [1992 and 1993].[18]

That, of course, is not the conclusion the Associated Press drew from the BJS news release issued a year earlier.

Was this apparently deliberate deception inspired by politics? Who can say? It did, though, give Charles Schumer a chance to put in another word for further gun control.

"It's no wonder crime is America's number one concern. We've become a society of victims or people afraid of becoming victims," Schumer said. To combat the trend (not shown on more objective studies), Schumer urged additional legislation to control handguns.[19]

Schumer is never at a loss for words. A few weeks after release of the new victimization study, the FBI released its latest Uniform Crime Reports. The UCR showed that the murder rate had dropped 2 percent in the first half of 1994. Violent crime in general was down 4 percent; rape, 6 percent; robbery, 4 percent; and aggravated assault, 2 percent.[20]

"One piece of bad news in this report is the gun murders," said Schumer, who apparently believes shooting a person to death is much worse than strangling, bludgeoning, or burning the same person to death.[21]

The *New York Times* seemed even more reluctant to accept the good news. It felt compelled to insert the following paragraph:

> Some experts have long criticized the FBI figures because some crimes are not reported to the police. A report by the Justice Department in Octo-

ber, based on interviews with 100,000 Americans, found that violent crime was rising and that more than half of all crimes were not reported to law enforcement agencies.[22]

We have already examined the DOJ's criminal victimization survey and compared it with the UCR.

Both Schumer and the *Times* exhibit a rather touching faith in the efficacy of legislation. The Gun Control Act of 1968—part of the Omnibus Crime and Safe Streets Act—had no negative effect on crime. Violent crime had gone from 288,460 cases in 1960 to 499,930 in 1967, the FBI's UCR reported. In 1968, it began a quantum jump. The 1968 figure was 595,010. Seven years later, in 1975, it was over a million. In 1993, 18 years later, it was still over a million but approaching two million.[23] The 1994 legislation had not had a chance to prove itself before Schumer was asking for still more gun control to stop crime.

To be fair, not all advocates of more gun control give crime as their only reason. Two of the most hard-line anti-gunners, Michael Beard and Josh Sugarmann, admit that gun control *won't* stop crime. Said Beard, executive director of the Coalition to Stop Gun Violence: "I would agree that clearly no law is going to prevent criminals from getting handguns or any kind of weapon they want. . . . You can't stop criminals from getting guns."[24] Sugarmann, founder of the Violence Policy Center, said, "Handgun controls do little to stop criminals from obtaining handguns."[25]

All three of the anti-gun lobby groups—the CSGV, the Violence Policy Center, and Handgun Control, Inc.—are concerned with other "wrong hands" than those of hard-core criminals. Spokesmen for all three organizations cite accidents, suicides, and spur-of-the-moment killings by persons "who are not really criminals" who kill in the heat of rage just because a gun is available.

Children killed by guns is a big talking point for the anti-gun lobby. To make their figures more dramatic, both HCI and the Coalition to Stop Gun Violence lump together children killed in gun accidents, children who kill themselves, and children who are murdered (almost always by other children). They further enhance their statistics by listing as "children" anyone 19 or younger.

By far, the largest number of "children" killed by guns are those murdered by other "children." From 1976 to 1993, the number per hundred thousand of boys 14 to 17 who murdered someone has more than doubled; so has the number who were murdered.[26] In the same period, killings by youths 18 to 24 went from 17.5 to 25.9 per 100,000.[27] Victims in that age group went from 14.7 to 24.2 per 100,000.[28] Juvenile murder is certainly a major problem in the United States. Most of those juvenile murderers, though, are the hard-core criminals that Beard and Sugarmann say will always get guns.

ACCIDENTS

Let's look at gun deaths that are not homicides. Take accidents. Literature from Handgun Control, Inc. frequently points out that the rate of auto accident fatalities in the United States has dropped. HCI doesn't try to claim that this is because cars are registered and drivers are licensed. That was true for eons, and the death rate from auto accidents kept growing. HCI does imply, though, that increased regulatory intervention, such as sobriety checks, has helped the situation. And, it concludes, more regulation can do the same for gun accidents.

There are a couple of problems with this analogy. One is that the rate of vehicle accidents hasn't declined that much. The National Safety Council gives the following figures for motor vehicle accident deaths: 1910, 1,900; 1920, 12,500; 1930, 32,900; 1940, 34,501; 1950, 34,763; 1960, 38,137; 1970, 54,533; 1980, 53,172; and 1990, 46,800.[29] Of course, there were more cars in 1960 than in 1900. But there weren't that many more in 1970 than in 1960. Certainly there were not 42.3 percent more, but that was the percentage increase in accidents between the two dates. During the same period, the population of the country increased 13.4 percent. The second problem is that the rate of gun accidents has been declining for most of a century. And it's declined a lot more than auto accidents. In 1905, the number of people per hundred thousand killed in gun accidents was 3.4. In 1991–92, it averaged .6.[30] Although the population of the United States has been steadily increasing, the number of accidental gun deaths has been steadily decreasing.

In 1987, less than half as many people under 19 died in shooting accidents as in 1974. In 1974, 85 children four years old or younger were killed in gun accidents; in 1987, 37. Among children aged 5–9, the decrease was from 142 to 66; in the 10–14 age group, 305 to 144; in the 15–19 group, 476 to 220. The decrease was not quite so steep among the population as a whole—from 2,513 to 1,440. Still, it's a pretty sharp decline. And 1,440 in a population of 255,000,000 is not a horrendous total.[31] It's not, especially when you understand that most experts agree that the accidents that occur "while cleaning a gun" are usually suicides.[32] Vincent DiMaio, a medical examiner and expert on gunshot wounds, said that in his extensive experience, he "has never seen a case of an individual fatally shooting himself while 'cleaning or oiling a weapon.' . . . Careful investigation of these deaths (where such an activity was alleged) . . . revealed all to be suicides."[33]

This decline in gun accident deaths cannot be attributed to increased regulation, the anti-gun lobby admits. It must be caused by improved gun safety education. And over the long period during which gun accidents declined, there was only one organization teaching gun safety—HCI's hated rival, the NRA.

Auto accident fatalities, although they have declined, are 29 times more numerous than firearms accidents. Even if you include only families that own both a gun and a motor vehicle, vehicle accidents kill 15 times more often. Incidentally, guns are far more common than swimming pools, but more Americans drown in swimming pools than die in gun accidents. They are also more likely to die in accidents involving boats or ships and in aircraft accidents.[34]

All of this is not meant to discourage gun owners from putting trigger locks on their weapons, locking them up, and, especially, storing them unloaded. It is meant to show that the anti-gun lobby's favorite image of a toddler picking up Daddy's pistol (although long guns figure in more gun accidents) and killing himself or his baby sister is a very, very rare occurrence.

SUICIDES

Accidents should not be lumped with suicides. Suicides are intentional. Even those who assert that murders often occur just because a gun was available seldom claim that suicides are *caused* by gun availability (although some advocates come close to that). The U.S. suicide rate hit its peak in the early 1980s, about the same time as the homicide rate.[35] Both peaks occurred, of course, a little more than a decade after GCA 68 ended the interstate sale of guns and importation of Saturday night specials, and otherwise made guns less available and—our leaders said at the time—made homicide and suicide less likely.

The anti-gun theory seems to be that guns increase the suicide rate because they are more likely to be fatal than other methods, such as taking sleeping pills. Also, after the would-be suicide pulls the trigger, he can't change his mind, as he might if he were trying carbon monoxide poisoning. Nor can anybody intervene successfully. Nobody could argue with either the lethality or swiftness of the gun as a suicide method, although some few do survive shooting themselves. On the other hand, jumping from a high place is just about as lethal. Nobody ever stopped her plunge from the Empire State Building or the Golden Gate Bridge and flew back up to safety. Hanging, if done so that the drop breaks the neck, is about as lethal as suicide methods get. There are, in fact, scores of ways of killing yourself.

Guns are a popular method of suicide in the United States, far more popular than in Japan, for instance. In Japan, almost nobody has a gun, while half of all the households in this country have one. Why is it, then, that the suicide rate in Japan is higher? The U.S. suicide rate is 12 per hundred thousand; the Japanese is 14.3. Hungary, which in 1989 was an Iron Curtain country with no guns available to ordinary citizens, had a horrendous suicide rate, 44.9 per hundred thousand. Gun control is also pretty strict in Denmark, which had a rate of 31.6. Switzerland, as noted above, has a high suicide rate, 24.5.[36] Strangely, although guns are widely available in Switzerland, few suicides choose to end their lives that way.[37] Canada also has one of the world's highest rates of gun ownership.[38]

Most of them are rifles and shotguns, but suicides with rifles and shotguns are quite common. In fact, of the shooting suicides in the United States where the type of weapon was recorded, 59 percent of the guns were rifles or shotguns; 41 percent were handguns.[39] In spite of the availability of guns, however, only 35 percent of Canadian suicides use them.[40] In the United States, 57 percent do.[41] Why guns are so popular for suicide in this country has never been explained, but there is no reason to think that, if deprived of guns, those suicidally inclined could not kill themselves.

Criminologist Gary Kleck studied all the data relating to gun ownership, control laws, and suicide in this country and analyzed them himself. There was some indication that laws prohibiting the mentally disturbed from having guns tended to reduce the suicide rate. In general, though, he found that gun control laws had no effect on the number of suicides.[42] The Centers for Disease Control studied the effect of waiting periods on the suicide rate for the U.S. Department of Justice. They found that there was no effect.[43]

SPUR-OF-THE-MOMENT SHOOTINGS

A common theme of the anti-gun lobby is how the presence of a gun induced someone "who was not really a criminal" to grab it in a moment of anger and commit murder. We'll look at these "moment of anger" murders in more detail in the chapter called "The Devil Gun Made Me Do It." A couple of observations are in order, though. First, almost everyone believes pistols are extremely lethal. (They aren't as lethal as generally believed, but the ability of the shooter to control that lethality is also far less than generally believed.) Anyone who points a pistol at someone else with the intention of shooting is a criminal—a very serious criminal—even if the intention lasts only a moment. A person with so little self-control is a continuing danger to society and should be locked up, whether he fires the gun or not. Second, almost all so-called domestic murders are preceded by many violent incidents. For instance, a study of domestic homicides in Kansas City, Missouri, showed that in 90 percent of the cases, police had responded to a disturbance call at that address during the previous two years. There was a median of five previous calls.[44]

THE BRADY BILL

The name of Jim Brady became attached to the first national restriction on guns since GCA 68, largely because of the efforts of Sarah Brady, the head of Handgun Control, Inc. It involved a lot of effort, and it was vigorously opposed by the gun lobby. But it wasn't much of a restriction. As originally introduced, the Brady bill would have mandated a seven-day waiting period before the purchase of a pistol anywhere in the country. Of the 50 states in the United States, 26 already had waiting periods before handgun purchase. Many of them were considerably longer than seven days. California, for instance, has a 15-day period. States that already had waiting periods of seven days or longer would not be affected. States that had no waiting periods would have them after the bill became law.

Waiting periods are not a new idea. In the early 1970s, before the Cincinnati Revolt, the NRA itself had stated, "A waiting period could help in reducing crimes of passion."[45] Even earlier, in the 1920s, it was part of the model firearms bill the NRA helped draft for Washington, D.C. But the NRA position changed after Cincinnati. When the Brady bill was introduced, Wayne LaPierre, then head of the NRA's Institute for Legislative Action, said his organization thought the mandate for a waiting period was a major anti-gun issue.

The bill first took the form of an amendment to the House Omnibus Drug Bill of 1988. Once again, the NRA sent out letters telling its members that the sky was falling. Rep. Thomas Foley of Washington, Speaker of the House, tried to prevent the amendment from being adopted in committee, but he lost. An amendment adopted by a committee is far harder to defeat than one offered on the floor. Rep. Bill McCollum of Florida saw a way to defeat the Brady amendment on the floor. The reason for the amendment, members of HCI-supported police organizations told Congress, was so police could check on the records of those who wanted to buy handguns. What if the police could do the background check without a waiting period? McCollum offered, as a substitute for the Brady amendment, one that instructed the U.S. attorney general to study the feasibility of a system, using computers and electronic communications, that could instantly check on a prospective buyer's record. The House adopted McCollum's substitute.

The next year, however, Attorney General Richard Thornburgh reported that though "a worthwhile goal," the instant record check would be too costly to implement at that time. The Brady bill came back to life. It was introduced as an amendment to the crime bill of 1990. And again, there was a substitute amendment. This time, instead of asking for a feasibility study of an instant check system as the McCollum amendment did, the amendment offered by Sen. Harley Staggers of West Virginia required implementation of a system within six months. That was not only more definite than the McCollum amendment, it was demanding something much more expensive and harder to accomplish. In other words, it was not likely to get as many votes. It didn't. The Brady amendment was added to the crime bill, passed both houses and went to a conference committee to iron out the differences between the versions passed by each house. The revised bill passed the House, but then President George Bush promised to veto the whole crime bill, including the Brady amendment. It wasn't tough enough on crime, he said. As a result, the crime bill died in the Senate.

In 1993, Bush, who had continually waffled on gun control legislation, was out, and Bill Clinton, a strong advocate of such legislation, was in. Rep. Charles Schumer introduced a new Brady bill.

In the course of its years-long hegira through Congress, the Brady bill had caused some interesting developments. The NRA had never, to put it mildly, been terribly interested in background checks on persons buying guns. With the introduction of McCollum's amendment, however, it became the leading proponent of instant background checks. The main reason—and about the only legitimate reason—for waiting periods is so the authorities can determine whether or not the prospective buyer is someone who is likely to do harm with the weapon. Nevertheless, Handgun Control, Inc. and its allies fought the instant check idea tooth and nail.

The anti-gun lobby denounced the idea as a pie-in-the-sky notion that would cost billions and could not be made to work. The National Rifle Association and its allies said checks on a person's record could be made as easily as credit card checks. As usual, the truth was somewhere in the middle. A great deal of police records are already computerized. Police frequently nab fugitives after stopping them for traffic violations. That's because they routinely check information from driver licenses and registration cards by radio with a computer in headquarters. Implementing the instant background check is simply a matter of adding information, such as commitments to mental hospitals, to the computer database. Some state computer databases have all the information now. Bringing the system up to the standards needed for an instant background check cannot be done in a week, but it's not a project rivaling the construction of the Panama Canal.

The other reason for a waiting period is expressed in one of its nicknames, a "cooling off" period. According to one theory, many murders occur when someone "who is not really a criminal" flies into a rage, rushes to a gun store, buys a weapon, and comes back to kill someone else. There are some flaws in the theory. One is that most homicides that are the result of fights occur between 8 P.M. and 3 A.M.[46] Almost all gun stores are closed at that time.

Even if the culprit's murderous rage lasted longer than a hour or two, the waiting period would still not have much effect on the crime rate. To be effective, several conditions would have to be met: (1) the killer would have to have no gun when he decided to kill the victim; (2) he would have to obtain his gun from a retail outlet; (3) the time between the purchase and the crime would have to be less than the specified waiting period; (4) if there were a waiting period, the killer would not simply have bided his time until it was over and then obtained the weapon and committed the murder.

In 1982, a study of 342 convicted killers in Florida found only three who had no other gun and who bought the murder weapon from a retail dealer and killed a victim in fewer than three days of the purchase. (The purpose of the survey was to see how many homicides would have been avoided had Florida's three-day waiting period been in effect at the time.) A national study of felons by Wright and Rossi found that Florida criminals were more than twice as likely to buy guns from retail stores than the national average. Even extending the waiting period to seven days, the criminologists concluded that the waiting period could have conceivably prevented only .5 percent of the homicides.[47] And that's assuming that none of the killers could have waited out the waiting period. That's a very big assumption. Colin Ferguson, perpetrator of the Long Island Railroad massacre, traveled to California, used an illegally obtained driver's license to establish his residency in that state, then waited the 15 days required by California law before purchasing a gun.

As the Brady bill moved through Congress for the last time, it picked up modifications. One was that it would not apply to states that already had waiting periods. Another was an amendment requiring that instant background checks be phased in over a five-year period. When the checks were instituted in a state, the waiting period would end. The anti-gun lobby reacted like a scalded cat. To the gun controllers, the waiting period itself—not a check to learn if the buyer was a homicidal maniac or a fugitive serial killer—was apparently the most important part of the bill. Deborah Mathis, a syndicated columnist with the Gannett News Service, wrote furiously:

> The Brady law does not—repeat, does not—require waiting periods, as people are wont to say. It did as originally designed, but the delay provision was too hot to handle on Capitol Hill.[48]

After the bill became law, several county sheriffs claimed it was unconstitutional because the federal government was commandeering state officials—them—to perform duties for it: background checks. They went to court, and the NRA, that great champion of background checks, gave them money and legal support.

In the struggle over the Brady bill, it became obvious that each lobby was really interested only in scoring points against the other. The common good was forgotten.

The Brady bill became the Brady law in 1993. Anti-gun lobby spokesmen hailed it as a great victory for law and order. But even as they spoke, their lobby and its allies were preparing legislation that, they promised, would again "make our streets safe" (something no gun control legislation had approached accomplishing so far).

CHAPTER 12

100,000 COPS AND BRADY II

THE POLITICS OF SCARING THE PUBLIC

Although, as we've seen, crime is actually decreasing, political discussion of crime is, at this writing, still increasing. Running against some sinister force is always attractive to candidates. Everybody wants to be against the bad guys. The candidate's job is to convince the voters that the bad guys are winning, but he has the way to beat them. The end of the Cold War hasn't made that kind of campaigning any easier. The candidate finds it hard to convince the voters that Joe Doakes, who's served with him in the state legislature for the last dozen years, is a sinister force. With Communism, Nazism, and the Demon Rum all out of the picture, almost the only sinister force left is crime.

The news media are in a similar fix—especially television. Television needs graphic news. The North American Free Trade Agreement doesn't make it. Neither does the stock market, unless brokers start jumping out of windows again. With no war on, television news consists mainly of fires, earthquakes, hurricanes, and murders. Any time you turn on the TV news there's usually some hyped-up crime or criminal trial getting nationwide coverage. But local television stations can't depend on news fed to them from Los Angeles, Long Island, or Union, South Carolina. Harry Tammen, co-founder of the *Denver Post*, once said, "A dogfight in a Denver street is more important than a war in Europe." And so we're treated to shots of detectives poring over taped-off areas surrounding where bodies were found or bodies being wheeled off on gurneys. And the TV viewer, who may never have seen as much as a fistfight in the last decade, gets the feeling that the country is dissolving into anarchy.

And if that TV viewer has a decent job and is making a decent living and all his family is in reasonably good health, what's he going to tell a poll taker when asked about the country's most serious problem? You guessed it—crime. For many years, the Gallup organization has asked respondents what they consider the most important problem the country is facing. From May 1981 until March 1991, "crime" was chosen by no more than 5 percent. In January 1993, it rose to 9 percent. And then in January 1994, it leaped to an amazing 37 percent. It climbed even higher the next August, hitting 52 percent. By January 1996, after months of officials from the president of the United States to local police chiefs congratulating themselves for a decline in crime already several years old, the percentage dropped to 27. That was a small step back to reality. But before 1994, no more than 9 percent of the population had considered crime the nation's most serious problem.[1] If crime is what concerns most of the population, crime will be the problem that causes the most expressed concern among politicians. That's particularly true of politicians on the national stage, even though the U.S. Constitution gives the federal government very little power to fight crime.

Nevertheless, the federal government and national politics in general makes a bully pulpit, and bullies from all branches of government take advantage of it. In December 1993, the U.S. Conference of Mayors called on President Clinton to present a "national action plan" to combat "an epidemic of violent crime."

"People in our cities are demanding action," Jerry Abramson, mayor of Louisville, Kentucky, and president of the conference, told Clinton. The mayor of Denver, Wellington Webb, added, "It's our belief that people are not dying by knife-throwing or rock-throwing; they're dying because of shooting—because of guns."[2] The mayors demanded that Clinton's plan include a comprehensive package of gun control laws. Reading statements like those of Abramson and Webb, is it any wonder the general public sees crime as our number one problem?

A survey by the Times Mirror Center for the People & the Press in December 1993 showed that 45 percent of the respondents thought the NRA had too much influence on gun laws.[3] That was up from 39 percent the previous August. The only national action on gun control in 1993 was that the Brady bill passed—a major defeat for the NRA. The poll didn't measure the respondents' reactions to what had happened but to the increased rhetoric. The same poll showed 57 percent being in favor of stricter handgun controls. (In a later chapter, we'll take a closer look at what polls like this really mean.)

Although nobody likes crime, the two political parties traditionally approached the problem in different ways. The Democrats had favored what they called "preventive" programs, which range from midnight basketball to Head Start programs for preschool children. The Democrats have been pushing preventive programs for the last couple of decades, but they don't seem to have prevented much, because the crime rate kept rising during most of that period.

The Republicans, on the other hand, say they want to "get tough" on crime. "Getting tough" often seems to be shorthand for wiping out constitutional rights. Preventive detention is one popular proposal. That's keeping a suspect in jail before he's proven guilty because you suspect he is. Warrantless searches, a direct violation of the Fourth Amendment, is another. So is letting evidence seized illegally be presented at trials. And so is—although it's never publicly advocated—torture (the "third degree") to make a suspect confess.

All of these "get tough" measures—except official sanction of the third degree—have been features of previous crime bills. So have mandatory minimum sentences and "boot camps" for young offenders.[4] Because of the different approaches the two major parties take to crime control, however, in 1993, no major crime bill had been passed since 1984. A crime bill that passed the House in 1991 died in the Senate after President George Bush announced that he'd veto it because it wasn't tough enough on crime. Bush, never famous as a risk-taker, managed to conciliate the gun lobby while at the same time looking tougher-than-thou on crime.

The election of Bill Clinton as president of the United States marked a change in Democratic policy. Clinton wanted to take both approaches—"get tough" measures and preventive programs. In a way, it was something like Lyndon Johnson's decision to fight both the war on poverty and the war in Vietnam. And the indications are that it will be no more successful.

THE CRIME BILL OF 1994

In his campaign for the presidency, Clinton promised "tough" measures against crime, including putting 100,000 new police officers on the streets of American cities and towns. He began working on a revival of the perennial crime bill soon after he took office. By December of 1993, he was beating the drums loudly.

On December 8, at a press luncheon at Blair House, Clinton said, "I am convinced that most Americans now understand how profoundly important these crime and violence issues are, and how it's time to face them."[5] He said he favored weapons registration and "stop and frisk" laws that would allow police to search persons suspected of carrying weapons without getting a warrant, or even without having what is usually considered probable cause. So much for the Fourth Amendment. December 11, in his weekly radio address, Clinton charged that "drugs and guns and violence fill a vacuum where the values of civilized life used to be." He referred to the Long Island Railroad massacre and the murder of 12-year-old Polly Klaas of California (abducted at knife-point, incidentally) and said, "These tragedies are part of the epidemic of violence that has left Americans insecure on our streets, in our schools, even in our homes."[6]

He urged the passage of a crime bill that would put 100,000 more cops on the streets, ban "assault weapons," and appropriate more money for military-style "boot camps" for young first offenders. The House had approved a bill that its sponsors said would provide 50,000 more police officers. A similar bill in the Senate aimed at 100,000 more police. Both Senate and House bills prohibited the transfer of handguns to juveniles, but the Senate bill also prohibited the sale of 19 types of semiautomatic guns called "assault weapons" (more on these gadgets in chapter 17 on "Devil Guns"). Manufacture and importation of the banned weapons or copies of them was prohibited under an amendment introduced by Sen. Dianne Feinstein of California. Possession was also prohibited unless such weapons already privately owned were registered. Clinton continued to press for further gun controls in the crime bill at every public appearance, and Secretary of the Treasury Lloyd Bentsen said the administration was considering a major hike—about tenfold—in license fees for gun sellers. The Brady law had just increased those fees from $30 to $200 for three years. Estimates of the new fees ran as high as $750 a year.[7]

In his 1994 State of the Union speech, Clinton asserted, "There is no sporting purpose on earth that should stop the United States from banishing assault weapons that outgun police and cut down children."[8] He got extended, standing applause from Democrats.

While Clinton was stumping for more gun control in the crime bills (particularly in the House version, which had passed without an "assault weapon" ban), Rep. Charles Schumer of New York said he planned to introduce a new gun control package that had been blessed by Sarah and Jim Brady. Handgun buyers would have to be fingerprinted and take a safety training course under Schumer's bill. The five-day waiting period of the recently passed Brady law would be supplanted by a seven-day period whether instant background checks were available or not.[9]

The House went back to work on a crime bill. Clinton lobbied furiously for an "assault weapons" ban. So did his allies in Congress. Rep. Rosa DeLauro of Connecticut stated that "assault weapons" are 18 times more likely than other guns to kill police officers.[10] The basis for this astounding claim was a letter from another congressman, Rep. Pete Stark of California, who said he had discovered it by analyzing information in the FBI's Uniform Crime Reports. There is no such information in the UCR, nor in the FBI's annual *Law Enforcement Officers Killed and Assaulted* report. Stark's claim could be charitably characterized as a gross exaggeration of a gross exaggeration based on creative accounting. An explanation appears in the notes on this chapter. Stark apparently combined figures on officers killed by rifles with a peculiar FBI concept—"Possible assault rifles." "Possible assault rifles" are *any* rifles or submachine guns of .22 rimfire, .223, .308, 9mm, or .45 caliber.[11] Only a tiny fraction of .22 rimfire and .308 rifles are even semiautomatic, and there are at least as many bolt-action .223 rifles as semiautomatics. Rifles with the pistol grips, long magazines, and other character-istics of "assault rifles" are but a fraction of the semiautomatics. Rifles in 9mm and .45 are usually semiautomatic, but not usually "assault rifles." There is no indication of how many of the type called "assault rifles" might have been in-volved in the killings. There were only four of these "possible assault rifles" involved in cop killings in 1986, eight in 1987, and seven in 1988.[12] In 1994, there were only six "possible assault rifles" involved in the murder of police officers, and the chances are that none of them was actually an "assault rifle."[13] Rep. Barbara Kennelly, another Connecticut legislator, dedicated her vote in favor of the crime bill to three Hartford residents shot in 1994—although none of them had been shot with any of the so-called assault weapons.[14]

On May 5, 1994, the House voted on an amendment banning 19 guns de-clared to be "assault weapons." It passed 216–214. Predictably, Representative Schumer said of the vote, "It means that our streets will be safer."[15]

Because other amendments had been added in the House, the crime bill had to go to a House-Senate conference committee. The bill, including the assault weapon ban, having passed the Senate once, crime bill supporters expected no trouble when the conference committee bill came out to be voted on by both houses.

They were wrong.

While the administration and HCI had relaxed their lobbying efforts, the NRA had stepped up its lobbying. Further, conservatives found that there was more money for preventive programs in the conference bill than in the bills they had previously voted for. African-American representatives objected to removal of a section aimed at ensuring that the death penalty would not be passed as a result of racial prejudice. And some Republicans resented what they felt was the ad-ministration ignoring them.

On August 11, 1994, the House voted 225–210 to block the conference com-mittee crime bill from coming to the floor. As we saw in chapter 7, Clinton responded by running against the NRA. With tear-jerker press conferences and behind-the-scenes arm-twisting, he managed to get the bill out on the House floor and passed, then avoided more roadblocks in the Senate. The *New York Times*, a tireless crusader for gun elimination, was not satisfied with the ban. In a summary of the crime bill, writer Gwen Ifill pointed to a "loophole" in the gun ban, saying it specifically exempted 650 types of semiautomatic rifles.[16] It did not. One reason is that 650 types of semiautomatic rifles do not exist. The act exempted 650 rifles of all types. (That is cold comfort to gun owners: what can be exempted today can be outlawed tomorrow.) Gun legislation is one of several topics on which the good gray *Times*'s errors are such that one could call the paper sloppy—if the errors were not all in favor of the *Times*' biases.

We'll take a close look at "assault weapons" and the effort to ban them in a future chapter. Before leaving the 1994 Crime Law, however, we should examine some of its other provisions.

100,000 COPS

It has been widely publicized by almost every news medium in the country that the bill will provide 100,000 new police officers. It will—if American states, cities, and towns can find 100,000 men and women willing to work as police officers for $15,000 a year.[17] That's how much money the federal government is providing. Of course, the local jurisdictions are expected to kick in, too. But the federal money runs out in six years. After that, either the local jurisdictions pay the whole freight (unless they can finagle extensions), or there will be wholesale layoffs. Have you seen any officials clamoring for a chance to fire hordes of police officers? Sen. Orrin G. Hatch called the 100,000 cops story "poppycock." He said the number of new police would be "20,000 at most."[18]

Hatch is not exactly a fan of Bill Clinton, but less biased experts agree with him. "It's simply not 100,000 extra police and everybody knows that," said Franklin Zimring, a law professor and criminologist at the University of California.[19] Jonathan Rubinstein, a former police officer who has written extensively on law enforcement, points out that hiring a police officer is a 50-year financial commitment—20 years of salary and 30 years of pension. "When the money runs out, you just can't lay these people off," he said.[20]

In spite of the impression President Clinton, campaigning against revision of the law in 1995, gave, money in the original bill could be put to other police uses than hiring more sworn officers. Under Title I (Public Safety Partnership and Community Policing Act of 1994) relating to hiring and rehiring police officers, grants may be used: (1) to rehire police officers who have been laid off as a result of budget cuts; (2) to hire new police officers; (3) in communities affected by military base closings, to hire police officers from former members of the armed forces involuntarily separated from the service; (4) to provide training for officers deployed in community-oriented policing; (5) to increase police participation in "multidisciplinary early intervention teams"; (6) to develop new technologies for preventing crime; (7) to develop programs to increase citizen participation in law enforcement; and (8) to decrease time spent by police for court appearances.[21]

This flexibility is why mayors and police chiefs had been clamoring for the crime bill. The money won't all go to hanging a 50-year financial commitment around their necks. Some of it—the part many are most interested in—will let them modernize their departments.

Then, too, there are hidden minefields for police forces that expand rapidly.

In 1989, Congress voted to withhold $430 million in aid to the District of Columbia until the District expanded its police force. The District hired 1,500 new officers in the next 20 months. Soon after the expansion, one of every 14 new officers had been arrested for crimes ranging from forgery to murder. Traffic accidents killed nine of the rookie cops. And dozens more proved so untrustworthy that prosecutors refused to let them testify.

A few years before, Miami had hurriedly expanded its police force. It hired some 600 new officers in 1981 and 1982. A short time later, about one in ten of them had been suspended or dismissed for drug-related offenses. Rapid expansion of a police force too often means background checks on the applicants for officer positions have been slighted and training has been skimped.[22]

On May 29, 1996, two years after the Crime Law had passed, how many new cops were on the street? Not 100,000. Not 50,000. Not even 20,000. The total deployed, according to Attorney General Janet Reno and George Stephanopoulos, senior presidential spokesman, was 17,000.[23]

''BOOT CAMPS''

Almost all our elected representatives in the federal government—Democrat or Republican, liberal or conservative, from President Clinton to the newest congressman—agrees that "boot camps" for young, first-time offenders are wonderful. The liberals say they will instill a sense of discipline that will keep youthful graduates out of trouble later. The conservatives agree with Gov. Zell Miller of Georgia, who said, "Nobody can tell me from some ivory tower that if you take a kid, you kick him in the rear end, and it doesn't do any good."[24] They agree with Miller, even if they raise their eyebrows at his grammar.

Just what are boot camps?

The name, in spite of Miller, doesn't have anything to do with booting people in the rear end. The program is supposedly based on military basic training. In the navy and marines, this training is called boot camp because, in the navy at least, the trainees used to wear rubber boots most of the time. The theory is that military boot camps develop discipline in the new sailors and marines. Actually, most of the recruits have a fairly healthy sense of discipline before they enter the service. What boot camp—or in the army, basic training—does is teach the recruits how to perform their duties. Future infantrymen, for example, learn close-order drill, marksmanship (in a way), squad tactics, and other military subjects as well as where they are in the military hierarchy (at the bottom). Some of the correctional boot camps may try to teach the kids to read and write or the rudiments of a trade, but there isn't enough time. Most don't teach them much except how to do pushups and clean up garbage. If more physically fit felons is what society needs, correctional boot camps are a success.

They are not much of a success in other respects. In spite of the president's enthusiasm for boot camps (which may be due to his lack of experience with even the military type), the General Accounting Office found that there was no significant difference in the recidivism rates of former boot campers and former inmates of conventional prisons. Doris L. McKenzie, a criminologist at the University of Maryland, found the same thing. No study indicates that the correctional boot camps do any good at all. Nevertheless, Congress rejected all information to the contrary, including the GAO report.

"It didn't tell them what they wanted to hear," said William Jenkins, Jr., assistant director of justice issues at the GAO, "so it died on the vine. Most people on the Hill believe that boot camps should be expanded."[25]

THROW AWAY THE KEY

More severe sentences are another feature of the 1994 crime law. Before the law, the death penalty could be imposed for two federal crimes. After the law, 60 crimes could be punished by death. Sentences in federal courts were made longer, and the federal code now incorporates a "three strikes and you're out" provision. The law also provides that states that do not adopt certain mandatory minimum sentences and delays in parole may not receive some federal subsidies.

Those who want to "get tough" on crime seem to forget that the criminal justice system is not infallible. Innocent people have been executed. According to the Death Penalty Information Center, 48 persons have been released from death row since 1970 because new evidence proved they were innocent.[26] The death penalty poses some other problems, too. The person who has committed any of the 60 federal crimes covered by the death penalty has nothing to lose. Threatened with arrest, he will fight to the death. And his may not be the only death. Then, of course, there's the question of just how much the death penalty deters criminals. England in the eighteenth century prescribed the death penalty for hundreds of crimes, but it also had a crime rate that is almost unbelievable today. Today, England has no death penalty, and it also has an extremely low crime rate. In the United States, states with the death penalty have no lower crime rate than states without it. What little difference there is indicates a higher homicide rate in the death penalty states.

The death penalty, of course, would be one way to make room in the jails, but electrocuting enough people to make a difference might result in national brownouts. There are already more than a million people in state and federal prisons. And that doesn't count people in local jails, where there are an estimated half-million or so. For the last few years, the United States has had the largest percentage of its people behind bars of any country in the world, having passed South Africa and the Soviet Union. Recently, Russia, where the violent crime and homicide rates are off the charts (in spite of an almost total prohibition on guns), has nosed ahead of us. But there are still a lot of Americans in jail, and we're incarcerating more at a record rate. In the first six months of 1994, the prison population increased nearly 40,000.[27] In 1980, there were 139 prisoners for every 100,000 residents in the country. At the end of 1994, there were 356. In 1980, there were 329,821 inmates in federal and state prisons; at the end of 1994, 1,053,738. Federal prisons were at 125 percent of capacity; state prisons at 117 percent.[28]

"Since the late 1970s we've had an uninterrupted growth cycle in the number of inmates, one that is longer now than any previous one in the twentieth century," said Franklin Zimring, the University of California criminologist.[29] The U.S. incarceration rate is four times higher than Canada's, five times higher than England's and 14 times higher than Japan's.[30] The new crime law's longer sentences may push us ahead of Russia and make the United States once again champion of the world.

There's one lesson that no one in government seems to have drawn from this situation: long sentences don't deter criminals. Since nobody seems to heed criminologists, maybe we should listen to criminals—someone like "Sneakers," a 21-year-old Milwaukee gang member. "Sneakers" has twice been convicted of felonies. The third conviction in Wisconsin means life without parole. "Sneakers" doesn't worry about "three strikes and you're out."

"The law don't make no difference to me," he says, "because I ain't gonna get caught. I mean, if I really thought I was going to get caught, I wouldn't commit a crime in the first place, now would I?"[31]

Most crime is committed by poor people who have no hope of otherwise getting ahead in this world. That's no secret. Most of those poor people belong to ethnic or racial minorities that are discriminated against, oppressed, even despised, by the majority. That's no secret, either. It's been a condition in our country for the last century-and-a-half. Crime was first an Irish problem. Then a Jewish problem. Then an Italian problem. Now it's a black and Hispanic problem. And unless we do something other than banning guns and creating ever-harsher punishments, it's going to be a problem in the United States for a long time to come.

It was a problem with the Irish for decades—as long as help-wanted advertisements included the phrase "No Irish need apply." The Irish eventually got jobs. Some became police officers on the nineteenth-century theory that you need thugs to keep thugs in their place. More dug coal in Pennsylvania and copper in Montana or laid track through the hunting grounds of hostile Indians or homesteaded lonely farms and ranches on the frontier. All of these lines of work were hard, dirty, dangerous, and low-paying. But they led the Irish to better things, including the education of their children. The history of the Jewish and Italian immigrations to this country is much the same.

Unless conditions change, it won't be the same for the African-Americans and the Hispanics. There are no jobs for unskilled people that lead to better things. We have a tax structure that encourages American corporations to move manufacturing jobs to foreign countries. What few jobs are available are usually part-time service jobs, without health benefits, pensions, or chances to advance. Pundits prattle about "the knowledge industry" supplanting manufacturing and agriculture as the basis of the economy—as if anybody ever ate an idea, wore an idea, or drove an idea to work. Entry into the "knowledge industry" requires a college education, but college tuition is rising so high it threatens to exclude not only the poor but the middle class from higher education. There is a welfare system that puts a premium on single parenthood, and there is an enormous increase in illegitimate births. For the last few decades, we have been unconsciously fostering the development of a permanent, increasing underclass. That will, in the long run, mean an ever-increasing crime rate and a steadily growing financial burden on the body politic.

Something must be done. But our leaders—and the voters who elect them—find it easier to clap more people in jail, ban more guns, and tell each other how tough they are. What they've been doing hasn't worked, so they want to do more of it. One of the new initiatives has been published under the imprimatur of Sarah Brady.

WITH BRADY II, HCI's ALL THROUGH?

"Handgun Control, Inc. is working for a comprehensive bill, dubbed Brady 2, including these measures [a ban on Saturday night specials and limits on gun purchases] and many more—like licensing handgun owners, registering transfers, safety training for purchasers and installation of safety devices by producers," wrote Sarah Brady in a letter to the *New York Times* published September 19, 1994. "The bill, introduced by Senator Howard M. Metzenbaum and Representative Charles E. Schumer, is the beginning of an overhaul of the way guns are bought and sold in this country.

"More important, it represents an end to incrementalism. The Brady law has proved a tremendous success in keeping guns out of criminal hands at the retail level. And the recent ban on military-style assault weapons will have a similar impact. The essence of Brady 2 is responsibility—from gun makers, dealers, and owners."[32]

Responsibility and an end to incrementalism—it sounds good. Everybody's in favor of responsibility, and almost everybody is tired of the yammering on both sides of the gun control "debate." If HCI, Metzenbaum, and Schumer could come up with something that doesn't threaten to destroy the billions and billions of dollars worth of firearms in private hands, even hard-core gunnies might be willing to listen.[33] There is one nagging doubt that comes from reading the letter, though. If Brady II is to end incrementalism, why is it "the beginning" of an overhaul of the way guns are bought and sold?

Let's take a closer look at Brady II. Metzenbaum retired before Congress could vote on it, but Schumer is still active—and, presumably, still ready and willing to push the bill.

The bill consists of four titles, covering licensing and registration, restrictions on firearms possession, restrictions on gun sellers, and prohibited weapons.[34]

The first title would require everyone who wishes to buy a handgun to have a license. The license would contain the licensee's name, address, date of birth, physical description, and photograph. License applicants would have to be at least 21 years old, present valid identification and proof of residence, be fingerprinted and have their backgrounds checked, and complete a safety course. Seven days would elapse before a sale to a license-holder could be completed, regardless of instant background checks. And a registration form recording each sale would be forwarded to the police. No sale between private individuals would be legal unless the buyer has a license and the sale is registered with the police. Some states, such as Connecticut, already have this provision.

Gun control advocates, including Attorney General Janet Reno, are fond of comparing proposed gun owner licenses to automobile licenses. They aren't comparable, though. Nobody needs a license to buy or own a car. A car doesn't have to be registered nor its owner licensed if it won't be driven on a public road. Although most people with cars do drive on public roads, thousands of farmers and ranchers confine their shooting to their own property. Unlike car owners who eschew public ways, they'd need a license. And, most important, a driver license is valid in any state, not just the state that issued it. That would not be the case if Brady II were law. You can drive in California with a Florida driver license, but if you tried to tour that state carrying a pistol, your Florida permit would be worthless. HCI continually calls for a uniform national firearms law, but this parochial proposal ignores many of the advantages of such a law.

The second title attempted to add some new restrictions on handgun possession. For many years, federal law has forbidden guns to anyone convicted of a felony or under indictment for a felony, a fugitive from justice, a drug addict, or an alien. The Brady law and the 1994 crime law added persons who had been confined to mental institutions, persons convicted of violent misdemeanors, persons under court restraining orders because of threats of violence, and persons under 21 years of age. These existing restrictions cover and exceed almost all the restrictions in Brady II. About the only new wrinkle is for what the bill terms "a federal arsenal license."

An "arsenal" seems to be what we used to call a gun collection. Any number of guns over 20 and any amount of ammunition exceeding 1,000 rounds would constitute an arsenal. This would require another fingerprint and background check (presumably the collector, or arsenal-keeper, would already have a gun owner license). And, of course, it would also require another fee. In this case, the fee would be $300 for three years. This provision would certainly add a little money to state coffers, but what it has to do with public safety is unclear. As a class, gun collectors (persons with 20 or more guns) are a notably peaceful sector of the citizenry. And while 1,000 rounds of ammunition may seem an enormous amount to the gunless population, it's a pretty small quantity to the target shooter. Most targeteers buy .22 caliber ammunition in "bricks" of 500 rounds, each about the size of a real brick. Firing rimfire, center-fire, and .45 stages in the Standard American match, a pistol shooter will burn up a *minimum* of 90 rounds. And that's not counting sighters and fouling shots before the match. A participant in an important match may fire several hundred shots for the record. To keep their eyes and nerves in condition, really dedicated target shooters fire hundreds of shots *a day* in practice. For those people, limiting ammo on hand to 1,000 rounds would mean daily trips to the gun store.

The only reason for this "arsenal" provision seems to be that the bill's sponsors don't like guns or ammunition, and think they are nasty in themselves and nobody should have them—at least, not that many—and that people who do have that many are also nasty and should be harassed. Harassment, too, seems to be the reason for the provision that holders of an arsenal license would have to put up with unannounced inspections of their collections. Gun control advocates say nobody needs 20 guns. True. But nobody *needs* more than one TV, more than two suits, or even one pair of downhill skis, and nobody badgers those who own those items to get rid of them. The United States is not a monastery, and few of its citizens have taken a vow of poverty. Busybodies who want to confine everybody's possessions to what they think other people need have no place here.

The third title raises the fee for gun dealers to $1,000 a year. Inasmuch as the fee before the Brady bill became law was $30 for *three* years and after the Brady law $200 for three years, the increase can fairly be called steep. Further, the BATF would be able to make applicants for a license wait 180 days and could make three warrantless, unannounced inspections of the business a year. Licensed dealers would be required to respond immediately to gun traces by the BATF and to report thefts or losses from their stock within 24 hours—both provisions already in force. They could sell only from their business premises, thus eliminating sales at gun shows. What this would accomplish is less than clear, as private individuals —other than dealers—could still sell at gun shows.

The fourth title puts a number of devices under the same proscription Mc-Clure-Volkmer applied to machine guns. Included are silencers, short-barreled shotguns, short-barreled rifles, "destructive devices" (hand grenades, cannons, rocket launchers, etc.), Saturday night specials (the name the bill applies to any pistol with a barrel three inches long or shorter), nonsporting ammunition (see chapter 17, "Devil Guns"), "semiautomatic assault weapons" (also discussed in chapter 17), and "large capacity magazines." "Large capacity" means capable of holding more than six rounds. Of the 273 semiautomatic pistols listed in the *Gun Digest Annual*, only 30 have magazines holding no more than six cartridges.[35] Whether newly manufactured six-round magazines for existing automatics would be legal is questionable. Forbidden are any magazines "which can be readily restored or converted to accept more than six rounds of ammunition."[36] In most semiauto pistols, the magazine fits into a hollow grip. Any magazine to fit such a pistol would have to be at least the same length as the grip. It's difficult to see how such a magazine could *not* be converted to take more cartridges.

The bill also has a provision that could be either an inadvertent technical error or one more bit of harassment. In the paragraph on safety devices, the bill would ban "any single action revolver which does not have a safety feature which by *manual operation* causes the hammer to retract to a point where the firing pin does not rest upon the primer of a cartridge."[37] Many single-action revolvers, and all of the Ruger series, have a safety device that does that *automatically*, a vastly safer arrangement. And while the safety devices the bill specifies are laudable, the bill outlaws all older guns that do not have such devices (the vast majority), which would make them almost impossible to sell or transfer. In effect, it penalizes all owners of such guns for what are sins neither of commission or omission.

"Prohibited weapons lawfully possessed prior to the effective date of the ban may be retained," HCI explains, "but if they are transferred they are subject to the registration and transfer tax requirements [$200 per item per transfer] presently imposed on the transfer of automatic weapons by the National Firearms Act of 1934."[38]

The act would make a huge number of guns illegal. Long-barreled, hand-operated rifles with nondetachable magazines holding five rounds or fewer and no evil "assault gun" trappings like bayonet lugs would be legal. So would long-barreled, hand-operated, double-barreled, or single-shot shotguns. Most handguns would be prohibited weapons. Prohibited weapons already legally owned could be retained, but their owners might well make plans to be buried with them. Transferring them legally, with the addition of a $200 transfer tax, would not be easy.

The inclusiveness of the prohibited weapons category, combined with such features of the bill as the "federal arsenal license" provision, the refusal to make gun owner licenses good nationwide, and the restrictions and sky-high fees on gun dealers, indicate that Brady II does not aim merely to control weapons—"to keep handguns out of the wrong hands," as HCI's motto has it. It aims to keep most handguns out of any hands, and along with handguns, "assault weapons" and a wide variety of other guns and ammunition. It would also greatly increase the difficulty and expense of owning *any* firearm. And as Sarah Brady wrote in her letter, it is to be the *beginning* of an overhaul of the way guns are bought and sold.

Altogether, Brady II would constitute the most complex and bizarre set of gun regulations of any country in the world. (There's more on other countries' regulations in chapter 21.)

HCI, however, will not be satisfied with even this legislation. It has begun a series of lawsuits against manufacturers of guns used in crimes. The suits are not based on the ancient common-law idea of negligence—that a person who manufactures a *defective* product is liable for any injury *caused by that defect.* The first HCI lawsuit is against the manufacturer of the pistols used by Gian Luigi Ferri to kill eight and wound six people in a San Francisco law firm. It does not charge that the manufacturer put defective guns on the market. The guns functioned perfectly. In Sarah Brady's words, "In these lawsuits we are charging the *manufacturers* of the assault pistols used in the killings—and the Las Vegas pawnshop that sold them to Ferri—with *negligence* in producing, marketing and selling these guns"[39] [emphasis in original]. Brady continues:

> It is imperative that we establish some principles of *legal accountability* for the gun industry, whose history is that of making products that have no *legitimate* purpose . . . but that are undeniably dangerous to the public safety [emphasis in original].
>
> Saturday Night Specials, cop-killer bullets, plastic handguns, exploding ammunition, high-capacity magazines—all pedalled [sic] to the general public because the gun industry had no fear it would ever be held accountable for the death and destruction these products cause. The gun industry must be made to bear the costs of its irresponsibility."[40]

In this case, Brady says, "[W]e are seeking a lifesaving legal precedent."[41]

To fully appreciate the impact Brady II and HCI's legal offensive would have on American life, we should take a look at the place of guns in U.S. civil society.

CHAPTER 13

DIGRESSION NO. 2: GUNS IN CIVIL LIFE

THE DOMESTIC ARMS RACE

All through the literature of gun control, a few phrases are repeated endlessly, like mantras. "The easy availability of guns" is one. "The domestic arms race" is another. In 1975, a couple of sociologists, Jeffrey H. Spiegler and John J. Sweeney of the Governmental Research Institute, concluded a study called *Gun Abuse in Ohio* this way:

> While the blessings of liberty should include shooting for hunt and sports, . . . it is doubtful whether the founding fathers could have foreseen the scope of the domestic arms race, especially in handguns, a device not well suited for either hunt or sport, but rather as a weapon, which has resulted in a gun in every other home.[1]

It's easy to see that Drs. Spiegler and Sweeney didn't get their degrees in history. If the founding fathers failed to foresee anything, it was that every other home would *not* have a gun. They might also be amazed that anyone thought they wrote the Second Amendment so that "the blessings of liberty" would include shooting "for hunt or sport." Further, ever since 1959, when surveys began to be taken on the subject, the results have *always* indicated that there was a gun in every other home. Compared to these errors of Spiegler and Sweeney, it's almost a cavil to note that anyone who made half an effort to investigate the place of guns in American life should know that handguns *are* used for hunting and other sports and that they are not, by any means, the most prevalent type of firearm in America.

As to the "easy availability of guns," guns are less easily available today than they ever have been in the United States. During the

1940s, just about every high school in southeastern Pennsylvania had a rifle team. That was probably true everywhere in the country, but I know it was true of the southeast corner of the Keystone State. It's no longer true. During the 1950s and 1960s, almost every corporation big enough to issue stock sponsored a pistol team. Now the very mention of a pistol brings the corporate frown of disapproval, and some corporations, such as fast-food chains and late-night delis, have fired employees for using guns to defend themselves against robbers. Years ago, you could buy guns and ammunition in a wide variety of hardware stores, sporting goods stores and department stores. Guns were sold by mail-order houses. In the 1930s, mail-order houses like Klein's in Chicago, which advertised mostly on the backs of comic books, featured cheap pistols along with tear-gas guns and books on judo and hypnotism. Today, five of the six largest retail chain outlets have discontinued gun and ammunition sales.

So why do people like Spiegler and Sweeney see a "domestic arms race"?

They see it because the manufacture and importation of firearms have continued steadily. Guns do not wear out quickly. There are thousands of guns in this country that were made a century ago but are still perforating targets and killing game in the woods. With production and importation continuing, and even increasing slightly, somebody must be buying more guns. An increasing share of the new guns are handguns, although handguns are still only about a third of all the guns in the country.[2] Gun control advocates refer to this situation as "the flood of handguns," "the domestic arms build-up," and "the domestic arms race." Charles Clotfelder of Duke University decrys "the almost breathtaking increase in the stock of handguns."[3] According to the Massachusetts Council on Crime and Corrections, "The unfortunate cycle continues: the rise in street crime causes nervous people to buy guns for protection, and these very guns eventually cause more accidents, more crime, and more national paranoia."[4] Pete Hamill, not an academic, but a reputedly close observer of the New York scene, asserts in *The White Majority*, "The revolt involves the use of guns. In East Flatbush and Corona, and all those other places where the white working class lives, people are forming gun clubs and self-defense leagues and talking about what they will do if a real race riot breaks out."[5] The consensus seems to be that people are buying more guns solely because they're afraid of crime or race riots. George D. Newton and Franklin Zimring do concede that some of the new long guns may be purchased for sporting purposes but say interest in sport shooting "does not account for the dramatic increase in handgun sales."[6]

The trouble with this consensus is that it is based on thin or nonexistent research. James D. Wright of Tulane University, Peter H. Rossi of University of Massachusetts, and Kathleen Daly of Yale University broke away from the pack. They did investigate the situation.

The problem was that it seemed almost certain, although nobody could be sure of the exact figures, that more guns were being added to the nonmilitary stock of guns than were being taken out of service due to wear, accidents, losses, or police confiscations. Still, every survey since 1959 showed that only about half of the households in the United States owned a gun.

Wright, Rossi, and Daly tried to estimate the increase in guns.[7] Considering all sources, their best guess was that there were 80 million guns in the country in 1968, when Newton and Zimring published *Firearms and Violence in American Life*. In 1978, they estimated, there were 120 million guns. In other words, there were 40 million new guns. Then the sociologists counted households. They found that there were some 20 million more households in 1978 than there were in 1968. That was more than could have been expected from the increase in population. It was due to the "baby boom" generation reaching the age where they were prone to start their own households. If the rate of gun-owning households remained constant (and it did), that would account for at least a quarter of the new guns. It would, that is, if each of the new households had only one gun. That turned out to be unlikely.

Next, the researchers studied trends in outdoor recreation.[8] Production of clay pigeons *doubled* in the 1960s. So did membership in trap and skeet clubs. Spending on sporting guns and ammunition increased 72 percent between 1960 and 1966. The trend continued through the 1970s. Hunting licenses increased by 3.7 million between 1970 and 1975. That increase was not merely due to the increased population. There were 119 hunters per thousand residents in 1970, and 132 in 1975. Altogether, the country had averaged an increase of about 540,000 hunters a year, or 5.4 million new hunters between 1968 and 1978. To meet the needs of those 5.4 million new hunters, the arms merchants would have had to sell a lot more than 5.4 million guns. A .22 rifle is fine for hunting squirrels, but it's not for hunting deer. (In fact, almost all states ban it for such use.) A .410 shotgun is an excellent weapon for hunting rabbits, but it's an invitation to failure when hunting ducks and geese. Very few hunters confine themselves to one type of game. If each new hunter got only two long guns, it would account for 86 percent of the increase in rifles and shotguns. And there is little reason to suppose that most hunters would be satisfied with merely one rifle and one shotgun. A bare minimum for an average hunter would be a .22 caliber rifle for small game, a center-fire rifle for big game, and a shotgun for birds. In addition, many hunters use handguns.

It's practically an article of faith among anti-gun lobbyists that handguns have no sporting value. That may be one case where there's a definite conflict between faith and reason. The oft-repeated statement about handguns' lack of utility for anything but shooting people would be easier to defend if it were qualified. But it seldom is. And even qualified, it's wrong. As we'll see, one person's "Saturday night special" is another's "trail gun." And some handguns are useless for anything but sport. Does Remington, for instance, sell its XP-100 series of pistols to people interested in self-defense? Imagine confronting a burglar in a darkened room with a Remington XP-100 Custom HB Long Range Pistol chambered for .223 Remington (also called 5.56 NATO, the NATO rifle cartridge). The muzzle flash from the first shot would blind the shooter, who would then have to find another cartridge to load his single-shot handgun. As for street carry, the Custom XP-100 weighs 5½ pounds and is almost two feet long. It's even bulkier when equipped with a telescopic sight (the heavy-barrel Custom has no iron sights). In other words, it's about as concealable as a 105mm howitzer. Is there a market for guns like this?

Remington sells four versions, and there are currently 23 other huge single-shot pistols competing for the market. Many of them have interchangeable barrels, chambered for a wide variety of cartridges.[9] Depending on what you choose, you can hit a woodchuck at 400 yards or drop an elk with a single shot. What you can't get is a good defense gun.

Not all hunting pistols are single shot. Several makers, notably Ruger and Smith and Wesson, make enormous, high-power revolvers designed for hunters rather than people interested in self-defense. A particularly popular number is the Ruger Super Blackhawk. This revolver weighs, depending on barrel length, 48 ounces (3 pounds) or 51 ounces, and is either 13⅜ or 16⅜ inches long. It's chambered for the .44 magnum cartridge—not as powerful as the .223 but hefty enough to make the gun point skyward after each shot. That recoil, and the fact that it's single action (the hammer must be separately cocked for each shot before the trigger is pulled, unlike a double-action revolver, which can be fired just by pulling the trigger), make it ill-adapted to rapid fire. And as each shell must be ejected and each cartridge loaded individually, it's slow to load. Police and crooks haven't carried single-actions for almost a century.

About 1.3 million persons went hunting with a handgun in 1980.[10] Many hunters and some fishermen also carried "trail guns," small, light pistols that most gun control advocates would call Saturday night specials.[11] They kept these light, small handguns to shoot any snakes they might see or, if they were hunters, to finish off wounded game.

The same interest in outdoor sports that created the increase in hunters also increased the number of "sport shooters." Sport shooters is a term that includes people who shoot paper targets with rifles and pistols, people who shoot clay pigeons with shotguns, and people who shoot tin cans with any sort of gun. Many of these people require more than one gun. Someone who specializes in pistol target shooting, for example, needs a .22 caliber, a center-fire (usually a .38 special), and a .45 ACP caliber pistol for the Standard American course. If he also shoots the International course, he'll need a free pistol (a highly specialized .22 caliber single-shot), a standard pistol (his .22 automatic will usually do), a center-fire pistol (like the one he uses for Standard American), and a rapid-fire pistol (a rather specialized semiautomatic in .22 short caliber). He may also shoot metallic silhouettes at distances of up to 200 meters. To place in all pistol silhouette events, he'd need one of the long-range single-shot pistols and a big revolver like the Ruger Super Blackhawk. If he wants to compete in the sport of "practical handgunning," he'll need a heavy semiautomatic pistol, like the old .45 caliber service pistol but heavily modified by gunsmiths.

Wright, Rossi, and Daly calculate that if hunters and sport shooters bought only two guns apiece, they would account for almost all the new long guns. They'd also account for a large part of the handgun production. Most of the rest of the pistols could be absorbed by new police armaments.

THE POLICE ARMS RACE

The police have always been a good market for handgun makers. Constant carriage in a holster that doesn't fit well may result in wear to the cylinder bolt of a revolver, resulting in loss of accuracy and the shaving of fragments of lead from the bullet when the bullet leaves the cylinder and enters the barrel. Some revolvers have been pulled from service after as little as three months.[12] In addition, police forces have expanded greatly. In 1970, there were about 450,000 armed police officers in the United States. In 1975, there were 556,000. Today, there are more than 600,000.[13] Each new cop means at least one new gun. As many police officers carry a "backup" handgun in addition to their service arm, the total is more like two new guns for each new cop. Counting weapons for off-duty carry and a spare in case something happens to the main gun, some cops may need as many as four pistols.[14] That's not counting the special weapons. It's a rare squad car these days that doesn't contain a shotgun or a rifle in addition to the sidearms the officers carry. In Philadelphia, "stake-out cars" each contain two high-power bolt-action rifles, two shotguns, a submachine gun, and an M-1 carbine. That kind of equipment isn't confined to big cities. A "command car" in Quincy, Illinois, contains two riot shotguns, a high-power rifle, and hundreds of rounds for each weapon.[15] Armament like this, and the almost universal existence of SWAT teams with the most sophisticated weaponry, makes it hard to accept the police complaint that they are "outgunned by the criminals" without a grain of salt.

In addition, there's been a revolution in police sidearms. For decades, almost all police officers carried revolvers chambered for the .38 special cartridge, with the Smith and Wesson Military and Police revolver being the most popular. (The frequently mentioned ".38 Police Special" exists only in the minds of writers.) After World War II, a few departments adopted revolvers for the much more powerful .357 magnum cartridge, and a handful tried the .41 magnum. In the

1970s, a few departments switched to semiautomatic pistols, usually in 9mm Luger. By the 1980s, this ripple of change had become a tidal wave, and it continues into the 1990s. Newspaper writers, with characteristic ignorance of small arms, usually say the police are switching to "more powerful" handguns. The most powerful loading of the 9mm Luger by the Federal Cartridge Company, for example, yields 355 foot-pounds of energy at the muzzle of a four-inch barrel, while Federal's top .357 magnum load yields 523 foot-pounds with a four-inch barrel. With an eight-inch barrel (unavailable in any new 9mm autos), it yields 800 foot-pounds.[16] The advantage of the 9mm is that it is generally used in a semiautomatic pistol, which may fire 15 or more shots without reloading. The average revolver can fire six shots before reloading. The advantage of the semiautomatic may be more apparent than real, however. According to the New York Police Department, in gunfights, the suspects fire an average of 2.55 rounds.[17] High-capacity semiautomatic pistols are in fashion for police sidearms, though, and the trend has undoubtedly accounted for a goodly share of the handguns produced in recent years. The gun makers certainly won't try to discourage the trend. Smith and Wesson, for instance, has put out so many versions of a few basic pistols that critics have derided the firm for producing "the gun of the month." Some have even charged that S & W spread rumors that their time-tried Combat Magnum couldn't handle the .357 magnum cartridge (which it had been firing since 1956) so they could sell more of their new Distinguished Combat Magnum models.

The 1994 crime law has given an ironic twist to the supposed "flood of handguns."[18] The crime law includes a ban on magazines that can hold more than 10 cartridges. After the law, such magazines could be sold only to the police and military. Magazines that hold more than 10 rounds are legal and can be resold if they were owned before the law went into effect. If they were suddenly made illegal, there would have to be confiscation on a mind-boggling scale; gun owners would lose immense amounts of money; and lots of voters would be very angry. The result has been that large-capacity magazines (and the guns that use them) have suddenly increased in value. Before the law, the magazine for a Glock 17 sold for about $17 new. Now it sells for $90 used. Why anyone would pay that much for a large-capacity magazine is something of a mystery, but with guns as with books, there's nothing like a ban to increase demand.

Gun wholesalers have taken advantage of the situation. They have begun to offer police departments brand-new large-capacity automatics with a huge discount when the cops trade in their slightly used large-capacity automatics. The guns and magazines the dealers want existed before the law, so they can be sold to all comers. So instead of getting guns "off the street," the crime law has increased domestic gun sales.

So far, though, in spite of all the alarmist statements, we still have the same proportion of gun ownership in the country—every other household—and no factions of militant citizens engaging in an arms race. There's no doubt, though, that some people have acquired guns for self-defense.

DEFENSIVE WEAPONRY

It's hard to say definitely why people own guns because most people who own guns give several reasons for having them. In a 1978 national survey, for instance, 74 percent of the respondents said hunting was one of the reasons they owned guns. In the same survey, 65 percent said protection was one of the reasons for their guns; 40 percent said target or sport shooting; and 21 percent said gun collecting.[19] Conceivably the same person could own a gun for all of those reasons, and no doubt many do. *Handgun* owners in that survey said that their *most important* reason for owning a pistol was: protection, 40 percent; target shooting, 17 percent; gun collecting, 14 percent; and hunting, 9 percent. In a survey of handgun owners taken a year earlier in Illinois, with heavy urban representation, 67 percent of the respondents said they owned their pistols primarily for protection with another 6 percent citing protection as a secondary reason. In an urban area, of course, opportunities for hunting and target shooting are limited.

An odd thing about this emphasis on protection by handgun owners is that of all types of firearms, pistols are the least accurate, least powerful, and least lethal. If a gun is to be kept at home for protection, a rifle or shotgun is far superior. A 12 gauge shotgun can fire—with one shot—nine to 18 round lead balls of .33-inch diameter at a greater velocity than most pistols produce. A .30-06 rifle can fire a mushrooming bullet with more than three times the velocity of the average pistol bullet. Both of these guns destroy a tremendous amount of tissue. They can usually be depended on to stop an assailant instantly. A shot from one of them is four times more likely to kill than a shot from any pistol.[20] And in a home, there's no need for concealment.

If a gun is to be carried on the person or in a car, there is no doubt that it should be a pistol. Even a short carbine is unwieldy in a car or pickup truck.

In many situations a pistol is the only practical self-defense weapon. John R. Salter, Jr., a civil rights activist who has worked with African-Americans in Mississippi, Hispanics in New York, and Indians in Arizona, found a .38 caliber revolver a lifesaver when he was working in Mississippi. While teaching at Tougaloo College, on the outskirts of Jackson, he had been helping the Jackson branch of the NAACP. During the Christmas season of 1962, Ku Klux Klan night riders fired a volley of shots into his house. One bullet narrowly missed his infant daughter.

"If anything, local law officials were strongly supportive of the night riders,"

Salter wrote.[21] "The U.S. Justice Department and the FBI had no interest in enforcing the Constitution in cases such as ours."

Salter and his colleagues in the civil rights movement armed themselves and took turns standing guard at strategic locations. They told the news media what they were doing. The attacks ceased. Salter carried his revolver with him everywhere. One night on a deserted road, "a large white car came up behind me— showing no inclination to pass. In the bright moonlight, I could see several persons therein and knew these were Klansmen.

"Although there was no question that they were quite open to shooting me, I was not surprised that they did not. Months before, we had diffused word on the local grapevines that we, and certainly myself, were armed. They knew full well that I was capable of returning fire—and willing indeed to do so."[22] The Klansmen had to settle for tailgating Salter and revving their engine to frighten him. He continued driving sedately. When he reached his destination, revolver still in his hand, the night riders drove on, frustrated and cursing.

Another veteran of the civil rights struggle in the South, Don B. Kates, Jr., also found it necessary to carry a gun at all times. "When Klansmen catch you in some deserted area and open fire," he wrote, "you take cover and shoot back—if you have a gun. Then both sides depart at great speed, because no one wants to get shot."[23]

Most people who have pistols for protection, however, do not carry them at all times. They keep them in bureau drawers. If a gun is to be kept in the home at all times, a rifle or shotgun is more effective than a pistol. The idea that a pistol is primarily for self-defense probably comes from movies and television, where the police and the bad guys typically shoot it out with pistols.

Another erroneous idea that most likely comes from film and TV is that guns are very lethal. Franklin Zimring did a study of bullet wounds in Chicago. He found that of those people wounded in the head, body, and extremities with a handgun, about 7.5 percent died.[24] Even with the more lethal long guns, a victim has two chances in three of recovering.

Zimring also stated that in spite of the low lethality of handguns, they are five times more lethal than knives. He got his data for this statement from the same hospital statistics he used for analyzing the lethality of bullets. Dr. Zimring had the misfortune never to have been a police reporter in Kansas City, Missouri. Once, when I was a very young reporter, an old hood in an amiable mood undertook to further my education.

"This is how you use a knife," the old hood said, taking a tiny pocket knife— the kind now called an "executive" knife—out of his pocket. "You hold it like this," he said and gripped the knife so that only about half an inch of the tip projected from his clenched fist. He explained that you should swing at the opponent's face, as if you were throwing a punch, but instead slash his cheek. That slash, he said, usually ends the fight. The tactic is non-lethal but effective. It is widely used in places where people resort to knives to settle disputes, and it explains why some criminologists think knives at close range are less lethal than guns. The point is important, because the statement is frequently made that guns are much more lethal than knives and eliminating guns could eliminate much homicide, especially domestic homicide. But if a knife is close enough to wound, and a knife-armed assailant has murderous intentions, homicide is extremely likely.

Take this incident from America's past: When Col. James Bowie rode home to Natchez after a trip to Texas, he was attacked by three men with knives. One grabbed the horse's bridle and stabbed the rider in the leg. Bowie beheaded that man with his knife, jumped off his horse and disemboweled the second attacker, then chased the third and split his skull with his knife.[25] Bowie's weapon, the famous Bowie knife, was about the size of a modern chef's knife. That's something to remember when you hear that only the presence of a gun makes domestic murder possible.

Another misconception is that you can easily wound a person with a gun without killing him. The idea may have started with the Lone Ranger, who shot guns out of people's hands on radio every weekday night from Monday through Friday. In real life, the Lone Ranger would probably have been hanged for murder before the end of a single broadcast season. In real life, Joseph "Crazy Joe" or "Joey the Blond" Gallo was shot in the buttock with a .32 automatic—a rather weak pistol bullet striking a supposedly nonvital spot. The bullet cut an artery, and Gallo bled to death in minutes. In fiction, the expert hit man always kills his victim. In real life, a young man known to Maj. Gen. Julian Hatcher, the late chief of Army Ordnance Field Service and an internationally recognized expert on guns and ballistics, tried to commit suicide by shooting himself in the head with a .22 pistol. The bullet glanced on his skull and traveled under the skin of his scalp. The young man passed out and was taken to the hospital where he completely recovered in a few days. The lethality of guns is even more unpredictable because bullets don't always travel in a straight line after entering a body. They can glance off bones and bounce around in all directions.

Still another misconception about defensive weaponry—and this is the biggest one—is about the people who own guns for defense. The usual stereotype is an anachronistic guy who keeps a gun because he's a rugged individualist and doesn't want to rely on the police for protection. Researchers found that the typical defensive gun owner was a woman, often a member of a minority group, who lives in a high-crime area and *knows* she can't rely on the police. David Bordua, one of the leading researchers on the effects of guns and gun laws, said: "The common stereotype held by gun control proponents of a Daniel Boone lingering on from yesterday should perhaps give way to that of a black nurse hoping to make it to tomorrow."[26]

PART III

CROSSFIRE— BULLETS FROM THE GUNNERS

CHAPTER 14

SLIDING DOWN THE SLIPPERY SLOPE

THE ORIGIN OF A FEAR

It's an article of faith among all followers of Harlon Carter that to give one inch on gun control legislation puts gun owners on a "slippery slope." The slide down that declivity can only end, they believe, in the total abolition of gun ownership in the United States. With Carter, the gun lobby believes that gun control is like potato chips. You can't pass just one law. That attitude has made gun control opponents an object of ridicule by their adversaries. The gun lobbyists' belief is not without reason, however.

The Brady bill was a pretty innocuous proposal. A short waiting period before buying a handgun is not a serious handicap for most people. NRA spokesmen, however, like to point to women who, upon being threatened by husbands, ex-husbands, or boyfriends, tried to buy handguns for self-defense but were delayed by waiting periods. As a result, they say, those women were killed by the threatening males. There really haven't been a lot of women like that. If all she needed was a gun, the threatened woman could have given up on getting a handgun and bought a shotgun instead. Just about all of the few killings recorded under these circumstances occurred in the home. A shotgun can be kept at home as conveniently as a pistol, and it is far more effective in stopping an attacker. The NRA didn't really oppose the Brady bill because it would delay a tiny number of people who wanted to get a pistol to meet an immediate emergency. It opposed the Brady bill because the bill was a potato chip to the anti-gun lobby.

The ink on the Brady law was hardly dry before the anti-gun lobby had an "assault weapon" ban moving through Congress. And although he promised that first the Brady bill, then the "assault weapon" ban, would "make our streets safer," before the crime law with its assault ban passed, Charles Schumer was already preparing—with Howard Metzenbaum and HCI—Brady II. At this writing, Sarah Brady is promising that Brady II will be "an end to incrementalism." It ought to be something close to that, as it would outlaw most existing handguns.

Still, remember the words of Brady's predecessor in the chair of Handgun Control, Inc. Pete Shields said, "The first problem is to slow down the number of handguns being produced and sold in this country." The more difficult the government can make buying, the higher the fees it puts on sellers, the more regulations it imposes on producers, the fewer handguns will be produced and sold. "The second problem," Shields said, "is to get handguns registered." Brady II is moving in that direction. "The final problem is to make possession of all handguns—and all handgun ammunition—except for the military, police, licensed security guards, licensed sporting clubs and licensed gun collectors—totally illegal."[1]

The second problem must be solved in order to solve the third. With registration, the authorities would know where each handgun was. Then they could confiscate them all. Actually, they could find out where most of them are right now, but it would take a lot of work to locate *all* handguns at the same time.[2] The exceptions Shields makes are interesting. The military obviously would have to have guns. The police, too, given the amount of violent crime in this country. But Brady II's language about the "federal arsenal license" makes one wonder how many gun collectors would be able to get licenses, even if they were willing to pay outlandish license fees and put up with unannounced inspections. The exception for private security guards—hired by large corporations and very wealthy individuals—shows that Shields shared the view of most other upper-class gun controllers: only the wealthy need protection.

Some people think there would never be confiscation of guns without some attempt at compensating the owners. But the Morton Grove law, although it's never been enforced, does precisely that.

The strategy of moving into gun control gradually motivates many members of the anti-gun lobby. In 1969, J. Elliott Corbett, secretary of a now-defunct anti-gun lobby organization called the National Council for a Responsible Firearms Policy, wrote to a correspondent who did not think the NCRFP's proposals went far enough:

I personally believe handguns should be outlawed. . . . Our organization will probably take this stand in time, but we are not anxious to rouse the opposition before we get the other legislation passed. It would be difficult to outlaw all rifles and shotguns because of the hunting sport. But there should be stiff regulations. . . . our movement will be towards increasingly stiff controls.[3]

The one-step-at-a-time approach is endorsed by many—not all professional lobbyists—who would like to get guns out of the hands of citizens. After the massacre of school children in Stockton, California, a television reporter asked the mayor why she supported a ban on "assault rifles" and not the much more powerful standard rifles. "I think you have to do it one step at a time," said the mayor. "Banning semi-assault [sic] military weapons is the first step."[4]

Or recall Josh Sugarmann's cynical words about "assault weapons:"

The weapons' menacing looks, coupled with the public's confusion over fully automatic machine guns versus semi-automatic assault weapons— anything that looks like a machine gun is assumed to be a machine gun— can only increase the chance for public support for restrictions on these weapons.[5]

Sugarmann, fairly knowledgeable for an anti-gun lobbyist, *knew* that those weapons were neither an important part of the total gun pool nor a serious factor in crime. But banning "assault weapons" would be one more step toward the desired goal of total firearms prohibition. The anti-gun lobby, as well as the gun lobby, believes in the "slippery slope."

At this moment, HCI's Brady II bill aims only at banning "assault weapons" and most handguns. But what reason is there to suppose it will stop with those weapons? HCI at first called only for controls on handguns until the "assault weapon" issue appeared. Most "assault weapons" are rifles. Some are shotguns. In many cases the difference between an "assault weapon" and a semiautomatic rifle is a cosmetic feature like a wire stock or a pistol grip. The logical next step would be to ban all semiautomatics. Then, because hand-operated guns are fully as deadly as semiautomatics, all guns.

PUTTING ON THE BRAKES

The psychology of the "slippery slope" is that once you take a small step, it becomes easier to take another small step, and so on. There is some truth in that. But not much. One thing does not inevitably lead to another. Making a carjacking that results in murder a federal crime subject to the death penalty does not mean the death penalty will someday be applied to driving without a license. The fact that a number of people would like to make guns totally illegal does not mean that they will get their way. A lot of people want all schools to teach that the universe was created in seven days (although they're hard put to define what constituted a day before creation). They're not likely to see such a course at Cal Tech or MIT, though.

The history of gun control efforts alone should convince the NRA and its allies that the slope is not *that* slippery. GCA 68 was followed by McClure-Volkmer, which reversed many of its more onerous provisions. Even the machine gun amendment to McClure-Volkmer would not have passed if the opposition had objected more strongly to Rangel's high-handed ruling on the voice vote. That they did not protest more strongly is because the only voters interested in the issue—the 100,000 machine gun owners—are the merest handful in a country of 255 million and because generations of propaganda have made the machine gun a "devil gun." Local initiatives banning handguns in some Illinois towns prompted a wave of state laws preempting local gun laws. The latest was passed over a governor's veto in Pennsylvania in 1994. While a few states were banning "assault weapons," other states were liberalizing laws regarding carrying concealed pistols.

What both the gun lobby and the anti-gun lobby forget is that legislation is not a natural force, like a glacier, that once started on a course proceeds steadily to a conclusion. Legislators are elected by voters, and if they value their jobs, they will try to follow the voters' wishes.

The NRA's "no retreat" strategy is counterproductive. It aims at legislators, promising dire results if they don't vote "right." It inspires small groups of activists to mail mindless messages and make harassing phone calls to legislators. Sometimes these activists even picket the offices of congressmen or state legislators. That's intimidation. It makes legislators mad. And if the angry legislator wants to retaliate, he'll hit all gun owners. The more the NRA takes positions most people see as unreasonable—such as opposing short waiting periods before buying handguns or demanding the discharge of officials who disagree with NRA positions—the less credible it becomes and the more public support it loses. That makes it easier for gun control advocates to lampoon the organization, its members, and all gun owners, and to pass more restrictive gun controls. The situation has gotten so bad (from the NRA point of view) that running against the gun lobby is often a good way to pick up votes.

In 1996, President Clinton appeared to feel frustrated because the anti-terrorism bill he had advocated was stalled in Congress. To move it forward, he blamed all the opposition on the NRA. The rifle association did oppose one part of the bill—putting chemical "taggants" into black powder as well as other explosives to help officials trace the origins of bombs. The NRA opposes any form of registration by reflex, but the "taggants" issue was hardly a major concern for the association.[6] Nor was the NRA opposition an important part of the overall opposition to the bill. The bill provided a lot of fuel for opposition. For one thing, the attorney general would be empowered to declare any ordinary crime committed outside U.S. borders "terrorism," making it a federal crime subject to the death penalty. And no court would be allowed to second-guess the ruling. The secretary of state could designate any organization as terrorist, whether Hamas, Irish Northern Aid, or the Iranian Children's Milk Fund. If such a law were in force during the Contra War, Alexander Haig could have certified the Sanctuary movement as terrorist. And anyone who contributed to that church-sponsored effort to help refugees would have been a criminal and subject to prison. The bill would greatly expand federal wiretapping, would allow the deportation of aliens without what used to be considered due process of law, and would cripple habeas corpus. Consequently the "anti-terrorism" bill aroused a storm of protest from civil libertarians. But the only opposition Clinton recognized was the NRA's. And in this, he was seconded by the Associated Press and a good part of the news media.[7] The bill finally was passed, but without "taggants" on gunpowder, the expanded wiretapping authority, and the authority to secretly check bank accounts and phone records. In the latter part of 1996, Clinton began campaigning to get the omitted portions incorporated in a new anti-terrorism bill. His ostensible reasons were the bombing of an Atlanta park during the Olympics—apparently by a maniac, rather than a terrorist—and the crash of TWA Flight 800, the cause of which, at this writing, has not been determined after extensive investigation. Once again, he blamed all opposition on the NRA.)

PUBLIC RELATIONS MEANS *PUBLIC* RELATIONS

The NRA's lobbying is anything but subtle, and the Clinton administration has taken full advantage of that. Sometimes it's easy to forget that Handgun Control, Inc. and the National Coalition also lobby legislators. They, too, make campaign donations and send charming, knowledgeable people to talk to lawmakers. They don't, however, encourage their members to mail vituperative letters and picket offices. Nor do they try to get public officials who do not agree with them fired. One reason is that the membership of all the anti-gun lobby groups combined doesn't approach that of the NRA, and the membership they do have lacks the strong financial motivation (loss of billions of dollars' worth of guns) of the NRA members. But the other reason is that they know bullying tactics don't work—at least, not until you have enough members to make bullying unnecessary. With three to three-and-a-half million members, even the NRA falls far short of that kind of clout.

It also appears that the anti-gun leaders, especially the HCI leaders, are a lot smarter politicians than the leaders of the NRA. The hard-liners who currently run the rifle association act as if their members are the dolts anti-gun propaganda makes them out to be. (Actually, polls show gun owners to be slightly more prosperous and slightly better educated than the national average.)[8] The NRA leaders think they can manipulate their members by scaring the daylights out of them and sending them stupid form letters to mail to congressmen and members of the media. In the first half of 1990, the NRA sent its members 51.3 *million* pieces of mail.⁹ The next year, it spent $10 million on mailing—"our biggest expense," said NRA official Richard Gardiner. Most of the mail is either prophecies of doom or appeals for money or both. The result is that although the NRA membership has grown rapidly since the Cincinnati Revolt (it had a million members in 1977), the association membership also has about the highest turnover rate of any group in the country.¹⁰

HCI and the National Coalition target not their members but the general public. They use tear-jerker demonstrations like the one in Washington in 1994 that piled a heap of shoes, allegedly from people killed by guns, around the Capitol reflecting pool.¹¹ They send out news releases by the gross about polls supporting gun controls (and sometimes twisting the results of polls that do not support them). Other news releases proclaim the good done by gun control legislation. One story in 1994 reported that the Brady law had foiled hundreds of felons who were trying to purchase handguns. Actually, the figure referred to sales that had been delayed for further checking, and most of those sales were in states already covered by state waiting periods. A large number of the sales were completed after checking. The Bureau of Alcohol, Tobacco, and Firearms (BATF) reported that—eight months after the Brady law went into effect—it had made one arrest under the law. And that arrest had nothing to do with an attempted purchase. The culprit had stolen a gun from a licensed dealer, an offense under the Brady law.¹²

This sort of distortion is not uncommon in the gun control debate. Sometimes the anti-gunners simply lie. Richard Aborn, president of HCI, wrote in the *Washington Post* that in the first three months of the Brady law, *33 percent* of handgun purchase applications in Georgia were submitted by *criminals*. Brady supposedly stopped this fantastic number of malefactors from getting guns and factoring more mal. Aborn offered no support for this unbelievable statistic. If this were the normal state of affairs in Georgia, you might reasonably expect everybody in Georgia to have been murdered several times. Actually, according to the BATF, nationally 6.4 percent of the applications were initially disapproved, and most of them were in the 26 states that already had waiting periods. According to the BATF, initial disapproval "does not mean that 6.4 percent of the initial query subjects had backgrounds that rendered them ineligible to purchase a firearm."¹³

The foregoing should not be construed as advice to the NRA to copy HCI by telling lies. The association already tells lies. But it directs its lies, like most of its other propaganda, to its members. HCI directs its propaganda to the public. One section of HCI's sister organization, the Center to Prevent Handgun Violence, directs all its efforts to relations with entertainment figures.¹⁴ That not only aids fund-raising efforts, it gets subtle bits of anti-gun propaganda to the public. That may explain why you get HCI's distorted view of gun ownership in unexpected places ranging from obscure comedy clubs to nationally syndicated comic strips like "Dick Tracy."

One of the rifle association's biggest problems is its tendency to preach to the choir instead of proselytizing the unconverted. Another is to confuse who is in the choir and who isn't. During the Vietnam War, the conservative NRA leadership strongly supported the war and President Richard M. Nixon. So strongly did the association support Nixon that when he broke the news of the invasion of Cambodia, Nixon made the announcement not to the Senate or the House, but to *a group of NRA officials.* In its voting recommendations at election time, the NRA has overwhelmingly picked Republican candidates.[15] J. Warren Cassidy, former Republican mayor of Lynn, Massachusetts, seemed to assume, during his tenure as NRA executive vice president, that Republicans were automatically pro-gun. The trouble with this is that Democrats are twice as numerous as Republicans in the NRA. Democrats make up 41 percent of the membership; Republicans, 21 percent; and unaffiliated voters, 38 percent.[16] And while many—but by no means the majority—of those NRA Democrats are generally conservative, they usually don't vote against their party.[17] This partisanship, which the NRA seems to be finally getting away from, has no doubt cost it some popular support.[18]

THE PRICE OF INTRANSIGENCE

The NRA's policy of hysterical opposition to any curb on unlimited gun ownership and use has not stopped a slide toward the abyss. It has greased the slope. The more unreasonable and inbred the organization becomes, the more popular support it loses. The more popular support it loses, the more clout it loses. And the more clout it loses, the more it loses, period.

The United States has a long and, in many cases, glorious tradition of gun ownership and gun use. That is not true of any country in Europe (not even Switzerland, which won its independence when pikes and halberds were the ultimate weapons), or perhaps of any country in the world. The argument is often made that this country should have gun laws like those of Europe—or even Japan. But the vast majority of people in this country came here, or their ancestors did, to get away from European laws. The founding fathers wanted their new country to be "a city on a hill"—an example for the rest of the world to imitate, not vice versa.

Gun lobbyists, however, cannot blithely ignore the fact that guns play a part in the high U.S. violent crime rate. They cannot say, with Harlon Carter, that serial killers getting guns is "part of the price we pay for freedom." They cannot, that is, if they want public support.

Instead of waiting for the anti-gun lobby to demand more restrictions, why doesn't the NRA publicize what it has already done to improve life in America? It can tell the public how its gun safety education program has drastically reduced gun accidents all through the twentieth century. It can publicize its efforts to preserve the country's natural environment. It can write news releases and features about its junior rifle program, which has been going on a lot longer than midnight basketball and has a lot more potential as a crime and delinquency deterrent.[19] If its leadership could get away from Carter's "potato chip" theory, it could even do some new things. It might start by pushing safety—for adults as well as children—a lot harder. It could try to distinguish between bad gun laws—registration comes immediately to mind—and good ones—such as reasonable limits on the number of handguns that could be purchased in a short time. (Why these and other laws are good or bad will be discussed in chapters 22 and 23.) It might even initiate some laws no one has thought of so far.

It will not, however, do any of those things as long as it clings to the various paranoid fantasies we'll look at next.

CHAPTER 15

THE FIVE-YEAR PLAN AND OTHER FANTASIES

PERVASIVE PARANOIA

In the NRA and HCI, the leading organizations in the gun and anti-gun lobbies respectively, the normal environment is paranoia.

"I never thought it could happen in America," NRA executive vice president Wayne LaPierre wrote to members early in 1994. "But before the end of this year, we may see thousands of NRA members, American gun owners and patriotic veterans—men and women who have risked their lives for our country—being marched off to jail. That's right, labeled as felons and being taken off to jail simply because they believe in the Constitution of the United States."[1]

The year came and went without long lines of veterans and gun owners shuffling into durance vile. What had alarmed LaPierre, though, had come to pass. It was the "assault weapon" and large-capacity magazine ban in the 1994 crime bill. The ban is silly and, to some people, an inconvenience, but it hasn't resulted in any incarcerations of law-abiding citizens. LaPierre's letter was pitched particularly at veterans. In discussing New York City's registration of rifles, he wrote:

> Remember what happened in New York City. In 1967, rifle owners were asked to register their guns under the promise that the information would *never* be used for confiscation.
>
> Then, in 1991, New York City passed a law banning possession of dozens of semi-automatic rifles. Thousands of residents who had obeyed the [first] law were ordered to surrender their guns. *Tens of thousands of New York veterans—many of them NRA members—who kept their rifles from World War II and Korea have now been turned into felons* [emphasis in original].[2]

One of the drawbacks of the Cincinnati Revolt that ousted the generals and other veterans from the NRA leadership was their replacement with nonveterans like LaPierre, who tend to write about things they don't understand. If the executive vice president had served in a war, he'd know that veterans of World War II and Korea did *not* take their rifles home. Or, if they did, it would be because they had stolen them. Any such veterans would not be "turned into felons" by the New York law. They would have been felons to begin with. Somebody at the NRA should have known that. But how important is accuracy if it spoils the picture of grizzled old-timers being separated from their beloved M-1s and herded into dungeons?

Fear of sinister forces seems to be more overt in the rifle association than in HCI. That may be because the NRA has been around so much longer than Handgun Control, Inc. It's had more practice in whipping up hysteria.

During World War II, both before and after the entry of the United States, gun control laws, the NRA professed to believe, were inspired by Nazi sympathizers or their dupes. Gun registration, especially, seemed to be an Axis plot to the true believers. NRA members were told that when the Germans overran a country, they first went to the gun registration records and used them to seize all the guns in that country. Thousands, if not millions, of NRA members still believe the gestapo or storm troopers went from house to house in occupied countries collecting small arms.

There's some truth in the story. The Germans did seize the gun registration records, but there were no national house-to-house searches. There were undoubtedly such searches in certain areas, particularly in Eastern Europe, and among certain populations, particularly Jews. But the Germans couldn't spare the manpower to search every house in occupied Europe. And if all the houses could not be searched in very short order, most of the guns might well be buried or otherwise hidden.

Instead, the Nazis merely made sure everybody knew they had the registration records and ordered all citizens to turn in their guns. The penalty for failure to do so was death. Most of the European populations complied with the order, especially after a few exemplary executions. The largest number of executions were carried out in Eastern Europe, the fewest in the Nordic countries.

In Norway, many guns were hidden. According to writer Nils Kvale, who was there, "Quite a few guns were turned in . . . and many more were undoubtedly thrown in lakes or otherwise destroyed. Still it was possible to find a gun for people engaged in the underground movement." The Germans, in Norway at least, seemed willing to accept a citizen's statement that his registered gun was lost or destroyed. It seems likely that many of the guns "lost or destroyed" were merely hidden. Again, Kvale: "When the surrender became a fact, and the underground forces came out into the open, everybody carried guns. It became the fashion to carry a gun, even for teenage girls."[3]

The German heel came down much harder in Poland than in Norway, which was inhabited, according to Nazi theorists, by "pure Aryans." Even in Poland, though, there were guns held by civilians. The Warsaw Ghetto uprising began with only ten pistols in Jewish hands. The ghetto fighters, however, were eventually able to buy enough long guns from their Christian neighbors to give the German army a fight it would never forget.[4]

World War II ended with an Allied victory, but there were still people in the United States who wanted to limit gun ownership. They couldn't be Nazis, so they must be Communists, the faithful believed. Time after time, the NRA reminded its members that "the first thing Communists do when they take over is register all guns."[5] One letter to members that reviewed pending gun control legislation included the statement, "I'm not sure how you define these gun-banners. Certainly, they cannot be called patriots."[6]

If consistency is the hobgoblin of little minds, the NRA leadership must in some respects be broad-minded. In 1951, during the height of the McCarthy-inspired red scare, many citizens were calling for the registration of all firearms to frustrate the Communists. Maj. Gen. Merritt Edson, president of the NRA, called for calmer reasoning, pointing out that registration "will contribute nothing to the defense of your community."[7]

Edward Leddy, who wrote *Magnum Force Lobby*, a book praising the NRA, borrowed a Communist term to attack the anti-gun lobby. He accused the anti-gun leadership of being the "new class."[8] Although popularized in this country by the liberal Lionel Trilling, the term was coined by Milovan Djilas, a Communist official in Yugoslavia who was imprisoned by Tito partially because he inveighed against the "new class"—the educated elite, who had grabbed the levers of power in his country. In a theoretically classless society, Djilas's term had some meaning: a new aristocracy that had replaced the old one. In the United States, the term itself is gobbledygook, although we certainly have an intellectual elite.

Leddy charged:

> The political temptation of the new class lies in believing that their intelligence and exemplary motive equip them to reorder the institutions, the lives and even the characters of almost everyone—that is the totalitarian temptation. This is also the reason that a politics featuring large roles for intellectuals is especially dangerous for human liberty . . . a society that cherishes liberty will do well to protect itself from the new class.[9]

Leddy wrote in 1987, on the eve of the total collapse of the Soviet Union and European communism. The red menace was no longer very menacing. There were still sinister forces, though. Now they were led by the homegrown totalitarians of the "new class."

This demonization of opponents works both ways, of course. To HCI, the NRA is the mouthpiece for "a gun industry that cynically puts profits before human lives." Or, as the lobbying group puts it in a letter to members, "an industry that has been *getting away with murder.*' " Handgun Control, Inc. promises "to expose the NRA-perpetrated *fraud that gun-control laws violate the Second Amendment to the U.S. Constitution* [emphasis in original]."[10]

The NRA's opponents, then, are would-be dictators who want to destroy the "American way of life." HCI's detractors are crooks and murderers. In this sort of climate, conspiracy theories grow like weeds in the summer. The "Rhino bullet" hysteria at the end of 1994 gave both sides a chance to display their worst qualities.

RHINO BULLETS AND RHINO BRAINS

The day after Christmas 1994, a research chemist named David Keen announced that he had invented two new bullets. One would shatter into razor-sharp fragments and inflict a fatal wound—almost instantaneously fatal—on any person it hit, no matter where it hit. The second would do the same, but it would do it after penetrating a bullet-resistant vest of the type worn by police officers (and professional criminals, although this class of vest-wearers is almost always forgotten by the news media). The bullets were called "the Rhino" and "the Black Rhino," respectively, and were made of plastic.

As in the "cop-killer bullet" episode (see chapter 10), this ballistic news made the police, the anti-gun lobby, and the gun lobby go ballistic. Each group charged into the fray like a hyperactive rhino with a toothache. The cops demanded immediate legislation to ban the armor-penetrating Black Rhino. (As it was made of plastic, this bullet was not covered by previous legislation.) The anti-gunners wanted immediate legislation to ban both bullets. The NRA's reaction was that David Keen was an anti-gun mole—a *provocateur* hired by somebody, probably HCI, to induce anti-gun hysteria.

All of these reactions followed the announcement in less time than it was supposed to take the Rhino bullet to kill bad guys. Nobody stopped to test the bullet. Nobody even hesitated long enough to inject a little common sense into the discussion.

In the first place, the idea that a 9mm bullet from a handgun would cause almost instant death no matter where it hit is absurd. There was already a bullet on the market, the Glaser Safety Slug, that would fragment into hundreds of small pieces after hitting its target. It was reasonably popular with the police, mostly because it would not ricochet from any object. There would be none of the bouncing around that made the KTW bullet such a menace. The Glaser also had excellent "stopping power," but it was by no means in a class with a shotgun of 20 gauge or larger. And the biggest 10 gauge magnum shotgun shell will not cause an invariably fatal wound wherever its load of buckshot hits.

If the claims for the Rhino bullet were absurd, those for the Black Rhino should have seemed obviously impossible even to a fifth-grader. A bullet hard enough to penetrate an armor vest could not at the same time be so soft it would disintegrate in soft tissue, like that of a human body. That is simply a physical impossibility.

Keen's language in announcing the bullet probably helped cause the flap. "The beauty behind it is that it makes an incredible wound," Keen said. "There's no way to stop the bleeding. I don't care where it hits, they're going down for good."[11] Keen, CEO of a company called Signature Products Corporation in Huntsville, Alabama, was making his first venture into the ammunition business. Signature had previously concentrated on making materials for the Air Force's "stealth" planes. Keen told reporters about the "thousands of razor-like fragments" the bullet explodes into when it strikes human flesh. "Each of these fragments becomes lethal shrapnel and is hurled into vital organs, lungs, circulatory system components, the heart, and other tissues. The wound channel is catastrophic. . . . Death is nearly instantaneous."[12] When fired into ballistic gelatin, a material that supposedly simulates the resistance of flesh, Keen told the press, it makes holes "the size of baseballs."[13]

No ammunition or firearms manufacturer before had ever gone on record describing "the beauty" of "an incredible wound." None had ever given such a gory account of the effects of a bullet striking human flesh. These words and a statement Keen made in favor of gun control and an "assault weapon" ban triggered the never-latent conspiracy perceptions of the NRA leadership.

"This has all the trappings of a hoax," said Tanya Metaksa, head of the NRA's Institute for Legislative Action. "Nobody I have talked to knows anything about this guy, and all we have here are the dubious claims of a would-be manufacturer."[14] She hinted that Keen might be a tool of the anti-gun lobby, using outrageous language to stir up anti-gun sentiment.

Curt Canon, president of Glaser Safety Slug, Inc., agreed with the NRA. "If he's not already a member, he [Keen] would make an ideal candidate for Handgun Control, Inc." said the maker of one of Rhino's competitors.[15]

Some independent experts shared Metaksa's doubts about Keen. "Is Mr. Keen a fool or a fraud?" asked Dr. Martin Fackler, a recognized authority on gunshot wounds.[16] "When someone makes a claim that he can pretty much guarantee a kill if you hit a person anywhere in the body, it doesn't pass the test of common sense. There is no magic bullet that makes a wound where you can't stop the bleeding."[17]

Jimmy Trahin, a firearms consultant to the Los Angeles Police Department, dismissed Keen's claims as nonsense. "No matter what you do, you can't get instant incapacitation with a handgun round," he said.[18]

Skeptics did not include either the press or the politicians. Just about every newspaper in the country ran editorials against the "high-tech death from Alabama," as the *New York Times* called it.[19] Robert Dvorchak of the Associated Press editorialized support for Keen's claims in the news story announcing the Rhino bullets. "As deadly as hollow points can be," he wrote, "they pale in comparison with the Rhino-Ammo. A typical hollow point loses about 10 percent of its mass to fragmentation upon impact, while 90 percent of a Rhino-Ammo bullet breaks into pieces."[20] Dvorchak's statement did not prove the Rhino's superior stopping power. It did prove that he is a victim of a failing all too common in the Fourth Estate—profound ignorance of everything about guns, including wound ballistics. Most bullets depend on deformation, not fragmentation, for stopping power. A bullet that fragments easily may not penetrate deeply enough to reach a vital area.

The politicians, too, were true believers. Rep. Charles E. Schumer of New York once again proved to be the fastest anti-gun in the East—or anywhere else.

"These bullets, their only real purpose is to go after the police officers of America," said Schumer.[21] After the "cop-killer" bullet fiasco, even Schumer must have known he was speaking utter nonsense. The number of people who want to kill police officers is extremely small (as the extremely small number of police officers killed shows). No manufacturer in his right mind is going to tool up for a product that appeals only to a minuscule group of sociopaths.

State legislators all over the country jumped on the bandwagon. Richard Tulisano, a state representative in Connecticut, announced that he would file legislation banning the Rhino bullets. "Just as dumdum bullets were banned internationally, we here in Connecticut should begin the movement to ban the Rhino bullets not only in our state, but throughout the nation and internationally as well," he said.[22] Tulisano apparently did not know that dumdum bullets, although banned for military use, are legal for civilians. In fact, almost all the bullets used by civilians for either hunting or target shooting would be classed as dumdums.[23]

Alas, all the hullabaloo over the vicious Rhinos faded away as the new year began. ABC Television's "Nightline" show tested the bullets—at least the Rhino; the Black Rhino has never been manufactured. Fired into ballistic gelatin, the Rhino produced a distinctly unspectacular hole. The cavity, about two inches in diameter, was not only not "the size of baseballs," it was only three-and-a-half inches deep, indicating the Rhino wouldn't have much penetration on even an unarmored human body. In fact, unless it struck an assailant in the head, the front of the body directly over the heart or the back of the body directly over the spine, it might not even stop him.

The Bureau of Alcohol, Tobacco and Firearms okayed the Rhino because it was no more deadly than a number of bullets already legal. The Black Rhino is not an endangered species, either. It seems there never was such an animal.

As for the NRA theory that David Keen was an HCI agent, that, too, appears to be a fantasy. Keen, the evidence indicates, just got into a business he didn't understand and thought his weird kind of hyperbole would stimulate the market.

It's possible that the bursting of the Rhino bullet bubble will dampen the NRA's enthusiasm for "gun-grabber" conspiracies. That's not likely, though. Earlier in 1994, it came up with one of the strangest conspiracy theories since the beginning of the gun control controversy.

HCI'S FIVE-YEAR PLAN

"The Final War Has Begun. A document secretly delivered to me reveals frightening evidence that the full-scale war to crush your gun rights has not only begun but is well underway," Wayne LaPierre wrote in the June 1994 issue of the *American Rifleman*. LaPierre went on to: "This document, and others almost identical to it, have been disavowed by Handgun Control, Inc., anti-gun politicians, and the Clinton White House. But you should read it and decide for yourself."[24] Spread over the next eight pages were various snatches of print.

The first two-page spread contained a photo of a page from *U.S. News and World Report* headlined "Crime report under White House seal" and clippings from what appear to be the writings of Josh Sugarmann of the Violence Policy Center. The "document" appears in the next three spreads—or, rather, photos of bits of pages from the document appear. At the top of each page are the typeset words "Confidential Document. DO NOT DISTRIBUTE OR COPY / NOT FOR GENERAL CIRCULATION." Below that, on the first page, is typed: "Confidential Information for use by Lobbyists or Senior Officers ONLY."

The first two of these spreads are concerned with licenses and license fees. A schedule of handgun license fees on the first spread goes from $50 to $650 a year, increasing in three steps. At the third step, it is noted "If private ownership has not been prohibited by this time, fees can be gradually increased to discourage private ownership." The second spread contains a list of licenses to be imposed: federal handgun license, federal rifle and shotgun license, state gun license, arsenal license, safe [for storing guns] license, ammunition license, reloading license, ammo safe license, ammo inspection fee. Total cost of all of these would be between $1,558 and $3,473 a year. The third spread features short clippings, apparently taken from the document. Among them: "Our eventual goal is to reduce the number of licensees to zero. The revenue itself can be utilized to achieve this goal. . . . Establish a nationwide system of toll-free numbers for reporting violator of the new gun restrictions and non-licensees. A certain sum may be set aside for cash rewards for tips which result in convictions. . . . Making possible the suing of owners of guns, as a group, for monetary compensation for victims of gun violence."

On the second spread are the words, "Get the whole story. For a copy of this document in its entirety, write to: NRA-ILA Research & Information, 11250 Waples Mill Rd., Fairfax, VA 22030 or call 1-703-267-1180."

I called. The result was almost as surreal as the document. The first call brought me a recorded announcement with out-of-date news on the crime bill. The second got me a young man who had never heard of the document his office was supposed to be distributing. I called the next day. I got another recorded announcement. On the fourth call, someone promised to send the document.

What arrived in the mail—quite promptly—was a document that was *not* the document pictured in the *Rifleman*. An introduction explained that the type had been set again to reduce the original 20 pages to five for mailing. But, it said, "Grammar, typographic, and usage errors in the original have been retained." Maybe. But the original words weren't retained. At least not if the pages pictured in the magazine were those of the original. Not one passage pictured can be found in the document mailed out. I tried twice more to get copies of the document pictured. Each time, I got another copy of the mailing piece.

It got curiouser and curiouser. In the June issue, LaPierre contended the "five-year plan" had been "secretly delivered" to him. But a notation of the document says it was posted on the Internet February 7, 1994. Why the secrecy? It must have been publicly accessible on the Internet, because its original distribution was not by a restricted Internet program. There are directions in the document that it should be "hand delivered" to people on the distribution list. There is a distribution list on the first page, mostly officials of HCI. But the list includes the name N. T. Shields. Pete Shields had died almost a year before the document was written. According to the introduction, the words "update list" were handwritten next to the distribution list. Somebody may have been trying to save stationery costs. The paper appears to be the letterhead of the Los Angeles office of HCI. According to the face sheet, it was posted on the Internet by Jeff Chen. Who Jeff Chen is, and how he got a supposedly confidential internal memo, are still mysteries.

Under the heading "CONFIDENTIAL! NOT FOR GENERAL DISTRIBUTION!" are "Notes and Minutes of Friday December 17, 1993. Rough Draft Proposal for Internal Memo and Five Year Plan."

According to the document, the minutes were forwarded to the national HCI office for reference. "A series of brainstorming meetings will be held at the White House through the winter of 1994. All suggestions should be collated and delivered to our policy team by then." What follows is certainly in the same spirit as the document pictured in the *American Rifleman*, but the words are different. The first suggestions, like "ban all clips holding over six bullets" and "arsenal licensing (for possession of multiple guns and large amounts of ammunition)" pretty much follow the features we've seen in Brady II. Then there are the various types of licenses, including licenses for safes to hold guns and ammunition, which the owners of guns and ammunition would be required to buy. Then it gets wilder, such as banning gun manufacture in counties with more than 200,000 people. That would put all large U.S. manufacturers out of business for no apparent reason. The definition of an arsenal would change from 20 guns to five, and no arsenals would be permitted in counties of more than 200,000 population. Finally, it gets downright bizarre, with suggestions for banning Revolutionary War reenactments and combat boots.

On February 24, 1994, soon after it appeared on the Internet, Sarah Brady denied that the five-year plan had anything to do with HCI. She pointed out that Shields's name was on the distribution list even though he had died well before the document was written. "Other inaccuracies include a reference to January being critical to the importance of Senator Feinstein's proposed ban on assault weapons. This amendment had already passed as part of the Senate's omnibus crime bill—in November of last year," she wrote. The amendment had not, however, passed the House, and the Clinton Administration began seriously campaigning for an "assault weapon" ban by the House in December 1993 and January 1994. It finally passed in May. Brady added: "This hoax document includes such ridiculous proposals as banning the wearing of combat boots and outlawing hunting parties of four or more individuals. These are but a few of the outlandish fantasies contained in this hoax document."[25]

Just whose five-year plan is it? HCI denies it came from there, and the NRA refuses to make a statement. Sarah Brady's statement that January was not critical because the Senate had passed Feinstein's amendment the previous November is rather disingenuous. Wayne LaPierre's statement that the document was delivered to him in secrecy just does not make sense. And why was the document pictured in the *American Rifleman* different from what was sent out to NRA members? Was some participant in a local HCI brainstorming session so delighted with his cleverness and that of his colleagues that he couldn't resist posting it on the Internet? As LaPierre and Metaksa say, decide for yourself.

And don't let your concentration be disturbed by that odor of old fish.

CHAPTER 16

PSEUDO MILITIA

"I've been hearing some strange rumors," said a gun-owning friend.[1] My friend is what might be called a grass-roots gun-rights activist. Before the 1994 elections, he and his wife had spent months organizing gun owners in their rural area to oppose political candidates—of any party—who favored increased gun control. They have since continued to lobby against restrictions on gun ownership. My friend and other activists around the country are linked by telephone, fax, and correspondence. A few of the other activists, he concedes, "are sort of off-the-wall." They were the source of the rumors.

"According to one rumor, U.S. troops are being asked to sign statements agreeing that they will, if ordered, enter civilian homes and arrest citizens who violate gun laws. That sounds pretty peculiar to me, but I wanted to hear your reaction," my friend said.

My reaction was to mention a material found in barnyards that is commonly used to describe something outrageously untrue. In the first place, the Posse Comitatus Act, passed in the 1870s, forbids any use of military personnel to enforce civilian law. Whether troops agree to do such work or not, it's still against the law. In the second place, troops are never asked whether they'd like to obey an order. They are simply ordered and expected to perform.

"There are other rumors, too," he said. "One is that the federal government has secret concentration camps around the country—unused military bases—that will be used to hold people arrested if martial law is proclaimed.

"Then there are some rumors that are even wilder. One is that the government is importing a lot of Russian military equipment which will be used to arm foreign troops—mostly Russian or Chinese—that are training here in the U.S. Some people say these troops will be used to confiscate guns from American civilians.

"I don't believe any of this stuff," he said, "but these are the kinds of stories that are going around. People around here are really uptight about gun control. Up in the counties north of here some guys are forming militias."

"Huh?"

"Militias. They're organized and connected by telephone networks. They have video cameras, and they're prepared to photograph any illegal actions the government takes against gun owners."

The conversation was disturbing. All political observers agree that the two most polarizing issues in the United States today are gun control and abortion. Everybody knows the violent turn the abortion controversy has taken. Is the gun control issue going to follow the same path? Already a sizable portion of the population has decided that it doesn't trust the government. That does not mean merely that they don't believe politicians' promises or that they doubt some of the pronouncements of the FBI. It means that they think their own government may want to deprive them of life, liberty, and the pursuit of happiness. This distrustful portion of the population is also armed, and some of them are preparing for what they think is an inevitable conflict.

THE MILITIAS

Information about these groups began appearing in the news media a short time after my conversation in mid–1994. The Associated Press, the *New York Times*, the *Chicago Tribune*, and *Time* magazine all carried stories on groups that call themselves militias. As we've seen, all males in the country between 17 and 45 belong to the militia whether they want to or not. These new "militia" groups are more like the old volunteer outfits. Like the volunteers, these units are composed of civilians from all walks of life who enjoy each other's company and are prepared to fight, if necessary. The difference is that whereas the volunteers were prepared to fight *for* their country, the new militia groups are preparing to fight *against* it.

"What's driving this movement is the lesson being taught by the American government," Ray Southwell, information officer for a militia group in Michigan, told Keith Schneider of the *New York Times*. "That lesson is that you're not in control of your life, your children, your home. The government is in control. And if you push back, if you cross the government, they will come down on you hard. We are preparing to defend our freedom. The way things are going, I think bullets will be as valuable as gold and silver some day."[2]

As well as poking fun at out-of-shape "militiamen" running obstacle courses, the press coverage inevitably raises the specter of such armed racist groups as the Aryan Nations. Schneider quotes the Anti-Defamation League of B'nai B'rith, which asserts, "There are hatemongers of long standing" in the militia groups, adding, "The question, which no one can answer just yet, is what, exactly, the militias intend to do with their guns."[3]

One answer is that most of them don't intend to establish racial, religious, or sexual discrimination. Of the 100 militia members at the camp Schneider attended, ten were women, one of them a black nurse from Detroit. The militias include Jews and Gentiles, blacks and whites, Catholics and Protestants, males and females. Jim Dupont, sheriff of Flathead County in Montana, said white supremacists tried to influence the militia group that was forming in his county. "They weren't successful at all. People here openly opposed that message."[4] Chip Berlet, an analyst with Political Research Associates, a Cambridge, Massachusetts, think tank, said, "White supremacy is not a principle of unity of this movement. Because of that, it has the ability to draw from a much broader constituency."[5]

Yet according to the Southern Poverty Law Center in Montgomery, Alabama white supremacist influence is growing in Deep South militia groups.[6]

Everybody may be right. Like many grass-roots movements, the militia movement seems to be made of people who take diverse views on many things other than their "principle of unity." According to militia spokespeople, there are 100,000 militia members in from 20 to 45 states. That's a lot of room for diversity. George de Lama of the *Chicago Tribune* called them "an angry stew of libertarians, right-wing isolationists, constitutionalists, tax-protesters and white supremacists."[7] They certainly impress the police in different ways. According to Sheriff Dupont, "I'd say 95 percent of the people who are interested in a militia are good, honest, hard-working people who were concerned about the federal government dictating to states about gun control. That is a big issue in this county."[8] But to Gary Krause, police chief of Fowlerville, Michigan, "As far as I'm concerned, they are a radical organization. . . . [T]hey called cops 'punks in badges' and said the next time one of them was stopped, they'd shoot a cop."[9]

If race hatred or cop hatred is not a unifying principle for the militias, what is?

In Montana, Sheriff Dupont says it's opposition to gun control. In Michigan, Ray Southwell says the federal government has become a tyrant. His evidence: the Brady law and the federal "assault weapon" ban.[10]

In rural areas like northern Michigan and Montana, this "evidence" is more likely to be accepted than in urban areas on the East and West coasts. Another friend, active in state politics in Connecticut, who believes that all guns—long or short, automatic or single-shot—in civilian hands are a menace, gave Southwell's complaint short shrift.

"I don't see how anyone could be excited about those laws," this friend said. "What freedom are they losing? The freedom to kill someone? You have to understand that the world is full of irrational people."[11]

FOOD FOR RUMORS

How could the bizarre ideas my friend heard develop and spread? Let's take one of the wilder rumors first. Why would the United States have to import Russian military equipment to arm foreign troops training on our soil? U.S. military equipment is quite adequate for any military task. Besides, American manufacturers would be delighted with the prospect of a new market. But the fact is that the United States *is* importing Russian military equipment. The breakup of the Soviet Union and the Russian Federation's need for dollars provided a marvelous opportunity for the U.S. intelligence services. They're buying Russian equipment so they can test it and see if our erstwhile rivals had any technological advantages. After all, a large part of the world other than Russia is armed with the same equipment.

What about foreign troops training on our soil? Of course there are foreign troops training here. There have been since the end of World War II. They weren't Russians or troops from the People's Republic of China, though. They were troops of U.S. allies, mostly the smaller allies, who wanted to learn the military techniques of their friendly superpower.

These facts are not exactly national security secrets. Add to them a latent isolationism and a feeling that sinister forces in the federal government are conspiring to take away your property and maybe your liberty or even your life. Putting all that together, it's not surprising that somebody came up with the nightmare scenario: The "one-worlders" in Washington are planning to turn over the sovereignty of the United States to the United Nations. They aim to have a single government for the world. A handful of the intellectual elite would rule the subservient, disarmed population of the earth. After all, didn't the federal government already seem to be bent on disarming the population? The UN army would just be a way to do it quicker.

Of course, some militia people think the bad guys in Washington plan to use U.S. troops instead of foreigners. Otherwise, why would the troops be signing those statements saying they consent to searching and arresting U.S. civilians? Maybe the foreigners are here only in case the government can't get enough U.S. troops to sign the consent statements.

It turns out that there is a basis for the consent statement story, too. A four-page questionnaire had been given to marines at the U.S. Marine Corps base at Twentynine Palms, California. Among its 46 questions was a series that followed a key question: "Do you feel that U.S. combat troops should be used within the

United States for any of the following reasons?" The reasons included drug law enforcement, environmental cleanup, security at national events, and use as an emergency police force. Another set of questions concerned possible duties while serving under UN command. The last question asked if the respondent would "fire upon U.S. citizens who refuse or resist confiscation of firearms banned by the U.S. government."

Joan Sanders, spokeswoman at the Naval Postgraduate School in Monterey, California, said the survey aimed to "examine the attitudes of marines who might be placed in non-traditional roles as some had been in Desert Storm and Somalia." The last question was to see how well they understood the Uniform Code of Military Justice and the U.S. Constitution. It represented, Sanders said, an unlawful order.[12]

And the martial law with concentration camps being prepared? Is there a basis for that, too?

Yes.

SUSPENDING THE CONSTITUTION

In 1987, during the Iran-Contra hearings, Rep. Jack Brooks of Texas attempted to question Oliver North on a plan "to suspend the Constitution of the United States." He was interrupted by Sen. Daniel Inouye, chairman of the Senate Select Committee.

"I believe that question touches upon a highly classified and sensitive area," said Inouye. "May I request you do not touch upon that, sir."

Suspending the Constitution? A highly sensitive area? That's not just sensitive. That's treason, isn't it? The Constitution is the *basic* law of the land. There is no provision in the Constitution that gives any individual or group the power to suspend it. No official or class of officials has any "inherent power" to do so.

A few months before, in a lawsuit filed against North and a number of other people, Daniel P. Sheehan, a well-known civil rights lawyer, charged that President Ronald Reagan had, on April 6, 1984, signed National Security Directive No. 52, which would have the effect of suspending the Constitution.[13]

"The plan was that the president of the United States, Ronald Reagan, would issue a declaration of a state of national emergency and the Constitution of the United States would be temporarily suspended," Sheehan said.[14] The reason for the emergency, he said, was to invade Nicaragua, where the Contras were fighting the Sandinistas. To insure tranquility at home, the federal government would round up 400,000 Latin American aliens and lock them up in detention camps set up on military bases. Arresting people who have broken no law and locking them up without a hearing obviously involves suspending the Constitution. Aliens legally residing in the United States are protected by the Bill of Rights as well as citizens. The government cannot, for example, deprive legal aliens of trial by jury or subject them to unreasonable searches.

Suspending the Constitution has been done before, of course. During the Civil War, Abraham Lincoln suspended the right of habeas corpus and locked up Confederate sympathizers after trial by a military tribunal. After the war, the Supreme Court, courageous as usual, condemned the action. In ex parte *Milligan*, the Court ruled that neither the Constitution or any stretch of the president's war powers allowed the military trial of civilians in areas where civilian courts were operating. Another case was Executive Order 1066, issued by President Franklin D. Roosevelt on December 8, 1941. The order divided the country into ten military districts and gave the military commanders the right to rule by decree. One of the decrees was interning people of Japanese ancestry, both aliens and citizens. One case went to the Supreme Court, *United States v. Hirobayashi*. The defendant argued that Executive Order 1066 was unconstitutional. The Court refused to hear the case until Congress passed a law authorizing the military commanders to exercise the power Roosevelt had given them. The Court then heard the case and ruled against the defendant, although its ruling was based on an ex post facto law, something specifically forbidden by the Constitution. After the war, the Court found that internment of the *nisei* and *isei* was also unconstitutional.

The invasion of Nicaragua never took place, probably because there was no great support for the Contras among the U.S. population and no incident occurred that would galvanize such support.[15] Evidence that the federal government has, since World War II, prepared to round up people and intern them without trial does not depend on Sheehan's lawsuit, however. Title II of the Internal Security Act of 1950 (the McCarren Act) set up six prison camps for the detention of subversives if the president should declare an internal security emergency. It was repealed in 1972. One camp was used as a regular prison; the others were sold. The FBI, however, continued to keep lists of persons who might be interned if a new emergency were declared.[16]

The rumor that U.S. troops might be used against civilians also has a basis in fact. The U.S. Army drew up a plan called "Garden Plot," which, according to the Federal Emergency Management Agency in 1982, "provides the basis for the deployment and employment of military resources, including National Guard personnel who are called-up, for use in civil disturbance operations in the fifty states, District of Columbia, Commonwealth of Puerto Rico, and U.S. territories and possessions, as directed by the President."[17] FEMA, which according to Sheehan's affidavit, would have directed the roundup of Latin Americans, drafted something called the Defense Resources Act that would be presented to Congress whenever the time seemed appropriate. The act not only provides for internment, it says, "Whenever the President shall deem that the public safety demands it, he may cause to be censored under such rules and regulations as he may from time to time establish, communications by mail, cable, radio, television, and other means of transmission crossing the borders of the United States."[18]

Considering the protection the U.S. Supreme Court has given to unpopular groups in the past, it may be understandable why gun owners, definitely unpopular with most of the press, are worried.[19] And it's not just the press that doesn't like gun owners. The federal government has demonstrated that as far as gun owners are concerned, Ray Southwell was right: "If you cross the government, they will come down on you hard."

RUBY RIDGE AND WACO

Randy Weaver crossed the government. Weaver lived in a plywood shack in Idaho, near the Canadian border. He and his family lived a hermit-like existence, subsisting chiefly on wild game and vegetables they raised in their garden. The federal government wasn't really after Weaver. It was after some of his neighbors, the Aryan Nations sect. Weaver was a white separatist and friendly with the Aryans. The government tried to turn him into an informer.

A BATF informer approached Weaver and bought a couple of shotguns from him. A condition of sale was shortening the barrels. Shortened, the barrels were 17¾ inches long—a quarter of an inch shorter than the legal limit. One day in June 1990 BATF agents told Weaver he could be arrested for selling sawed-off shotguns—but if he kept them informed of what the Aryans were up to, he wouldn't have to go to jail. Weaver refused. January 17, 1991, Weaver and his wife, Vicki, stopped to help a pickup truck owner in trouble. Suddenly agents appeared, threw Vicki to the ground and pressed a pistol against Randy's neck. He was arraigned and went home on bond. He did not show up for a hearing in federal court. One reason was that the government had changed the date for his court appearance without telling him.

Several more months went by. On August 21, the Weavers' yellow Labrador began barking. Thinking the dog was chasing a deer, Weaver, his 14-year-old son, Sam, and Kevin Harris, a young man who lived with the Weavers, grabbed rifles and ran out.

The dog was barking because it had smelled a special strike force of U.S. marshals sneaking up on the shack. They wore camouflage suits and ski masks. They carried walkie-talkies and automatic rifles. Little (4 feet, 11 inches) Sammy found the dog. He found him just as one of the marshals fired a burst into the animal. Startled, Sammy fired his rifle. The marshal fired at Sammy, hitting him in the arm. Kevin Harris ran toward the sound of the shots. Randy Weaver called to his son.

"I'm coming, Dad," the kid yelled back and ran toward his father.[20] The marshal fired again. He hit Sammy in the back, killing him instantly. Kevin Harris fired his rifle in the direction of the sound and ran back to the cabin. Harris's bullet killed a marshal.

That shot caused a law enforcement panic. In a couple of days, federal marshals, state police, National Guardsmen, and FBI agents surrounded the cabin.

The day of the shooting, Weaver went out when it got dark and brought Sam's body back to an outbuilding. The next day, he, his daughter, Sara, and Harris went out to wash the body. As soon as they appeared, snipers began shooting. They hit Weaver and Harris. Vicki Weaver, carrying her baby, held the door open for her family. A federal sniper shot her dead, narrowly missing the baby.

What followed was the "siege of Ruby Ridge." In the press, the Weavers' shack, perched on a hill called Ruby Ridge, became a "mountaintop fortress." The U.S. government and the state of Idaho surrounded one plywood shack with armored personnel carriers, helicopters, high-tech robots, and a small army of law enforcers. The FBI took over the siege. It sent in its negotiating team. Their techniques were unusual, to say the least.

"They'd come on real late at night and say, 'Come out and talk to us, Mrs. Weaver. How's the baby, Mrs. Weaver?' in a real smart-alecky voice," recalled Sara Weaver. "Or they'd say, 'Good morning, Randall. How'd you sleep? We're having pancakes.' "[21]

One time the feds sent a robot holding a telephone up to the cabin. The Weavers didn't try to use the phone, though, because the robot also held a shotgun pointed right at the cabin door.

Weaver finally surrendered when the authorities promised to get a famous criminal lawyer named Gerry Spence to talk to him. As soon as he met Weaver, Spence told him he hated bigotry, white separatism, and everything Weaver stood for.[22] He said he'd listen to Weaver's story but that was all he agreed to do. When he heard the story, though, Spence took the case.

Spence didn't even call a witness. He let the FBI agents, the BATF agents, and the marshals destroy their own case. The jury found Harris not guilty of murder or anything else. It found Weaver not guilty of murder and not guilty of selling a sawed-off shotgun, as the BATF had entrapped him. He was found guilty of not appearing in court.

Spence said, "A jury today has just said that you can't kill somebody just because you wear badges, then cover up those homicides by prosecuting the innocent."[23]

Spence spoke too soon. Less than a year and a half later, the BATF and the FBI did just that to a group of gun owners near Waco, Texas.

The Branch Davidians were, of course, pretty odd.[24] But so was Randy Weaver. Randy Weaver, by not appearing in court, had obviously broken the law. Law-breaking was not so obvious in the Branch Davidians' case. The BATF had an arrest warrant for sect leader David Koresh, but it also had a search warrant. The search warrant was to find evidence that Koresh and his followers did what the arrest warrant charged that they did. As in Weaver's case, the charge involved firearms. Also as in Weaver's case, it was a nonviolent offense. The Branch Davidians were supposed to have turned semiautomatic rifles into full automatic rifles. Nobody, though, ever claimed to have seen the rifles. It would seem, then, that the search warrant should have preceded the arrest warrant. Questioned about the rifles over the telephone, David Koresh, the Davidian leader, had previously invited BATF agents to come to his compound and inspect what he had. They did not accept the invitation.

Quite a while later, the federal agents did come, hidden in cattle trailers. They announced their presence by shooting a dog and throwing hand grenades into the windows of the compound the Davidians called "Mount Carmel."[25] At the same time, they began firing from National Guard helicopters and killed a man working on the compound's water tank.[26] The Branch Davidians, seeing masked men attacking them from all sides, began shooting. A videotape of the initial shootout shows BATF agents firing rapidly. The cars and trucks behind which they are hiding, however, show no evidence of return fire—no holes or broken windows. No dust is kicked up behind them. The windows of the compound are curtained, and no one is visible. Fire from the compound was apparently both lighter and later than from the BATF.[27] Another siege took place. Finally, the FBI, which had taken over from the BATF, got tired. They sent tanks to punch holes in the compound and pump in tear gas in quantities that could have been fatal, especially to the many children in the buildings.[28] One tank aimed at a cinder-block section where the feds decided Koresh must be hiding. It didn't punch a hole: it just smashed into the wall. It didn't hit Koresh. But according to survivors, it did flatten a propane tank and knock over some oil lamps.[29] Within seconds, the compound was an inferno. A few of the cult members shot themselves. A handful escaped with their lives. Most of the rest burned to death.

As it had done in Idaho, the federal government charged the few survivors with murder and other offenses.

The jury found no one guilty of murder. It did find five of the 11 defendants guilty of voluntary manslaughter, which according to Federal Judge Walter S. Smith, Jr., is a killing "in the sudden heat of passion, caused by adequate provocation." He did not explain the difference between voluntary manslaughter and killing in self-defense, which many people would think was "caused by adequate provocation." One was convicted of possession of a grenade and another of aiding in the unlawful possession of a machine gun. The jury found seven of the Davidians guilty of carrying a firearm in the commission of a violent crime. The judge threw that verdict out, however, because the jury did not find them guilty of committing a violent crime. Two days later, those convictions were reinstated. Government lawyers had cited case law to show that a conviction is not necessary for a jury to find a defendant guilty of using a firearm in a crime. So the jury found them guilty of using firearms in a violent crime that they had not committed. The judge then imposed the maximum possible sentences.[30]

In 1996, FBI besieged another peculiar group near Jordan, Montana. The "Freemen," as they called themselves, unlike the Weaver family or the Branch Davidians, were alleged to be career crooks, having perpertrated various scams and swindles, as well as threatening public officials and refusing to pay either mortgages or taxes. In spite of this, the FBI showed commendable patience, resisting pressure by some elements of the news media to do something dramatic. The agents waited almost three months outside a Montana ranch house until the "Freemen" surrendered. The public outcry over Ruby Ridge and Waco seems to have had some effect.

JOINT RESPONSIBILITY

When it comes to finding guilt for polarization that might conceivably result in armed conflict, there's plenty to go around. Some of it certainly belongs to the gun lobby for its endless, hysterically paranoid propaganda about the evil "gun grabbers" in Washington.

The NRA, of course, denies any responsbility for the "militias" and their wild ideas, such as the UN effort to take over the country. It has not, however, shrunk from taking advantage of that fear of the "one-worlders." In a letter to NRA members mailed in May, 1996, Tanya Metaksa, the association's chief lobbyist, charged that "Bill Clinton has joined forces with the United Nations to push an international gun ban scheme hatched in Tokyo."

The mailing includes post cards that the members are urged to send to the ambassador from Japan, the secretary general of the UN, the chairman of the Senate Foreign Relations Committee, and the chairman of the House Appropriatons Committee. The card to be sent to the ambassador reads:

Dear Ambassador Owada:

I am writing to urge that Japan end its participation in the United Nations international gun control project.

I reject any U.N. attacks on my Constitutional rights or the sovereignty of the United States . . . and using my tax dollars to meet those ends.

I have written Senator Helms and Congressman Livingston to urge that they cut off U.S. funding for the U.N. until the U.N. cuts off its global gun control scheme.

Sincerely,

The other three cards are similar.[31]

Another portion of blame for the developing polarization, just as surely, belongs to the anti-gun lobby for its endless prevarication. Each of the anti-gun crowd's "final demands" has led to another. That has convinced many gun owners, especially in rural areas where a gun is considered a necessity, that the anti-gun lobby wants the government to confiscate all guns.

A very large portion of guilt, perhaps the biggest piece, belongs to the federal government for its ruthlessness, its continual attempts to evade constitutional limits, and its Big-Brother-knows-best attitude.

Not the least of the federal flaws has been the whole-hearted acceptance of the concept of devil guns.

PART IV

CROSSFIRE—
BLASTS
FROM THE
ANTI-GUNNERS

CHAPTER 17

DEVIL GUNS

"ASSAULT WEAPONS"

During World War II, German ordnance specialists got an idea. They'd build a new rifle firing both semiautomatically and automatically, able to replace both the rifle and the submachine gun, and, in some cases, the light machine gun. To fire automatically, the new weapon would have to be much less powerful than the standard rifle. The standard army rifle of the time has a hefty recoil. The gun comes back hard against the shooter's shoulder, and since the top of the stock is lower than the axis of the barrel, the gun then rotates upward. This jump is no problem when the shooter is firing semiautomatically. But the usual automatic rate of fire is around 600 shots a minute—ten shots a second. If a standard army rifle fired that fast, the gun would be aimed at the sky before the shooter could take his finger off the trigger.

In addition to the lower-power cartridge, the new gun would have to have a straighter stock. That would also reduce the tendency to climb in automatic fire. To aim a rifle with that kind of stock, though, the sights would have to be much higher above the barrel. Another problem with the straight stock was that a shooter holding the rifle with his right hand on the stock couldn't reach the trigger. A pistol grip at the bottom of the gun solved that problem.

The technical difficulties were not the biggest obstacle. The biggest problem was *der Führer*. Hitler absolutely rejected the idea of a rifle with a lower-power cartridge. He apparently thought it was unmacho, or whatever the German equivalent to that may be. His ordnance people went on producing the gun, but called it a submachine gun instead of a rifle and hoped the dictator wouldn't notice. The MP (for *Maschinenpistole*) 43, and its successor, the MP 44, were great successes with the German troops.

Hitler, the story has it, remained blissfully unaware of the new gun until some generals on the Russian front requested more MP 44s.[1] Suddenly the new rifle was acceptable. Its developers, instead of being in danger of a firing squad, became heroes. The Germans then renamed the new gun. It changed from a Maschinenpistole (machine pistol) to a *Sturmgewehr* (assault rifle), a more macho name that pleased Hitler. The name caught on and was applied to all low-power rifles capable of both semiautomatic and automatic fire.[2]

The National Rifle Association of America, with the cooperation of the Department of the Army, has long run national rifle matches. The matches have a military, or militia, purpose—to encourage citizens to become proficient riflemen. That being the case, one series of matches is for contestants using the service rifle. When the United States adopted the M-14, then the M-16, there was a problem. Both weapons could fire automatically as well as semiautomatically. They were machine guns. So the match rules specified semiautomatic versions of the service rifle. Colt brought out their AR-15, a semiautomatic version of the M-16. It sold well.

Importers started bringing in semiautomatic versions of foreign assault rifles. These sold to weapons buffs who wanted guns as close as they could legally get to such foreign rifles as the Belgian FN-FAL and the Soviet Avtomat Kalashnikova 1947g, better known as the AK-47. Because they make a lot of noise and muzzle flash (when firing blanks), assault rifles are also a favorite prop in action movies and TV shows. Inevitably, that led to a lot of commando wannabes buying them. To tap the wannabe market, foreign and some domestic manufacturers began producing a variety of grotesque weapons. There were three-pound pistols that looked like submachine guns and were no easier to carry. There were perfectly decent .22 semiauto rifles tarted up with pistol grips, barrel jackets, and flash hiders. There were shotguns with pistol grips and no stocks and all the instinctive pointing qualities of a medieval hand cannon.

If some grownups wanted to shoot military-looking rifles and fantasize about being Green Berets or SWAT team members, nobody seemed to care. Other grownups fire muzzle-loading rifles and fantasize about being mountain men or Civil War soldiers. Then Patrick Purdy appeared. Purdy was a nut, a homicidal maniac. Nuts appear occasionally. There was Howard Unruh with his Luger and Richard Speck with his knife. Purdy, unfortunately for gun buffs, used a semiautomatic version of the AK-47.

On January 17, 1989, Purdy took his AK-47 look-alike to a school yard in Stockton, California, and started shooting at Asian children. He killed five of them and wounded 33 other children and a teacher. Then he killed himself. He just wandered around mumbling to himself while he shot kids for four minutes.

He lay dead for another four minutes before any police arrived. It was cold-blooded, crazy murder. But he didn't need any kind of special weapon to accomplish the massacre. He could have shot that many people with a six-shot revolver or a single-shot rifle.

The greatest public interest after the massacre was not in how someone like Purdy happened to be at large. This should have been the question. Purdy had a long record of violent behavior and arrests. Some were felony arrests, but they were plea-bargained down to misdemeanors. Instead of focusing on Purdy or the justice system, though, public interest centered on Purdy's gun.

Dozens of anti-gun spokesmen suddenly broke into print complaining about the "easy availability" of these "high powered" weapons. Joseph McNamara, then police chief of San Jose, California, told reporters "one bullet hitting a child in Stockton took out his entire stomach."[3] The statement was not only an example of gratuitous bad taste but an out-and-out lie. Dr. Martin Fackler, then director of combat trauma management at the Letterman Army Institute of Research, analyzed the autopsy reports. He said, "The magnitude of the tissue disruption reported from fatal wounds inflicted by the AK-47 bullets fired by Purdy was, in fact, no greater than that produced by many common handgun bullets."[4] Most common handgun bullets produce small holes, not massive tissue destruction.

The anti-gun lobby had already targeted semiautomatic rifles with a "military" appearance to be the new Saturday night specials. The year before Purdy's crime, William Bennett had, on March 14, 1988, suggested to Attorney General Edwin Meese, "We should consider supporting legislation to better manage the production, importation and sale of automatic weapons."[5] The production, importation, and sale of automatic weapons had already been totally banned. Bennett obviously meant semiautomatic weapons. Here was a high federal official, later to become President Bush's "drug czar," who didn't know the difference. Six months after Bennett's memo, Josh Sugarmann wrote his own memo, *Assault Weapons and Accessories in America*, to the leadership of the National Coalition to Ban Handguns. In it, you remember (chapter 8), he wrote of "the public's confusion over fully automatic machine guns versus semi-automatic assault weapons."[6] Obviously, he wasn't exaggerating.

Sugarmann and his allies, the National Coalition to Ban Handguns (which then became the Coalition to Stop Gun Violence), seized on the Stockton massacre to whip up popular support for a ban on what they called "assault rifles"— really assault rifle look-alikes. In naming its Sturmgewehr, the German army had inadvertently given the American anti-gun lobby a strong talking point. Who could be in favor of a rifle meant to assault people?

At first, most gun control advocates railed against "assault rifles." Then, it seemed, "assault rifles" became too limiting a term. They adopted Sugarmann's term, "assault weapons." Before Sugarmann, an assault rifle was a definite type of weapon—a selective-fire military rifle using a cartridge more powerful than a pistol but much less powerful than a standard military rifle. After Sugarmann, an "assault weapon" was any kind of firearm that "looked real mean." Most had detachable magazines sticking out and pistol grips. Some had flash hiders; others had screw threads around their muzzles. Most of the rifles and shotguns had folding stocks. Guns classed as "assault weapons" vary from hoked-up .22 pistols to the Barrett Light Fifty, a 28.5-pound, five-foot-long monster that fires .50 caliber machine gun cartridges.[7]

A Handgun Control, Inc. pamphlet attempts to define "assault weapons" covered by the 1994 federal crime bill. Quotes from the pamphlet and my comments (in italics) follow:[8]

"Assault weapons are commonly equipped with some or all of the following *combat* [emphasis added] hardware:

- "Large-capacity ammunition magazine, enabling the shooter to continuously fire dozens of rounds without reloading. Standard hunting rifles are equipped with no more than 3- or 4-shot magazines."

   Most standard bolt-action hunting rifles have five-shot magazines. Lever-action center-fire hunting rifles have six- to 13-shot magazines. Most semi-automatic "standard hunting rifles" have four- or five-shot magazines. Only the Browning Automatic Rifle (not the military BAR) and a few bolt-action rifles, mostly "elephant guns," have three-round magazines.

- "Folding stock on a rifle or shotgun, which sacrifices accuracy for advantages such as concealability and mobility in close combat."

   Even with a folding stock, you can't carry one of these things in your pocket. A folding stock makes a military rifle easier to store in a crowded tank or armored personnel carrier.

- "Pistol grip on a rifle or shotgun, which facilitates firing from the hip, allowing the shooter to spray fire the weapon. A pistol grip also helps stabilize the weapon during rapid fire."

   A pistol grip does NOT facilitate firing from the hip. The shooter's arm has to reach around the stock, making hip-shooting marginally more difficult. The pistol grip is required because of the straight stock, which is an advantage only for automatic fire.

- "Barrel shroud which is designed to cool the barrel so the firearm can shoot many rounds without overheating. It also allows the shooter to grasp the barrel area without incurring serious burns, during rapid fire."

Nobody is going to fire enough shots from a low-power semiautomatic to get serious burns. Further, the barrel jacket (or shroud) has no effect on overheating. The barrel will get just as hot with or without a jacket. If it gets too hot (which would take work with a low-powered semi-auto) it will lose accuracy.

- "Threaded barrel is designed to accommodate a flash suppressor, which serves no useful sporting purpose. The flash suppressor allows the shooter to remain concealed when shooting at night, an advantage in combat but unnecessary for sporting or hunting purposes. In addition, the flash suppressor is useful in preventing barrel climb during rapid fire, helping the shooter maintain control of the firearm.

The last sentence is stupid. A device called a compensator, not a flash suppressor, helps control climb. Because the compensator directs some of the white-hot gases emerging from the muzzle straight up, it tends to increase—not decrease—the visible flash. There is no climb except in automatic fire. Compensators are useful on specialized rapid-fire target pistols (never considered "assault weapons,") but useless on any semi-auto rifle or carbine.

- "Threaded barrel designed to accommodate a silencer, which is useful to assassins but has no purpose for sportsmen."

Sportsmen in France regularly use silencers to cut down noise pollution. So do sportsmen in some parts of Switzerland and other countries. They are illegal in the United States, however.

- "Barrel mount designed to accommodate a bayonet, which obviously serves no sporting purpose."

How many bayonet-point robberies have you heard of?

An interesting feature of the HCI description of "combat" features is the assumption that there is no reason to have a gun except for hunting. The corollary is that guns not used for hunting are "illegitimate" and should be banned. That's something like saying no one needs a horse except to commute to work; any other use is illegitimate and ownership of a horse for such other purposes should be banned.

Not one of the features in the HCI list makes a weapon more deadly. People who own these guns got them so they can either compete in "service rifle" matches or because they collect guns and want examples of modern firearms technology.

People who own or want to own these rifles understandably opposed the ban. But why did people uninterested in guns with such cosmetic features as flash hiders, pistol grips, and folding stocks oppose it? One reason is that because the features that make an "assault weapon" out of a standard gun are mostly cosmetic, restrictions on "assault weapons" can easily be applied to standard rifles. For example, the Ruger Mini 14 semiautomatic rifle with a wood stock is legal, but it is banned as an "assault weapon" if it has a folding wire stock. Except for the stock, both guns are identical. Suppose the legislators suddenly had an attack of logic. Couldn't they reason that if the wire-stocked gun is so dangerous it should be banned, shouldn't its identical twin, the wood-stocked gun, be banned, too?

If guns considered "assault weapons" are no more deadly than weapons not classed as "assault weapons," why would a congresswoman write the following to her constituents?

> I worked hard to pass the assault weapons ban which prohibits the possession and manufacture of 19 specific types of assault weapons including the Uzi, Street Sweeper, and AK-47. If these weapons sound familiar, it is because they are weapons favored by drug dealers, cop killers, and terrorists."[9]

The answer, of course, is that the congresswoman had been misinformed (see chapter 12 and notes).

Why would a police officer tell the *Los Angeles Times*, "We're tired of passing out flags to the widows of officers killed by drug dealers with Uzis"?[10] In that case, the answer is that he lied. From 1980 through 1989, only one police officer was killed by an Uzi, and he was in Puerto Rico. And the killer wasn't a drug dealer.[11] The L.A. cop was merely mouthing the standard police line about the "carnage of our police." As we've seen (chapter 10) that "carnage" is mostly imaginary.

We've already seen the figures on police officers killed by "assault weapons." Here are some other statistics:

- A survey of prison inmates in Virginia between November 1992 and May 1993 indicated that 10 percent had, at one time or another, possession of an "assault weapon," but none of them did at the time of their arrest.[12]

- Of 375 guns seized by Chicago police in drug raids in 1988, six could be classed as "assault weapons."[13]

- Of guns seized by police under all circumstances in 1988, less than 3 percent were "assault weapons" in Los Angeles; .5 percent in New York; and 0 percent in Washington, D.C.[14]

- Of 271 homicides committed in Dade County, Florida, in 1989, 3 percent were done with "assault weapons;" of 295 gun homicides in Massachusetts outside of Boston from 1984 to 1988, five were committed with "assault rifles."[15]

Even HCI admitted in 1989 that "assault weapons" play "a small role in overall violent crime," although they could become a problem in the future.[16]

Why, then, is it trying so hard to ban them?

Basically, it's because they are guns. Every gun out of circulation is a step in the right direction, from the anti-gun lobby point of view. As Sugarmann wrote, the effort to ban pistols had bogged down, but similar efforts against "assault weapons" might be successful. Comparatively few people owned them. Owners of other types of guns might not worry too much about a ban of these ugly-looking weapons. Further, they were called *assault* weapons, and the public was likely to confuse them with machine guns. Then too, anti-gun lobby sympathizers, like the *New York Times*, said these rifles could be readily converted to the oldest of devil guns . . .

. . . MACHINE GUNS

At least, that's what they said some of the time. In an editorial from November 2, 1988, the *Times* asserted that "many semiautomatics can be made automatic with a screwdriver, even a paperclip."[17] Eight months later in a feature on the importation of guns, it said:

> The staff of the [Bureau of Alcohol, Tobacco, and Firearms] disassemble, test, and examine samples of all semiautomatic weapons marketed in the United States to make formal determinations on this question [whether they can be converted into full automatic weapons]. Any weapon found to be readily converted to automatic fire would be declared illegal. None of the five types included in the import ban have been declared readily convertible, nor have any semiautomatics now on sale.[18]

Was there a shortage of screwdrivers at the BATF? Or maybe paperclips?

Then there's the question of how diabolical automatic weapons really are. Machine guns have been pariahs in the American gun world since 1934—all kinds of machine guns. But how many water-cooled Browning M-1917s or Maxim Model 1908s or Browning .50 caliber machine guns have ever been involved in a civilian homicide or robbery? The automobile bandits of the 1930s did use military BARs, and both they and the Prohibition-era gangsters used Thompson submachine guns. Some bad guys today use submachine guns, actually more than in the 1920s,[19] in spite of Senator Kennedy (chapter 7), although they still make up only a small percentage of the guns used in crime. But the BAR is never seen in crooked hands.

The reason does not seem to be the ban on automatic weapons. More likely, it's that most machine guns (certainly the BAR) are just too darn big. What submachine guns are used tend to be small. The Uzi, the MAC 10, and the MAC 11 are favorites. The Uzi is only two-thirds as long as the Thompson, and the MAC 11 is one-third the length of the Uzi. Concealability is important in modern crime.

Another reason why submachine guns are not used more may be that they just aren't that effective. In military use, automatic fire is effective. It encourages the enemy to keep his head down while your troops advance. It wastes ammunition, but the army has practically unlimited resources. But compare the results Capt. Henry Lum got (chapter 6) firing automatically with his score in semiautomatic mode. In most situations, the semiauto can kill more people faster.

Because most Americans may not have or use automatic weapons, they learn to handle them only in the service. And most service marksmanship training is often inadequate, to put it charitably. Sweden, a country with a low rate of violent crime, does not view automatic weapons for civilians as dimly as the United States. Members of the Swedish National Rifle Association compete with submachine guns and light machine guns as well as rifles. "Actually," writes Nils Kvale, a Norwegian firearms expert currently living in Sweden, "the organization uses today all the small arms of the Swedish army, except the service pistol."[20] In 1957, a factory-new submachine gun cost a Swede the equivalent of $25, and a like-new bolt-action rifle the same amount.[21] The Swedes obviously consider plain, old pistols more dangerous in civilian hands than machine guns.

SHORT GUNS

Sawed-off shotguns were used by the gangsters of the 1920s and 1930s. Like the tommy guns also used, they were subjected to a prohibitive tax under the National Firearms Act. "Sawed-offs" include any shotgun with a barrel shorter than 18 inches and any rifle with a barrel shorter than 16 inches. Pistols with shoulder stocks are considered short rifles. The law, however, cannot prevent anyone from obtaining a sawed-off rifle or shotgun. Hacksaws are available at every hardware store.

"Saturday night specials," cheap, short-barreled revolvers, have also been the target of gun-banners.[22] Like "assault weapons," they were said to be the "weapon of choice" of professional criminals. Those who want to ban them say they have no legitimate purpose. It's true that they'd be nobody's "weapon of choice" for deer, or even rabbit, hunting. (Although some use them as trail guns.) But when the anti-gun lobby says they have no defensive use, that they are useful only to criminals, it runs into a problem in logic. How can a weapon be useful in the hands of a criminal but not in those of an honest citizen?

Apparently criminals aren't that crazy about them. A report of the Police Foundation in 1977, when Saturday night special fever was at its height, states, "This evidence clearly indicates that the belief that the so-called Saturday Night Specials (inexpensive handguns) are used to commit the great majority of these felonies is misleading and counterproductive."[23]

The proposed Brady II bill gets around that problem by classifying any revolver with a barrel of three inches or shorter—regardless of cost—a Saturday night special.[24]

DIABOLICAL AMMO

Although it's been firmly established that the "cop killer" KTW bullet never killed any cops and the "Black Rhino" bullet does not exist, and although legislation prohibits any metallic bullet capable of penetrating a police-type armor vest when fired from a handgun, media like the *New York Times* continue to dredge up the "cop killer" bullet myth. In an editorial from January 30, 1995, the Good Gray *Times* proclaimed, "A responsible Congress should be seeking . . . to cut down on the manufacture of bullets that kill cops."[25] The paranoid NRA view of the press is not entirely without foundation.

The Brady II bill would prohibit what it calls "non-sporting ammunition." That includes, besides such projectiles as tracers and explosive shells, "any handgun ammunition measuring more than .45 inches in diameter." Why a bullet .45 inches in diameter is "sporting" and one a ten-thousandth of an inch larger is not, nobody in the anti-gun lobby has tried to explain. The authors of the legislation presumably don't know that the .45 ACP, one of the most popular U.S. handgun cartridges, has an actual diameter of .4505 inches and the .45 Colt, another popular cartridge, is .455 inches wide.[26] The whole idea is supremely silly. But Brady II's other classification of a devil round is counterproductive if you're opposed to concealable firearms. The bill would also prohibit "any handgun ammunition that produces a force at the muzzle of 1,200 foot pounds." The only handguns that develop that kind of power are those enormous hunting handguns mentioned in chapter 13. Anyone seriously concerned about weaning the public away from pocket pistols would *want* to encourage the use of these hand cannons.

On the other hand, there may be more to this provision than meets the eye.

When pistols use cartridges like the .223 Remington, the .30-30 Winchester, and the .308 Winchester, these rifle cartridges become handgun cartridges. In 1994, the BATF prohibited the importation of steel-cored 7.62 x 39mm cartridges because handguns were being chambered for these Russian rifle cartridges: their bullets' construction was outlawed for handguns by legislation prohibiting "cop-killer bullets."[27] Almost any center-fire rifle cartridge in one of these big handguns generates muzzle energy in the proscribed amount. Outlawing such cartridges would mean most of the most popular sporting rifles would become useless. That would be the biggest step toward disarming the nation ever proposed, short of total confiscation of all firearms.

Josh Sugarmann, head of the Violence Policy Center, also wants to ban caseless ammunition. This ammunition, which does away with the traditional brass cartridge shell, is the latest development in ammunition technology. The brass shell made breech-loading guns practical. The new ammunition is almost as big a step forward. It will eliminate the need to build extractors, ejectors, and ejection ports into weapons. Sugarmann objects to it because police will not be able to trace such guns from the cases they eject.[28] But ordinary revolvers, which are involved in far more homicides than any high-tech "assault weapons," don't leave cases, either. Further, you can't *trace* an individual gun from its case. You can narrow down the possible *types* of gun that ejected the case. But one type of gun may include, as is true of the AK-47, about 50 million individual weapons.[29] Cases found at the scene of a crime may be compared with those fired from a suspect's gun. That does permit identification of the individual weapon. But you can make the same comparison with bullets, and even caseless ammunition uses bullets.

Caseless ammunition is in an early stage of development. Whatever we do about it in this country, it will undoubtedly be the military small arms ammunition of the future in other countries. Stopping development now would do little to help the police but much to hurt the military.

"As with plastic handguns" [remember them?] Sugarmann writes, "Caseless ammo may be an example of technology outpacing common sense."[30] Sugarmann's position may be an example of gun-hatred outpacing common sense.

The same may be true of his position on laser sights. The laser sight is a small laser attached to a gun. It projects a thin beam of red light straight ahead of the gun. At short ranges, the spot of light projected by the laser shows the shooter where his bullet will land. Introduced on military weapons, and still being developed, the laser would be an ideal device for a homeowner confronting an intruder in the dark. Sugarmann and Kristen Rand, the VPC's lawyer, however, see it only as an assassination tool and demand that it be banned.[31]

WHY DEVIL GUNS?

When you analyze it, the whole idea of banning certain types of weapons, as it is done in the United States, is rather bizarre. All studies show that "assault weapons," machine guns, and even Saturday night specials are not responsible for a large portion of crime in the nation. Most crime involving guns involves mainstream semiautomatic pistols and revolvers. Mainstream handguns, though, are owned by large numbers of people. Several statewide attempts to ban them have been made. Each was shot down by a wide margin. The anti-gun lobby, therefore, has concentrated on peculiar weapons owned by relatively few people. And in the case of Saturday night specials, by poor people with no political clout.

The devil gun approach, however, opens possibilities for back-door disarmament. Brady II's magazine ban and safety requirements (chapter 12) could eliminate large numbers of handguns. Its nonsporting handgun ammunition ban could effectively eliminate huge numbers of rifles.

And in any case, banning any gun is a step in the right direction if you believe, as much of the anti-gun lobby does, that guns themselves *cause* homicide.

CHAPTER 18

THE DEVIL GUN MADE ME DO IT

GUNS AS EVIL OBJECTS

As we've seen, both Michael Beard and Josh Sugarmann, ardent proponents of strict gun control, concede that no law can keep guns out of the hands of criminals (chapter 11). Why, then, do they want gun control laws?

They do because they don't see crime as the principal trouble caused by guns. Sugarmann says, "Although drug-related violence has recently escalated, it isn't criminals who are killing most of the 22,000 people who die each year from handguns. Crime is merely the most publicized aspect of the widespread public health problem created by the easy availability of handguns."[1]

According to Sugarmann, "The turning point will come when handgun violence is recognized for what it is: a broad-based public health problem stemming from the widespread and virtually unregulated distribution of a hazardous consumer product."[2]

Beard's group, the Coalition to Stop Gun Violence, advertises a study done by Drs. John Henry Sloan, Arthur L. Kellermann, and Donald T. Reay on murder rates in the two cities of Seattle, Washington, and Vancouver, British Columbia. Sloan, Kellerman, and Reay are among a group of physicians who have conducted study after study sponsored by the U.S. Centers for Disease Control—all aimed at showing that guns are a public health hazard. The murder rate in Seattle was one-and-a-half times higher than in Vancouver. According to CSGV, "Both cities have large white majority populations with similar numbers of minority population. They even watch the same TV shows.

"The most significant difference between the two is the way each city regulates firearms. In Vancouver, it is virtually impossible to own a handgun, while in Seattle handguns are relatively easy to obtain."[3]

The study concerned all murders, not merely those committed with guns, of course. Only Rep. Charles Schumer and some of the more extreme anti-gun lobbyists seem to think "gun murders" are worse than other murders.

Dr. Kellermann has done numerous studies on the danger of firearms in the home. Describing a 1993 study, he wrote in the *Atlanta Constitution*, "Gun ownership was found to be linked with an increased risk of homicide in the home."[4]

Dr. C. Everett Koop, former surgeon general of the United States, has been pushing a program called STOP—Steps to Prevent Firearm Injury. Speaking to the American Academy of Pediatrics, Dr. George Cohen of the Children's National Medical Center in Washington, said, "The main message of the STOP program is simple: A gun in the home is a danger to your family. Parents need to know that the safest thing to do is to remove the gun from your home."[5]

Andrew J. McClurg, an associate professor at the University of Arkansas School of Law, says, "Handguns are perhaps the paradigmatic case of a product unreasonably dangerous per se."[6] He describes the handgun as "an ugly instrument designed principally for the purpose of killing human beings."[7]

The message of all of these people has been echoed more crudely in editorials from coast to coast. The line goes like this: "Common sense tells you that with 100 million or more guns in private hands, some of them are going to be used for murder. The more guns there are, the more murders."

Of course, at one time common sense once told people the world was flat. Common sense does not explain why there are so few murders in Switzerland, a country loaded with guns, or in Sweden, where any honest person can buy a submachine gun for a reasonable price. And if handguns really were, as McClurg charges, "designed principally for the purpose of killing human beings," a lot of people have wasted a lot of money. Handguns are still selling briskly, at a median price of around $500, but only a tiny fraction have ever been used to kill a human being. If killing people is all a handgun is good for, why do so many people who wouldn't think of killing a person buy them?

If you take this anti-gun message to its logical conclusion, you get a paraphrase of the well-known NRA slogan. In this case, it's "People don't kill people. Guns kill people." That's even more ridiculous than the original.

What about the surveys, by Kellermann and others, that prove the murder rate goes up when guns are more available?

GETTING SURVEY RESULTS YOU WANT

Take the most famous—the Seattle-Vancouver study. There were a couple of differences between the two cities the CSGV doesn't mention. First, there was the matter of minorities. In Seattle, 12.1 percent of the population is black or Hispanic and 7.4 percent Asian. Vancouver's population is .8 percent black or

Hispanic and 22.1 percent Asian.[8] Much more important, although the *average* per capita income in each city is about the same, its distribution varies greatly. The per capita income of Seattle's non-Hispanic white population is vastly greater than that of its African-American and Hispanic populations. No comparable diversity of income exists in Vancouver. The low end of the income scale in Seattle is largely occupied by blacks and Hispanics who have long suffered from discrimination and the ills that afflict inner city Americans—broken families, lack of jobs, and lack of hope.[9] The homicide rate for non-Hispanic whites in Seattle was 6.2 per 100,000 in the period studied. For non-Hispanic whites in Vancouver, it was 6.4 per 100,000. The homicide rate among the economically depressed African-Americans and Hispanics of Seattle was quite different. For Seattle's blacks the homicide rate per 100,000 was 36.6, and for its Hispanics, 26.9.[10]

The study was financed by the U.S. government's Centers for Disease Control, a federal agency with a long history of nonscientific, unobjective advocacy of gun control.[11] It aimed to show that the lower homicide rate in Vancouver was a result of the Canadian federal government's tight new restrictions on handgun possession. Even disregarding the way the study glossed over minority incomes and homicide rates, there were problems. One was that Vancouver's homicide rate began dropping *before* the new gun laws took effect in 1978. The same thing was true nationally. Canada's murder rate had increased from 1961 to 1975. In 1975—three years before the new gun law took effect—it began to decline. It continued to decline until 1981, when, in spite of the new law, it began to edge upward.[12] In Vancouver, but not the country as a whole, the use of guns in homicides dropped dramatically. The overall murder rate, though, did not change much, proving that if you take away one weapon, the murderer will find another. Like the rest of Canada, Vancouver's murder rate declined slowly until 1981. Then it began to increase.[13] There were still about as many murders in Vancouver, but the murderers didn't make as much noise. Quieter murder is a rather dubious advantage.

Evidence now indicates that Vancouver may not even be enjoying that advantage. The murder rate has continued to rise. From 1978, when the gun law took effect, until 1994 Vancouver's homicide rate increased 26 percent.[14] In 1982, the Vancouver Police Union declared that the city was afflicted with a great surge in armed robbery. It demanded more powerful handguns and a shotgun in each patrol car. At the same time, the Vancouver chief of police was calling for a total ban on all handguns (something Vancouver was already close to). He said, "The only reason for a handgun is protection, but we don't have a community that needs that kind of protection."[15]

Kellermann's 1993 study, which purportedly shows that a gun in the house increases the risk that a member of the household will be murdered, shows other forms of bias. According to Kellermann, he and his colleagues studied every household where a homicide had occurred in three counties and compared them with a sample where there had been no homicide. And, he said, "Gun ownership was found to be an increased risk of homicide in the home." He also said, "More than three-fourths of the homicides in the study involved a family member, spouse, or someone else who knew the victim well."[16]

However, only a quarter of the homicides in the counties involved took place in the victim's home. They were the homicides Kellermann and his team studied. Considering the location, it's hardly surprising that "strangers were involved in only 3.6 percent of the cases."[17] The FBI's Uniform Crime Reports, covering *all* murders, give a different picture. In 1993, only 12 percent of murder victims were related to their killers. More—35 percent—were acquainted with their murderers. That does not mean they were friends. A drug dealer and his customer are acquainted. So are members of rival gangs. Fourteen percent of the killers were known to be strangers to their victims, and in 39 percent of the cases (a substantial portion of which must have involved strangers), the relationship was unknown.[18]

Kellermann's study shows a much more egregious error, however. Edgar A. Suter, another physician interested in social issues, pointed out that the households studied were not socially and demographically representative of the areas studied or of the nation as a whole:

> The groups had exceptionally high incidence of social dysfunction and instability. For example, 52.7% of case subjects had a history of household members being arrested, 24.8% had alcohol-related problems, 31.3% had a household history of illicit drug abuse, 31.8% had a household member hit or hurt in a family fight, 17.3% had a family member hurt so severely in a family fight that medical attention was required.[19]

These characteristics did not come close to being representative of the populations of the three counties. As we saw in the Kansas City study (chapter 11), domestic homicides, whether by gun, knife, or broken bottle, almost always occur in households with a history of violence. Despite what Sugarmann says, people who beat up other people and send them to the hospital ARE criminals. They aren't "ordinary folks" who are tempted to violence by the presence of a gun.

Nor is a gun even necessary. Marvin Wolfgang, a professor of criminology who believes in gun control, wrote, after studying murders in Philadelphia: "It is the contention of this observer that few homicides due to shooting could be avoided merely if a firearm were not immediately present, and that the offender would select some other weapon to achieve the same destructive goal. Probably only in those cases where a felon kills a police officer, or vice versa, would homicide be avoided in the absence of a firearm."[20]

Another famous criminologist, Franklin Zimring, found that in almost every shooting he studied, the opponents were within eight feet of each other.[21] At that distance, a knife, a hatchet, a poker, or any number of weapons could be effective—fatally effective.

After the passage of Massachusetts's Bartley-Fox Law, providing a mandatory year in prison for anyone carrying a pistol without a permit, Harvard Law School's Center for Criminal Justice studied the results of the law during the first year it was in effect. In domestic homicide and other unpremeditated crimes, the use of guns did decrease. But the number and severity of the crimes did not.[22]

A GUN FOR SELF-DEFENSE

In his article, Kellermann said, "We have been criticized for failing to count nonfatal uses of a gun for self-defense. If keeping a gun in the home provides substantial protection against homicide, we should have found that fewer homes where a homicide occurred contained guns. The opposite was true."[23]

If only 3.6 percent of the homicides involved outsiders, and the households studied were filled with unstable, violent people, that would be a most unreasonable expectation. Further, it should be obvious that "self-defense" does not always involve intruders. It would be foolish to assume that in all cases of domestic homicide, especially where the victim is a husband, an ex-husband, or a boyfriend, that the killer was always the aggressor. Men, as a rule, are larger and stronger than women, which means that a woman's only chance of survival may have been a gun. Prosecutors and courts often recognize that fact. In Detroit, 75 percent of wives who shoot and kill their husbands are not prosecuted. In Miami and Houston, the figures are 60 and 85.7 percent, respectively.[24] The number of self-defense killings by wives and girlfriends is probably even larger. Unfortunately, cases where a woman does kill an aggressive, abusive man with whom she has been intimate are often not classed as self-defense slayings. Sociologist Cynthia Gillespie points out that the rules for legal self-defense were written by lawmakers who apparently were thinking of conflicts between two normal-size men. Force can only be met with approximately equal force. For example, if one man punches another, the second can punch him back. He can't shoot him.[25] But a 110-pound woman cannot be expected to repel a 220-pound man with her fists. Gillespie, who studied many domestic killings, concluded that in the vast majority of cases in which a women killed a man in a domestic dispute, the woman acted in self-defense. But in case after case, women who killed in self-defense were convicted of criminal homicide.[26]

Kellermann's 1993 study, conducted with Drs. F. P. Rivara and N. B. Rushforth, is similar to one he conducted in 1986 with Dr. D. T. Reay. And that was almost a duplicate of a 1975 study conducted by Rushforth with three other physicians. All used the same flawed logic. And all were roundly criticized by most sociologists and criminologists. The 1975 study stated that there were 148 accidental gun deaths in Cuyahoga County, Ohio, from 1958 to 1973, of which 77 percent occurred in homes. There were 23 "burglars, robbers, or intruders who were not relatives or acquaintances" shot to death by householders defending their homes. Because, the authors claimed, there were six times as many fatal accidents as burglars killed, "the possession of firearms by civilians appears to be a dangerous and ineffective means of self-protection."

In the first place, there were 115 (77.7 percent of 148) fatal accidents (or, as we'll see, other types of deaths) in the home. So the authors' math was incorrect. In other words, there were five, not six, times as many of these deaths as there were deaths of burglars, etc. Then it turned out that all of the deaths weren't accidental. Most of them were suicides. The authors added all suicides to the accidental deaths in Cuyahoga County during the period studied. Nationally, there are 44 gun suicides to every gun accident, even when you don't count the highly suspicious "killed-while-cleaning-a-gun" accidents as suicides. The result is to exaggerate the frequency of accidents about 4,400 percent.[27]

More important, the whole statement is a non sequitur. People keep guns to protect themselves, their families, and their property, not to kill burglars. If the burglar flees at the sight of a gun, nobody is happier than the householder. No normal person relishes killing another human being. Chances are that if the householder has to fire, he or she will try to hit a nonvital spot. And, of course, the number of accidental deaths has nothing to do with the gun's effectiveness as a means of defense. Further, as criminologist Gary Kleck points out, "gun accidents are largely concentrated in a very small, high-risk subset of the population—for everyone else, the risks of a fatal gun accident are negligible."[28]

Kellermann's injunction, "Keeping a loaded gun is not the answer," is in accord with the endlessly repeated statement by gun control advocates that guns are useless in self-defense—at least, guns in the hands of "civilians." This high regard for the firearms skills of police officers may cause some amusement among competitive pistol marksmen who have fired against police teams (the pick of police marksmen). Nevertheless, it is a widely held belief. Don B. Kates assigned some of his law students to collect from 30 daily newspapers accounts of the use of firearms to counter criminal attacks—both successful and unsuccessful attempts, by either police or other citizens. They collected 296 incidents, which they then analyzed. If a criminal were driven off, captured, or killed, the attempt was considered successful. It turned out that the "civilians" were successful in 84 percent of the cases, the police and security guards in 73.3 percent.[29]

Few cities keep good records of what criminologists call civilian justifiable homicides, or CJHs. Chicago does. Any time someone not a police officer kills someone, the killing is extensively investigated. If it is declared a justifiable killing, you may be sure it is. Police killings do not get such investigation. All police killings have traditionally been declared justifiable, although one sociologist said 14 percent of those he investigated appeared to be murder or manslaughter.[30] Anyway, "civilian" justifiable killings in Chicago annually outnumber those by police three to one.[31]

In many cities, including Chicago, some persons found to have committed CJHs were originally arrested on criminal charges. Their cases go into the FBI's Uniform Crime Reports as murder or non-negligent manslaughter. The FBI classification is not changed after further investigation, prosecutors, or courts establish that the killers' actions were justified. Such CJHs as are reported go into the FBI's unpublished Supplementary Homicide Reports. The number of justified homicides in the SHR, therefore, is under-reported. The number is still further diminished because some police departments do not bother to report civilian justifiable homicides: they see that as unnecessary paperwork.[32] Then there is the legal distinction between justifiable homicide and excusable homicide. Excusable homicides include some accidents, but not motor vehicle accidents and some other common types. Most of them are intentional killings that the authorities do not want to say are justified, but which they don't want to prosecute because they really weren't criminal. An accidental shooting that was not the result of criminal negligence on the part of the shooter might be one. Another might be a self-defense shooting in which the shooter wrongly, but reasonably, thought his life was in danger. Most are what criminologists call civilian legal defensive homicides or CLDHs. This may sound like splitting a hair six ways, but there are a lot of these excusable homicides. In Detroit, between 1969 and 1980, there were 344 justifiable and 741 excusable homicides.

Estimation of the number of CLDHs varies widely from city to city, from 1.6 to 19.5 percent of intentional, non-police homicides in six jurisdictions Kleck studied. Detroit and Dade County, Florida, were in the middle range. Kleck tried to extrapolate the number of CLDHs nationally from those two jurisdictions. One way was to determine the ratio of CLDHs to murder and non-negligent manslaughter. There were .1365 CLDHs to each murder and NNM in 1980. Multiplying .1365 by the total murders and non-negligent manslaughters in 1980 gave Kleck an estimate of 3,146 civilian legal defensive homicides.

The 1980 homicide rate—10.2 per 100,000—was the highest for any year between 1960 and 1995. There were 23,040 murders and non-negligent homicides known to the police.[33] According to Kleck's calculations, some 3,000 of those killings were justifiable. If we deduct 3,000 from the total, we get 20,000 murders and non-negligent manslaughters, giving the United States a rate of 8.8 per 100,000 instead of 10.2. This would give the United States a lower homicide rate than some European countries, assuming the Europeans don't fold excusable and justifiable homicides into their murder and non-negligent homicide figures the way we do. Police procedures being somewhat different from country to country, that's not an unreasonable assumption. (More on this later.)

Kleck tried another method of estimation. There were 145 CLDHs in Dade County and Detroit in 1980, but only 36 were reported to the FBI as civilian justifiable homicides. Extending that nationally would mean that for every CJH counted by the FBI, there were 4.167 CLDHs. He multiplied the 423 recorded CJHs by 4.167 and got an estimate of 1,704 CLDHs.

Of the 423 CJHs, 89.6 percent involved guns. Kleck multiplied his two estimates by that figure and got 2,819 legal defensive fatal shootings for the first estimate and 1,527 for the second. He concluded that people using guns to defend themselves killed between 1,500 and 2,800 attackers in 1980. Since only about 15 percent of gunshot wounds are fatal, he further estimated that legal defensive shooters wounded 8,700 to 16,600 attackers that year.[34]

SHOWING A GUN

Data indicate that guns are used far more than 16,000 times a year for defense. A person who confronts a would-be felon with a gun, or even fires a warning shot, would not be included in any of the estimates above. Several national surveys have been taken to determine how often guns have been used for defense by ordinary citizens. Some asked the respondent if he or she had *ever* used a gun in that way; others asked if such use occurred within five years. Some asked about the respondent's personal use; others about such use by anyone in the household. Because time makes memory fade, the surveys with a five-year time limit are no doubt more accurate than those that ask about lifetime experience.

Two of the most informative surveys are one taken by Hart Research Associates, Inc. in 1981 and one by Gary A. Mauser in 1990. The Hart survey asked, "Within the past five years, have you yourself or another member of your household used a handgun, even if it was not fired, for self-protection or the protection of property at home, work or elsewhere, excluding military service or police work?" Six percent of the respondents said they had. The next question was whether they were defending against a person or an animal. Of the total sample, 2 percent said "animal," 3 percent said "person," and 1 percent said "both." In other words, 4 percent were defending against persons. The Mauser survey asked essentially the same questions. It found that someone in 3.8 percent of the households had used a gun defensively against a person in the previous five years. The difference could have been due to sampling error, or it might reflect slightly less use of guns nine years later.[35] In 1980, the Bureau of the Census listed 80,622,000 households in the United States. Four percent of that is

3,224,880. So, according to the Hart survey, more than three million persons used guns defensively in the 1975–80 period. That would be an average of almost 650,000 instances a year. That figure, incidentally, is just slightly higher than the number of times a gun was used in a crime in the same period, according to the *Uniform Crime Reports*.[36]

It would appear, then, that handguns, even those kept strictly for defensive purposes, have a use. That's especially true if the user is a woman, in spite of the horror expressed by the Violence Policy Center in Sugarmann and Rand's *Cease Fire* at the firearms companies marketing guns for women.[37] In fiction or films, the woman who brandishes a gun is often disarmed by a man. In real life, that almost never happens. Lorraine Copeland, a Canadian authority on rape and director of the Queen's Bench Foundation Rape Victimization Project, told Carol Ruth Silver, an American civil rights lawyer, that to the best of her knowledge, a prospective rapist has *never* disarmed a gun-armed woman.[38]

A favorite statement of gun control advocates, when they have run out of other arguments, is that if additional gun controls save only one life they would be worth it. It's about time to think about how many lives may be *lost* because of some gun controls.

DETERRENCE

From October 1966 to March 1967, the Orlando, Florida, police department, facing an epidemic of rape, trained thousands of women in the use of guns, especially pistols. The program was well publicized. Rape decreased by 88 percent in 1967,[39] and in 1968, Orlando was the only city of 100,000 or more to report a decrease in violent crime.[40]

Responding to retail businessmen's complaints about store robberies, police in Kansas City, Missouri, conducted pistol training for 138 area merchants from September through November 1967. The next year, robbery increased 35 percent in Missouri outside the Kansas City area and 30 percent nationally. It did not increase in Kansas City and dropped 13 percent in Kansas City suburbs.[41]

In Detroit, during the same period, a merchants' association undertook to train its members—over the strong protests of the chief of police. That, too, turned back a rising wave of retail robberies.[42]

When Kennesaw, Georgia, passed an ordinance requiring every household to have a gun, many urban Northeasterners predicted a wave of burglaries in the Atlanta suburb—thieves trying to steal the guns they now knew were in all houses. The exact opposite happened. Residential burglaries declined 89 percent. That was somewhat offset by burglaries of businesses, where the thieves knew there would be nobody inside who might shoot them.[43] (Few people live in stores.) Publicity about the Kennesaw ordinance was probably responsible for the sharp decline in home burglaries immediately after the ordinance passed. The benefits continued for years, however. Between 1981 and 1993, burglaries in Kennesaw dropped 16 percent.[44]

When James D. Wright and Peter H. Rossi surveyed convicted felons in prison, 74 percent agreed with the statement, "One reason burglars avoid houses when people are at home is that they fear being shot."[45] In the same survey, 57 percent also agreed with the statement, "Most criminals are more worried about meeting an armed victim than they are about running into the police."[46]

It is well known that the United States has a relatively high crime rate. Not so well known is that the United States has one of the world's lowest rates of one type of crime—burglaries of occupied houses. In 1977, 48 percent of all burglaries in the Netherlands were of occupied homes. In the United States, the rate was 9 percent. In 1982, 59 percent of all burglaries attempted in England and Wales, and 29 percent of those completed were of occupied homes. In 1978 in Toronto, where gun ownership is much lower than the Canadian average, 44 percent of the residential burglaries occurred while someone was at home, and 21 percent of these resulted in a confrontation between the criminal and an occupant.[47]

The U.S. burglary rate in general is very low. Here, according to Interpol, are the burglary rates (instances per 100,000 population) of all types of burglaries for the United States and seven countries with which the United States is often compared: Japan, 2,351.2; New Zealand, 2,243.1; Scotland, 2,178.6; Australia, 1,754.3; England and Wales, 1,639.7; Canada, 1,420.6; United States, 1,263.7; and Switzerland, 976.8.[48]

The two last-place countries have something in common. In Switzerland, every man from 21 to 50 is in the militia and must—by law—keep a gun in the house. In the United States, every other house contains a gun. The American burglar doesn't know which home has a gun and which doesn't. All householders benefit because some Americans have guns.

But what if nobody had guns? That's something to consider.

CHAPTER 19

CONSIDERING THE ALTERNATIVE

LOOK-WHAT-HAPPENS-IN-AMERICA

Colin Greenwood, a superintendent of the West Yorkshire Metropolitan Police in England, in 1978 wrote an article entitled "Another Syndrome" for a British sporting magazine. This new syndrome he called the Look-What-Happens-in-America Syndrome. As an example, he quoted an official of the Home Office (the branch of government responsible for the police) who was asking for further controls on firearms:

"I can only say that in America, where there are no controls, there were in 1974, 197,752 robberies involving the use of a firearm," she said. "In England and Wales, there were 645 such robberies that year."[1]

On this, Greenwood commented: "Most Americans would be more than a little surprised to learn that there are no gun controls in their country. In fact there are rather more than 20,000 at Federal, State and local levels which are concerned with the acquisition, ownership and carrying of firearms."[2]

The Violence Policy Center says of those 20,000 regulations, "What is rarely mentioned is that most of those laws do not relate to firearms sale or possession, but have to do with zoning regulations for guns stores, the transport and discharge of firearms within municipal boundaries, etc."[3] Like much of what the Violence Policy Center says, this ain't necessarily so. There are very, very few zoning regulations concerning gun stores. (In my 12 years as both a town and a regional planning and zoning commissioner, I have never seen any.) And if laws concerned with transport and use don't relate to possession, to what do they relate? And what is "etc."? After you've covered purchase, possession, transport, and use, there's nothing left to regulate.

The British, of course, can be excused for

not knowing much about U.S. gun laws. As we'll see in the chapter on public opinion polls, most Americans don't know much about them, either. But it is curious that members of the anti-gun lobby can be ignorant of a matter that apparently concerns them so vitally. Still, Josh Sugarmann of the VPC can write of "the *widespread and virtually unregulated* [emphasis added] distribution of a hazardous consumer product [handguns]."[4]

As a matter of fact, there is not one of the fifty states or the District of Columbia that does not have gun laws—usually of mind-boggling complexity. Every state but Vermont requires a permit to carry a concealed weapon. In addition, 27 states and the District of Columbia forbid carrying guns openly. In New York, the state permit does not permit carriage in the state's largest city. Until 1995, that was true in Pennsylvania, too. More than half of the states had waiting periods for handguns before the Brady law. Eight states have waiting periods for long guns, too. Nine states in 1993 and 16 states in 1994 had instant background checks—that measure the anti-gun lobby said was impossible. Ten states have termed a variety of guns "assault weapons," "Saturday night specials," and "high-capacity" weapons, put them on lists that do not necessarily correspond to the federal list, and banned them outright. In 27 states, records of sales are sent to the police. That's theoretically true in the District of Columbia, too, but in practice, sales are totally eliminated. There is registration of pistols in eight places and of long guns in five. No state's permit to carry is good in another state. South Carolina and Virginia limit the number of handguns that can be purchased by one individual to one a month.[5]

In addition to these state laws, there are a host of local laws. In some Chicago suburbs, as we've seen, possession of a handgun is absolutely outlawed. Sales of handguns are prohibited in Chicago. In New York City, only a tiny minority of the rich and celebrated can legally possess a handgun or a semiautomatic rifle. Some cities in Ohio and Illinois have banned certain types of guns.[6]

Enforcement varies. In 30 states, licenses are issued at the discretion of the issuing authority. In 13 of those, the issuing authorities almost never issue licenses. Issuance of carry permits in the state of New York is restrictive, but in the city of the same name, it's practically impossible to get a permit. (It's almost impossible to get a permit to even possess a pistol.) In 15 states (including the District of Columbia), a prospective purchaser has to have a license to buy a handgun, and in seven states, to buy a long gun. In some states, the issuing authority must give the license to anyone who meets statutory requirements. In other states, the authority may issue the permit or not, at its discretion. The state of New Jersey is extremely restrictive on both handguns and long guns.[7]

England and Wales (Scotland has a separate body of law) are often held up as models to emulate by the anti-gun lobby. Superintendent Greenwood, however, says [legal] private ownership of handguns in New York City "is far below the level of such ownership in any part of England. At least four cities, New York, Chicago, Detroit, and Washington, have gun control measures which are much more stringent than anything found in England."[8] Then the police superintendent throws in a zinger: "Incidentally, over 20% of the country's homicides are committed in those four cities, though they have only 6% of the population."[9]

HOW EFFECTIVE ARE GUN LAWS?

Since Greenwood wrote his article, the percentage of national homicides committed in those four cities has dropped to 17 percent. But the populations of the cities have also dropped proportionately. In general, though, Greenwood's point about the effectiveness of gun control is still good. Among states and the District of Columbia, the worst homicide rates tend to be among the states with the most restrictive gun laws.

The worst homicide rate among states (including the District of Columbia) in the United States—a horrific 78.5 persons per 100,000—belongs to the District of Columbia, the most restrictive major jurisdiction in the United States.[10] No resident can legally acquire a handgun, and very few get permits for long guns. Louisiana, runner-up in the homicide sweepstakes with 20.3 cases per 100,000, has relatively mild gun laws, but that's not typical of the ten most murder-ridden states. Where Louisiana is typical is in the official attitude toward carrying a pistol. According to the U. S. Department of Justice, Louisiana has one of the 13 most restrictive permit systems in the United States.[11] Mississippi, third on the list, is more relaxed than most of these states about guns, but it requires the registration of both pistols and center-fire rifles. New York, fourth on the list, has a moderately restrictive permit system except in New York City, which is almost as restrictive as Washington, D.C. New York City, incidentally, accounts for 81.7 percent of all the murders in the state.[12] California, the fifth worst with 13.1 per 100,000, invented the "assault weapon" ban. It has the longest waiting period, for both handguns and long guns, and rarely grants permits to carry. Right behind it, with a rate of 12.7, is Maryland, home of the gun-hating Neil Behan, chief of the Baltimore County police, the Saturday night special ban, waiting periods for both handguns and long guns, and an extremely restrictive permit-to-carry system. Baltimore accounts for more than half of the murders in the state. Texas, with 11.9 killings per 100,000, until 1995 prohibited carrying a concealed handgun. Now it gives permits to carry concealed guns to those who are not felons, insane, drug addicts, fugitives, or aliens and who can pass an examination testing their knowledge of guns and gun safety.[13] Eighth is Alabama, with 11.6, followed by Georgia and Illinois with 11.4. The two Deep South states both have less stringent gun laws than most of the most murderous states. Tied with Georgia for ninth place, however, Illinois has virtually every gun restriction practiced in the

United States, plus one huge city and a number of small towns that ban handguns outright.

The ten least murderous states present a contrast. Maine, with 1.6 murders and non-negligent homicides per 100,000, has no waiting period but that provided by the Brady law and permits open carriage of handguns without a permit and concealed carriage with a mandatory permit system. North Dakota, with 1.7 murders and non-negligent homicides, is as relaxed as Maine. New Hampshire, third safest state with a rate of 2.0, has an instant background check and a mandatory (no official discretion) carry permit system. Iowa, with a rate of 2.3, has a permit-to-purchase system for handguns that is, in effect, a three-day waiting period. It does not issue carry permits freely. Idaho, with 2.9 murders and non-negligent homicides per 100,000, on the other hand, is as permissive as any state but Vermont. Montana, just behind Idaho with 3.0 per 100,000, is no more restrictive than Idaho. A third Rocky Mountain state, Utah, has a rate of 3.1 per 100,000. It has an instant background check, issues concealed carry permits freely, but requires that pistols carried openly without a permit be unloaded. South Dakota and Wyoming are tied for eighth place, with 3.4 homices per 100,000 each. Wyoming has no waiting period except that required by the Brady law and issues carry permits freely. It has no prohibition against carrying pistols openly. South Dakota has a waiting period of two days before obtaining a handgun, but that does not apply if the applicant has a carry permit. Carry permits are issued freely, and there is no prohibition against carrying pistols unconcealed. Vermont, tenth of the safest states with 3.6 murders and non-negligent homicides per 100,000, has one basic gun law: no one may carry a gun with the intention of harming someone else. The only waiting period is the one mandated by the Brady law, and no permit is required to carry a pistol either concealed or openly.[14]

In summary, five of the ten states with the worst murder rates have the most stringent gun laws in the United States. All are more restricted than nine of the ten states with the lowest murder rates. Those nine states have the least restrictive gun laws in the country. It might be supposed that gun laws really have very little effect on homicide.

Studies of towns in Illinois—big, medium, and small—tend to confirm that suspicion. In April 1982, Chicago prohibited possession of any handguns not previously registered with the police. In 1982, there were 384 homicides in Chicago. The next year, there were 428. The trend continued upward with only a couple of dips. In 1993, there were 629 murders and non-negligent homicides. Evanston, a medium-size Chicago suburb, banned handguns in 1982. Its robbery rate rose 8 percent by the end of 1982. By the end of 1992, the robbery rate had increased 33 percent. Its homicide rate remained steady, but the homicide rate in other U.S. suburbs declined 11 percent. Oak Park, a small Chicago suburb, has seen its burglary rate increase 35 percent since it banned handguns.[15] Nationally, the burglary rate has declined 28 percent.[16]

Authorities in cities like New York and Washington, of course, always argue that the killers in their towns get their guns in other states "where the gun laws are lax." There are a couple of flaws in that argument.

The first is that it is absolutely illegal to buy a handgun in a state in which you are not a resident. (Residents of adjacent states can buy long guns, but rifles and shotguns figure in very little crime.) Violating that law brings ten years in a federal prison, no matter how "lax" the laws in the state of purchase may be.

And the laws in those states really aren't lax. Ohio, often singled out as the state where New York criminals get their guns, has about every gun restriction known to the human race, including out-and-out prohibition in some municipalities. Virginia has also been attacked as the source for guns in both the New York and Washington underworld. Virginia has one of the most restrictive sets of state gun laws in the country. It's one of two states with a one-handgun-per-month law, which brought howls from the NRA but which greatly hampers gunrunners.

The third flaw is that if guns are so easily available in places like Virginia and Ohio, why don't the homicide rates there—Virginia, 8.3, and Ohio, 6.0 [17]—even approach those of Washington and New York?

There has to be a reason why the homicide rate is so high in cities like Washington and New York, but it has nothing to do with gun laws. It has nothing to do with race, either: Virginia has an enormous African-American population. It has everything to do with poverty, broken families, and loss of hope.

WHAT IF?

The anti-gun lobby says there would be none of this "leakage" of guns into the metropolitan centers if there were uniform national gun laws (meaning, probably, uniform national prohibition). Ignore, for the moment, the possibilities of smuggling, bootleg manufacture, and other means of evading a gun prohibition. Suppose that all handguns except those for the police and the military were made to disappear. Would robbers who previously toted pistols give up their trade? Or would they buy long guns and hacksaws? Cutting most of the stock and most of the barrel off a rifle or shotgun makes it much more concealable. It's not something you can carry in your pocket, but it can be tucked into the belt and hidden by a bulky coat, carried in a bag or a briefcase, or disguised as a bundle. If the robber has to use such a weapon, it would be four times more deadly than a pistol.[18] James Wright and Peter Rossi found that the worst of the convicts they surveyed in prison (chapter 18), would do just that. Of the felons they termed "predators," three-quarters said that if pistols were unavailable, they would saw off a long gun.[19]

A totally effective handgun prohibition, then, would leave the armed robber with three alternatives: (1) Go into another line of work. This is the least probable. (2) Obtain a long gun and cut it down. This would quadruple the number of murders committed in the course of a robbery. (3) Instead of a gun, use a knife or a club. This would have several effects, almost all of them bad.

First, robbers with guns are much more likely to rob commercial establishments than robbers with less effective weapons. The loot from these robberies is greater than that from robberies of individuals. To maintain his standard of living, therefore, the robber without a gun would have to commit more robberies. Such a robber looks for the frail elderly, the crippled, or other easy victims. A knife-armed robber is more likely to wound his victim than one with a gun. One who uses a club is likely to attack first, catching the victim by surprise, and then taking the valuables. One criminologist found that gun-armed robbers injured their victims in 17 percent of the cases; knife-wielders, in 32 percent; and those using other weapons (clubs or fists) in 53 percent of the robberies. Serious injuries occurred in .3 percent of the gun robberies, .4 percent of the knife robberies, and .7 of the "other weapons" robberies.[20]

Presumably the object of handgun prohibition is not to make life safer for bankers and storekeepers and much more hazardous for old ladies. That's what it would do, though, if robbers gave up guns. If, instead of giving up their pistols, they switched to rifles and shotguns, the only result would be a lot more dead bodies.

As for domestic disputes, it's just as easy to pick up a rifle or shotgun as a pistol. And it's much more lethal. There are a lot more rifles and shotguns around than pistols, and new ones are no more expensive.

What if all guns, long and short, were magically eliminated?

That would, as we've seen, ensure that life would become more hazardous for old ladies—and old gentlemen, too. There would certainly be an increase in burglaries of occupied houses. Such burglaries would probably be at least as frequent as they now are in Toronto, England, or the Netherlands. In domestic disputes, women would be even worse off than they are now. A knife can never be as efficient an equalizer as a gun. In general, there would be at least as much violence as there is now. Getting rid of the tools is not the same as getting rid of the impulses that lead to the misuse of those tools.

Changing the hardware is a poor substitute for changing murderous proclivities. English society in the thirteenth century was even more unsettled than American society today. War between the monarchy and the barons had its effect on the lives of the common people. The old certainties of medieval life were disappearing; law and order began to break down. The result was a homicide rate almost three times higher than that of the present-day United States. The murderers were poor, disturbed, despairing, and often alcoholic. Their victims were their relatives and acquaintances. None of the murderers, of course, had guns. They killed their victims with knives, agricultural tools, or large rocks.[21] Knives, axes, pitchforks, and brush hooks are just as deadly today as they were in the 1200s. And there's no way to ban rocks.

Because all the men wore knives, some commentators have blamed the prevalence of knives for the high homicide rate. But all men carried knives in the century before and the century after, and the homicide rate was lower. In more modern times, in some African societies, every man was expected to carry a spear—a more deadly weapon than a knife—but those societies had remarkably low homicide rates.[22]

It's true that without guns there would be no more "drive-by" shootings—a type of crime that has been greatly exaggerated by the press. But how about "drive-by" bombings? There are a large number of books now on the market describing how to make explosives and bombs. One publisher's catalogue lists 46 of them.[23]

Of course, there will be no magical disappearance of all guns, nor even of all handguns. There is no magic in the real world. Let's look at that real world.

THE PROBLEM THAT WON'T GO AWAY

Suppose the federal government were to pass a national version of the Morton Grove ordinance (see chapter 10). And suppose it were to apply to all guns, not just handguns. What would happen?

One thing that would *not* happen would be that all those guns would be turned in. Some of them, war souvenirs and the like, have never been registered. Some were registered as many as 30 or 40 years ago. Many of them have new owners. Some have had several owners since they were registered. Some states have required individuals transferring guns to notify the authorities, but these requirements have been widely ignored. The BATF has said it can trace 90 percent of all guns sold since 1968.[24] It meant tracing individual guns, such as those involved in a crime. That sort of trace may involve interviewing a number of previous owners. To attempt to trace between 100 million and 200 million guns that way would be impossible.

The chances are that a very large number of guns would remain hidden. The number of guns turned in could be much larger if the government would pay fair market value for them, but that would cost billions of dollars. Even then, some gun owners would keep their weapons. People who have guns solely for target shooting or hunting would be most likely to turn their weapons in because those sports would be forbidden. Collectors would be more likely to keep their guns. Criminals, for whom guns are capital equipment, would be the last to surrender their guns.

Guns that have been withheld for one reason or another might well enter the black market. Proscribed drugs now retail for more than 100 times their true value. The same kind of inflation would no doubt affect the price of black market guns. Look what happened to the price of Glock 17 magazines overnight (chapter 17)—and that was only a magazine, not a gun. In 1979, when there were fewer guns in the country, Mark K. Benenson, a civil rights lawyer and student of crime, estimated that a 95 percent reduction in the number of handguns would still leave 20 handguns for each violent criminal in the country.[25] When you consider that a well-cared-for gun can last several lifetimes, it's obvious that gun prohibition will not quickly end crime.

It will take even longer than that. An unmechanical dolt with two left hands can make a single-shot, muzzle-loading pistol with a bit of pipe, a piece of wood, some string, a nail or two, a couple of inches of heavy wire, and a rubber band. Crushed match heads, instead of gunpowder, could propel a large chunk of metal or many small bits of metal. A match or a smoldering cord could provide the ignition. With slightly more skill, he could make his own black powder and primer mixture. Even so, such a gun would be hopelessly inefficient compared to a modern weapon. Used against someone without a gun, however, it would be the Ultimate Weapon. If cartridges are available—either factory-made or reloaded cases—the same inept mechanic could make a traditional zip gun. Against unarmed people, that too would be effective. Only the police would be relatively safe.

Someone with skill and a few tools could do far better. A clandestine film made during World War II shows members of the Resistance assembling submachine guns from parts manufactured at night in a Danish machine shop. Today, on Pakistan's Northwest Frontier, tribesmen with the most primitive tools make copies of Lee Enfield bolt-action rifles, semiautomatic pistols, and AK-47s. They may not be as accurate or durable as the original models, but they'd be quite sufficient to commit any sort of crime. And holders of these weapons would be able to shoot it out with the police.

These underground gun manufacturers would be something like American cultivators of marijuana or producers of "designer" drugs. They would be competing with products smuggled in from abroad. Belgium, the Czech Republic, Germany, Italy, Spain, and other European countries, plus Argentina and Brazil, now produce tons of guns for the U.S. market. It would be naive in the extreme to suppose that no one would try to smuggle these weapons into the country.

On May 22, 1996, in San Francisco, more than 90 Customs and BATF agents seized 2,000 fully automatic AK-47 rifles worth $4 million. They had been produced by Norinco and Polytech, two Chinese government arms factories. This, the U.S. authorities said, was not the first Chinese shipment of illegal weapons into the United States. The market for automatic weapons in this country is infinitesimal compared with the market for standard rifles, shotguns, and pistols. If *all* guns were made illegal, we could expect a tremendous increase in smuggling.[26]

There's another consideration, too. All drug smugglers are outlaws in their own countries. That's not true of gun makers. Many of them, like the Chinese organizations, are government-owned. Most of the rest are government-subsidized. All are considered eminently respectable. The U.S. officials would not say whether all the management of the Chinese factories was involved in the shipment or whether it was directed by a few crooked bureaucrats. You can bet that evidence showing Chinese government involvement will never appear. And you can also bet that if widespread smuggling of weapons into the United States began, the great gun factories of Europe, Latin America, and the Far East would never achieve the pariah status of the Cali and Medellín cartels.

Like drugs, guns and ammunition take up very little space, and, under prohibition, their "street value" would be astronomical. Smugglers annually bring in tons of drugs. They could do the same with guns and ammunition. The profits possible in the illegal gun trade would also bring the Pakistani and Afghan copyists into the market. Those profits, like those from illegal heroin, would greatly increase the flow of contraband from those Middle Eastern countries.[27]

It's true that most drugs are sold to addicts. But there are people addicted to violence, too. Like many hard-core drug addicts, they live in inner cities. For many people, a gun has become both a way to earn a living and a symbol of status. Such people will pay a healthy price for a gun and for the ammunition to make it effective. Serving their needs will enormously increase the numbers of one type of criminal specialist, the gunrunner. All gunrunners by definition are armed, and, competing for the huge and profitable illegal gun market, they would be at least as violent as our current illegal drug dealers.

A national gun prohibition, then, could be expected to increase violent crimes against those least able to protect themselves and to create virtually a new class of violent criminals. Those, certainly, are not the aims of people who tell pollsters they favor "more gun control."

CHAPTER 20

UNDERWHELMING POPULAR DEMAND

WHAT WAS THAT AGAIN?

According to "An Analysis of Public Attitudes Toward Handgun Control," a report prepared by Cambridge Reports, Inc., a well-known polling firm, "It is clear that the vast majority of the public (both those who live with handguns and those who do not) want handgun licensing and registration."[1]

According to "Attitudes of the American Electorate Toward Gun Control in 1978," by Decision Making Information, Inc., another well-known polling firm, "Majorities of American voters believe that we do *not* need more laws governing the possession and use of firearms and that more firearms laws would *not* result in a decrease in the crime rate."[2]

Both reports were based on surveys taken by reputable polling firms and taken at about the same time. The Cambridge report was commissioned by the Center for the Study and Prevention of Handgun Violence (CSPHV), an anti-gun group run by a collection of prominent anti-gun lobbyists. The DMI report was sponsored by the NRA. Nevertheless, in spite of their diverse sponsorship, both surveys used impeccable procedures, and their results are statistically valid.

To know how this can happen is to know how polling companies can keep busy taking surveys for groups as different as the CSPHV and the NRA.

One of the first things all poll designers learn is that the opinions of most people on most subjects are held very lightly. People are polled on an enormous number of subjects, from gun control to their state's policy on garbage disposal. Most of these subjects come to mind only when a representative of a polling company asks about them.

Gun control—in spite of all the protestations of both the anti-gun lobby and the gun lobby—is a subject most Americans do not think about much. A Harris poll taken in February 1994 asked "What do you think are the two most important issues for the government to address?" and "What do you think are the two most serious problems facing the country?" To the first question, 3 percent answered "gun control." That compares with 45 percent who answered "health care." There were 12 more subjects considered more important. On the second question, only 4 percent thought gun control was one of the most serious problems. It got the same rating as sex on television, with nine other subjects, such as health care, employment, and drugs, ahead of it.[3]

For years, polling companies have asked respondents if they thought gun laws should be more strict. One trouble with that question is that there's no separation of respondents from areas with strict controls, like New York City, or with few controls, like Vermont. What would be less strict for one would be stricter for another. More basic, most respondents don't know what the current gun laws are. The only poll that ever measured public knowledge of federal gun laws found that 79 percent of the public couldn't identify three out of five of the most basic federal restrictions on gun sales. That's a poorer score than a body of totally ignorant respondents would get by just guessing.[4] A local poll in Missouri had respondents favoring stricter gun controls. But follow-up questions on what sort of controls they would like produced a surprise. The respondents thought some of the laws that had been in existence for 65 years (unknown to them) were too strict. The results of this poll were published in a St. Louis paper under the headline, "Voters Back Gun Control."[5] Media bias? Perish the thought.

In general, people who hold opinions lightly are liable to endorse measures that they think will not adversely affect themselves or their neighbors. These are the measures that criminologists James Wright, Peter Rossi, and Kathleen Daly call "Why Not?" items.[6]

The way a question is worded can greatly affect the answer if the subject is one the respondent does not care much about and has not really thought about. The Cambridge Reports survey asked respondents if they favored several measures. One was to "Require prospective handgun purchasers to get a permit or license to purchase." A majority (72 percent) favored that measure. The DMI survey asked the question differently: "Would you favor or oppose a law giving police the power to decide who may or may not own a firearm?" Only 31 percent favored such a law.[7]

Many of the respondents in both surveys lived in areas that require a permit to purchase a handgun. In many of these jurisdictions, a permit is given automatically if the prospective purchaser is not a convicted criminal, a drug addict, or in some other legally proscribed category. Such permit laws affect nobody except those most people think should not have a gun anyway. In other areas, though—New York City is the prime example—the police *do* decide who may or may not own a firearm. That kind of selective law enforcement proved to be objectionable to most people.[8]

Another example of how wording affects answers is a question used by Gallup repeatedly: "Here is a question about pistols and revolvers. Do you think there should or should not be a law which forbids the possession of this type of gun except by police *and other authorized persons*" [emphasis added]. In 1988, 37 percent endorsed the idea. "Other authorized persons" could be construed by some respondents to mean those who have pistol permits. That this is indeed the case is indicated by a similar question in a Time/CNN survey in 1989, just seven months later. The Time/CNN pollsters left out the "other authorized persons" and just asked about "making it illegal for civilians to own handguns." Only 28 percent favored that.[9]

Designers of polls would have to be pretty dumb—and none of them are—not to know how to phrase a question so that people will tend to give the desired answer.

PICK A SUBJECT—NOT JUST ANY SUBJECT

There are many varieties of what is called gun control. Picking the right ones to ask about is part of the pollster's art. In general, people seldom want more laws. "If it ain't broke, don't fix it" is a popular motto. So the DMI, but not the Cambridge, pollsters asked, "In general, would you say there are: already too many laws governing the possession and use of firearms, the present laws are about right, or that we need more laws"? The majority (54 percent) said there were too many laws (13 percent) or that the present number was about right (41 percent). Those who wanted more laws were 44 percent, and 2 percent didn't know.[10]

Taking advantage of the same public feeling about laws, the Cambridge people asked an entirely different question: would their respondents favor "a crackdown on illegal sales?" A total of 85 percent favored a crackdown—72 percent strongly, 13 percent somewhat.[11] People don't want *more* laws; they think the ones we have are about right, but they want those laws enforced.

Registration and licensing are popular subjects for pollsters representing gun control advocates. That's because most respondents are familiar with automobile registration and driver licensing. Neither of these measures makes anyone feel his or her freedom is being jeopardized. Even public officials (who should, and probably do, know better) make registering cars and guns, and licensing drivers and shooters, sound like the same thing. Interestingly, respondents don't think registering guns will do much, if anything, to reduce crime, but they favor it anyway. That's true of many gun laws, not just registration. A 1990 national survey showed that 46 percent of the people favoring more gun control laws did not believe the laws would reduce crime even slightly.[12] Criminologist James D. Wright concludes:

Just as licensing and registration seem to have very little effect in reducing automobile accidents, so too do most people anticipate that stricter weapons control would have little or no effect on crime. . . . The underlying concept here seems to be that weapons, as automobiles, are intrinsically dangerous objects that governments ought to keep track of for that reason alone.[13]

What escapes most respondents is that there is a reason for registering cars—to identify vehicles involved in crime. The license plate obtained through registration is clearly visible; a gun's serial number is not. There's an entirely different reason for local registration of guns—to facilitate their confiscation. Respondents in all surveys are overwhelmingly against banning or confiscating common handguns and long guns, but majorities favor registration. For them, registration is a "Why Not?" subject. Also, they feel that factory and retail sales records constitute registration, as, in one sense, they do. Such recording seemingly presents no threat. But there are other types of registration. New York's registration of rifles and shotguns was a prelude to making it illegal to possess certain types of long guns.

Several years ago, the city of Cleveland demonstrated the utility of local registration. In 1976, the city council banned all handguns with barrels shorter than three inches and calibers smaller than .32. A municipal judge declared that this "Saturday night special law" was unconstitutional because it discriminated against the poor. The Cleveland city council then passed a handgun registration ordinance. While residents were registering their pistols, the city appealed the decision on its SNS law. A higher court upheld the original law, and once again all the handguns originally banned were illegal. The police then told everybody who had registered such guns that their registration cards were revoked. They had to immediately dispose of the guns, give them to the police, or have them confiscated.[14]

Another theory about why such measures as gun registration are popular is that, although they won't do much to stop crime, "we have to do something." That's sometimes called "sending a message." The message, of course, is that "we don't like crime." But nobody does, not even criminals—except the crimes they profit from. Most people recognize that this is a futile activity, but if it doesn't hurt anyone, "Why Not?"

The situation is not, as Cambridge Reports implies, that a majority of people are clamoring for gun registration and licensing. They're simply saying, "Why Not?"

REDNECK CONTROL

Nevertheless, it seems likely that a minority of the public actively desires more restrictions on gun ownership, even while they recognize that these measures will not affect the crime rate. The reason for this is the feeling that some people who do not own guns have about gun owners as a class. Surveys show that more men than women own guns and that more rural people than urban people do. More people from the South and the Rocky Mountain states own guns than people from the Northeast. But other than sex and geography, there are few differences between gun owners and non-gun owners. On the average, gun owners are slightly more affluent and slightly better educated than non-gun owners, but the margin is very small. And it's most unlikely that gun ownership is a causal factor. Study after study has tried to discern a link between gun ownership and violent behavior. There is none.[15] Many non-gun owners, however, persist in believing that gun owners as a class are low-brow, violent ignoramuses, both reactionary and racist—in a word, rednecks, if not a "sordid race of gunsels."

Because of this, Gary Kleck writes, "[I]t is possible that some people support gun control as a way of stigmatizing another, disliked, group and its culture, using the criminal law to declare that some kinds of activities, such as owning guns, are shameful and morally objectionable, and should be limited for this reason alone. Some gun control support, therefore, would be unrelated to either the specifics of the particular measures asked about, or to concerns about reducing crime."[16]

EXPLOITATION OF IGNORANCE

Because most people don't think much about guns or gun control, they can be manipulated by those who do. Josh Sugarmann was totally candid in his paper on "assault weapons": because the public confused these cosmetic oddities with machine guns, it would be easy to ban them.

The free press, which is supposed to enlighten the public, has, as we've seen repeatedly, fallen down on the job. It's most unlikely that journalists are, as some NRA members think, part of a vast conspiracy to disarm the public. What would they gain? The problem is that most big newspapers and broadcasting stations are staffed by people who think the proper intellectual attitude toward guns (and for some, gun owners) is utter contempt. Consequently, they learn nothing about these contemptible objects. And so the public is bombarded with foolish stories about Saturday night specials, "assault weapons," "cop-killer" bullets, plastic guns, and other nonsense.

For this hokum, news people can be excused on the grounds of ignorance. It's harder to excuse the way they have exaggerated the incidence of crime at a time when crime is actually declining. In that case, there has been something to gain—more readers and higher ratings.

All of this has an effect on the poll respondent. A person who has no strong opinions on a subject gets his ideas from the news media. And such a person usually likes to think he agrees with the majority. All of this leads to such claims from the anti-gun lobby that "an overwhelming majority of the public wants a ban on assault weapons."

The only thing the average person knows about the guns labeled "assault weapons" is that they are horrible. She gets that impression from television and the newspapers. Ask that average person about "assault weapons." This is what she'll tell you:

Assault weapons—weapons designed to assault people—have no purpose except killing large numbers of people very quickly. They are the favored weapons of drug dealers, gangsters, and serial murderers. They are more powerful than any other weapon that can be held in the hands. They are available everywhere. They outgun the police and have been responsible for the slaughter of hundreds of police officers.

Of course, the press isn't alone in spreading this nonsense. The President of the United States, the attorney general, congressional leaders, and police chiefs have all been saying the same thing. But the press is supposed to set the record straight. It hasn't.

It's no wonder, then, that the polls show majorities favoring the banning of "assault weapons," although neither they nor the pollsters can explain what an "assault weapon" is. Polls also show majorities in favor of banning Saturday night specials, described by interviewers as "cheap, low quality handguns." It might be interesting to see what the public thinks about banning "cheap, low quality toasters."

Accepting poll results at face value can lead to serious mistakes. Sometimes the anti-gun lobby itself inadvertently shows how unreliable survey data can be. In 1978, the Carter administration was considering a national gun registration program. The National Coalition to Ban Handguns wrote to all its members—who also contacted their members. "This is our first opportunity in some time to show the Carter administration that the *majority* of the public wants reasonable gun control," they wrote [emphasis in original]. The National Council to Control Handguns (another anti-gun lobby group) wrote to its sympathizers, "The majority of Americans want stronger handgun control, but they must be heard. Write a letter or postcard. Urge friends and family to do the same." The NRA also urged its members to write. Congress got 7,800 letters and postcards supporting registration. It got 337,000 opposing it.[17]

That kind of experiment shows that opponents of gun control feel more strongly than advocates. But what about the great, largely uncommitted mass of voters? That's when gun control measures supposedly favored by the public are tested in the voting booth.

THE PEOPLE SPEAK—REFERENDA

A classic test of the validity of public opinion polls took place in Massachusetts in 1976. A referendum was held on whether to ban the possession of handguns in the state. Massachusetts, then considered the most "liberal" of the states, seemed to be the perfect place to introduce such a measure. In June 1976, the powerful *Boston Globe*, which ardently championed the ban, reported the ban was supported by 55 percent of the public. The NRA, of course, began campaigning against it, but its paid ads were matched by those of ban proponents. And the *Globe* and the Boston broadcasting stations gave the ban enormous free support. By September, public support had dropped to 40 percent. The *Globe* stepped up its "crusade." In October, support for the ban was up to 51 percent, the *Globe* reported. In November, the people voted. Only 29 percent voted for the ban.[18]

Such "devil guns" as Saturday night specials and "assault weapons" have proved to be less popular with the public than mainstream weapons. The state of Maryland banned small, cheap pistols called Saturday night specials. In 1988, a group of citizens introduced a referendum to repeal the ban. According to the polls, repeal didn't have a chance: it was behind three to one. What followed was one of the dirtiest modern campaigns in a state renowned for dirty politics. Repeal advocates concentrated on black areas of Baltimore, trying to convince people that the SNS ban was aimed at disarming black people and leaving them defenseless. Repeal opponents got the director of the Peace and Justice Commission of Baltimore's Roman Catholic archdiocese to write to all priests urging sermons supporting the ban. (Many gun-owning Catholics replied by dropping empty cartridge shells in the collection basket.)[19] As the campaign went on, the polls showed public support for the Saturday night special ban dropping from more than 60 percent to between 49 and 44 percent.[20] The day before election day, when pro-repeal workers were desperately calling supporters to get out the vote, Baltimore police raided the repeal campaign office, closed it, and carried off all its files. The files had been subpoenaed by Baltimore's chief prosecutor, who charged the repealers with "irregularities." No irregularities were ever proven, but the publicity from the raid was believed to have caused a massive switch in voter sentiment.[21] Repeal was defeated 58 to 42 percent.

Earlier the same year, the state of California put an initiative on the ballot that would "freeze" all handguns in the state. Under Proposition 15, no new handguns would be sold or manufactured in the state; no handguns could be brought into the state by individuals, either.

"The measure would have allowed handguns to be exchanged," Osha Gray Davidson writes, "and, as an additional sop to gun owners, forbidden the state legislature from passing legislation to confiscate existing handguns or to restrict the sale of rifles and shotguns.[22]

Some sop. No legislation can forbid the legislature from taking any action in the future. The legislature can always change its collective mind. A future legislature could forbid the sale of long guns. It could even confiscate all existing guns. But it could not give back guns it had confiscated and melted down.

Proposition 15 touched off another hurricane of conflicting claims, with all major news media predicting success for the freeze. So much pro-freeze information reached the East that it was something of a shock when the freeze lost 63 to 37 percent.[23]

In recent years, the idea of banning handguns locally has moved north from the Chicago area and into Wisconsin. In Wisconsin, however, the initiatives have not been taken solely by city or village councils. They have resulted in referenda. In 1993, Madison, a liberal university town, voted on a ban. The ban lost 51 to 49 percent in the referendum. That close vote may have encouraged handgun ban advocates, however. They introduced similar measures in Milwaukee and Kenosha the next year. The Milwaukee ban went down 67 to 33 percent, and Kenosha voters rejected the same idea 73 to 27 percent.[24]

All of which indicates that when gun control advocates talk about the public "demanding" this or that form of gun control, the statement should be taken with more than a grain of salt.

CHAPTER 21

DIGRESSION NO. 3: GUNS IN THE REST OF THE WORLD

MOST VIOLENT WHERE?

"The rest of the civilized world looks with horror on the lack of gun controls in the United States," wrote Pete Shields.[1]

In an article entitled "Death by Gun," *Time* asked, "How can America think of itself as a civilized society when day after day the bodies pile up amid the primitive crackle of gunfire across the land?"[2]

Rev. Robert Drinan, S. J., former congressman from Massachusetts, did not accuse the United States of being a disgrace to all civilization. Just to the Western nations: "Alone among the Western nations, the United States permits the unrestricted availability of handguns, and alone it suffers an astronomical crime rate."[3]

Father Drinan, a renowned legal scholar, was letting his hatred of guns overpower his scholarship. (Neither Shields nor *Time* has ever been accused of scholarship.) As we've seen, the availability of handguns is hardly unrestricted in the United States. And in only eight nations in the world—Albania, Cyprus, Greece, Guinea, Ireland, Morocco, Tanzania, and Russia—is there an unrestricted prohibition of handguns.[4] We'll examine gun laws in some other nations later in this chapter. But for now, how about violence? Is the United States really the most violent, or the most crime-ridden, country in the world? In the "civilized" world? Among the "Western nations"? Among the "industrialized nations?" Among the "advanced nations?"

The last category is often mentioned by those denouncing U.S. gun laws and violence, but it's a bit too vague to permit a good answer. What makes a nation "advanced"? Perhaps Japan would be considered advanced by most gun control advocates: it has almost no guns and a low homicide rate. But it also has a high suicide rate and an extraordinarily high burglary rate. And its police routinely conduct warrantless searches and torture prisoners. The Tokyo Bar Association charges, "Even in cases where suspects claimed to have been tortured and their bodies bore physical traces to back their claims, courts have still accepted their confessions." Of all those arrested, 95 percent confess to crimes. And they usually are not allowed even to read the confessions they sign. There is no right to trial by jury.[5] Amnesty International calls the Japanese practice of holding suspects without bail for up to 28 days a "flagrant violation of United Nations human rights principles." After the 28-day period is up, it may be renewed or the suspects rearrested. Some people have been held, interrogated, and tortured for several months before seeing a judge.[6] That's advanced?

One point about the low Japanese homicide rate is seldom mentioned: Japanese-Americans and Japanese citizens living in the United States, have a *lower* homicide rate than their relatives in Japan.

Britain's gun laws, in general, are stricter than those in the United States, and it, too, has a low level of homicide. Maybe it's advanced. But the British government censors newspapers, radio, and television broadcasts, and bans books. British television stations, for instance, cannot show old film clips of Eamon de Valera, because the late Irish leader was a member of the Irish Republican Army in the 1920s. The police can search anybody without what would be considered probable cause in the United States, and they can arrest anyone they "reasonably suspect" of "supporting" an illegal organization. Detention without trial has been used frequently in Northern Ireland. In Britain itself, under the 1989 Prevention of Terrorism Act, police can hold suspects for eight days without charges to interrogate them. The new Criminal Justice and Public Order Act lets a suspect's silence be used as evidence of his guilt. And juries are no longer told, as they are in the United States, to view skeptically the uncorroborated word of a criminal against the accused. Under the same act, the police, not a magistrate, set bail for a suspect. Under its Official Secrets Act, the British government can classify anything it cares to, and divulging such secrets is a major felony. There is no Freedom of Information Act. Torture has been a common police practice in Northern Ireland, and the fabrication of evidence is not unknown in Britain. Trial by jury for "political violence" has been abolished in Northern Ireland. Jury trial has also been abolished in Britain itself for almost all civil cases and most criminal cases. During the Gulf War, the song "Give Peace a Chance" was banned on the BBC.[7] Those who value civil rights would hardly call the United Kingdom advanced.

Maybe the United States is the most violent and criminal of the industrialized nations? But is Russia—that country with the orbiting space station—part of the Third World? In 1993, there were 29,900 murders in Russia—a country of 150 million.[8] The same year, the United States, a country of 255 million, had 24,530 cases of murder and non-negligent homicide.[9] The murder rate in Russia is more than double that of the United States. Fifty top executives of Russian corporations were murdered in 1993; about every business in Russia, from sidewalk peddlers to giant corporations, pays tribute to at least one of the hundreds of gangs comprising Russia's "Mafiya."[10] In the last few years, Russia passed the United States in the percentage of its people incarcerated, but crime continues to grow and murderers to thrive.

Although most Americans don't realize it, Brazil is a major industrial power. It's not only the greatest in South America, its industrial production exceeds that of most European nations. It certainly exceeds that of Australia, listed by HCI as one of "other industrialized countries."[11] Brazil exports manufactured goods of all types, from candy to cannons. And it sells them to the "developed" countries of Europe. Brazil is also one of the world's most crime-ridden and murderous nations. A Gallup survey there showed that 34 percent of all Brazilian families experienced some sort of crime, compared to 13 percent of families in the United States. Murder is so common that few killings are even mentioned on the TV news shows. Everett G. Martin, a *Wall Street Journal* reporter in Rio de Janeiro, wrote, "There is so much crime here, and so much toting of weapons, that news of violence just doesn't generate much excitement anymore."[12]

Brazil has trouble counting its homicides. "I don't have much confidence in our crime statistics," said João Baptista Peterson, a public prosecutor and advisor to Rio's state minister of justice.[13] Everyone, however, knows there is a lot of crime. Police even advise motorists in Rio de Janeiro and São Paulo not to stop for anything at night, not even traffic lights. Gallup ranks the country the second most violent in the world.[14]

Colombia is number one. Colombia does not belong to Interpol, so its homicide statistics are not available from that organization. It is known, though, that Medellín, a city of about a million, has about 5,000 murders a year.[15] That's a rate of 500 per 100,000. And most of them are *not* caused by the drug trade. Next to Medellín, Washington, D.C., looks like the Peaceable Kingdom.

Since Brazil and Colombia, as well as Mexico, another horrendously homicidal nation, are indisputably Western nations, that takes care of Drinan's accusation. In Mexico, the homicide rate (49.4 per 100,000) is about five times that of the United States.[16] If "Western" refers less to geography than to countries dominated by Europeans, we can't leave out South Africa. In 1989, South Africa had a homicide rate more than double that of the United States.[17] By 1995, the South African homicide rate had risen to ten times that of the United States.[18] Finally, take another look at Europe. In 1989, according to the World Health Organization, the United States had 10.8 homicides per 100,000, while East Germany had 36.7.[19] East Germany, of course, is no more, but all the East Germans didn't disappear.

The U.S. homicide rate from the WHO seems high. In 1989, according to the FBI's Uniform Crime Reports, the homicide rate was 8.7 per 100,000.[20] That's an unusually wide discrepancy. In 1980, the WHO gave the U.S. rating as 10.5, while the FBI's was 10.2.[21] The 1989 figure is probably the result of the World Health Organization not having kept up with the increase in the U.S. population.

If we take the actual number of murders and non-negligent homicides in the United States in 1989—21,500—and deduct an estimated 3,000 that proved to be justifiable or excusable (see chapter 18), we have 18,500 in a population of about 250 million for a rate of 7.4 per 100,000. That would put the United States below Sweden, as well as East Germany.[22]

Since the United States is not the most violent industrialized nation, nor the most violent Western nation, it can't be the most violent nation in the world, or even in civilization. Unless, that is, if by "advanced" and "civilized" you mean only those nations with low rates of violence. If you do, the assertion is a tautology.

Counting all known homicide and violent crime statistics, the United States is right in the middle. About half of the world's nations have higher homicide rates, and about half have lower rates.[23]

WAR . . . OR MURDER?

So far, we've been discussing only individual violence, the type usually called criminal violence. Both El Salvador and Zimbabwe have enormous homicide rates—129.4 per 100,000 in El Salvador and 126.2 per 100,000 in Zimbabwe.[24] In both of these countries, the homicide rate falls into a kind of twilight zone between criminality and war. Until recently, El Salvador was in the grip of a brutal civil war, with troops perpetrating massacres of entire villages and informal "death squads" murdering hundreds of people. Those unsolved and officially mysterious murders by the "death squads" were recorded as ordinary homicides. Probably the massacres by troops, which were officially denied, were also—if they were recorded at all. Zimbabwe, too, was the scene of fighting by various factions.

The gory massacres in Rwanda could also fall into this category because most of the killing seems to have been done not by troops but by ruffians supporting a political party. So far there's been no official body count, but the Rwandan homicide rate must be astronomical. The killings in Bosnia, including "ethnic cleansing," more nearly approximate war, a war of nonstop atrocities, like the Thirty Years War of the seventeenth century. It gets difficult at times to separate murder from war.

If one is to consider the violence quotient of individual countries, however, war must be considered. And when it is considered, the United States looks pretty good.

Take Europe, that continent so admired by the anti-gun lobby for its low homicide rates. (At least until Russia's murder rate exploded.) Europe has about the same area as the United States and about two-and-a-half times the population. It has had in this century, however, far more than twice the organized violence. There were, of course, two world wars fought with dreadful slaughter on European soil during the twentieth century. But there's been a lot more war than that.

Early in the century, the Balkan states fought the two Balkan Wars. Greece and Turkey fought a war right after World War I. So did Poland and the Soviet Union and Finland and the Soviet Union. Finland and the U.S.S.R. fought a separate war during World War II before either got into the big show. Ireland had an abortive rising in 1916, a successful war for independence after World War I, and a civil war immediately after that. Russia had two civil wars (not including the 1991 coup and counter coup). Both Germany and Austria had periods of confused fighting right after World War I that could be called civil wars. Spain had a civil war in the 1930s. Greece had another in the 1940s. Hungary's war for independence was crushed by the Soviet Union in 1956. There was a short, bloody war in Romania following the collapse of the Soviet Union. There is fighting now in some of the Caucasian nations that broke away from the Soviet Union. As this is being written, Russia, the U.S.S.R.'s largest successor state, is trying to establish an armistice with would-be secessionists in Chechnya. A truce ended more than a quarter of a century of low-key war in Northern Ireland, but at this writing, the cease-fire has broken down, bombs have gone off, and more low-key warfare may follow. In addition to all this fighting on European soil, European nations like Spain, France, Italy, Britain, Russia, and Germany carried war to Africa and Asia before and after World War I.

We've already looked at the European propensity for assassinating national leaders (chapter 8). Another European blood sport is called the "purge." Hitler's Germany purged six million Jews and about an equal number of Slavs, Gypsies, and Resistance members. Stalin's purges of kulaks and others came to some 20 million people. The Turks purged millions of Armenians in Europe and Asia Minor. And Russian purges of Jews, called pogroms, were conducted regularly to take the peasants' minds off their own troubles. And, of course, let's not forget the recent purges in what once was Yugoslavia.[25]

When you combine both individual and collective homicide, the United States is far behind the European average. Do strict gun control laws affect individual homicide, but not collective homicide? That's possible. But as we've seen in chapter 11, they haven't affected suicide. And how strict are those foreign laws, anyway? As we've seen in chapter 5, the laws of Switzerland are, by U.S. standards, anything but restrictive. Let's look at a few other countries.

BRITAIN

Before the First World War, there were no gun laws in Britain. The police were unarmed, and the homicide rate was so low as to be almost invisible. During the war, Defense of the Realm regulations required anyone purchasing a rifle, a pistol, or ammunition for either to get a permit.[26] The Easter Rising of 1916 in Dublin was followed by stringent controls on rifles and pistols in Ireland.

The Defense of the Realm regulations disappeared after the war. In Ireland, though, the war for independence, known to the Irish as the Black and Tan War, began in 1919.[27] Private ownership of guns in Ireland was all but prohibited while Britain was in control. After the foundation of the Irish Free State, the prohibition continued.[28] In 1920, the British government introduced the Firearms Act, which required all Britons desiring a rifle or pistol to show the police a need for ownership. Gradually, the police began adding further restrictions. All "firearms" (rifles and pistols, not shotguns) had to be stored in a secure place, and the police demanded the right to inspect how the weapons were stored. During all this time, the homicide rate remained at about the prewar level. There were no controls on shotguns, which an English police official called "a toy of the landed gentry."[29]

World War II started in 1939. In 1940, the British army was forced to evacuate the continent at Dunkirk, leaving most of its weapons behind. The British militia, neglected for centuries, was unarmed. The government issued buckshot cartridges of SG (equivalent of American 00) size to shotgun owners. Nevertheless, most of the older men who enlisted in Home Guard units had to drill with canes. No guns were available. The British government took out advertisements in the United States, asking American civilians to "send a gun to defend a British home."

Gun laws remained unchanged in the immediate postwar period. But in the 1960s, the crime rate, including murder and non-negligent manslaughter, began to rise. In 1967, England and Wales had 414 murders and non-negligent manslaughters.[30] In 1992, they had 689.[31] That's a 59 percent increase in 25 years. In spite of increasingly restrictive gun laws, however, the rate of gun killings has remained the same—between 8 and 10 percent of the total.[32] Of those gun murders, handguns are used in between 30 and 40 percent of the cases.[33]

A widely distributed Handgun Control, Inc. pamphlet proclaims, "In 1990, handguns killed 22 people in Great Britain . . . and 10,567 in the United States. God bless America."[34] The pamphlet doesn't mention that the United States has 4½ times the population of the United Kingdom or that handguns are used in about 3 or 4 percent of English murders and about 60 percent of U.S. murders.[35] The truth is bad enough. The U.S. murder rate is about ten times the English. But HCI's statistical juggling is thoroughly dishonest.

The British Criminal Justice Act of 1967 attempted to stop the increasing violence. It required a license to buy a shotgun and restricted shotguns with barrels shorter than 24 inches. Shotgun certificates were mandatory, however. If an applicant met the qualifications (98 percent did), the police had to issue a certificate. After obtaining a certificate, a purchaser could buy as many shotguns as he or she wanted, and the police were not notified. Pistols and rifles were further restricted. Only members of recognized shooting clubs could buy pistols. Prospective rifle owners found it harder and harder to convince the police they had a "good reason" for owning one. Self-defense is not considered a good reason for owning any kind of weapon in Britain. Rifle and pistol owners had to prove to the police that they had secure places, such as safes, to store their weapons. And to get a license, they had to follow police recommendations for storage. An owner of a rifle worth five pounds, therefore, might have to spend 100 pounds on a safe to store it. And an owner of several pistols might have to invest 1,000 pounds in an electronic security system. Once again, weapons were being restricted to the affluent. Another part of the 1967 act eliminated the requirement that a jury verdict be unanimous.[36]

In 1989, after a madman killed 16 people with a pistol and a semiautomatic rifle, the gun laws were tightened again. Shotguns were subject to the same storage requirements as rifles, and all shotguns were registered. Shotguns holding more than two rounds were subject to the same restrictions as rifles. Semiautomatic rifles were banned, as were pump-action rifles and shotguns with barrels under 24 inches. All banned guns were confiscated.

While it was restricting guns, the government attempted to do battle with knives. Sword canes, long a common weapon for urban Britons, were banned. So were double-edged knives with blades longer than three inches and martial arts weapons. In fact, carrying any sort of sharp object in a public place was forbidden. In 1991, an American woman was given a suspended prison sentence for using a penknife against men who attacked her on a subway.[37]

And how have all these laws affected the increasing violence and homicide in Britain? Violence and homicide are still increasing.

IRELAND

Ireland's gun laws are similar to Britain's. The country is much more restrictive on pistols: they are banned completely. Center-fire rifles are severely restricted. Ireland's attitude toward shotguns, however, is considerably more relaxed. In 1975, every room in a government-subsidized bed-and-breakfast in Straid, County Mayo, contained a fishing rod and a single-shot shotgun.[38] That was a convenience for guests who wanted to sample the famous (in Europe) fishing and shooting of western Ireland. A large proportion of those guests were aliens. Such a practice would be considered foolishly liberal anywhere in the United States.

Nevertheless, Ireland's homicide rate (two per 100,000) is below such low-homicide countries as Canada, Scotland, and Denmark.[39]

Ireland's gun laws resemble Britain's for at least two reasons. First, Ireland inherited British law, and during the civil war years and later when the IRA went underground, the government found it convenient to keep restrictions on guns. Second, Ireland is in much the same position regarding Britain as Finland is regarding Russia. Ireland and Finland are both small nations cheek by jowl with large, powerful nations they don't particularly like but can't afford to offend. One way to avoid offending Britain is to avoid giving any aid or comfort to the Irish Republican Army. Therefore, Ireland outlaws any military weapons in private hands, from rifles and pistols to antitank missiles; raids IRA arms caches; and vigorously tries to intercept any arms aimed at crossing its coasts or its border with Northern Ireland.

Britain, of course, is even more vigorously cracking down on privately held military weapons in Northern Ireland. Ireland is a small country and an island. The Irish navy is quite a respectable force for a nation that size, and all the waters around the island are patrolled by Britain's Royal Navy, which is still one of the world's largest.

If civilian guns were prohibited in the United States, there would no doubt be attempts to smuggle firearms in. The United States, with its long borders and thousands of miles of coast, is difficult to seal off. Ireland should be much easier. How well have the Irish and British governments succeeded in keeping guns from the Irish Republican Army? It's interesting to read what a leading British writer on intelligence matters says of the IRA:

What impresses the security forces is that this generation of IRA terrorists has an understanding of the technology of warfare that no other terrorist group in the world has demonstrated. Despite the restriction of operating on an island where all their arms have to be imported, they have managed to fight a war, which while not conclusive, has in their terms continued to be effective.[40]

Ireland is not the only example of the futility of trying to stop smuggled arms from entering even a small island. There's another, more extreme, example close to the United States.

JAMAICA

When Jamaica got its independence in 1962, it had a rather unremarkable homicide rate. It had a healthy democratic tradition and a strong judiciary. It had also, however, sharp class distinctions. There were distinctions not only between white and black, but between upper- and upper-middle class blacks and lower-class blacks. The upper-class blacks moved into positions that had been held by whites in past centuries. The lower-class blacks didn't move at all. They called themselves "the sufferers."

To forget their troubles, many turned to marijuana, locally called *ganja*. Many joined the Rastafarians, a religion that considers Haile Selassie, the late emperor of Ethiopia, divine. (Before he took the title Haile Selassie, the emperor was a noble named Ras Tafari Mekonnen.) Rastafarians make sacramental use of ganja. Many other "sufferers" used ganja for worldly, not spiritual, ends. They raised, sold, and exported ganja. Before long, there was a lively trade between the Jamaican gangs and the United States. For their marijuana, the Jamaican gangsters received both money and guns.

Politicians began to surround themselves with bodyguards of gangsters. Michael Manley, a labor leader, became the most powerful politician in Jamaica by ostensibly supporting the cause of the "sufferers." He also recruited the biggest private army of gunmen. Opposing him was Edward Seaga, who led an almost equally large group of street warriors. Each eventually became prime minister. Political campaigning in Jamaica began to resemble war. Gunmen would break up rallies, frighten away poll watchers, and intimidate people who wanted to vote for the other party.

Nurtured by the politicians, crime in Jamaica took a quantum leap during the 1970s. The bodyguards had begun to branch out into armed robbery and contract murder. Gang warfare became intense.

"It was the politicians who first brought guns" into his Kingston neighborhood, Delroy Edwards said. "Seaga was the biggest gangster of all."[41] Edwards, nicknamed "Uzi" for the weapon he usually carried, achieved a kind of fame in the United States. He founded the first Jamaican posse here and started the widespread merchandising of crack. Edwards began as one of Seaga's bodyguards. He left Jamaica when the politicians started to crack down on the gunmen.[42]

From the politicians' point of view, the gunmen had served their purposes and it was time to disarm them. The politicians found that it was easier to encourage gunmen than to get rid of them. Manley had been elected by promising "power to the people." But the mass of the people, "the sufferers," received no more power than before. More and more turned to what seemed the only way to better themselves—crime. In 1974, after several prominent citizens were murdered, the press and civic leaders began to demand that the government "get the guns." Prime Minister Manley declared, "There is no place in society for the gun, now or ever."[43] The Jamaican House of Representatives passed laws increasing penalties for possessing and selling ganja; requiring children over 14 to be tried as adults for gun offenses; allowing warrantless searches of homes, vehicles, and persons; and—with a law called the Gun Court Act—outlawing the private ownership of guns and ammunition.

To enforce the last law, the government set up a "Gun Court." Gun Court tried offenders in secret. There was no bail and no jury. Those convicted were sent to the "gun stockade," a concentration camp built in the middle of Kingston and painted blood red. Possession of a single cartridge could mean a sentence of life in prison.[44] Persons who had licenses for guns—exclusively members of the upper class—were allowed to keep one gun.

The government was dedicated to the eradication of the "gun culture." Scenes in movies and television programs showing gunplay were forbidden. Police made house-to-house raids in poor sections of Kingston. And police used the utmost violence in enforcing the law. Killings by police became common.

The violence, however, kept increasing. Guns seemed more plentiful than ever, and automatic weapons became common. In 1980, 933 Jamaicans were killed—556 by gunmen and 234 by police and soldiers.[45] Most of those killed by the security forces were killed under circumstances that in other places would be called murder. As the nation had a population of approximately 2.5 million, that was a homicide rate of 37.3 per 100,000. Even assuming all the killings by police were justified (a rather large assumption), it was a rate of 22.2—well over twice the U.S. rate. And the homicide rate in Jamaica is still going up.

Gun Court was obviously a failure. Seaga, who replaced Manley, modified it, but did not eliminate it. All the warrantless, house-to-house searches, the jury-less trials, and Draconian sentences have not disarmed one small island nation. Of course, the Jamaicans have had only about 20 years to do the job. Let's look at a country where the most repressive sort of gun controls have been in place more than 70 years.

RUSSIA

Russia's murder rate, and crime rate in general, began to climb before the breakup of the Soviet Union. In 1989, according to the World Health Organization, the Soviet homicide rate was 6.2 per 100,000, about 60 percent of the U.S. rate.[46] The next year, Interpol says the U.S.S.R. had 24,875 homicides in a population of 287 million.[47] That's a rate of 11.5, well above the U.S. rate. From that point, it skyrocketed.

Why that happened is the subject of many theories. Some things are certain. The nonmilitary side of the Soviet economy had been slipping for many years, and things were getting worse. Agricultural production was down, as was the availability of consumer goods generally. There was less food, less clothing, less housing, and longer lines. People, of necessity, had begun to evade the law. The black market flourished, bribe-taking increased, and theft, particularly from the military, increased. The Afghan War became as unpopular in the U.S.S.R. as the Vietnam War was in the U.S.A., and respect for the government and the law declined.

When the Soviet Union collapsed in a mostly bloodless revolution, Russia's turn toward a market economy caused further hardships. Controls on food prices and guaranteed employment both began to disintegrate, but neither jobs nor salaries increased. Life became harder for ordinary people. The black market exploded, law evasion became the norm and ruthless people, many of them former Communist bosses, formed criminal gangs to take advantage of the situation.

The laws against guns remain on the books. Pistols are forbidden to anyone but the police and the military. From the beginning, however, high government and Communist party officials could keep pistols. After the passing of the Soviet Union, persons of influence—officials, rich men, and their bodyguards—could also have pistols, in spite of the law. Writer David Remnick in 1995 described a visit to the Moscow Commercial Club, where Russia's nouveaux riches entrepreneurs meet to overawe each other. "Well dressed men and their sable-swathed women negotiated the icy sidewalk and headed for the entrance. Their bodyguards, with pistols and machine guns bulging their jackets, stayed close."[48]

Pistols, in spite of this, are still absolutely forbidden to civilians. But as in Sweden, civilians can obtain weapons that are absolutely forbidden in the United States. Russian television personality Vladislav Listyev, murdered March 1, 1995, told an interviewer a few months before his death that he was afraid of being killed and had thought about getting a license to buy "a Kalashnikov or a pump-action shotgun."[49] A Kalashnikov is a full-automatic rifle—in the United States, about as illegal as any weapon ever made.

The Soviet Union and later Russia have manufactured hunting rifles, both center-fire and rimfire, and shotguns both for export and for domestic use. Only professional hunters or very well-connected Russians got to use them domestically, though. Myron Cohen, an American manufacturer of medical equipment, has made several business trips to Russia. Cohen, an avid hunter and fisherman, says he has several times been invited to hunt with local clubs in Russia. "Each time," he says, "I was told I'd have to take an oath of secrecy so that no one would know they had guns. The guns were all stolen from the army." Cohen politely declined the invitations.[50] There are an estimated 30 million illegal guns in private hands in the Commonwealth of Independent States—the former U.S.S.R. About a million are in Moscow.[51]

Different traditions, economic conditions, and other factors all affect gun laws and gun use in other countries. Because something works in one country does not mean it will work in another. In no country (e.g., Britain) do restrictive gun laws seem to have reduced crime, violence, or homicide. And in no country (e.g., Switzerland) do permissive gun laws seem to have increased these evils. Perhaps it might be worthwhile to look at two countries with which we share a continent, much history, and some traditions—Canada and Mexico.

THE NEIGHBORS

English-speaking Canada was founded by American loyalists who fled the 13 colonies so they could remain subjects of the British monarchy. In the first few years after the Revolution, it was settled mainly by American farmers who cared little about politics and much about cheap, fertile land.[52] The infertile Laurentian Shield blocked the sort of stampede for western land that touched off so much fighting with the Indians in the United States. When settlers began to move west, via railroad in the late nineteenth century, the government and the Mounties were well established.[53] Although Americans and Canadians drive the same cars, count their money the same way, and, outside Quebec, speak the same language (with almost the same accents), there is a basic difference. As Canadian historian Pierre Berton says, "While Americans opt for 'life, liberty and the pursuit of happiness,' Canadians are more concerned with 'peace, order, and good government.' "[54]

Handgun ownership has never been as widespread in Canada as in the United States. However, as owners of one of the greatest expanses of almost-uninhabited land on the globe, Canadians have always owned large numbers of rifles and shotguns. Restrictions on handguns began in Canada before Britain's gun laws. The first law requiring a permit to carry a handgun passed in 1892 and was strengthened in 1913. A 1920 law required prospective purchasers of handguns to get a permit. In 1930, all handguns had to be registered. In 1977, a permit to purchase long guns was also required. However, only 1 percent of permit applicants have been denied, and if the police deny an application, they must produce a written statement explaining why, and their decision may be appealed. Further, Canadians can buy their guns through the mail, something prohibited in the United States since 1968.

Some weapons were on the "restricted list." These included all handguns and many center-fire semiautomatic rifles, especially those with short barrels or folding stocks. To purchase a restricted weapon, a Canadian had to prove the gun will either "protect life where other protection is inadequate," or be used "in connection with a lawful profession or occupation," or for target practice under the auspices of a shooting club, or be part of the collection of a "bona fide gun collector."[55] Sawed-off shotguns, sawed-off rifles, silencers and machine guns are completely illegal.

Until recently, Canadian laws about rifles and shotguns have been more liberal than U.S. laws. What Canada called restricted rifles are called "assault weapons" in the United States and totally prohibited. Canadians can buy guns by mail, and permits to buy rifles are almost automatic. Canadian laws concerning pistols were more restrictive than in many parts of the United States, but less restrictive than others. In 1995, the law was changed to ban outright the formerly "restricted weapons" and all handguns with barrels shorter than 4½ inches. All other weapons must be registered—even crossbows. Possession of an unregistered gun could bring up to five years in prison. To enforce the law, police can make warrantless searches of gun owners' homes. The bill met "unusually fierce opposition from gun owners," according to the *New York Times*.[56] But it passed.

In spite of the freedom Canadian gun owners have enjoyed, Canada has had one of the world's lowest homicide rates—2.2 per 100,000—lower than Scotland, Denmark, Finland, Sweden, and many other notably peaceful lands.

Looking toward our other border, we see about as great a contrast with Canada as possible. Mexico shares some of our worst traditions—wars against the Indians, frontier violence, and even, to a small extent, slavery. It also shares some of our best. Armed citizens were instrumental in driving the would-be emperor Maximilian's army out of Mexico. Armed citizens, following such leaders as Pancho Villa, also overthrew the dictatorship of Porfirio Díaz and made possible the Mexican Revolution. Mexico also adopted a written constitution that contained an article guaranteeing the right to keep and bear arms. But as we saw in chapter 1, that article contains a "catch-22." Mexican citizens can keep and bear any arms *it is lawful for them to have*. There are no such arms for almost all Mexican citizens. Plutarco Elías Calles and his political heirs, the people who drew up the rules that guaranteed their party more than 60 years of unbroken rule over Mexico, did not want any armed citizens messing up their plans.

Mexico produces rifles, pistols, and machine guns for its security forces. About the only widely merchandised civilian guns, though, are the Cabanas rifles. These strange devices shoot an air gun pellet, which is propelled by a separately loaded .22 caliber blank cartridge.[57] For self-defense, hunting, or competitive target shooting, the Cabanas rifles are simply useless. The Mexican arms industry, which is capable of producing guns as fine as any in the world, can't even make a real gun for export.

Mexico has the most complete gun prohibition this side of Japan. And Mexicans enjoy about the same civil liberties as the Japanese. Mexican police with nothing else to do stop cars to look for guns—no warrants, no probable cause, not even suspicion. But unlike Japan, Mexico has a homicide rate five times greater than that of the United States. Why the difference?

Japan, to the Japanese, is a family. The government is the father and mother. The corporations are big brothers. Family members look after each other. The family will not let anyone get really hurt. Even convicts, after they are convicted, fare better than their counterparts in most countries. Sentences are short, and the justice system seeks to help the convict see the error of his ways and to reintegrate him into society. There are divisions of rank, prestige, and wealth that everybody accepts as part of life. But nobody starves.

Mexico is different. A lot of people starve. A few people are staggeringly wealthy. There are sharp distinctions—of prestige, of wealth, even of race. People do not publicly question their "betters." In a rich country, the bulk of the people are poor. The revolution that was to bring them equality has been betrayed. Like millions of people all over the globe, the majority are frustrated, angry, and hopeless. The Indians in Chiapas have revolted, but their chances of defeating government forces are just short of nonexistent. Most Mexicans will take out their frustrations on each other. Hence the murder rate.

There's no need to take a trip to Mexico to see the process. It's going on in all large American cities. Wherever the homicide rate and the crime rate are up, you'll find the same thing. In Mexico, in Russia, in Colombia, in Jamaica, and in Washington, D.C., you'll find a breakdown in society—people are being squeezed against the wall, being pushed into violence.

In this situation, most gun laws are irrelevant; some are even harmful. Call them snake oil. Some gun laws could help the situation—a little. Call them Band-Aids. The great advantage of gun laws is that they are cheap (except to gun owners). But to make any substantial progress against crime, violence, and murder, we need radical surgery.

PART V

WHAT CAN WE DO?

CHAPTER 22

SNAKE OIL

THE GUN LOBBY SOLUTIONS

Even if the United States' homicide rate is but one-thirteenth of El Salvador's or one-thirtieth of Colombia's, it's far too high. That's something on which all parties to the gun control "debate" agree. They also agree that something should be done. It's on the somethings that they disagree.

The gun lobby prescriptions for the malady are simple. First, remove all gun controls. Second, execute more criminals and lock the rest up for so long they'll forget why they're there.

If you get down to specifics, the gun lobby's call for an end to controls becomes less sweeping. There is, for instance, no groundswell for removing the prohibitions on automatic weapons. The NRA's allies didn't even bother to fight when Congressman Charles Rangel rammed through (probably illegally) William Hughes's machine gun amendment to the McClure-Volkmer Bill. Nor is there any talk of following Switzerland's lead by making mortars, antiaircraft guns, and other "destructive devices" available to the populace. Instead, the NRA and its allies would like to see an end to waiting periods, however short. They might also like to see no instant background checks, unless they were an alternative to waiting periods.

In early 1995, the rifle association began a campaign to liberalize laws restricting the carrying of pistols. This has brought the usual barrage of denunciations, wild predictions, and simple untruths from the anti-gun lobby. For example, in its Winter 1995 *Progress Report*, HCI states, "In 32 states, carrying concealed weapons (CCW) is either prohibited or requires a license or permit issued by police." In fact, that's true in 49 states.[1] Only Vermont does not require a license to carry a concealed pistol. Vermont, as we saw, has one of the lowest homicide rates of all states. Of the states that have permits, 28 are mandatory: if the applicant meets the requirements, the permit must be issued. Another 14 have optional permits: the authorities can decide whether or not to issue a permit. In the remaining eight states, carrying concealed guns is not permitted.

Where HCI got its statistics from is puzzling. Even more puzzling is its attempt to prove these are "dangerous laws." It charges that since Florida passed a mandatory permit law in 1986, "the violent crime rate in that state between 1987 and 1992 increased 17.8%." But even the gun-hating *New York Times* reports, "Florida's experience has generally provided strong arguments for proponents of right to carry laws. . . . In any event, handgun-related homicides in Florida dropped 29 percent from 1987 to 1992, declining to 3.6 per 100,000 residents annually from 5.0, according to FBI statistics."[2] Violent crime, it should be noted, consists of homicide and non-negligent manslaughter, rape, robbery, aggravated assault, and simple assault. Even if you leave out simple assault, guns are involved in only than 30 percent of these crimes.[3] It appears that HCI was just looking for any figures that could make Florida look bad after it changed its law on carrying concealed weapons.

If the gun lobby's advocacy of mandatory gun carrying permits stopped there, it would be a positive contribution. But it's hard to believe that the professional gun advocates don't want to end *all* restrictions on carrying pistols. That might be harder to justify. It would be fine if unrestricted weapons-carrying resulted in a homicide rate like Vermont's everywhere. But that's most unlikely. There are many factors that affect the homicide rate, and most licensing laws can't change it much in either direction. We'll take a closer look at this fact a little later.

The NRA's desire to "get tough" with criminals is one of the few aims it shares with HCI. Unfortunately, they're both wrong. We've examined the drawbacks of "toughness" in chapter 12. Here are some more thoughts:

The death penalty is usually sold as a deterrent to murder. It's difficult for its advocates to explain, however, why the state with the largest number of executions in 1993—Texas—had the third highest murder rate among all the states that year.[4] Texas was tied with California in the murder rate, and California had even more people than Texas on death row.[5]

Long sentences and mandatory minimum sentences also present problems. Not allowing time off for good behavior greatly complicates the job of keeping order in a prison. And "three strikes and you're out" is clogging courts. California court officials are finding that suspects are no longer willing to plea-bargain if they have two strikes. Jails in the state are crammed with prisoners awaiting trial, court dockets are growing like Jack's beanstalk, and there are endless delays in trials. To prevent total gridlock, judges are reducing felonies to misdemeanors, and prosecutors are ignoring "strikes." So far, only one in six "three strikers" has been sent up for the 25-year minimum.

"I've been a Republican all my life, and I'm afraid I'm starting to sound like a Democrat," Judge Carol Fieldhouse of California said. "I've never seen something before where DAs, defense lawyers, and judges agree. This thing [the three strikes law] isn't working."[6]

Mandatory sentences for crimes committed with a gun are a particular favorite of both the NRA and HCI. Of this concept, criminologist Gary Kleck says:

It is no overstatement to say that the very survival of the criminal justice system depends on court officials evading the intent of legislatively mandated sentencing enhancements. If legislative intent were actually implemented and long prison sentences were imposed on every person arrested for violent crime with a gun (or 1 year sentences imposed on every unlawful carrying arrestee), the system would collapse. Nationally, there were only about 600,000 state and federal prison spaces available in 1988 (U.S. Bureau of the Census, 1988, p. 185), but about 155,000 persons were arrested for violent crimes with a gun (computed from U.S. FBI 1989, pp. 12, 21, 24, 168, assuming 10% of rape arrestees used a gun) with another 220,000 arrested on weapons charges, most of which were probably unlawful carrying or something similar. We could empty the prisons of every killer, rapist, drug dealer, and other offender who did not use a gun in the crime for which they were imprisoned, and make each weapons violator serve just one year, and would still not have enough prison space to make each violent gun crime arrestee serve even three years in prison.[7]

Not all the minimum mandatory sentences are for gun offenses, of course. Many are for drug offenses, and some of these are quite nonviolent. Possession of drugs, like carrying a gun, is not in itself a violent crime, but sentences for both have forced the early release of violent criminals.[8]

A trouble with just about all of the gun lobby's proposed solutions is gross oversimplification. That's true also of the anti-gun lobby's.

THE ANTI-GUN LOBBY SOLUTIONS—BANS

Some of these proposals have been dealt with at some length previously. This is basically a summary of suggestions from the anti-gun lobby.

1. *Ban all guns. Make possession of any kind of gun illegal for any private individual. Only military and police organizations could own guns. Confiscate all guns in private hands.*

   This suggestion is legally and politically impossible. It's legally impossible because the ban would violate the Second Amendment to the U.S. Constitution (see chapters 1–5) and the confiscation would violate both the Fourth and Fifth amendments. The Fourth Amendment forbids "unreasonable searches and *seizures*," and the Fifth says, "nor shall private property be taken for public use without just compensation." It's politically impossible because whenever statewide referenda have been taken on banning pistols—the type of weapon most often used in crime—the proposed ban has been overwhelmingly defeated (see chapter 20). Bans have been passed on some highly specialized weapons— "assault weapons" and Saturday night specials—owned by relatively few people, but never on mainstream pistols, rifles, or shotguns.

If such a ban could be passed, we've seen in chapter 19 that it would not decrease crime. If anything, it would increase crime. The best estimates are that there are more than 200 million guns in the country today.[9] Many would undoubtedly be hidden. Many of these would eventually appear on the black market—far more than enough to supply every criminal using guns for several generations. Further, the ban would create gun-smuggling and bootlegging gangs, just as the "war on drugs" has created drug-smuggling and bootlegging gangs. The result would be a net increase in criminality.

2. *Ban all guns, but buy back those in private hands.*
This would eliminate problems with the Fourth and Fifth amendments. It would also greatly increase cooperation from gun owners. It would, however, be extremely expensive, if gun owners received "just compensation" for their weapons (see chapters 9 and 19). Of the 200 million guns in private hands, a *low* estimate of their average value is $250. That's $50 billion.

Most buy-back programs have brought in few guns because the would-be buyers, either from ignorance or parsimony, put too low a price on the guns. Connecticut had another sort of trouble with a "guns for goods" program instituted in 1993.

A number of retailers agreed to exchange purchase certificates for guns turned in to police stations. Nonworking guns would be worth $50 in merchandise; working long guns and handguns, $100; and "assault weapons," $500. As anyone familiar with the market might expect, the state got a large number of hopelessly unrepairable wrecks, including at least one rusted relic that had been buried for 20 years. It also got a large number of cheap and marginally workable rifles, shotguns, and handguns, most of which had not been used in years, let alone used in crime. But in addition to these junkers and klunkers, it also got a large number of former Chinese army rifles in excellent condition. These guns were all the same type, the Chinese type 56 carbine, a copy of the Russian SKS carbine—a weapon that had recently been declared obsolete in the Chinese army and had been exported to the United States in large numbers. The police had declared these guns "assault rifles," although they were not automatic, could hold no more than ten cartridges, and were not among the guns the state had listed as "assault weapons." The type 56 carbines sold in gun shops for the unusually low price of a little more than $100. But people turning them in were receiving $500 merchandise certificates. In a very short time, the Chinese guns lost their "assault rifle" status, but by then they had accounted for thousands of dollars in certificates.

They had accounted for much more, in fact, than the business people had agreed to pay out. For a while, a nasty situation seemed to be developing. People who had turned in guns did not receive the promised certificates, and Connecticut's rabidly anti-gun governor, Lowell Weicker, refused to return the guns. The gun owners threatened to sue. Eventually Weicker found some state funds to add to what the merchants had pledged, and the gun providers got their merchandise.

A ban-and-buy-back program would not violate the Fourth and Fifth amendments, but it would still violate the Second. Further, criminals, to whom the guns are capital equipment, would be unlikely to turn them in. The ban-and-buy-back would make life much more pleasant for criminals because most potential victims would be unarmed.

3. *Ban the manufacture and sale to the public of new guns. Grandfather those now in private hands.*

This might well evade constitutional problems. But with 200 million guns out there, none of us would live long enough to see it make an impact on crime.

4. *Ban handguns, the type most used in crime.*

We've seen in chapter 19 what results this would have. Crooks would switch to other weapons. If they go to long guns, much more deadly, they would kill four times as many people as they do now. If they go to clubs or edged weapons, they'd injure many more people than they do now, and they'd switch their targets from commercial establishments to individuals—especially the old and infirm.

5. *Ban certain types of guns, such as "assault weapons" or machine guns.*

Chapter 17 explores this option. It won't reduce crime.

6. *Ban certain types of ammunition.*

Sen. Daniel P. Moynihan has proposed banning .25, .32, and 9 mm pistol cartridges because they are most used in crime. Does anyone except Senator Moynihan think crooks wouldn't immediately switch to other, more powerful pistols, such as the .45 ACP, .357 magnum, or .44 magnum?

7. *Give municipalities and counties local option to ban some types or all types of guns.*

This has been done. It hasn't helped. If anything, it has increased crime. See chapter 19.

OTHER ANTI-GUN LOBBY SOLUTIONS

1. *Increase taxes on guns and ammunition to shrink the pool in private hands.*

This revives Henry VIII's idea that guns should be available only to the wealthy. Make the taxes high enough, and you guarantee the development of a violently criminal black market. It should be noted that ammunition is even easier than guns to make at home or to smuggle over borders.

2. *Load gun owners down with so many licenses, taxes and security regulations that they'll give up their guns.*

This idea is not the exclusive property of the authors of the strange "Five-Year Plan" (see chapter 15). It's being done in England. While it may work in England, it wouldn't work here. There are already too many guns in private hands. Like the bans, this barrage of regulations would be widely evaded.

3. *Require a high-priced "arsenal license" for gun collections.*

As we saw in chapter 12, this sort of licensing seems to be the by-product of a hatred of guns and gun owners. Its probable aim is to reduce gradually the number of guns that make up an "arsenal," and thereby phase most guns—and gun collectors—out of existence. It, too, would be widely evaded.

Like all of the anti-gun solutions listed previously, and like many of the Brady II regulations looked at in chapters 12 and 17, this is a technique for getting guns out of private hands. That would leave guns only in criminal hands, as even Michael Beard and Josh Sugarmann concede (see chapter 11). The black market in guns would become a major criminal enterprise. Even without the black market, crime would increase because the deterrent effect of an armed citizenry that we examined in chapter 19 would be absent.

4. *Instead of concentrating on guns, concentrate on people. Screen potential gun owners by requiring them to get a license from their local police, who can decide if they are suitable.*

This leads to selective law enforcement, the kind now practiced in New York City. Whether this kind of license is required to purchase, to possess, or to carry, it is—judging by New York's experience—undemocratic, and more to the point, ineffective.

5. *Require license applicants to show a need to have a gun, buy a gun or carry a gun.*

This is as subjective as letting the police screen the applicants. Nobody knows when he or she will have to repel an attacker. Almost nobody these days *needs* to hunt for food. Nobody *needs* to engage in target shooting. On the other hand, nobody *needs* to go swimming, but millions of people do—even though hundreds drown every year.

Self-defense is a genuine need, but the police hierarchy is generally convinced that they alone can protect the public. Actually, the police can't protect anyone. It's seldom indeed that cops can arrive in time to interrupt a crime in progress, and the courts have maintained that they have no obligation to do so.[10]

6. *Register all guns.*

When I was a child in California, all of us kids believed that state law required professional boxers to register their hands as deadly weapons. Just what such registration would accomplish, we didn't ask. Certainly, no one thought that if a boxer misused those deadly weapons the state would amputate his hands. It just seemed that registration was what you did with deadly weapons. Considering the poll results discussed in chapter 20, most people still think so.

As discussed in chapter 20 and other places, the only real reason for registration is to facilitate confiscation. There is already a wide enough paper trail to let the authorities trace any individual gun used in a crime. Registration is favored by the public, but confiscation is not (chapter 20). Registration by itself is the perfect bureaucratic solution to the problem of gun violence. It requires a great deal of paperwork, filing, record-keeping, and hordes of new employees, but it doesn't change the situation. New Zealand adopted gun registration in 1920. In the 1980s, the police decided that it was doing no good. "Whatever law you have, if criminals decide they want to commit a crime with a gun, they will get a gun," said a police spokesman.[11] In 1983, the police persuaded the government to drop registration.[12]

Although many of the proposed solutions to the problem of gun violence are useless or counterproductive, gun violence remains a problem. And a solution is not hopeless. There are some things that we can do. Many of them—those that relate directly to guns—will do some good, but not a vast amount. Although the problem requires radical surgery, we should not despise Band-Aids. They'll help, and as we'll see, they are much easier to apply.

CHAPTER 23

BAND-AIDS

LIMITED ASPIRATIONS

Nobody familiar with the subject expects any sort of gun control law to result in a sharp, immediately noticeable improvement in either the crime or homicide rates. The experience of more than a century of gun control laws and their results, both in this country and abroad, supports that conclusion. That, of course, is contrary to the views of many opinion leaders in and out of government. But it seems that each time a law to "make our streets safe" passes, muggings and murders move up the chart. This effect is not confined to the United States. In 1919, New York had the Sullivan Law, and several other states had concealed weapons laws, but Canada had only one law on gun-toting. It required those who wanted to carry a pistol to get an almost-automatically issued permit, *unless they "had reasonable cause to fear an assault."* In that case, they didn't need any permit.[1]

At that time, the U.S. homicide rate was 13.8 times that of Canada. In 1977, Canada severely restricted pistols, a move that might have been expected to widen the gap between the Canadian and U.S. homicide rates. It did not. The Canadian homicide rate had been moving up slowly for most of the twentieth century. As noted in chapter 18, it began dropping in 1975, three years before the new pistol law took effect. It continued to drop until 1981, and then it began increasing. The gap did not widen under the new restrictions. It narrowed. The U.S. homicide rate for the years 1983–86, after Canada's handgun restriction had time to make itself felt, was only 2.92 times that of Canada.[2]

In spite of such discouraging figures, it seems probable that certain gun control measures could be instituted that would improve life in the United States. But they would not result in revolutionary change. According to criminologist Gary Kleck, "If crime control strategies are rejected because they can produce no more than, say, a 5–10% reduction in crime rates, there is little point in considering most of them."[3]

One reason gun control measures are so popular with many political leaders is that they are usually cheap and require no effort beyond what it takes to write a bill. Improving life in America's inner cities, on the other hand, would be complicated and expensive, require extraordinary effort, and be politically risky. But only such work can make revolutionary changes in the crime and homicide rates. We'll look at this core problem—and the radical surgery it demands—in the last chapter. For now, let's consider some more modest measures. All of these, incidentally, would apply to both long guns and handguns, concealed or unconcealed. There is no profit in banning pistols and encouraging felons to switch to the much more deadly rifles and shotguns.

TIGHTENING RETAIL SALES

Just about everyone but the hardest-core gun lobby fanatics agrees that some people should not have guns. On the other hand, just about everyone agrees that most of these people will always be able to get guns. In spite of that, making it as hard as possible for high-risk people to obtain firearms would seem to be a worthwhile public policy goal.

The federal and various state governments have already made strides toward this goal. They ban certain classes of people—felons, fugitives from justice, drug addicts, aliens, those committed to mental hospitals for violent acts, and those convicted of violent misdemeanors—from obtaining guns. Some laws deny permits to anyone who has been in a mental hospital within a certain time, usually five years. This all-inclusiveness is counterproductive. The vast majority of mental patients are not violent, and denying the nonviolent along with the violent the right to buy a gun does not improve public safety one iota. But, Kleck points out, denying the privilege creates a disincentive to seek treatment.[4] How many this would discourage is pure speculation, but it's no advantage to society to have mentally ill, untreated people wandering around. One other disqualification could profitably be added to those above. Any person convicted of an offense involving alcohol—from public drunkenness to drunken driving—could be denied a permit for five years after the offense. Alcohol figures in a majority of homicides.

Until recently, these disqualifications meant only that those purchasing guns from licensed firearms dealers had to sign a paper affirming that they were not members of one of the prohibited classes. Most of the states also had waiting periods that allowed police to check on the prospective purchasers.

Under the federal Brady law, local authorities are required to check on pro-spective gun buyers. Several sheriffs have challenged the constitutionality of the federal government ordering state officials to do anything. Whatever the result of their lawsuits, it won't change the situation much. The Brady law also mandates that each state have an instant background check system within five years after the law takes effect. This is by no means the impossible dream that anti-gun lobby spokesmen charged. Instant check systems were up and running in many states in 1994. When all systems are up, they will effectively choke off licensed retail sales of guns to high-risk individuals—felons, fugitives, assaulters, wife-beaters, violent nuts, and drug addicts. Excluding aliens probably won't help much. That provision is part of the traditional U.S. xenophobia. Similar provi-sions are not seen in most countries, including such tight-control lands as Britain and Ireland.

Kleck mentions a couple of provisions that are not now part of any instant record check, but that should be: (1) When a dealer calls the record center for a check, the call would be logged with its time and date. That would let law enforcers inspecting the dealer's records know that the dealer had gone through the checking process before each sale. (2) The purchase applicant's name would *not* be retained in the system.[5] The purpose of the instant check is to ensure that high-risk persons do not buy guns. It should not be a way to sneak in gun registration.

THE U.S. ARMS BAZAAR

Closer control of retail sales will take care of only part of the problem. A small part. Only a minority of criminals get their guns from a dealer. Criminologists James Wright and Peter Rossi surveyed hundreds of convicted and imprisoned felons to find out, among other things, how they acquired their guns.

"How did you get your most recent handgun?" they asked.

The largest number of felons, 43 percent, said it was a cash purchase, but only 21 percent said it was from a licensed dealer, such as a gun shop, a pawn shop, or a hardware or department store. The others bought it from individuals. Of those who didn't buy the gun, 32 percent stole it; 9 percent rented or borrowed it; 8 percent received it as a gift; and 7 percent got it in a trade with another private party.

The figures for rifles and shotguns were similar. Forty-two percent were pur-chased, 32 percent from a licensed dealer; 23 percent were stolen; 22 percent were gifts; 7 percent were traded, and 6 percent were rented or borrowed.[6] With only 21 percent of the handguns and 32 percent of the long guns being purchased from licensed retailers, it's obvious that we need more controls.

Other than theft and purchases from licensed dealers, the convicts said they got their handguns from "the street," 14 percent; a fence, 5 percent; a drug dealer, 4 percent; their families, 4 percent; and "the black market," 3 percent.

Friends, 33 percent, and families, 22 percent, were the biggest sources of rifles and shotguns. Only 5 percent came from "the street," and 2 percent each from drug dealers and the "black market." It's interesting to note that, in spite of all the talk about criminals getting guns in other states, only 23 percent of the felons got their handguns out of state, and they were not from licensed dealers.[7]

As you might expect, many were purchased from family members and friends. Many others were stolen from the same people. In fact, more guns were stolen from family and friends than from any other source—almost as many as were purchased. The most popular way of obtaining a gun from friends or family was by renting or borrowing.[8] Renting guns has become a profitable enterprise in parts of big cities where violence is a problem.

In the most common scenario, a gun owner gets the word out that he has a gun or guns to rent. Say it's a shotgun worth $100. The renter, who plans to use it in a robbery, puts down a deposit greater than the worth of the shotgun, say $200. When he returns it, he gets back a large part of the deposit, perhaps $150. But many cagey gun owners add a proviso. If the gun has been fired, the renter keeps it, and the former gun owner keeps the deposit. Nobody wants a "hot" gun.

The figures above are for all the felons interviewed. Wright and Rossi found, however, that there were distinct groups in their sample. There were the unarmed felons, who used no weapons; the "improvisers," violent, impulsive men who flew into rages and attacked with anything handy; the knife users; the one-time handgunners; the sporadic handgunners; the handgun predators, who always used pistols; and the shotgun predators, who always used sawed-off shotguns. The last two classes, the most dangerous and violent, stole almost half of the guns they used.[9]

There were other qualifications. Many of the guns the criminals purchased from other than licensed dealers had previously been stolen. And many of the purchases from licensed dealers were not made directly but through "straw men," persons with no personal convictions who buy guns for criminals. The illicit drug trade was deeply involved in illicit arms trafficking. Smugglers who brought cocaine into this country often took guns back. In countries like Colombia and Bolivia pistols bring prices almost as inflated as the price of cocaine in the United States.[10]

Even without criminal transactions, the gun business in the United States is far more chaotic than you might think from reading federal laws. A large part of the *legitimate* gun transfers do not involve licensed gun dealers. According to a DMI survey in 1979, 36 percent of gun owners in general did not get their weapons from licensed dealers, but from private individuals.[11] In most of the

United States, gun sales between private individuals are totally unregulated. For some reason, sales at gun shows, where exhibitors, most of them dealers, display weapons and accessories, are considered sales between private individuals. (Brady II, as noted in chapter 12, would prohibit dealers from selling at gun shows as individuals, but not non-dealers.)

For gun control laws to have any effect at all, they would have to take into consideration straw men and thieves.

BURNING THE STRAW MEN

Two legislative approaches strongly opposed by the NRA would make life difficult for straw men. One law, in effect in Virginia and South Carolina, limits handgun purchases to one in a 30-day period.[12] NRA spokesmen call this "rationing" and say that if a state can limit a citizen to one pistol a month, it can limit him to one a year, one a decade, or one a lifetime. That's the "slippery slope" argument again. But legislation depends not on precedent but on the will of the people. Very few of the people who favor one gun a month would favor one gun a lifetime, or even one gun a year.

Handguns, as mentioned before, are expensive. It's fairly obvious that anyone who regularly buys several handguns a month is up to no good. Unless he is fabulously wealthy, he must be reselling them. And unless he is being subsidized by someone forbidden to buy guns, he must be reselling them above list price. And anyone paying more than list price is probably someone who could not legally buy a gun. The law makes exceptions. A collector who wants to buy an intact collection could get permission to do so. The "rationing" law could stand further modification. Suppose a collector has just bought a pistol and then sees one he has been looking for all his life but for the first time at a price he can afford. He wouldn't be able to take advantage of the opportunity. He could, though, if the law allowed him to sell one gun (through a dealer, of course) so he could buy another. Or the law could be written so the limit was, instead of one gun per month, six guns per six months. Very few people would reach either limit often.

Applying this law nationally would do much to clip the wings of straw men. Another law that might be desirable would be to require holders of dealer licenses to sell a certain number of guns each year. Before the Brady law, when a federal dealer's license cost only $20 for three years, many people who had no interest in retailing guns or anything else held dealer licenses. That allowed them to buy guns by mail and across state lines at a discount and avoid paying some taxes on the purchases. There is no doubt that many guns obtained by these freeloaders ended up in the underworld.

FREEZING THE THIEVES

At a minimum, the law should require that any theft of a firearm be reported as soon as possible. There should be criminal penalties if that is not done. Such a law should apply not only to licensed dealers but to individuals. Another law could require that guns not under the direct control of a responsible adult be locked up. Carrying the gun, or the responsible adult having it in a car or in a room where she can quickly reach it, would be considered having it under control. A gun kept in a bedroom at night where it could be easily reached by the owner would also be under control.

To promote safety, the law might also require that even these guns (except those carried on the person) be unloaded. Speed loaders for revolvers and stripper clips, or detachable magazines for rifles and semiautomatic pistols, allow a gun to be brought into action almost as quickly as if it were loaded. If the ammunition, in its quick-loading device, were in a different place from the gun, it would lessen the chance of children finding it and causing damage. Some gun control advocates are calling for the return of child-proof guns like the old Smith and Wesson New Departure. The New Departure had a hard double-action-only trigger pull and a grip safety. Even so, it was proof against tampering only by very small children, and it was useless for anything except close-range self-defense.

The storage requirement would not allow police to inspect arrangements, as in England. If a gun were stolen, though, the owner would have to show that she had taken reasonable precautions to keep it safe.

A few states have laws on safe storage of guns, but most of them are vague and seldom enforced.

The law could also attack the problem of thievery from the other side. It could make it a crime to knowingly possess a stolen gun. Conviction would result in jail. Possession of more than one stolen gun would be a presumption of guilt. Such a person would be required to prove he didn't know the guns were stolen.

LIGHT ON PRIVATE SALES

As mentioned above, most sales of guns between private individuals are not recorded. In a few states, sales must be reported to the authorities, but the law is widely ignored. In some places, anyone who sells a gun illegally may be civilly liable for damage done by the gun. Kleck proposes that all private sales be conducted through a licensed dealer acting as a broker.[13] A dealer would have instant access to the electronic records check and, with his license and livelihood at stake, would not cut corners. The small brokerage fee she could charge would be a bargain, considering how this system could bring order to the chaotic firearms bazaar. The law would not prohibit sales at gun shows. Most exhibitors are licensed dealers anyway. Their sales would be considered part of their business. Persons not licensed dealers could easily find a dealer to broker their sales.

LICENSES

Licensing gun owners is a proposal that worries many people, not just NRA officials. First, many license laws are written like New York's, giving local officials, usually police chiefs, almost total discretion about who gets a license. There are no objective standards. Second, gun owners fear that their licenses would make them a target if the federal, state, or local government passes a law banning firearms.

The first objection is easily overcome. Make the licenses mandatory. *Require* that each applicant who meets certain objective standards be issued a license. As for the second objection, do not tie the license to gun ownership. You don't have to own a car to get a driver license. Why couldn't we have gun user licenses? Anyone using a gun or having one in his possession would have to have one of these licenses. Possession of such a license would not be as clear an indication of gun ownership as membership in a sports association, such as the NRA. Particularly the NRA—which now sells name lists of former members to anyone willing to pay the price.[14]

The purpose of the gun user license would be the same as the purpose of the driver license—to ensure that the operator of dangerous equipment knows how to use it competently and safely. The applicant for a gun user license would have her background checked and would pass an examination on safety and competence. Ideally, the examination would not be administered by the police. In any case, it would have to be completely objective. Persons who failed would have the right of appeal. And officials who falsify test results or otherwise seek to fail applicants without reason would be punished.

Like a driver license, the gun user license would be valid in all states, although it would be issued in the state in which the gun user lived. A person with such a license would be someone with a clean record, someone who knows how to safely store and carry a gun, someone who can use a gun efficiently and safely. The license would apply to both handguns and long guns. A license holder would be allowed to carry a gun concealed in urban areas and either concealed or openly in less populated districts.

The deterrent effect of guns in houses, shown in U.S. burglary rates, would be magnified. If there were a lot of licensed gun users around, it would discourage muggers. It would, in fact, pay governments to offer gun-handling and gun-safety classes in school, as driver-training classes are now offered.

A proposal to have gun classes in school would, no doubt, drive some anti-gun fanatics berserk. Many have objected to having the NRA's Eddie Eagle gun safety course in schools because it "legitimizes gun ownership." *Gun ownership is legitimate.* It has been as long as the United States has been in existence. And in a country where 200 million guns are in private hands, refusing to teach gun safety is madness.

OTHER MEASURES

As one who has written several hundred thousand words on military subjects, I'd like to see something resembling the Swiss system. The Swiss class-based officer-enlisted person system is a reflection of the class-conscious Swiss society and would not have to be duplicated here. Officers could be elected, and the militia might have a looser organization, something like the South African model. It would be a great advantage if everyone in the militia (now all men from 17 to 45) had standard weapons and government-sponsored training. The standard weapons, issued by the government, should be the type used by the armed forces. The rifles would be selective fire, able to fire full automatic or semiautomatic. The training could include, besides small arms use, marksmanship with machine guns, mortars, and light antitank and antiaircraft weapons. And, as in Switzerland, the government might also encourage marksmanship with privately owned weapons. Ideally, submachine guns and automatic rifles would be available for private use, as in Sweden, Israel, and Switzerland, and many other countries, including Russia.

Switzerland, as Metternich said, is an army. Switzerland is also a small country without overseas commitments. If Switzerland calls up its army, it's for all-out war. Its military is less a standing army than a cadre around which its militia can form.

The United States is different. It needs fairly powerful standing military forces to meet a variety of commitments. These forces could be quickly augmented by calling up portions of the militia—a modern version of the eighteenth-century minutemen. The minutemen would have sufficient training to let them take their places in the military forces without delay. The remaining militia, loosely organized in regional units—commandos, if you will—could be used much like the old Revolutionary War militia. They could be home guard forces—guerrillas, if necessary—and could join in any large scale battle in their part of U.S. territory.

Large scale battles on U.S. territory sounds pretty far-fetched in the mid-1990s. But war "in my time or in the time of my children" seemed pretty far-fetched to Alonzo Cornell in the 1880s.[15] Before Cornell's time was up, there was a small war with Spain, a larger one in the Philippines, an invasion of Mexico, numerous skirmishes in the Caribbean, and World War I. His children saw World War II.

A well regulated militia, as mentioned in the Bill of Rights, could not harm the

United States. It would confer all the advantages James Madison and Alexander Hamilton explained in the Federalist Papers. A country in which the people hold the power, in fact as well as in name, is no goal to be despised.

But to be realistic, such a militia system, if it ever comes to pass, is years, maybe generations, away. A far more urgent problem must be solved first—the growth of violence and lawlessness, particularly among young people in our larger cities. That's the point—ostensibly—of all gun control laws. But as we've seen, gun control laws, even the most carefully thought out, are at best just short of futile. We need a new approach.

CHAPTER 24

RADICAL SURGERY

We've seen that there seems to be no correlation between strictness of gun control and violent crime or homicide. In the United States, there is something like a reverse correlation, with low-crime jurisdictions like South Dakota having looser controls than high-crime jurisdictions like the District of Columbia. In that case, though, there's a question of causation. Which came first—the high crime rate or the tight controls? There are also a whole host of sociological conditions that probably have more to do with the crime rate than the presence or absence of gun controls.

Looking at other countries, it becomes even more obvious that gun controls are a negligible factor in crime and violence rates. Guns are scarce in England and Wales, and those countries enjoy low rates of crime and violence. Guns are plentiful in Switzerland, and it, too, has low rates of crime and violence. Controls are Draconian in Mexico, Russia, and Jamaica, and the homicide rates in those countries far exceed that of the United States. Controls exist in Brazil, but they are generally ignored. Brazil is the second most violent country in the world.

Low-violence countries do not share similar gun laws. Neither do high-violence countries. Are there some characteristics they do share? Let's look at some features that are alleged to influence low violence countries.

LOW VIOLENCE COUNTRIES

Homogeneity

Certainly, Japan is a homogeneous society. England is also homogeneous to a lesser extent, in spite of the immigration of West Indians, East Indians, and Pakistanis. Switzerland

257

isn't really homogeneous. There are three major languages—German, French, and Italian—and some minor dialects—Romansch and Ladin. Iceland is extremely homogeneous, but Belgium, with the same low homicide rate, is divided between French speakers and Flemish speakers. Racial and ethnic homogeneity itself, it seems, is not important. If different ethnic groups have lived together for centuries in peace and cooperation, as in Switzerland, the crime and homicide rates will tend to be low. If they have lived in communal warfare, as in the former Yugoslavia, the opposite will be true.

Family and Community Pressure

In most of Europe outside of major cities, there is little mobility. Everyone in the community knows everyone else. Peer pressure to conform to common ethical standards is quiet but intense. So is family pressure. In Japan, where the whole nation is considered one family, pressure is intense beyond anything known in the West.

Distribution of Wealth

In most of Western Europe, real wealth is distributed more evenly than it is in the United States. Nobody starves; everybody's basic health needs are taken care of. That's true even in England, with its aristocracy and ostentatious royal family. In Japan, too, taxes are enormous, and CEOs are rewarded with perks instead of cash. In none of the major industrialized nations are heads of large corporations paid as much more than their workers as in the United States.

What characteristics do high-violence countries share? Let's take a sample—Russia, Mexico, Brazil, Colombia, Jamaica, East Germany, Egypt.

HIGH VIOLENCE COUNTRIES

Homogeneity

Russia, as the largest successor state of the old Soviet Union, has a number of diverse ethnic groups. There has always been considerable tension in their relations with each other. Some groups, like the Chechens, have been the targets of discrimination and, occasionally, horrendous oppression.[1]

Mexico has a history of racial tensions: whites against Mestizos and vice versa, and both groups against Indians. Among the whites, Spaniards were especially disliked. Pancho Villa used to kill any he came across. The Indians of Chiapas are currently revolting against the Mestizo-and-white-run government.

Brazil is a mixture of white, black, and Indian. The blacks, like those in the United States, were originally slaves. Also, like those in the United States, they were freed in the late nineteenth century. Most blacks are poor, and in spite of the official line, there is much prejudice against them. Some of Brazil is still frontier country, like the United States 100 years ago. There is still fighting between settlers and Indians, and Indians are occasionally massacred to make way for ranches and timber companies.

Colombia, like Mexico, has a mixture of races. It also is anything but homogeneous politically. For generations, the Liberal and Conservative parties swapped power in Bogotá. The transitions were not peaceful. When the Liberals were in power, the Conservative leaders went into exile. When the Conservatives returned, the Liberal leaders left the country. Both Liberal and Conservative leaders were termed *los oligarcos* by the mass of Colombians. Some time in the late 1950s, the so-called Marxists took a hand. There were a number of these leftist guerrilla groups, and they soon came to resemble bandit gangs more than revolutionary soldiers.

At one point, Fidel Castro thought he had found a revolutionary bonanza. He dropped agents into guerrilla country. Most of them were killed by the "Marxist" guerrillas.

This civil war is still going on. If that isn't enough, Colombia also has some of the richest and most ruthless gangsters in the world—the men who control the cocaine trade.

In Jamaica, the lack of homogeneity is not so much racial as economic and cultural. The whites and the wealthy blacks run everything. The wealthy blacks model their lives on those of the English aristocracy, with "public" schools, large estates, etc. The poor blacks call themselves "the sufferers" and seek escape in marijuana and crime.

East Germany seems to be the odd one out in this lineup. The population was overwhelmingly German—even more so than in West Germany, where there has been a heavy Turkish immigration. But according to the WHO 1989 report, West Germany's homicide rate was 1.2 per 100,000. East Germany's was 36.7 per 100,000—almost four times the U.S. rate.[2]

Egypt has diverse racial and ethnic groups—Arabs, Copts, Berbers, and blacks. Racial strife, though, has never been a feature of Egyptian life. Religious strife has. Muslims have long discriminated against Coptic Christians. Now Muslim fundamentalists are at war with the government and all nonfundamentalists.

Family and Community Pressure

In Russia, until its collapse, the Soviet state took the place of the family in many ways. It told people where they would move to, where they would live when they got there, where they would work. It made sure everyone had a place to sleep, however crowded, and enough to eat, however tasteless. To a large extent, the state was the community, too. Most of the clubs, associations, and social activities

were run by the state or the Communist party. When the state and party collapsed, most people were without moorings.

The family is important in Mexico, but the cult of machismo has weakened it
considerably. The macho man has many mistresses. He gets his way, or he gets
violent. Community pressure counts for something, but poor communities are
ground down by the local rich families and the police they employ. At the head
of the country is a handful of fabulously wealthy, intermarried political aristocrats who have kept all of the power for the last six decades. The poverty and
lack of opportunity in Mexico may be the reason so many Mexicans have become
macho men. It's the only way they can nourish their self-esteem.

In Brazil, huge numbers of people live in ramshackle slums built of packing
boxes and trash. The typical family in one of these slums is a woman and her
children. The woman keeps busy scrounging to stay alive; the kids join gangs.
The communities are thrown-together conglomerations of strangers unable to
exert any pressure.

Colombia is much like Brazil. The communities may be a little more stable,
but decades of war and violent crime have taken a toll.

In Jamaica, things started to go downhill when politicians began arming street
gangsters. Poor kids who had nothing were not going to follow poor parents who
had nothing when the politicians gave the kids Uzis and a chance to take anything they wanted.

East Germany underwent massive chaos following World War II. Masses of
people were evicted from land that had been given to Poland and Czechoslovakia
sent west to find new homes for themselves. Living standards were vastly better
in West Germany, so many families broke up when people walked into one of the
western zones and never came back. When the wall went up, people still tried to
escape at the risk of their lives. Families were disrupted, and communities were
disrupted even more. East German Communism was more doctrinaire than in
most of the Eastern Bloc countries. As in the Soviet Union, it largely supplanted
family and community. When it began to crumble in 1989, crime and murder
increased. In an article in the January 8, 1996 *New Yorker* and in his recent
book, Ingo Hasselbach gives an inside view of the growth of street gangs and
homicide while he was a neo-Nazi in East Germany.

In Egypt, nationalistic, fundamentalist Islam has, like similar movements of
religious enthusiasm, affected the young primarily—especially young men. This
has the effect of splitting both families and communities. That's especially bad
because of the homicidal nature of the movement itself.

Distribution of Wealth

Distribution of wealth is more of a problem in Russia than in most other countries. For more than 70 years, this "classless" society liked to believe that each

contributed according to his ability and each received according to his need. Actually, each contributed as little as possible and most received little but the barest necessities. Government and party biggies lived well (and embezzled millions), but did not flaunt their wealth. There were few consumer goods and even less advertising. Then the economy collapsed, the Soviet Union fragmented, and the Communist party fell into disgrace. Into the vacuum charged a crazy mixture of freebooters—professional criminals, ousted party bosses, and young men on the make. These nouveaux riches flaunt their wealth. They drive big foreign cars, hire armies of bodyguards, and send their children to private schools abroad. Russian television advertises consumer goods most Russians had not even dreamed about a few years ago, goods far beyond the means of all but a few. Stephen Handelman's book, *Comrade Criminal*, details the origin and operations of the Russian "Mafiya" that has grown up in this new environment and is responsible for most of Russia's internal violence.

Brazil, Colombia, Mexico, and Jamaica are alike in that a few people hold most of the wealth in each country and the majority of the people live in grinding poverty. Brazil probably has the largest middle class, but it is by no means the majority of the population, as it is in the United States. In Colombia, the wealth is held by both the old families, whose hobby is politics, and the upstart drug gangsters. In Mexico, the old families have kept most of the wealth, as they have in Jamaica.

In Egypt, a wealthy, cosmopolitan elite run everything. The mass of the people live in utter poverty. That's true in many Arab countries, but it's worse in Egypt because there are so many poor people and they are so tightly jammed together.

THE TANTALUS SYNDROME

In Greek myth, Tantalus was confined in a well with water up to his neck. When he tried to drink, the water drained away before he could moisten his lips. Delicious fruits hung over his head, but when he tried to get one, they receded out of reach.

Each of the more violent countries is caught in the Tantalus Syndrome. Russians see gangsters and shrewd operators making millions and enjoying all kinds of luxuries while they can't even buy necessities. Egyptians see hordes of foreign tourists with more money than they know how to spend, as well as their own ruling classes, and they know they can never live like that. Education and jobs are limited in what is essentially an agricultural economy. Inhabitants of Brazil's shanty towns, too, see wealthy foreigners enjoying their luxurious beach resorts. They see Brazilian politicians living in luxury and stealing public money. They can't see how they can get out of the slums. Colombians see gangsters living in almost unimaginable luxury. Like the rest of Latin Americans, they are bombarded with advertising—advertising for products they could never afford. Mexicans have all of these problems—rich foreigners flaunting wealth most people can never achieve, advertising for products they can't afford, successful gangsters and oligarchic old families controlling the wealth and political power. They know that the Mexican Revolution, which was supposed to bring the good life to all Mexicans, has been betrayed. Jamaicans, too, feel betrayed. They elected Michael Manley, a socialist who promised "power to the people," but they got no power. Their lives improved not at all. Instead, they got a plague of crime and the excesses of the Gun Court. They, too, see wealthy Jamaicans and wealthy foreigners turning their island into a paradise for the rich.

WHAT MAKES A NONVIOLENT SOCIETY?

From this look at foreign countries, it would seem that homogeneity, often cited as the reason for Europe's low homicide rate, is not the most important factor. The Swiss, Belgians, and Canadians all have low homicide rates in spite of combining two or more groups with different cultures and different languages. If none of these groups is seriously oppressed and all have lived peacefully together, homogeneity is a nonissue.

A stable society, such as obtains in much of Europe, where people live in the villages of their ancestors, does keep down the crime and homicide rates. People live in stable communities, where most people know not only each other but each other's parents, grandparents, and children. In such communities, family pressure is also a strong incentive to harmony. Developing this sort of community and family stability would be difficult, if not impossible, in modern America's mobile society. The example of Canada, however, shows that a low level of violence does not require families living in the same place for the last couple of millennia. Stable communities don't need roots in the Bronze Age.

A fairly equitable distribution of wealth is also an incentive to harmony. "Fairly equitable" does not mean a nation living like a colony of ants. It does mean that nobody is homeless, nobody lacks important medical care, and everyone has enough to eat, adequate clothing, and the opportunity to work and get a good education. Along with these minimum benefits, everyone should have a reasonable opportunity to advance, socially and economically.

All of the low-homicide nations we've examined have these characteristics. All of the high-homicide nations lack them. The high-homicide nations, in addition, suffer from the curse of Tantalus. They see the good life in the lifestyles of rich people, foreign and local. They also see consumer goods they could never afford advertised incessantly. Each ad repeats the same message: "Without this product, you can't live as you deserve to."

THE AMERICAN TEST

Would these criteria—lack of family and community stability, lack of equitable distribution of wealth (which in classless America includes opportunities to improve oneself), and the presence of the Tantalus curse—be found in the most violent U.S. cities? It's necessary to look at cities because some areas in the United States have lower homicide rates than England or Japan; in others, the rate is as high as Mexico's.

Here are the ten worst cities in 1994 (the latest figures available): Gary, Indiana, 89.1 murders and non-negligent homicides per 100,000; New Orleans, Louisiana, 80.3; Washington, D.C., 78.5; St. Louis, Missouri, 69.0; Detroit, Michigan, 56.8; Richmond, Virginia, 54.5; Atlanta, Georgia, 50.4; Baltimore, Maryland, 48.2; San Bernadino, California, 47.1; Birmingham, Alabama, 45.0.[3]

What do these cities have in common? One obvious thing, from our point of view, is that most have strict, even Draconian, gun laws. Washington, Detroit, and Baltimore are notorious. St. Louis, on paper, doesn't look too strict—but see note 8 in chapter 20. Another obvious point is that all have large minority, mostly African-American, populations. Less obvious, but more important, is that those large minority populations are, on the average, extremely poor. Even less obvious, but still more important, is that except for San Bernadino, all of these cities have long, ugly histories of racial oppression. Birmingham, after all, is the city made famous by "Bull" Connor and his police dogs.

These huge minority blocs have all the troubles that have become typical of poor minority groups in U.S. cities. They are not only poor, they can see no way to end their poverty. There are few entry-level jobs that, like those in the recent past, lead to substantial careers. This is largely because of the decline in manufacturing, due to some tax laws we'll look at soon. There is a superabundance of broken families and unwed mothers, almost eliminating the chance for substantial family pressure to create stability. To a great extent, this can be blamed on a poorly thought-out welfare system. The hopelessness young people feel makes it difficult for them to get an education. Many don't think learning is worth the effort. Those who do are often subjected to jeers that they are "acting white."

In these cities, as in most American cities, distribution of wealth is quite inequitable. Not only are the lives of the rich very different from those of the poor, but the poor are constantly exposed to the most powerful messages of those apostles of consumption, the advertisers. And while rising out of the black ghetto is difficult in any U.S. city, it's doubly difficult in nine of these ten cities, where the legacy of racial prejudice remains strong.

Too often in cities like these, girls get pregnant in their teens, leave home, and live on welfare. Boys join gangs. Many of them use dope. The children of those kids, knowing nothing better, do the same as their parents. The United States is fostering a growing, violent underclass. Unless we can reverse the trend, the U.S. Congress and the state legislatures can pass gun control laws every month, and the homicide rate will—in the long run—keep edging upward.

ARE THERE SOLUTIONS?

There are solutions, but they aren't easy and they certainly won't fit into the last chapter of a book like this. It's hard even to say which steps should be taken first.

There must be jobs. There must be some kind of financial opportunity. Before blacks and Hispanics made up the U.S. urban underclass, the bottom rung in cities was held successively by the Irish, the Jews, and the Italians. They provided most of the dope addicts, drunks, and criminals of their day. But there were alternatives to crime. The members of those past underclasses worked their way out of their ghettos because there was work that didn't take much education. Some farmed on the frontiers. Some laid track across the prairies. Some dug coal and copper from mines in the East and West. Some slaved in sweatshops. Some put together a little money and worked around the clock in mom-and-pop stores. They were able to send their children to school and watch their grandchildren go to college. They were able to get out of the underclass. That won't happen to the present underclass unless its members have some opportunity for honest work.

Instead of creating jobs, though, we've rewritten tax laws so that investors are encouraged to take over corporations by financing the purchase with highly speculative bonds. Then, to pay the interest on those bonds, the entrepreneurs are allowed to sell off the assets of century-old companies and throw thousands of people out of work. If that's not enough to take care of the interest, they can opt for Chapter 11 bankruptcy—let the courts reorganize their companies while they retain their jobs and their handsome salaries. And their former employees are out on the street.

We've made it profitable to close down factories in the United States, putting Americans out of work, and open them in Mexico, where peasants can be paid starvation wages. The age of the multinational corporation has encouraged American business to move thousands of jobs to the Far East and to manipulate their books so they don't even pay much in taxes to the United States.

We must change the welfare system so that it doesn't penalize two-parent families. We should get rid of the enormous public housing projects that have become breeding places for crime. We should replace them with small, scattered projects. That will get rid of the all-minority schools and the classmates who keep telling kids, "Stop acting white." We should, as a nation, invest more in college education for deserving students. One of the country's best investments ever was the college tuition and board program in the post-World War II G.I. Bill of Rights. It shouldn't require a war for us to do something like that again.

Programs like this could build stable communities and stable families. But it would be tough work. Tough to sell, and tough to do. It's infinitely easier to build prisons than to build communities. Creating gun control laws is a snap compared with creating jobs. It's a lot more fun to tell each other how tough we are on crime than to take on the tough job of eradicating the roots of crime.

The history of this effort is discouraging. Bill Clinton, a Rhodes scholar, is far from stupid. It does not seem likely that Charles Schumer, a Harvard graduate, is stupid, either. Nor were any of the leading gun control advocates in American politics in years past. Clinton has to know that hardly any "assault weapons" have been used to murder children and outgun cops. Still, he could say of the "assault weapon" ban in his 1995 State of the Union speech, "A lot of people laid down their seats in Congress so that police officers and kids wouldn't have to lay down their lives under a hail of assault weapon attack, and I will not let that be repealed."[4] Schumer has to know it's ridiculous to say of the Rhino bullets, "These bullets, their only real purpose is to go after the police officers of America."[5] As if any company would make bullets whose only real purpose is to kill cops.

If Clinton, Schumer, and scores of other politicians know better, why do they mouth such drivel? Can it be that they read the poll results, see that majorities favor banning "assault weapons" (without knowing what they are), and conclude that attacking these gadgets and other supposedly exotic weaponry like Rhino bullets is a good way to pick up votes? And that, therefore, it's a worthwhile thing to do, whether it has any effect on crime or not?

Both President Clinton and former Senator Bob Dole are running hard for president as this book is being written. Crime, according to the polls, is a major campaign issue. And both candidates are trying to outdo each other in being "tough on crime." But the "tough" measures they advocate are easy to do, although, as we've seen, totally ineffective. Both, and Schumer and every other politician, shy away from the really tough decisions that could have a major effect on crime.

Building very small public housing units and scattering them throughout our cities would be a tremendously unpopular program, even though it would do more to lessen crime and violence than all the gun control laws ever enacted. No politician will touch it. No politician will try to change the tax laws, deregulation, and the international trade treaties that over the last couple of decades have had the effect of driving good entry-level jobs (pushing hamburgers in a fast-food place is not an entry to anything) out of the country. Thanks to these policies, the poor are increasingly left with two alternatives—welfare or crime. Of course, the poor make no campaign donations and hire no lobbyists. The World War II G.I. Bill of Rights, which let hundreds of thousands of veterans go to college, probably did more to increase the wealth of this country than any measure in the twentieth century. Does such a law have to be preceded by a war?

Debate on gun control proposals has taken a tremendous amount of time and legislative energy in the national capitol and in state houses across the country. The measures enacted create a false sense of security and in some cases, as we've seen, increase the danger of crime. But worst of all, this effort has diverted us from doing something meaningful about violent crime and the growth of an underclass—developments that are on the verge of becoming a true national disaster.

Conditions cry out for a change.

ENDNOTES

Introduction

1. Kristen Rand, *No Right to Keep and Bear Arms*, pamphlet of the Violence Policy Center, Washington, D.C.; Charles Cozic, ed., *Gun Control*: "Gun Control Is Constitutional," by Sarah Brady, pp. 83–86; "U.S. Court Decisions Support the Constitutionality of Gun Control," by Daniel Abrams, pp. 94–98; "The Second Amendment Does Not Guarantee the Right to Own a Gun," by Warren E. Burger, pp. 99–102; "The Second Amendment Does Not Prohibit Gun Control," by Michael K. Beard and Kristen M. Rand, pp. 103–06.

2. "Civilian" is in quotation marks because when used in this sense, it is meant to separate citizens from police. Municipal, state, and federal police (like the FBI) are not military. They, too, are civilians.

3. Nevertheless, some types of guns are obviously more suitable than others. A snub-nose revolver, for instance, would have limited value in war. And a military rifle would hardly be the ideal weapon to provide personal protection on the street.

4. Newspaper columnists have called gun owners "lunatics," "nuts," "bulletbrains," and "bumpersticker cretins." Former Governor Mario Cuomo of New York once characterized his critics as "NRA hunters who drink beer, don't vote and lie to their wives about where they were all weekend." David B. Kopel, *The Samurai, the Mountie and the Cowboy*, pp. 304–05.

5. Osha Gray Davidson, *Under Fire*, pp. 50–51. Most of those decrying "jackbooted Fascists" wouldn't know a jackboot if it kicked them. A jackboot was a heavy boot covering the leg from the sole of the foot to mid-thigh. It was worn by seventeenth- and eighteenth-century cavalrymen (known as "jackmen").

6. *Ibid.*, pp. 204–05.

7. *Yale Law Journal* 99 (1989) pp. 637–59, "The Embarrassing Second Amendment," by Sanford Levinson.

8. Josh Sugarmann, *NRA: Money, Fear and Firepower*, p. 45.

Chapter 1
AN OLD, OLD PROBLEM

1. Aristotle, *Politics*, book IV, in *The Basic Works of Aristotle*, Richard McKeon, ed., pp. 1208, 1224–25; J.B. Bury and Russell Meiggs, *A History of Greece*, pp. 94–95.

2. Marcel Dunan, ed., *Larousse Encyclopedia of Ancient and Medieval History*, p. 92; A.M. Snodgrass, *Arms and Armour of the Greeks*, pp. 61–63; Maj. Gen. J.F.C. Fuller, *A Military History of the Western World*, pp. 12–13.

3. Sean Morrison, *Armor*, pp. 53–54; Fuller, p. 12.

4. Arnold J. Toynbee, *A Study of History*, vol. II, pp. 313–14; Dunan, p. 183; Morrison, pp. 57–58.

5. 26 Matthew 51, 14 Mark 47, 22 Luke 50, 18 John 10.

6. 22 Luke 36.

7. In at least one Swiss canton, male citizens traditionally go to the polls armed with a sword or dagger to show that they are free men.

8. R. Ewart Oakeshott, *The Archaeology of Weapons*, pp. 164–65; Morrison, 101–05.

9. A.V.P. Norman and Don Pottinger, *English Weapons and Warfare*, pp. 39, 44–45; also Oakeshott, p. 293; John Beeler, *Warfare in Feudal Europe 730–1200*, p. 107.

10. Norman and Pottinger, p. 60; Oakeshott, p. 294; Beeler, p. 196.

11. William Weir, "Hand Launched Missiles," *Military History*, April 1985.

12. *Ibid.*; Frederick Wilkinson, *Edged Weapons*, p. 119; Sir Ralph Payne-Gallwey, *The Crossbow*, p. 36; C.W.C. Oman, *The Art of War in the Middle Ages*, p. 144.

13. Lee Kennett and James LaVerne Anderson, *The Gun in America*, pp. 8–16.

14. David B. Kopel, *The Samurai, the Mountie and the Cowboy*, p. 112; David T. Hardy, *Origins and Development of the Second Amendment*, p. 22.

15. Kennett and Anderson, p. 11.

16. *Ibid.*, page 9.

17. Norman and Pottinger, pp. 60, 77.

18. *Ibid.* pp. 177–79.

19. *Ibid.*, pp. 39, 44–45, 60, 78; Kennett and Anderson, pp. 60, 77–78, 147–48, 178, 182; Kopel, p. 63.

20. Joyce Lee Malcolm, *To Keep and Bear Arms*, p. 8, quoting John Pocock, *The Political Works of James Harrington*.

21. Malcolm, p. 9.

22. *Ibid.*

23. Kopel, p. 62; Malcolm, p. 104.

24. Wilkinson, *Edged Weapons*, p. 37.

25. Kennett and Anderson, pp. 16–26.

26. *Ibid.*, page 21.

27. *Ibid.*, p. 20.

28. *Ibid.*, pp. 21–22.

29. Included were some of the author's ancestors.

30. Kopel, p. 62.

31. *Ibid.*; Kennett and Anderson, p. 23; Malcolm, pp. 9–10.

32. Wilkinson, pp. 40–41.

33. Kopel, p. 64.

34. Not stockbrokers or commodity traders, but vintners, guild leaders, and merchants—the people who had really ruled London for several centuries.

35. Kennett and Anderson, p. 24.

36. Hardy, p. 28; Malcolm, p. 28.

37. Kopel, pp. 64–65.

38. *Ibid.*, p. 64.

39. *Ibid.*, p. 65; Hardy, pp. 31–32.

40. Malcolm, pp. 69–76, 105–06.

41. Kopel, pp. 111–12, quoting *Blackstone's Commentaries* (star edition), Vol. I, p.*412.

42. Kopel, p. 65; Malcolm, p. 105.

43. *Kopel*, pp. 65, 112; Malcolm, p. 105.

44. The king compounded the mistakes of his brother by becoming a Catholic. The English majority, rabidly anti-Catholic, believed James was trying to disarm them so he could use his large standing army to force all Protestants to become Catholic.

45. Kopel, p. 66; Kennett and Anderson, p. 24.

46. During the eighteenth century, a series of judicial and legislative initiatives liberalized weapons ownership for Englishmen. In the American colonies, where every householder was *expected* to have a gun, these developments in the old country re-enforced the colonists' notion that their "rights as Englishmen" included gun ownership. See Malcolm, pp. 128–34; 138–43.

47. Kopel, p. 112, quoting Thomas Macaulay, *Critical and Historical Essays, Contributed to the Edinburgh Review* (Leipzig: 1850) Vol. I, pp. 154, 162.

48. Kopel, p. 113, quoting Blackstone, I, p.

139 (facsimile of original edition, University of Chicago: 1979); Hardy, pp. 49–50.

49. About 54 percent of the English common law was rejected by the Revolution. And the most important rejection was the supremacy of the legislature. Instead, the framers of the Constitution made a written Constitution the supreme law of the land. The point is important, because some advocates of gun control try to maintain that American law is merely a continuation of English law and use English precedents to justify proposed gun restrictions in the United States.

Chapter 2
THE MILITIA IN AMERICA

1. Kennett and Anderson, p. 35.
2. The story of the roast pork is the Indian version of what happened at the village of Wessagusset. Standish later claimed an enormous Indian chief was taunting him. He invited the chief and two of his companions to step into a nearby hut. Standish and two of his companions followed them, and at a signal from Standish, one of the Pilgrims barred the door. Then Standish attacked the Indian, disarmed him after a terrific struggle and stabbed him to death with his own knife. The captain's two companions did the same to the other Indians. Considering the difference in size between Standish and the chief and the fact that all of the white men emerged victorious, the Indians' story seems more likely.
3. Hardy, p. 43.
4. Harold L. Peterson, *Arms and Armor in Colonial America 1525–1783*, p. 17; ———, *The Treasury of the Gun*, p. 48.
5. Peterson, *Arms and Armor*, p. 43; Kennett and Anderson, p. 45.
6. Peterson, *Arms and Armor*, pp. 22–25; ———, *The Treasury of the Gun*, pp. 57–71.
7. Malcolm, p. 139.
8. Hardy, p. 43; Malcolm, p. 139.
9. Hardy, p. 42; Malcolm, p. 139.
10. Malcolm, p. 139.

11. Peterson, *Arms and Armor*, p. 45.
12. *Ibid.*, p. 42; Kennett and Anderson, p. 36.
13. Kennett and Anderson, p. 41.
14. *Ibid.*, p. 42.
15. *Ibid.*
16. *SNAFU: Great American Military Disasters* by Geoffrey Regan gives a good short account of this campaign, pp. 8–22.
17. Kopel, p. 351.
18. Samuel Eliot Morison, *The Oxford History of the American People*, p. 158.
19. See William Weir, *Fatal Victories*, pp. 99–135, for a short account of this engagement and hostilities through Bunker Hill.
20. Robert Leckie, *The Wars of America*, page 80.
21. See David Hackett Fischer, *Paul Revere's Ride* for a complete and fascinating account of the opening of the Revolution.
22. The Redcoats did find some supplies. They threw sacks of bullets and barrels of flour into a pond without destroying the containers. All were recovered intact. They also burned some artillery carriages. The smoke from that fire made the militia think they were trying to burn the town and caused them to move toward North Bridge.
23. Fischer, pp. 243–44.
24. *Ibid.*, pp. 254–55.
25. *Ibid.*, p. 257.
26. Richard M. Ketchum, *The Battle for Bunker Hill*, p. 122.
27. Thomas J. Fleming, *Now We Are Enemies*, p. 329; Leckie, p. 121.
28. Ketchum, p. 137.
29. Peterson, *Arms and Armor*, pp. 195–203.
30. *Ibid.*, p. 160.
31. Harold L. Peterson, *The Book of the Continental Soldier*, p. 15. Military sermons were part of every training day for New England militia, and the Yankees continued the practice in wartime. See Marie L. Ahearn's fascinating *The Rhetoric of War: Training Days, the Militia, and the Military Sermon*. The sight of black men carrying weapons was, of course, a totally new experience for a man from the South.
32. Kopel, p. 316.

33. Peterson, *Arms and Armor*, p. 197. Major George Hanger, a British officer, described a rifleman's attempt to kill either him or Banestre Tarleton from 400 yards: "A rifleman passed over the milldam, evidently observing two officers, and laid himself down on his belly; for in such position they always lie, to take a good shot at a long distance."
34. Peterson, *Continental Soldier*, p. 20.
35. Even Burgoyne's expedition into the interior was to be largely waterborne. First he traveled down the Richelieu and Lake Champlain, then he marched overland a short distance to reach the Hudson. During that march, he met disaster at Bemis Heights in what became known as the Battle of Saratoga.
36. Kopel, p. 315.
37. *Ibid.*
38. Ferguson, inventor of the Ferguson breech-loading rifle, was a brave and chivalrous soldier who sometimes showed poor judgment. As the leader of a sharpshooter detachment, he had Washington himself in his rifle sights at Brandywine. He didn't know who the distinguished-looking officer was, but he couldn't bring himself to shoot him from cover. At King's Mountain, this expert rifleman tried to drive away the backwoods militia with bayonet charges. Wounded several times, he continued leading charges until he died.
39. Tarleton himself was one of the few survivors. He escaped the carnage to lead more of Cornwallis's cavalry.
40. Kenneth Roberts, *Rabble in Arms*, p. 8.

Chapter 3
". . . THAT EVERY MAN BE ARMED . . ."

1. Some have said that the words, "But as for me, give me liberty or give me death," were added to written versions of the speech after Henry made it.
2. Benjamin Franklin, *Franklin: Writings*, p. 608.
3. The first state constitution of Massachu-

setts was strongly weighted in favor of the wealthy in Boston. A disproportionate share of the tax burden fell on the small farmers, particularly in the western counties. Daniel Shays was made a leader of the movement against his will, by discontented fellow farmers.
4. Morison, p. 305.
5. *Ibid.*, p. 311.
6. *Ibid.*, p. 315.
7. Hardy, p. 67; Malcolm, p. 156.
8. Hardy, p. 64; Kopel, p. 385; Malcolm, p. 157.
9. Bejamin Fletcher Wright, *The Federalist by James Madison, Alexander Hamilton and John Jay*, pp. 334–35.
10. *Ibid.*, p. 335.
11. *Ibid.*, p. 223.
12. *Ibid.*, p. 224 (paper 28).
13. Hardy, p. 67; Kopel, p. 319; Malcolm, p. 156.
14. Hardy, p. 68; Malcolm, p. 158.
15. Hardy, p. 69; Malcolm p. 158.
16. Malcolm, p. 159.
17. *American Rifleman*, March 1991, "Madison and the Bill of Rights," by Michael T. McCabe; Hardy, pp. 71–76.
18. Hardy, p. 72, quoting *1 Debates and Proceedings in the Congress of the United States 433–434*. Madison wrote about his plan: "Fourthly, in that article 1st, section 9, between clauses 3 and 4, there be inserted these clauses, to wit: . . . The people shall not be deprived or abridged of their right to speak, to write, or to publish their sentiments; and the freedom of the press, as one of the great bulwarks of liberty, shall be invincible.

"The people shall not be restrained from peaceably assembling and consulting for the common good. . . .

"The right of the people to keep and bear arms shall not be infringed; a well armed and well regulated militia being the best security of a free country; but no person religiously scrupulous of bearing arms shall be compelled to render military service in person. . . ."
See also Kopel, p. 355.
19. *American Rifleman*, March, 1991, "Madison and the Bill of Rights," by Michael T.

McCabe; Hardy, pp. 71–76; Malcolm, pp. 159–61.

20. Malcolm, pp. 159–61; Hardy, pp. 76–77; Kopel, p. 439, quotes Howard Owen Hunter's article, "Problems in Search of Principles: The First Amendment in the Supreme Court from 1791 to 1930" in *Emory Law Journal 39* (Winter 1986), p. 85, to show how the United States rejected much of English common law:

> But the religion clauses, the second amendment provisions on arms, the third amendment provisions on quartering soldiers, and the eighth amendment prohibition of cruel and unusual punishment were patent breaks with English practice. . . . In addition, the two major structural components of the American system—the federalism which dispersed power, and the concept of a government of limited powers delegated by the people—were radical departures from English government in both fact and theory.

21. Kopel, pp. 67–68; Malcolm, pp. 159–61.

22. In 1941, in the case of *Bridges v. California*, the U.S. Supreme Court emphasized the break between U.S. and British law. Harry Bridges, a labor leader, had been convicted of contempt for criticizing a judge. Justice Felix Frankfurter argued that criticism of judges was not protected by the First Amendment. Judicial power to punish criticism, he said, was "part and parcel of the Anglo-American system of administering justice," recognized in "the judiciaries of the English-speaking world." Justice Hugo Black countered that the clearest purpose of the Bill of Rights was to give "far more security to the people of the United States with respect to freedom of religion, conscience, expression, assembly, petition and press than the people of Great Britain have ever enjoyed." The Court voted five to four to set aside Bridges's conviction.

23. Malcolm, p. 164.

24. Hardy, pp. 79–80; Kopel, pp. 106, 318, 355.

25. Kopel, p. 355.

26. Hardy, p. 81.

27. Hardy, pp. 93–95; Kopel, p. 319.

28. Title 10, United States Code, paragraph 311(a), (lawyers' edition, Lawyer's Cooperative Publishing Company, vol. 17, p. 146).

Chapter 4
SECOND THOUGHTS ABOUT THE SECOND AMENDMENT

1. The American attempts to invade Canada were disastrous. U.S. troops were defeated not only by British regulars but by Canadian militia. British incursions into the United States ended the same way. A seaborne British force did burn Washington, where no one expected such a thing could happen, and the militia were grossly unprepared. The same force next attempted to burn Baltimore. This time the American militia were prepared. British General Robert Ross, who led the invasion, was killed, his force repulsed, and Francis Scott Key wrote "The Star-Spangled Banner" while watching Ft. McHenry drive away the British fleet. British Admiral Alexander Cochrane sailed back to the West Indies to prepare for the next invasion. That ended in the fantastically lopsided British defeat at New Orleans.

2. New Orleans has often been called an indecisive battle because it was fought after the peace treaty had been signed (although well before it was ratified). It was hardly indecisive. The most important cause of the war was the impressment of American seamen—a matter not even mentioned in the treaty. After New Orleans, though, impressment was a dead issue. It never occurred again. Nor were there any more British conspiracies to detach groups of states or territories from this country. Nor did Britain ever again dare to treat the United States as if it were still a colony.

3. Hardy, pp. 86–87, quoting *Bliss v. Commonwealth* 12 Kentucky 90 (1822).

4. In April of 1860, Rep. Roger A. Pryor of Virginia challenged Rep. John Fox Potter

of Wisconsin to a duel. As the challenged party, Potter chose Bowie knives of equal size and weight, with the duelists to fight in a closed room until one fell and was unable to get up. Pryor withdrew his challenge. A year and a month before that, Rep. Dan Sickles of New York accosted Philip Barton Key, a Washington socialite alleged to be his wife's lover, and shot him dead with a Deringer pistol in front of the White House. Sickles became a general in the Civil War.

5. Hardy, pp. 88–89, quoting *Nunn v. State*, 1 Ga. 243.
6. Kopel, pp. 334–35, 347, 366; Hardy, pp. 90–92, quoting *United States v. Cruikshank* 92 U.S. 542 (1876).
7. Kopel, p. 336; Don B. Kates, Jr., "Toward a History of Handgun Prohibition in the United States," in Don B. Kates, Jr., ed., *Restricting Handguns: The Liberal Skeptics Speak Out*, p. 14.
8. Kates, "Toward a History of Handgun Prohibition in the United States," in Kates, *Restricting Handguns*, p. 17.
9. Kopel, pp. 353–54, 372–73; Kennett and Anderson, pp. 77–78; Hardy, pp. 92–93.
10. Rand, *No Right to Keep and Bear Arms*.
11. In the United States, many people speak of "pistols and revolvers" as if they were different things. Since the disappearance of revolving rifles, all revolvers have been pistols. Revolving rifles had a nasty habit of burning the left hand of right-handed shooters (and the right hand of southpaws), so they are probably gone for good. In this book, "pistols" means pistols, whether single-shot, revolver, or semiautomatic.
12. Kennett and Anderson, p. 171.
13. Kennett and Anderson, p. 175. Compare Sullivan's oratory to President Bill Clinton's statement in the *New York Times*, August 27, 1994 after the passage of the 1994 crime bill: "This crime bill is going to make every neighborhood in America safer." Sure.
14. Kennett and Anderson, p. 185.
15. *Ibid.*
16. The opposite of "discretionary" licensing is "mandatory" licensing, such as fol-

lowed in New York's neighbor, Connecticut. Under mandatory licensing, the licensing authority *must* issue a license if the applicant meets certain objective criteria.
17. Kates, Introduction, p. 5.
18. Carol Ruth Silver and Don B. Kates, Jr., "Self Defense, Handgun Ownership, and the Independence of Women in a Violent, Sexist Society," in Kates, *Restricting Handguns*, p. 153.
19. *Ibid.*
20. Quoted in Kates, "Toward a History of Handgun Prohibition in the United States," in Kates, *Restricting Handguns*, p. 17.
21. Kopel, p. 343; Kennett and Anderson, p. 183.
22. Kates, Jr., pp. 21–22.
23. *Hartford Courant*, December 12, 1993, "Courts Haven't Supported Rights of Individuals to Own Firearms," by Laurie Asseo, Associated Press; also *New Haven Register*, December 12, 1993, "Courts Leaning Toward Gun Control View," by Associated Press.
24. Hardy, pp. 89–90, quoting *Dred Scott v. Sanford*, 60 U.S. 393, 420 (1856).
25. Hardy, pp. 90–92; Kopel, pp. 334–45, quoting *United States v. Cruikshank*, 92 U.S. 542 (1876).
26. Kopel, pp. 353–54, 372–73; Kennett and Anderson, pp. 77–78; Hardy, pp. 92–93, quoting *Presser v. Illinois*, 116 U.S. 252 (1886).
27. Hardy, pp. 93–95; Kopel pp. 319, 355–56, quoting *United States v. Miller*, 307 U.S. 174 (1939).
28. Rand, *No Right to Keep and Bear Arms*.
29. Kopel, p. 354, quoting *United States v. Verdugo-Urquidez*, 494 U.S. 259, 265 (1990).

Chapter 5
WHERE HAVE ALL THE MILITIAMEN GONE?

1. Peterson, *Arms and Armor*, p. 185.
2. 1994 Congressional Calendar: "August 27, 1794: Sec. Hamilton wrote to Gov.

Henry Lee that 1500 weapons were waiting for VA militia."

3. Walter Millis, *Arms and Men*, pp. 37–38.
4. *Ibid.*, pp. 38–39.
5. *Ibid.*, pp. 45–46.
6. William Weir, *Written With Lead*, p. 40.
7. *The Telephone Bulletin*, Nov. 1966, "The Last Gallant War," by William Weir.
8. Millis, p. 129.
9. *Ibid.*
10. *Ibid.*, pp. 159–62.
11. Hardy, p. 66.
12. Davidson, p. 29; Sherrill, *The Saturday Night Special*, pp. 57–60; Sugarmann, *NRA*, pp. 29–32.
13. Weir, *Written With Lead*, pp. 229–48 (Dillinger) and 211–28 (Barrow).
14. Sugarmann, page 30.
15. *American Rifleman*, Sept. 1957, "Almost a National Affair," by Nils Kvale.
16. Even the Afrikaner militia, so powerful in defensive war, failed in a war of conquest against a neighboring African tribe.
17. *The Journal of the Medical Association of Georgia*, March 1994, "Guns in the Medical Literature: A Failure of Peer Review," by Edgar A. Suter, MD, (hereafter, Suter, *JMAG*) graph 10, p. 142.
18. The United Kingdom is not the gun-free paradise the anti-gun lobby pretends. It is easier to get a pistol anywhere in England, Scotland, or Wales than it is in Washington, D.C., Evanston or Morton Grove, Illinois, or even New York City. See Colin Greenwood (superintendent of the West Yorkshire, England, police), "Another Syndrome," reprinted in Kates, p. 35.
19. Kopel, pp. 278–94.
20. Kopel, pp. 283–84.
21. *Handgun Laws in Other Industrialized Countries*, an HCI pamphlet
22. This information on Swiss gun laws was correct as of mid–1996. There is a possibility that they may be tightened, but very little chance that they will become as tight as those in the United States.
23. All Swiss men from 21 to 50 are required by law to have a fully automatic assault rifle in their homes unless they are militia officers. If they are officers, the law requires that they keep a pistol until they are 55. Retired militia officers keep their pistols. Retired militia enlisted men receive either an assault rifle or a bolt-action rifle from the government on retirement.
24. Related by the author's brother, a former resident of Switzerland.
25. Kopel, p. 284.
26. *American Rifleman*, August 1994, letter, p. 10.
27. Abraham N. Tennenbaum, "Israel Has a Successful Gun Control Policy," in Charles P. Cozic, *Gun Control*, pp. 249–51.
28. *Ibid.*
29. Robert W. Lee, "Gun Control Would Not Reduce Crime," in Cozic, *Gun Control*, pp. 52–53.
30. Michael Howard, *The Franco Prussian War*, pp. 245, 249–56.
31. For more on the Afrikaner military organization, see Thomas Pakenham, *The Boer War*; Oliver Ransford, *The Battle of Majuba Hill*; Rayne Kruger, *Goodbye Dolly Gray*, and Deneys Reitz, *Commando*.

Chapter 6
DIGRESSION NO. 1: WEAPONS AND WARFARE

1. Neil Sheehan, *A Bright Shining Lie*, pp. 141–42.
2. William Weir, *Fatal Victories*, p. 233.
3. Bill Gunston, "Air Warfare," in Ray Bonds, ed., *Advanced Technology Warfare*, pp. 92–127.
4. Col. Richard S. Friedman, "Land Warfare," in Bonds, *Advanced Technology Warfare*, pp. 135–39. Another innovation is Chobham armor, a laminated material including ceramics as well as steel. It is said to have improved resistance to shaped charges, HESH (high explosive squash head) projectiles, and solid shot.
5. *Ibid.* p. 137.
6. *New York Times*, Jan. 4, 1995, "Russian War: Corpses and Wild Dogs," by Michael Spector.
7. In the eastern (mountainous) area of Korea, tanks were most useful as prefab

pillboxes after having been winched to the top of ridges.

8. The Diagram Group, *Weapons: An International Encyclopedia from 5000 B.C. to 2000 A.D.*, pp. 156–57, 200–1; John Marriot, "Missiles and Rockets," in J.I.H. Owen, *Infantry Weapons of the World*, pp. 149–95; Shelford Bidwell, "Anti-Tank Guns and Guided Weapons," in Shelford Bidwell, ed., *Artillery of the World*, pages 156–93.
9. John Marriot, "Missiles and Rockets," in Owen, *Infantry Weapons of the World*, pp. 149–95.
10. Diagram Group, p. 285.
11. Edward Clinton Ezell, *Small Arms of the World*, p. 319.
12. *Ibid.*, p. 17.
13. Ken Warner, ed., *1993 Gun Digest Annual*, ballistics tables, p. 220.
14. Friedman, "Land Warfare," in Bonds, *Advanced Techology Warfare*, p. 143.
15. W.H.B. Smith, *Small Arms of the World*, p. 213.
16. Ezell, p. 573.
17. John Weeks, *World War II Small Arms*, pp. 15–16. Firearms expert John Weeks has this to say about the heat generated by rapid firing: "But the heat is not entirely confined to the barrel alone. It travels along the metal of the body and breech block and warms up all the working parts, so that after a few hundred rounds the entire gun is substantially hotter than when it started. This heat affects the clearances between moving parts and also can reduce the effectiveness of the many little springs which operate the various components."
18. W.H.B. Smith, *Small Arms of the World*, p. 43.
19. NRA, *High Power Rifle Rules*, pp. 14–15.
20. *American Rifleman*, July 1969, letter, "M 16 Automatic Fire," by Henry Lum.
21. Diagram Group, p. 284; Ezell, pp. 64–67.
22. Ian V. Hogg, *The Complete Machine-Gun*, p. 27.
23. Friedman, "Land Warfare," in Bonds, *Advanced Techology Warfare*, p. 144.
24. Ernesto "Che" Guevara, *Guerrilla Warfare*, pp. 54–56.
25. Stanley C. Crist, "Small Arms Master

Plan," in Warner, *Gun Digest Annual*, 1993, 102–10.
26. W.H.B. Smith, *Small Arms of the World*, p. 213.
27. Kurt Saxon, *The Poor Man's James Bond*, pp. 6–13; *The Poor Man's Armorer*, Volume 1, Number 9, "Improvised Munitions Handbook," reprinted from U.S. Army TM Number 31–210.
28. See also Larry Collins and Dominique LaPierre, *O Jerusalem!* for descriptions of how weapons and even armored vehicles were improvised.

Chapter 7
THE SEEDS OF DISCORD

1. Sugarmann, *NRA*, p. 90.
2. Davidson, p. 23.
3. *Ibid.*, p. 26.
4. *Ibid.*, p. 26; Sugarmann, *NRA*, pp. 26–27.
5. Sugarmann, *NRA*, pp. 26–27.
6. *Arms and the Man*, May, 1911, editorial; Sugarmann, *NRA*, p. 27.
7. Sugarmann, *NRA*, p. 17.
8. *Ibid.*, p. 15.
9. *New Haven Register*, Aug. 19, 1944, "Crime Bill Opposers Got NRA Cash"; *Hartford Courant*, Aug. 19, 1944, "Key Lawmakers on Crime Bill Got NRA Cash."
10. *ConnPIRG* newsletter, Fall 1994, "Special Interest PACs Thwart Action on Clean Water."
11. Federal Election Commission news release, April 4, 1996.
12. Ann McBride, "Campaign Money Chase Turns Off Quality Challengers, Incumbents, Too." Common Cause pamphlet.
13. Sugarmann, *NRA*, p. 87.
14. *Ibid.*, p. 88.
15. Wilfred Ward, "SHOT Show '91 . . . As Seen Through British Eyes," in Warner, *Gun Digest Annual, 1992*, pp. 68, 70.
16. Kates, Jr., "History of Handgun Prohibition," in Kates, *Restricting Handguns*, pp. 25–26.
17. *Ibid.*, p. 25.
18. *Washington Post*, April 11, 1986. The

House had just passed the McClure-Volkmer Bill.

19. Davidson, p. 80.
20. *Ibid.*, p. 46.
21. NRA mailing to members, summer, 1994.
22. *Hartford Courant*, Aug. 13, 1994, "Clinton Vows to Fight for Crime Bill," by Ann Devroy and Kenneth J. Cooper of the *Washington Post*.
23. *Hartford Courant*, Aug. 16, 1994, "Compromise May Be Tried on Crime Bill," by combined wire services.
24. *Hartford Courant*, Aug. 5, 1994, editorial: "Don't Give in to Gun Bullies."
25. *Philadelphia Inquirer*, May 17, 1981, "Gun Rules . . . or Worldwide Gun Control," by Garry Wills.
26. *Webster's Encyclopedic Unabridged Dictionary of the English Language*.
27. *Ibid.*
28. The Prohibition movement and the evils of alcohol are discussed more fully in Weir, *In the Shadow of the Dope Fiend*.
29. How this may be accomplished is the point of Weir, *In the Shadow of the Dope Fiend*.
30. Jay Robert Nash, *Bloodletters and Badmen*, pp. 409–10; Weir, *Written With Lead*, p. 285.
31. See William J. Helmer, *The Gun that Made the Twenties Roar*.
32. See Weir, *Written With Lead*, pp. 211–48.
33. The "BAR" used military rifle cartridges, not pistol cartridges like the submachine gun. Barrow obtained his BARs (he used a number in his brief career) by robbing National Guard armories.
34. Helmer, p. 108.
35. L.L. Edge, *Run the Cat Roads*, p. 4–10.
36. Sugarmann, *NRA*, p. 30.
37. Sherrill, p. 58.
38. Sugarmann, *NRA*, pp. 32–33.
39. Kopel, p. 74.
40. Sugarman, p. 33.
41. *Ibid.*
42. Weir, *Written with Lead*, pp. 270–71.
43. Sherrill, p. 60.
44. *Ibid.*, p. 61.
45. Guy Gugliotta and Jeff Leen, *Kings of Cocaine*, pp. 9–13.
46. Weir, *In the Shadow of the Dope Fiend*,

pp. 184–85; *New York Times*, Oct. 31, 1994, "Modern 'Fagins' Admit to Series of Bank Robberies," by Robert Reinhold.

Chapter 8
TIME OF TROUBLES

1. James F. Kirkham, Sheldon G. Levy, and William J. Crotty, *Assassination and Political Violence*, p. 150.
2. Hugo Byars, *Government by Assassination*.
3. Gary Kleck, *Point Blank*, p.5.
4. Sherrill, p. 68.
5. *Ibid.*
6. *Ibid.*, p. 72.
7. *Ibid.*
8. *Ibid.*
9. Ezell, pp. 408–09.
10. Sherrill, p. 73.
11. *Ibid.*
12. Sugarmann, *NRA*, p. 39.
13. Sherrill, p. 286.
14. Handgun Control, Inc., pamphlet, *Twenty Years of Steady Progress to Save Lives*.
15. Nelson "Pete" Shields, *Guns Don't Die—People Do*, p. 23.
16. Interview with Jennifer Jackson, June 1994.
17. Interview with Shawn Taylor Zelman, October 1994.
18. *The New Yorker*, July 26, 1976, "A Reporter at Large: Handguns," by Richard Harris; Kopel, p. 125.
19. Shields, p. 145.
20. Sugarmann, *Assault Weapons and Accessories in America*, p. 26.
21. Sugarmann, *NRA*, p. 254.
22. Davidson, p. 30.
23. *Ibid.*, pp. 30–36; Sugarmann, *NRA*, pp. 46–52.
24. Davidson, pp. 48–49.

Chapter 9
HARLON "CANUTE" VERSUS THE TIDE

1. Davidson, p. 56.
2. *Ibid.*, p. 54. Contrary to the statements of Josh Sugarmann and other anti-gun lob-

byists, very few of those 20,000 U.S. laws regulating guns are zoning regulations. In my 12 years as a member and chairman of a town planning and zoning commission and a regional planning commission, I found *no* references to guns, gun stores, shooting ranges, and the like.

3. Davidson, p. 59, quoting Michael Beard of the NCBH.

4. Kleck, pp. 20–21, 54–55.

5. Davidson, p. 62.

6. *Ibid.*, p. 75.

7. *Ibid.* p. 78.

8. Sugarmann, *NRA* p. 222, quoting *Insider Gun News*, Aug. 1987.

Chapter 10
GREEN APPLES, PLASTIC PISTOLS, AND PARALLEL PARANOIA

1. Davidson, pp. 85–114; Sugarmann, *NRA*, pp. 183–98.

2. The M-14 was intended to be an assault rifle, that is, capable of firing both semi-automatically and automatically. But the shoulder stock is at an angle with the line of the barrel, causing the gun to climb in automatic fire. Further, its cartridge, the 7.62 NATO, is almost as powerful as the old .30-06—far too powerful to control in automatic fire in a rifle as light as the M-14. The army did consider rifle designs with a straight stock before adopting the M-14, but the brass thought they looked funny. They also were reluctant to reduce the power of the cartridge. All they did was prove that you can't make any rifle into an assault rifle by giving it automatic capability. NRA literature, however, continued to compare the M-14 favorably to possible rivals, such as the AR-15, until the army stopped buying M-14s and adopted the AR-15 (as the M-16) for all troops.

The pistol ballistics tests were a cooperative effort by the Pentagon and the LEAA. The Pentagon wanted to replace the .45 ACP pistol cartridge with the 9mm Luger cartridge. There was a good reason:

all our allies used the 9mm, so the U.S. use of it would simplify supply in time of war. But the Pentagon wanted to make it look as if the 9mm was also more deadly than the .45. According to the tests, even the .38 special had more stopping power than the .45. The tests were based on the size of a temporary cavity made by bullets striking a block of gelatine and on a computer model of a human being. The premises were fallacious for reasons that would take too much space to explain here, but the results were contrary to the experience of soldiers, police, and hunters for more than a century.

3. The military has sold weapons to NRA members at far below cost; it has loaned weapons to NRA-affiliated clubs; it has supplied ammunition to those clubs; and military personnel have operated the Camp Perry, Ohio, range for the NRA's national matches.

4. Davidson, p. 98.

5. Weir, *Written With Lead*, p. 124.

6. I was there.

7. Davidson, p. 87.

8. U.S. Department of Justice, Bureau of Justice Statistics. *Sourcebook of Criminal Justice Statistics—1994*, (hereafter, DOJ, *Sourcebook 1994*), table 3.143, p. 357.

9. By telephone from Bureau of Justice Statistics, confirmed by the FBI's *Law Enforcement Officers Killed and Assaulted, 1994.*

10. DOJ, *Sourcebook 1994*, table 3.101, p. 320; table 3.98, p. 317.

11. *Ibid.*

12. *Ibid.*

13. *Ibid.*, table 3.98, p. 317.

14. *Hartford Courant*, Nov. 21, 1993, "A Corner Where Crack Is King," by Edmund Mahony.

15. A bullet, contrary to the usage of many journalists and gun control advocates, is not a cartridge. It's one of four components of a modern cartridge—bullet, propellant, primer, and case. The bullet is the part that comes out of the muzzle of the gun when the cartridge is fired.

16. Inside a pistol or rifle barrel is rifling, spiraling grooves that impress themselves on

the bullet when the gun is fired and make it rotate. The spinning keeps the bullet traveling nose first, which improves its accuracy. A bullet too hard to be impressed by the grooves does not "take" the rifling.

17. Sugarmann, *NRA*, p. 186.
18. Davidson, p. 45.
19. *Ibid.*, p. 89.
20. *Ibid.*, p. 90.
21. *Ibid.*
22. Sugarmann, *NRA*, p. 185.
23. Davidson, p. 90.
24. *Ibid.*
25. *Ibid.*
26. *Ibid.*, pp. 90–91.
27. *Ibid.*, p. 96.
28. *Ibid.*
29. *Ibid.*, p. 97.
30. *Ibid.*
31. *Ibid.*, p. 112.
32. Sugarmann, *NRA*, p. 192–93.
33. Davidson, p. 100.
34. Sugarmann, *NRA*, p. 192.
35. Davidson, p. 103.
36. See Weir, *In the Shadow of the Dope Fiend*.
37. Davidson, p. 103.
38. *Ibid.*, p. 107.
39. Letter to *The American Rifleman*.
40. Sugarmann, *NRA*, p. 194–97.
41. Davidson, p. 130.
42. *Ibid.*, p. 131.
43. *Ibid.*
44. *Ibid.*, p. 132.
45. *Ibid.*

Chapter 11
POLITICIANS VERSUS CRIME

1. *Hartford Courant*, Oct. 31, 1994, "Survey: Violent Crimes Rose 5.6% in 1993," by Associated Press.
2. FBI, *Crime in the United States, 1993: Uniform Crime Reports*, chart 2.7, p. 12.
3. *New York Times*, Apr. 2, 1994, "Crime Levels Fell in 1993, Report Says," by Clifford Krauss.
4. *New Haven Register*, Nov. 1, 1994, "Candidates Find They Can Make Points on Crime," by Gregory B. Hladky.

5. *New York Times*, May 6, 1996, "Major Crimes Fell in '96, Early Data by FBI Indicate," by Fox Butterfield; *New Haven Register*, May 6, 1996, "Crime Rate in U.S. Dips a 4th Year," by Associated Press.
6. DOJ, *Sourcebook 1994*, table 3.99, pp. 318–19; table 3.94, p. 305.
7. *Ibid.*, table 3.99, p. 318.
8. DOJ, *Sourcebook 1994*, table 3.100, p. 319; Kleck, p. 170. The DOJ figures are for robberies *involving* guns, which may include involvements other than robbers using guns to commit the robbery. Kleck, using 1986 figures, says robberies in which the criminal was armed with a gun amounted to only about 20 percent of the total.
9. DOJ, *Sourcebook 1994*, pp. 175–76.
10. DOJ, *Sourcebook 1993*, table 3.2, p. 247.
11. *Ibid.*, table 3.107, p. 352.
12. Interview, Oct. 31, 1994.
13. *Hartford Courant*, Oct. 31, 1994, "Survey: Violent Crimes Rose 5.6% in 1993," by Associated Press.
14. Bureau of Justice Statistics, *Questions and Answers About the Redesign*, p. 1.
15. BJS, *Criminal Victimization 1993*, p. 6.
16. BJS, *Questions and Answers About the Redesign*, p. 6.
17. BJS, *Questions and Answers*, p. 1.
18. BJS, *Criminal Victimization 1993*, p. 5.
19. *Hartford Courant*, Oct. 31, 1994, "Survey: Violent Crimes Rose 5.6% in 1993," by Associated Press.
20. *New Haven Register*, Dec. 4, 1994 "Overall Crime Rate in Country Decreases," by Associated Press; *New York Times*, Dec. 5, 1994 "Serious Crime Is Still Declining, but Fears Remain, FBI Reports," by Keith Bradsher.
21. *Ibid.*
22. *New York Times*, Dec. 5, 1994, "Serious Crime Is Still Declining, but Fears Remain, FBI Reports," by Keith Bradsher.
23. DOJ, *Sourcebook 1994*, table 3.94, p. 305.
24. Kopel, p. 415.
25. *Ibid.*
26. DOJ, *Sourcebook 1994*, table 3.122, p. 342.
27. *Ibid.*, table 3.121, p. 342.

28. *Ibid.*, table 3.116, p. 339.
29. National Safety Council, *Accidental Facts*, 1992 Edition, p. 32.
30. Suter, *JMAG*, graph 4, p. 379.
31. Kleck, table 7.5, p. 310.
32. To clean a gun, it's necessary to at least open the action—pull back the breechblock or disengage the cylinder—if not disassemble the gun. A gun in such condition cannot fire even if there is a round in the chamber.
33. Kleck, p. 271.
34. *Ibid.*, p. 272.
35. Suter, *JMAG*, graph 3, p. 135.
36. *Ibid.*, graph 6, p. 138.
37. Kopel, p. 287.
38. *Ibid.*, p. 136.
39. Kleck, p. 236.
40. Kopel, p. 156.
41. Kleck, p. 223.
42. *Ibid.*, pp. 223–68.
43. Wayne LaPierre, *Guns, Crime and Freedom*, p. 43., quoting Centers for Disease Control, "Suicide Surveillance, 1970–1980."
44. Kleck, p. 170.
45. Davidson, p. 194.
46. LaPierre, p. 47.
47. Kleck, p. 334.
48. *Hartford Courant*, March 30, 1994, "Gun Lobby Distorts Brady Law," by Deborah Mathis.

Chapter 12

100,000 COPS AND BRADY II

1. DOJ, *Sourcebook 1994*, table 2.1, p. 140.
2. *Hartford Courant*, Dec. 10, 1993, "Clinton Seeks 'Action Plan' to Stop Crime," by Robert A. Rankin, Knight-Ridder Newspapers.
3. *Ibid.*
4. For more on the fallacy of boot camps, see Weir, *In the Shadow of the Dope Fiend*, pp. 202, 205–07.
5. *Hartford Courant*, Dec. 9, 1993, "President Says Time Has Come to Consider Strengthening Gun Laws," by *Los Angeles Times* syndicate.
6. *New Haven Register*, Dec. 12, 1993, "Clinton Urges All to Replace Violence with Values for Kids," by Associated Press.
7. *New Haven Register*, Dec. 21, 1993, "Clinton Wants to Boost Fees for Gun Sellers," by Associated Press.
8. *New Haven Register*, Jan. 30, 1994, "Congress Eyes Weapons Ban," by Associated Press.
9. *Hartford Courant*, Dec. 9, 1993, "President Says Time Has Come to Consider Strengthening Gun Controls," by *Los Angeles Times* syndicate.
10. *New Haven Register*, May 6, 1993, "Assault Guns Banned," by Tamara Lytle; Interview with Mary Jo Hoeksema, DeLauro's guns and crime specialist, Nov. 16, 1994; interview with Bureau of Justice Statistics spokeswoman, Dec. 1, 1994; copy of letter dated May 4, 1994 to all members of the House from Rep. Fortney "Pete" Stark of California; FBI, *Crime in America: Uniform Crime Reports 1993*; FBI, *Law Enforcement Officers Killed and Assaulted 1992*; FBI, *Law Enforcement Officers Killed and Assaulted 1994*; FBI, *Killed in the Line of Duty*; Kleck, p. 96.

Stark took an estimate from the BATF that "assault weapons" are less than 1 percent of all guns in the United States, and changed "less than 1 percent" to .5 percent. Then he wrote, "After examining data provided by the FBI on police killed between 1986 and 1993, it becomes clear that although less than 1% of all privately owned American guns are assault weapons, they are 9% of guns used by cop killers."

Neither the latest issue of the FBI's annual *Law Enforcement Officers Killed and Assaulted* nor its long-term study, *Killed in the Line of Duty*, says a word about "assault weapons." According to Kleck, p. 96, the FBI lists as "possible assault weapons" any rifle or submachine gun in the following calibers: .22 rimfire, .223, 7.62 NATO (.308 Winchester), 9mm Luger, or .45 ACP.

Stark assumed that "possible assault

rifles" were really "assault weapons"—as we've seen, a huge jump at conclusions. He said he learned from the FBI that 8.9 percent of officers killed between 1896 and 1993 were killed with these weapons. Stark changed 8.9 to 9, not as great an exaggeration as changing "less than 1 percent" to .5 percent. That gave him his estimation that "assault weapons" were 18 times more likely to kill police officers than any other kind of weapon.

Any estimate of the number of "assault weapons" or any other type of guns is no more than a guess. The BATF is, unfortunately, a highly unreliable source for the number of guns in private hands. Both the BATF and the Bureau of the Census estimate handgun imports. The BATF estimate is always higher—*as much as 200 percent higher*—than the Census Bureau's. A larger number of guns in the country makes the BATF's job seem more important. It does nothing for the Census Bureau. Similarly, a low estimate of the number of "assault weapons" makes voting for their ban seem like a low-risk political choice. That kind of accounting makes it easy for people like Stark to play further games. If there are, as most estimate, 200 million guns in private hands in the United States, the number of "assault rifles" has to be more than .5 percent. One maker, Colt, has probably produced enough of these military-looking rifles to exceed .5 percent of all guns. By 1977, Colt had produced and sold more than 300,000 of its AR-15 series, and it's been producing the AR-15 and its sibling, the Colt Sporter, ever since (Ezell, p. 630). It's a safe bet that there are more than a million of the AR-15 series at large. That's more than .5 percent by itself. Ruger's Mini 14 series—the Mini 14, the Ranch Rifle, and the Mini 30—also has sold in massive quantities. The Chinese Type 56 Carbine, better known here by its Russian name, the SKS, has been imported into the United States in huge quantities. The SKS, which has a fixed magazine and no pistol grip, has only been occasionally classified as an

"assault rifle," but the AK-47, imported from China and elsewhere, has also been a big seller. The catalogue section of the 1993 *Gun Digest* lists no fewer than 28 semiautomatic rifles with the characteristics of what journalists and politicians call "assault rifles." It seems likely, then, that "assault rifles" make up a far larger share of the total of privately owned firearms. All of the foregoing concerns the so-called assault rifles. Stark's letter, though, referred to "assault weapons." "Assault weapons" is a term used by the press and politicians to include not only funny-looking rifles, but funny-looking pistols and shotguns. The number of "assault weapons," therefore, is considerably greater than the number of "assault rifles," further distorting the situation.

For the record, the latest—1994—total of police officers killed was 76. Of them, 75 were killed by firearms. Eight were killed by rifles and three by shotguns. Of those killed by rifles, one was killed by a .22 caliber rimfire gun, very few of which have ever been classified as "assault rifles." Two were killed by .223 caliber weapons, which may or may not have been an "assault rifle"—the chances are against it. One was killed by a .30 caliber rifle, no further identification. One was killed by a .30-06 rifle, which could not have been an "assault rifle." Two were killed by .308 rifles, and the chances of either of them being an "assault rifle" are even slimmer than for the .223. One was killed by a rifle using the former Russian service cartridge, 7.62 x 39mm. The odds on that weapon being an "assault rifle" are about 50–50. (Information by phone from Bureau of Justice Statistics, confirmed by *Law Enforcement Officers Killed and Assaulted 1994*.)

Chapter 17, "Devil Guns," presents verified and verifiable figures on these weapons and their importance.

11. Kleck, *Point Blank*, pp. 80–81, 96.
12. *Ibid.*, p. 96;
13. Information by telephone from Bureau of Justice Statistics, confirmed by FBI's *Law*

Enforcement Officers Killed and Assaulted 1994.

14. *New Haven Register*, May 6, 1994, "Assault Guns Banned," by Tamara Lytle.
15. *Hartford Courant*, May 6, 1994, "House Passes Weapons Ban in Close Vote," by Kenneth J. Cooper, *Washington Post*.
16. *New York Times*, Aug. 28, 1994, " 'Victory' Over Crime at Least Politically," by Gwen Ifill.
17. *Hartford Courant*, Sept. 11, 1994, "Stories on Crime Bill Misled Readers," by Henry McNulty.
18. *New York Times*, Aug. 27, 1994, "President Foresees Safer U.S.," by Neil A. Lewis.
19. *Ibid.*
20. *Ibid.*
21. 1994 Crime Control Act, Title I.
22. *New York Times*, Sept. 18, 1994, "The Perils of Police Hiring," by Clifford Strauss.
23. *New York Times*, May 29, 1996, "Revisiting the Issue of Crime, Dole Offers List of Remedies," by Katharine Q. Seelye.
24. *New York Times*, Dec. 19, 1993, "As Boot Camps for Criminals Multiply, Skepticism Grows," by Adam Nossiter.
25. *Ibid.*; Weir, *In the Shadow of the Dope Fiend*, p. 206.
26. *New York Times*, Nov. 19, 1994, "The High Cost of Death," by Anna Quindlen.
27. *New York Times*, Oct. 28, 1994, "Ranks of Inmates Reach One Million in 2-Decade Rise," by Steven A. Holmes.
28. Bureau of Justice Statistics Bulletin, "Prisoners in 1994," p. 1.
29. *New York Times*, Oct. 28, 1994, "Ranks of Inmates Reach One Million in 2-Decade Rise," by Steven A. Holmes.
30. *Ibid.*
31. *Time*, Nov. 14, 1994, "Going Soft on Crime," by Jill Smolowe.
32. *New York Times*, Sept. 19, 1994, letter to the editor from Sarah Brady. In HCI publications, the bill is called Brady II, but the *New York Times* apparently frowns on Roman numerals used this way.
33. There are most likely more than 200 million guns in private hands in the United States. A reasonable guess on their average market value would be $250. Multiply $250 by 200,000,000 and you get $50,000,000,000. Fifty billion dollars is a lot of money.
34. Text of Senate Bill 1882, *A Bill to Amend Title 18, United States Code, to Promote the Safe Use of Guns and Reduce Gun Violence*; *"Brady II" the Gun Violence Prevention Act of 1994, S. 1882/H.R. 3932*; *Licensing and Registration; The Gun Violence Prevention Act—Brady II, Questions and Answers*. Except for the text of the bill, all are pamphlets of Handgun Control, Inc.
35. Warner, *Gun Digest Annual, 1993*, catalogue section.
36. Senate Bill 1882, *A Bill to Amend Title 18, United States Code, to Promote the Safe Use of Guns and Reduce Gun Violence.*
37. *Ibid.*
38. *"Brady II" The Gun Violence Prevention Act of 1994, S. 1882/H.R. 3932*, an HCI pamphlet.
39. Sarah Brady letter to HCI members late in 1994 asking for donations to the Center to Prevent Handgun Violence, which is sponsoring the lawsuits.
40. *Ibid.*
41. *Ibid.*

Chapter 13
DIGRESSION NO. 2: GUNS IN CIVIL LIFE

1. James D. Wright, Peter H. Rossi, and Kathleen Daly, *Under the Gun*, p. 83, quoting Spiegler and Sweeney, *Gun Abuse in Ohio*, Cleveland: Government Research Institute, 1975.
2. Wright, Rossi, and Daly, p. 52.
3. *Ibid.*, p. 49.
4. *Ibid.* p. 81.
5. *Ibid.*
6. George D. Newton and Franklin Zimring, *Firearms and Violence in American Life*, p. 22.
7. Wright, Rossi, and Daly, pp. 51–52.
8. *Ibid.*, pp. 55–57.

9. Warner, *Gun Digest Annual 1993*, catalogue section, pp. 300–27.
10. Kleck, p. 42.
11. Wright, Rossi, and Daly, pp. 58–62.
12. *Ibid.*, pp. 70–71.
13. *Ibid.*, p. 68.
14. *Ibid.*, pp. 68–71.
15. *Ibid.*, pp. 71–72.
16. *Shooter's Bible*, 1993 edition, Stoeger Publishing Co., p. 496.
17. Kleck, p. 79.
18. *Hartford Courant*, Dec. 9, 1994, "Police Gun Swap Could Help Dealers Through Legal Loophole," by John Springer.
19. Kleck, pp. 25–26.
20. Don B. Kates, Jr., and Mark K. Benenson, "Handgun Prohibition and Homicide: A Plausible Theory Meets the Intractable Facts," in Kates, *Restricting Handguns*, p. 111.
21. John R. Salter, Jr., "Gun Owners Can Protect Themselves Against Assault," in Cozic, *Gun Control*, p. 159.
22. *Ibid.*, p. 158
23. Kates, Jr., "The Necessity of Access to Firearms by Dissenters and Minorities Whom the Government Is Unwilling or Unable to Protect," in Kates, *Restricting Handguns*, p. 186.
24. Kates, Jr., and Benenson, "Handgun Prohibition and Homicide: A Plausible Theory Meets the Intractable Facts," in Kates, *Restricting Handguns*, p. 107.
25. Harold L. Peterson, *American Knives*, p. 29.
26. Kleck, p. 29.

Chapter 14
SLIDING DOWN THE SLIPPERY SLOPE

1. *The New Yorker*, July 26, 1976, "A Reporter at Large: Handguns," by Richard Harris.
2. The BATF says it can trace more than 90 percent of the guns made since 1960. Manufacturers must record to whom each gun is sold. Wholesalers must record which retailers buy each gun. Retailers must record every individual who buys a gun with the serial number and description of the gun he buys. The retailer must keep these records for ten years and turn them over to the BATF if he goes out of business. In many states, the retailer must also send the records to state or local police, and in a number of others, the buyer must get a permit from state or local police to buy a particular gun. In addition, in several states, such as Connecticut, a private individual must also record any proposed transfer to another private individual and get police permission to complete the sale. This paper trail makes it fairly easy to trace a particular gun, such as one used in a crime. If each gun owner registered his weapons with local or state police, however, mass confiscation would be infinitely easier.
3. Kleck, p. 10, quoting *Congressional Record*, Mar. 4, 1969.
4. *Ibid.*, p. 10, quoting ABC News presentation "Guns," Jan. 24, 1990.
5. Sugarmann, *Assault Weapons and Accessories in America*, p. 26.
6. Every high school chemistry student and, of course, every terrorist, knows how to make black powder at home, using materials that could not include a "taggant." The NRA's position was on behalf of the minority of its members who like to fire muzzle-loading guns, antique or reproductions.
7. For example, the New Haven Register, Mar. 14, 1996, "NRA wins battle on fight against terrorism," by Associated Press.
8. Kleck, pp. 21–23, 56–57.
9. Davidson, p. 149.
10. *Ibid.*, pp. 157–58.
11. *New Haven Register*, Sept. 21, 1994, "Shoes in Capitol Symbolize Footsteps Lost to Gunfire," by Tamara Lytle.
12. *American Rifleman*, Nov./Dec. 1994, "ILA Report."
13. *Ibid.*
14. *Handgun Control, Inc. & The Center to Prevent Handgun Violence*, an HCI pamphlet.
15. I personally know of one Republican state legislator who made no secret of his position that no private citizen should own a

handgun but who was repeatedly endorsed by the NRA.
16. Davidson, p. 142.
17. "Conservative" and "liberal" are words
that have little meaning in the gun control
controversy. Many of the most hard-line
opponents of gun control support unions
and distrust all corporations. Many extreme conservatives, like William F.
Buckley, support strict gun control.
18. In 1989, Patrick McGuigan, writing in
Policy Review, blasted the NRA for not
supporting conservative causes, particularly the nomination of Judge Robert Bork
(Davidson, p. 178). Before the 1994 elections, Tanya Metaksa, executive director
of the NRA's Institute for Legislative Action, said, "The Second Amendment isn't
Democratic or Republican. It's not 'conservative' or 'liberal.' And neither is the
NRA" (*American Rifleman*, October
1994).
19. Height is a great advantage in basketball,
and weight is a great advantage in foot-
ball. Rifle shooting requires no unusual
physical equipment, so excellence is accessible to many more youths. In addition,
it teaches kids to handle guns safely and
channels the attraction weapons have for
most boys (and many girls) into a safe direction.

Chapter 15
THE FIVE-YEAR PLAN AND OTHER FANTASIES

1. NRA/ILA Alert (undated).
2. *Ibid.*
3. *American Rifleman*, Jul. 1966, "Gun Laws
in Scandinavia," by Nils Kvale.
4. *American Rifleman*, Feb. 1988, "The
Warsaw Ghetto: 10 Handguns Against
Tyranny," by David I. Caplan; LaPierre,
pp. 168–70.
5. Davidson, p. 156.
6. *Ibid.*
7. *Ibid.*
8. *Ibid.*, p. 43.
9. *Ibid.*, p. 43, quoting Leddy, *Magnum
Force Lobby*.

10. HCI application for 1994 year-end report.
11. *New Haven Register*, Dec. 28, 1994, "Ban
on Rhino Pursued," by David Ross.
12. *Hartford Courant*, Dec. 27, 1994,
"Deadly Bullets for Handguns to Go on
Sale," by Robert Dvorchak, Associated
Press.
13. *Ibid.*
14. *New York Times*, Dec. 29, 1994, "Company Puts a Hold on Plastic Bullet," by
Fox Butterfield.
15. *Ibid.*
16. *New York Times*, Jan. 1, 1995, "Maker of
Ammunition Defends Himself," special to
New York Times.
17. *New York Times*, Dec. 29, 1994, "Company Puts a Hold on Plastic Bullet," by
Fox Butterfield.
18. *Hartford Courant*, Dec. 29, 1994, "Production of New Bullet Put on Hold," by
combined wire services.
19. *New York Times*, Dec. 28, 1994, editorial:
"High Tech Death from Alabama."
20. *Hartford Courant*, Dec. 27, 1994,
"Deadly Bullets for Handguns to Go on
Sale," by Robert Dvorchak, Associated
Press.
21. *New York Times*, Dec. 28, 1994, "Congressman Wants to Ban Ammunition," by
Associated Press.
22. *Hartford Courant*, Dec. 28, 1994, "Tulisano to Introduce Legislation Prohibiting
Rhino-Ammo in State."
23. Soft-point bullets, hollow-point bullets,
and plain lead bullets are all considered
dumdums (named for the soft-point bullets produced at the British arsenal in
Dumdum, India). There are those who
think that banning dumdums and permit-
ting flame-throwers and napalm is typical
of the stupidity of most weapons legislation, local, national, or international.
24. *American Rifleman*, June 1994.
25. Sarah Brady letter to HCI members, Feb.
24, 1994.

Chapter 16
PSEUDO MILITIA

1. Telephone conversation, Sept. 1994.
2. *New York Times*, Nov. 14, 1994, "Fearing

a Conspiracy, Some Heed a Call to
Arms," by Keith Schneider.

3. *Ibid.*

4. *Ibid.*

5. *Ibid.*

6. *Ibid.*

7. *New Haven Register*, Nov. 2, 1994,
"Rumor of Foreign Takeover Finds Be-
lievers in America," by George de Lama,
Chicago Tribune.

8. *New York Times*, Nov. 14, 1994, "Fearing
a Conspiracy, Some Heed a Call to
Arms," by Keith Schneider.

9. *Ibid.*

10. *Hartford Courant*, Oct. 10, 1994, "Gun
Activists Organizing Independent Militias," by Associated Press.

11. Conversation, January 1995.

12. *New Haven Register*, Nov. 2, 1994,
"Rumor of Foreign Takeover Finds Be-
lievers in America," by George de Lama,
Chicago Tribune.

13. Affidavit of Daniel P. Sheehan, filed Dec.
12, 1986 in the U. S. District Court,
Southern District of Florida, in the case of
*Tony Avirgan and Martha Honey v. John
Hull et al.*

14. Interview, June 1990.

15. For more on this situation, see Weir, *In
the Shadow of the Dope Fiend*, pp. 82–
131.

16. *The Nation*, April 5, 1971, "Detention
Camps," and July 1, 1978, "Internment
Camps for Citizens: The FBI's Forty-Year
Plot," by Robert Justin Goldstein.

17. *The Progressive*, May 1985, "The Take
Charge Gang," by Keenen Peck.

18. *Ibid.*

19. The Media Research Center of Alexan-
dria, Va., studied network television coverage of the Brady bill fight. It found a
three-to-one bias in favor of the bill. It
also checked 78 stories over a two-year
period and found that 29 were what it considered neutral, three were slanted
against gun control, and 46 contained "an
aggressively pro-gun control agenda."

20. *American Rifleman*, Nov. 1993, "The
Randy Weaver Case," by Jim Oliver.

21. *Ibid.*; LaPierre, p. 185.

22. Gerry Spence, *From Freedom to Slavery*,
pp. 4–5.

23. *American Rifleman*, Nov. 1993 "The
Randy Weaver Case," by Jim Oliver. See
also Weir, *In the Shadow of the Dope
Fiend*, pp. 218–221.

24. But not nearly as odd as the FBI made
them out to be. The FBI agents "negotiating" with Koresh were almost totally ignorant of the Bible and so unable to
understand Koresh at all, because Koresh
spoke of nothing else. See Tabor and Gal-
laher, *Why Waco?*, and Reavis, *The Ashes
of Waco.*

25. The grenades, called "flash-bang" grenades, are often described as harmless.
They are intended to disorient opponents
by their noise and flash. They are actually
enhanced concussion grenades. Concussion grenades are used in war by troops
on the offensive because, as they spew out
no fragments, their lethal range is not
great enough to injure the thrower. They
are, however, capable of blowing arms,
legs, and heads off persons near them
when they explode. The BATF agents
used these lethal weapons in a building
full of small children.

26. Dick J. Reavis, *The Ashes of Waco*, pp.
124, 129–36, 145, 222, 289–90.

27. James D. Tabor and Eugene V. Gallagher,
Why Waco?, p. 213, n. 4.

28. The Davidians had gas masks, but none to
fit children. Amnesty International reported that heavy exposure to CS, the gas
used, can be fatal. There is evidence that
milder doses can be fatal to children.
Among its other effects, CS, according to
the U.S. Army, "may make them [partici-
pants in civil disturbances] incapable of
vacating the area." When burned, CS produces deadly fumes. Reavis, pp. 264–65.

29. Not all of the tanks sprayed in powdered
CS. Some shot in "ferret bombs," which
contain methylene chloride, a petroleum
derivative. Methylene chloride, according
to a standard chemical text, "forms in-
flammable vapor-air mixtures in larger
volumes. May be an explosion hazard in a
confined space. . . . Combustion by-prod-
ucts include hydrogen chloride and phos-

gene." Phosgene was the most poisonous gas used in World War I.

30. For a fuller treatment of the Branch Davidian mess, see Weir, *In the Shadow of the Dope Fiend*, pp. 214–18.

31. Tanya Metaksa, *Tell Bill Clinton and the United Nations to Get Their Hands Off Your Guns and Your Constitutional Rights! Sign, Stamp and Send the Enclosed Postcards Today*, mailing from the NRA Institute for Legislative Action.

Chapter 17
DEVIL GUNS

1. Weeks, pp. 106–08.

2. The United States was late in climbing on the assault rifle bandwagon. Its M-14 rifle fired a cartridge almost as powerful as the old .30-06. As a result, it was a disaster in automatic fire and was replaced by the M-16 when the Vietnam War began to heat up.

3. Davidson, p. 202.

4. *Ibid.*

5. *Ibid.*, p. 194.

6. Sugarmann, *Assault Weapons and Accessories in America*, p. 26.

7. Connecticut's ban on "assault weapons" specifically bans the Barrett, a rifle useless for crime or suicide or any purpose except target shooting at immensely long range.

8. HCI, *Assault Weapon Ban Questions and Answers*.

9. Letter dated June 17, 1994, from Rep. Rosa DeLauro to the author.

10. Kleck, p. 80, quoting *Los Angeles Times*, May 25, 1990.

11. *Ibid.*

12. Bureau of Justice Statistics, *Guns Used in Crime*, July 1995.

13. Kleck, p. 73.

14. *Ibid.*

15. *Ibid.*

16. *New York Times*, April 7, 1989; Kleck, p. 73.

17. Kleck, p. 89, quoting *New York Times*, Nov. 2, 1988.

18. *Ibid.*, p. 90, quoting *New York Times*, April 3, 1989.

19. Kates, Jr., and Benenson, "The Effects of Handgun Prohibition in Reducing Violent Crime," in Kates, *Restricting Handguns*, p. 99.

20. *American Rifleman*, Sept. 1957, "Almost a National Affair," by Nils Kvale.

21. *Ibid.*

22. Police in Kansas used to refer to these weapons simply as "Saturday night guns." They were used by town toughs, not professional criminals, who, when confronted with more than they could handle, would threaten to "shoot my way out." Another term for these guns was "suicide specials." "Saturday night special" may be a combination of the two terms.

23. Kleck, p. 84.

24. 103rd Congress, 2nd Session, Senate Bill 1882, Title IV—Prohibited Weapons, p. 36.

25. *New York Times*, Jan. 30, 1995, editorial: "Stand Up Again to the N.R.A."

26. W.H.B. Smith, *The NRA Book of Small Arms, Vol. I, Pistols and Revolvers*, pp. 486, 496–97.

27. *New York Times*, Feb. 6, 1994, "Firearms Agency Bans Armor Piercing Bullets," by Associated Press.

28. Violence Policy Center pamphlet, *Phantom Ammo: The Advent of Caseless Ammunition*.

29. Ezell, p. 38.

30. Violence Policy Center pamphlet, *Phantom Ammo: The Advent of Caseless Ammunition*, p. 4.

31. Josh Sugarmann and Kristen Rand, *Cease Fire*, p. 22.

Chapter 18
THE ~~DEVIL~~ GUN MADE ME DO IT

1. Sugarmann, *NRA*, p. 255.

2. *Ibid.*, p. 263.

3. CSGV pamphlet, *Public Health Studies on Gun Control*.

4. *Atlanta Constitution*, Nov. 10, 1993, "It's

Not the People—It's the Guns," by Arthur L. Kellermann.

5. *New Haven Register*, June 23, 1994, "Koop Says Pediatrician Should Warn About Guns," by Associated Press.

6. Andrew J. McClurg, "The Danger Posed by Handguns Outweighs Their Effectiveness," in Cozic, *Gun Control*, p. 176.

7. *Ibid.*, p. 177.

8. Suter, *JMAG*, p. 141; *New England Journal of Medicine* 319:1256–62, 1988; "Handgun Regulations, Crime, Assaults, and Homicide: A Tale of Two Cities," by John Henry Sloan, Arthur L. Kellermann, Donald T. Reay, James A. Ferris, Thomas Koepsell, Frederick P. Rivara, Charles Rice, Laurel Gray, and James LoGerfo.

9. *Ibid.*; Kopel, p. 153.

10. Suter, *JMAG*, p. 141.

11. Kopel, p. 154. The funding came from $20 million the CDC had allocated to prove that the United States is suffering from an "epidemic" of guns. Conducting research to prove a foregone conclusion is hardly the scientific method. It indicates how much trust can be put in the CDC's vaunted campaign to treat gun violence as a public health problem.

12. *Ibid.*, p. 151.

13. *Ibid.*

14. LaPierre, p. 173.

15. *Ibid.*, p. 154.

16. *Atlanta Constitution*, Nov. 10, 1993, "It's Not the People—It's the Guns," by Arthur L. Kellermann.

17. *Ibid.*

18. FBI, *Crime in the United States, 1993: Uniform Crime Reports*, p. 17.

19. Suter, *JMAG*, pp. 136–37.

20. Greenwood, "Crime, Suicide and Accidents: Some Cross-National and Cross-Cultural Comparisons," in Kates, *Restricting Handguns*, pp. 50–51.

21. *Ibid.*; Kates, Jr., and Benenson, "Handgun Prohibition and Homicide: A Plausible Theory Meets the Intractable Facts," in Kates, *Restricting Handguns*, p. 107.

22. *Ibid.*, p. 51. A pamphlet published by the Coalition to Stop Gun Violence reprinted in Cozic, pp. 208–13, asserts, "In Boston, after two years under Massachusetts'

Bartley-Fox law, homicides declined 39 percent." The statement is typical of the CSGV. The Bartley-Fox amendment provides a mandatory year in prison for carrying an unlicensed pistol. No reputable criminologist has ever held that it affected the homicide rate. Why would a murderer worry about an extra year in jail? And why did the CSGV pick two years after the passage of Bartley-Fox? Because in 1977, the Massachusetts homicide rate dipped to 3.1—its lowest point in 20 years. (Boston accounts for half of the homicides in Massachusetts.) In 1978, it popped back up again to a more normal 3.7. For the last couple of decades, the Massachusetts homicide rate has bounced between 3.1 and 4.2 per 100,000 (data on Massachusetts murder and non-negligent manslaughter rates from a telephone interview with an FBI statistician).

23. *Atlanta Constitution*, Nov. 10, 1993, "It's Not the People—It's the Guns," by Arthur L. Kellermann.

24. Kopel, pp. 417, 436.

25. *Ibid.*

26. Cynthia Gillespie, *Justifiable Homicide*, quoted in Kleck, pp. 114–15.

27. Silver and Kates, Jr., "Self-Defense, Handgun Ownership, and the Independence of Women in a Violent, Sexist Society," in Kates, *Restricting Handguns*, p. 152.

28. Kleck, pp. 128, 269–319.

29. Silver and Kates, Jr., "Self-Defense, Handgun Ownership, and the Independence of Women in a Violent, Sexist Society," in Kates, *Restricting Handguns*, pp. 154–55.

30. *Ibid.*, p. 156.

31. *Ibid.*

32. Kleck, p. 112.

33. DOJ, *Sourcebook 1993*, table 3.107, p. 352.

34. Kleck, pp. 112–16.

35. *Ibid.*, pp. 105–06.

36. *Ibid.*, pp. 106–08.

37. Sugarmann and Rand, *Cease Fire*, pp. 18–19.

38. Silver and Kates, Jr., "Self-Defense, Handgun Ownership, and the Indepen-

dence of Women in a Violent, Sexist Society," in Kates, *Restricting Handguns*, p. 159.

39. Kleck, p. 134.
40. Silver and Kates, Jr., "Self-Defense, Handgun Ownership, and the Independence of Women in a Violent, Sexist Society." in Kates, *Restricting Handguns*, p. 167.
41. Kleck, pp. 134–35.
42. *Ibid.*, p. 135.
43. *Ibid.* pp. 136–37.
44. *A Tale of Two Towns*, an NRA pamphlet.
45. Kleck, p. 139; James D. Wright and Peter H. Rossi, *Armed and Considered Dangerous*, p. 145.
46. Wright and Rossi, p. 145.
47. Kleck, p. 140.
48. Kopel, p. 407.

Chapter 19
CONSIDERING THE ALTERNATIVE

1. Colin Greenwood, "Crime, Suicide, and Accidents: Some Cross-national and Cross-cultural Comparisons," in Kates, *Restricting Handguns*, p. 34.
2. *Ibid.*, p. 35.
3. Sugarmann and Rand, *Cease Fire*, p. 9.
4. Sugarmann, *NRA*, p. 263.
5. DOJ, *Sourcebook 1994*, table 1.99, pp. 132–33.
6. *Ibid.*
7. *Ibid.*
8. Greenwood, "Crime, Suicide, and Accidents: Some Cross-national and Cross-cultural Comparisons," in Kates, pp. 35–36.
9. *Ibid.*, p. 36.
10. All homicide rates for states from DOJ, *Sourcebook 1994*, table 3.99, p. 318.
11. *New York Times*, March 6, 1995, "States Seek to Let Citizens Carry Concealed Weapons," by Sam Howe Verhovek; DOJ *Sourcebook 1994*, table 1.99, pp. 132–33.
12. Homicide rates for cities of more than 250,000 from DOJ *Sourcebook 1994*, table 3.102, pp. 323–28; number of

crimes per state from *Sourcebook 1994*, table 3.96, pp. 307–15.
13. Telephone call to Citizens' Assistance Office, Office of the Texas Attorney General, Austin, Texas.
14. DOJ, *Sourcebook 1994*, table 1.99, pp. 132–33.
15. NRA, *Fact Sheet*, "Handgun Bans: A History of Failure."
16. DOJ, *Sourcebook 1993*, table 4.2, p. 419.
17. DOJ, *Sourcebook 1994*, table 3.99, p. 318.
18. Kates, Jr., and Benenson, "Handgun Prohibition and Homicide: A Plausible Theory Meets the Intractable Facts," in Kates, *Restricting Handguns*, p. 111.
19. Wright and Rossi, p. 220.
20. David T. Hardy and Don B. Kates, Jr., "Handgun Availability and the Social Harm of Robbery: Recent Data and Some Projections," in Kates, Restricting Handguns, pp. 121–22.
21. James Given, *Society and Homicide in Thirteenth Century England*; Benenson and Kates, Jr., "Handgun Prohibition and Homicide: A Plausible Theory Meets the Intractable Facts," in Kates, *Restricting Handguns*, p. 109.
22. Kopel, p. 94.
23. Delta Press, Ltd., Winter 94/95.
24. Greenwood, "Crime, Suicide, and Accidents: Some Cross-national and Cross-cultural Comparisons," in Kates, *Restricting Handguns*, p. 35.
25. Benenson and Kates, Jr., "Handgun Prohibition and Homicide: A Plausible Theory Meets the Intractable Facts," in Kates, *Restricting Handguns*, p. 97.
26. *New York Times*, May 23, 1996, "China Arms Aides Are Sought by U.S. in Smuggling Plot," by David E. Sanger.
27. For details on how drugs are smuggled into the United States, see Weir, *In the Shadow of the Dope Fiend*, pp. 144–57.

Chapter 20
UNDERWHELMING POPULAR DEMAND

1. Wright, Rossi, and Daly, p. 215.
2. *Ibid.*

3. DOJ, *Sourcebook 1993*, table 2.2, p. 155.
4. Kates, Jr., "Toward a History of Handgun Prohibition in the United States," in Kates, *Restricting Handguns*, p. 27.
5. *Ibid.*
6. Wright, Rossi, and Daly, p. 232.
7. Kleck, p. 360.
8. Professor Don B. Kates, writing about Missouri's discretionary permit system, said, "Permits are automatically denied . . . to wives who don't have their husbands' permission, homosexuals and non-voters. . . . As one of my students recently learned, a personal 'interview' is not required for every St. Louis application. After many delays, he finally got to see the sheriff—who looked at him only long enough to see that he wasn't black, yelled 'he's alright' to the permit secretary and left" (in Cozic, "Gun Control Would Not Reduce Crime Against the Poor and Minorities," by Stefan B. Tahmassebi, pp. 64–65). At the other end of the state, in Kansas City, I once asked the police how to get a pistol permit. "You don't need a permit, we know you," the officer said and dropped the matter. At the time, I had a .38 caliber revolver that I later swapped to a detective for his .45. The transaction was, of course, extremely illegal, but it was done openly in the KCPD detective bureau. But I wasn't black, either.
9. Kleck, pp. 359–60.
10. Wright, Rossi, and Daly, p. 227.
11. Kleck, p. 363; Wright, Rossi, and Daly, p. 223.
12. Kleck, p. 371.
13. Wright, "Public Opinion and Gun Control," *Annals* 455:24–39, quoted in Kleck, pp. 370–71.
14. LaPierre, p. 92.
15. Kleck, pp. 22–25.
16. *Ibid.*, pp. 375–76.
17. Kates, Jr., "Toward a History of Handgun Prohibition in the United States," in Kates, *Restricting Handguns*, p. 27.
18. Kleck, p. 363.
19. Davidson, pp. 139–40.
20. Kleck, p. 363.
21. Sugarmann, *NRA*, p. 229.
22. Davidson, p. 137.

23. *Ibid.*
24. NRA, *Fact Sheet.*

Chapter 21

DIGRESSION NO. 3: GUNS IN THE REST OF THE WORLD

1. Shields, p. 82.
2. *Time*, July 17, 1989.
3. Kates, Jr., "Crime, Suicide and Accidents: Some Cross-national and Cross-cultural comparisons," in Kates, *Restricting Handguns*, p. 31.
4. Kopel, p. 346.
5. *Ibid.*, p. 26.
6. *Ibid.*, p. 25.
7. *Ibid.*, pp. 99–106; *The New York Times*, Feb. 27, 1995, editorial: "British Justice, No Longer a Beacon."
8. Handelman, *Comrade Criminal*, p. 178.
9. DOJ, *Sourcebook 1994*, fig. 3.94, page 305.
10. *The New Yorker*, Feb. 20 and 27, 1995, "The Tycoon and the Kremlin," by David Remnick.
11. HCI, *Handgun Laws in Other Industrialized Countries*.
12. *Wall Street Journal*, "Want to Play Safe? It Might Be Sensible to Stay Out of Brazil," by Everett G. Martin.
13. *Ibid.*
14. *Ibid.*
15. *The New Yorker*, April 22, 1991, "Letter from Medellín," by Alma Guillermoprieto.
16. Suter, *JMAG*, graph 10, p. 142, using 1989 data from the World Health Organization.
17. *Ibid.*
18. *New Haven Register*, May 1, 1996, "Mandela's South Africa Beset by Problems," by Holger Jensen.
19. Suter, *JMAG*, graph 10, p. 142, using data from World Health Organization.
20. DOJ, *Sourcebook 1993*, table 3.107, p. 352.
21. DOJ, Bureau of Justice Statistics, Special Report: *International Crime Rates*, table 5, p. 5.
22. Suter, *JMAG*, graph 10, p. 142.
23. *Ibid.*; Kates, Jr., and Benenson, "The Ef-

fect of Handgun Prohibition in Reducing Violent Crime," in Kates, *Restricting Handguns*, p. 117.

24. Suter, *JMAG*, graph 10, p. 142, using 1989 data from the World Health Organization.

25. For more on European wars and purges, see Weir, *Written With Lead*, pp. x–xi.

26. Kopel, pp. 73–74.

27. So called for the largest component of the British forces, unemployed army veterans, some of them released from jails, who made up a special unit of the police. They were dressed in a combination of army uniforms (khaki) and police uniforms (dark green).

28. Kopel, p. 78

29. Greenwood, "Crime, Suicide and Accidents: Some Cross-National and Cross-cultural Comparisons," in Kates, *Restricting Handguns*, p. 44.

30. Interview with Steve Smith, Bureau of Justice Statistics.

31. *Ibid*.

32. Kopel, p. 91.

33. Greenwood, "Crime, Suicide and Accidents: Some Cross-National and Cross-cultural Comparisons," in Kates, *Restricting Handguns*, p. 46.

34. HCI, *Stop Handguns Before They Stop You*.

35. FBI, *Crime in the United States, 1993: Uniform Crime Reports*, table 20, p. 202.

36. Kopel, p. 82.

37. *Ibid*., p. 124.

38. I was there.

39. Suter, *JMAG*, graph 10, p. 142.

40. James Adams, *Engines of War: Merchants of Death and the New Arms Race*, p. 44.

41. Kopel, p. 268.

42. For more on the Jamaican posses in the United States, see Weir, *In the Shadow of the Dope Fiend*, pp. 188–90.

43. Kopel, p. 260.

44. *Ibid*., p. 261.

45. *Ibid*., p. 266.

46. Suter, *JMAG*, graph 10, p. 142.

47. Interpol report, 1990.

48. *The New Yorker*, Feb. 20 and 27, 1995, "The Tycoon and the Kremlin," by David Remnick.

49. *The New York Times*, March 3, 1995, "Celebrity's Killing Stirs Talk of Intrigue in Russia," by Alessandra Stanley.

50. Interview, January, 1994.

51. Handelman, p. 208.

52. Pierre Berton, *Flames Across the Border*, pp. 23–24.

53. Kopel, p. 140.

54. Berton, p. iii.

55. Kopel, pp. 142–48.

56. *New York Times*, Feb. 19, 1995, "Registration of All Guns Proposed in Canada," by Clyde H. Farnsworth.

57. Warner, *Gun Digest*, p. 366.

Chapter 22

SNAKE OIL

1. The following statistics on permits are from DOJ, *Sourcebook 1994*, table 1.99, p. 132.

2. *New York Times*, March 6, 1995, "States Seek to Let Citizens Carry Concealed Weapons," by Sam Howe Verhovek.

3. DOJ, *Sourcebook 1994*, table 3.99, p. 318.

4. DOJ, Bureau of Justice Statistics, Bulletin: *Capital Punishment 1993*, p. 1; DOJ, *Sourcebook 1993*, table 3.111, p. 365.

5. DOJ, *Capital Punishment*, p. 1.

6. *Time*, Nov. 14, 1994, "Going Soft on Crime," by Jon D. Hull, Sylvester Monroe, and David Seidman.

7. Kleck, pp. 338–39.

8. Weir, *In the Shadow of the Dope Fiend*, pp. 197–99.

9. Kleck, p. 432.

10. Kates, pp. 144–45; Kopel, pp. 394, 395; LaPierre, p. 31.

11. Kopel, p. 238.

12. *Ibid*.

Chapter 23

BAND-AIDS

1. Kopel, p. 141.

2. Kleck, p. 394.

3. *Ibid*., p. 432.

4. *Ibid*., p. 438.

5. *Ibid*., pp. 434–35.

6. Wright and Rossi, table 9.1, p. 183.
7. *Ibid.*
8. *Ibid.*, table 9.2, p. 185.
9. *Ibid.*, table 9.3, p. 186.
10. *Ibid.*, p. 203.
11. Kleck, p. 45.
12. DOJ, *Sourcebook 1994*, table 1.99, p. 132.
13. Kleck, pp. 435–37.
14. *New Haven Register*, March 2, 1994, "For a Price, NRA Lists Ex-Members' Names," by Associated Press.
15. Davidson, p. 26.

Chapter 24
RADICAL SURGERY

1. During World War II, Stalin deported thousands of Chechens from the homes they'd lived in for a millennium to Central Asia, where their remote ancestors had lived. After the dictator's death, the Chechens painfully made their way back to Chechnya.
2. Suter, *JMAG*, graph 10, p. 142.
3. DOJ, *Sourcebook 1994*, table 3.101, pp. 320–22; table 1.99, pp. 132–33.
4. *New York Times*, March 18, 1995, "Dole, in a 2d Nod to Right, Pledges to Fight Gun Ban," by Jerry Gray.
5. *Ibid.*, Dec. 28, 1994, "Congressman Wants to Ban Ammunition," by Associated Press.

BIBLIOGRAPHY

BOOKS

Adams, James. *Engines of War: Merchants of Death and the New Arms Race*, New York: Atlantic Monthly Press, 1990.

Adcock, F.E. *The Greek and Macedonian Art of War*, Berkeley: University of California Press, 1962.

Ahearn, Marie L. *The Rhetoric of War: Training Days, the Militia and the Military Sermons*, Westport, CT: Greenwood Press, 1989.

Aristotle. *The Basic Works of Aristotle*, New York: Random House, 1941.

Bakal, Carl. *The Right to Bear Arms*, New York: McGraw-Hill, 1986.

Bartlett, Donald L., and Steele, James B. *America: What Went Wrong?* Kansas City, MO: Andrews and McMeel, 1992.

Beeler, John. *Warfare in Feudal Europe 730–1200*, Ithaca, NY: Cornell University Press, 1971.

Berton, Pierre. *Flames Across the Border: The Canadian-American Tragedy, 1813–1814*, Boston: Little, Brown, 1981.

Bidwell, Shelford. *Brassey's Artillery of the World*, New York: Bonanza Books, 1979.

Bonds, Ray, ed., *Advanced Technology Warfare*, New York: Cresent, 1985.

Burrows, William E. *Vigilante!* New York: Harcourt Brace Jovanovich, 1975.

Bury, J.B., and Meiggs, Russell. *A History of Greece*, New York: St. Martin's, 1951.

Byars, Hugo. *Government by Assassination*, New York: Alfred A. Knopf, 1942.

Caulfield, Max. *The Easter Rebellion*, New York: Holt, Rinehart and Winston, 1963.

Chant, Christopher. *The New Encyclopedia of Handguns*, New York: W.H. Smith, 1986.

Clark, Ramsey. *Crime in America*, New York: Simon and Schuster, 1970.

Cleator, P.E. *Weapons of War*, New York: Thomas Y. Crowell, 1967.

Collins, Larry, and LaPierre, Dominique. *O Jerusalem!*, New York: Simon and Schuster, 1972.

Cozic, Charles P., ed. *Gun Control*, San Diego, CA: Greenhaven Press, 1992.

Craige, Capt. John Houston. *The Practical Book of American Guns*, New York: World Publishing, 1950.

Cruickshank, C.G. *Elizabeth's Army*, London: Oxford University Press, 1966.

Cumming, William P., and Rankin, Hugh. *The Fate of a Nation: The American Revolution Through Contemporary Eyes*, London: Phaidon Press, 1975.

Currie, Elliott. *Reckoning: Drugs, the Cities, and the American Future*, New York: Hill and Wang, 1993.

Davidson, Osha Gray. *Under Fire: The NRA and the Battle for Gun Control*, New York: Henry Holt, 1993.

Davis, Richard Harding. *Notes of a War Correspondent*, New York: Scribner's, 1911.

Diagram Group, The. *Weapons: An International Encyclopedia from 5000 B.C. to 2000 A.D.*, New York: St. Martin's, 1990.

Dunan, Marcel, ed. *Larousse Encyclopedia of Ancient and Medieval History*, New York: Harper & Row, 1963.

Edge, L.L. *Run the Cat Roads: A True Story of Bank Robbers in the Thirties*, New York: Dembner Books, 1981.

Ellis, John. *The Social History of the Machine Gun*, New York: Pantheon, 1975.

Ezell, Edward Clinton. *Small Arms of the World: A Basic Manual of Small Arms*, 11th rev. ed., Harrisburg, PA: Stackpole Books, 1977.

Fischer, David Hackett. *Paul Revere's Ride*, New York: Oxford University Press, 1994.

Fleming, Thomas J. *Now We Are Enemies*, New York: St. Martin's, 1960.

Franklin, Benjamin. *Franklin: Writings*, New York: The Library of America, 1987.

Fuller, Maj. Gen. J.F.C. *A Military History of the Western World* (vol. I), New York: Minerva Press, 1967.

Gillespie, Cynthia. *Justifiable Homicide*, Columbus: Ohio State University Press, 1989.

Given, James. *Society and Homicide in Thirteenth Century England*, Palo Alto: Stamford University Press, 1979.

Graham, Hugh Davis, and Gurr, Ted Robert. *The History of Violence in America: A Report to the National Commission on the Causes and Prevention of Violence*, New York: Bantam Books, 1969.

Greene, Lt. Col. T.N. *The Guerrilla and How to Fight Him*, New York: Praeger, 1962.

Guevara, Ernesto "Che." *Guerrilla Warfare*, New York: Vintage Books, 1961.

Gugliotta, Guy, and Leen, Jeff. *Kings of Cocaine*, New York: Simon and Shuster, 1989.

Handelman, Stephen. *Comrade Criminal: Russia's New Mafiya*, New Haven, CT: Yale University Press, 1995.

Hardy, David T. *Origins and Development of the Second Amendment*, Southport, CT: Blacksmith Corp., 1986.

Hatcher, Maj. Gen. Julian S. *Textbook of Pistols and Revolvers*, Plantersville, SC: Small-Arms Technical Publishing Co., 1935.

———. *Hatcher's Notebook*, 3d ed., Harrisburg, PA: Telegraph Press, 1966.

Helmer, William J. *The Gun That Made the Twenties Roar*, Highland Park, NJ: Gun Room Press, 1969.

Hogg, Ian V. *The Complete Machine-Gun 1885 to the Present*, New York: Exeter Books, 1979.

Holmes, Oliver Wendell, Jr. *Representative Opinions of Mr. Justice Holmes*, Alfred Lief, ed., New York: Vanguard Press, 1931.

Holy Bible, New Catholic Edition, New York: Catholic Book Publishing Company.

Howard, Michael. *The Franco-Prussian War*, New York: Collier, 1969.

Kates, Don B., Jr., ed., *Restricting Handguns: The Liberal Skeptics Speak Out*, Croton-on-Hudson, NY: North River Press, 1979.

Kennett, Lee, and Anderson, James LaVerne. *The Gun in America: The Origins of a National Dilemma*, Westport, CT: Greenwood Press, 1975.

Kessler, Ronald. *The FBI*, New York: Pocket Books, 1993.

Ketchum, Richard M. *The Battle for Bunker Hill*, Garden City, NY: Doubleday, 1962.

Kirkham, James F.; Levy, Sheldon G.; and Crotty, and William J. *Assassination and Political Violence: A Staff Report to the National Commission on the Causes and Prevention of Violence*, New York: Bantam, 1970.

Kleck, Gary. *Point Blank: Guns and Violence in America*, Hawthorne, NY: Aldine de Gruyter, 1991.

Konvitz, Milton R., ed. *The Bill of Rights Reader*, 3d ed., Ithaca, NY: Cornell University Press, 1965. *(Special Note: 941 pages and not one page—even a sentence—on the Second Amendment.)*

Kopel, David B. *The Samurai, the Mountie and the Cowboy: Should America Adopt the Gun Controls of Other Democracies?* Buffalo, NY: Prometheus, 1992.

Kruger, Rayne, *Goodbye Dolly Gray*, Philadelphia: Lippincott, 1960.

LaPierre, Wayne. *Guns, Crime and Freedom*, Washington, D.C.: Regnery, 1994.

Leckie, Robert. *The Wars of America*, New York: Harper & Row, 1968.

Machiavelli, Niccolo. *The Art of War*, New York: Da Capo, 1965.

Malcolm, Joyce Lee. *To Keep and Bear Arms: The Origins of an Anglo-American Right*, Cambridge, MA: Harvard University Press, 1994.

Millis, Walter. *Arms and Men: A Study of American Military History*, New York: New American Library, 1958.

Montross, Lynn. *War Through the Ages*, New York: Harper & Row, 1960.

Morison, Samuel Eliot. *The Oxford History of the American People*, New York: Oxford University Press, 1965.

Morrison, Sean. *Armor*, New York: Thomas Y. Crowell, 1963.

Nash, Jay Robert. *Bloodletters and Badmen*, Philadelphia: M. Evans and Company, 1973.

National Commission on the Causes and Prevention of Violence. *Final Report: To Establish Justice, to Ensure Domestic Tranquility*, New York: Bantam Books, 1970.

Newton, George D., and Zimring, Franklin E. *Firearms and Violence in American Life: A Staff Report to the National Commission on the Causes and Prevention of Violence*, Washington, D.C.: U.S. Government Printing Office, 1969.

Norman, A.V.P., and Pottinger, Don. *English Weapons and Warfare, 449–1660*, New York: Dorset Press, 1985.

Oakeshott, R. Ewart. *The Archaeology of Weapons*, New York: Praeger, 1960.

Oman, C.W.C. *The Art of War in the Middle Ages*, Ithaca, NY: Cornell University Press, 1953.

Osanka, Franklin Mark. *Modern Guerrilla Warfare*, New York: Free Press of Glencoe, 1962.

Owen, J.I.H., ed. *Brassey's Infantry Weapons of the World*, New York: Bonanza Books, 1978.

Pakenham, Thomas. *The Boer War*, New York: Random House, 1979.

Payne-Gallwey, Sir Ralph. *The Crossbow*, London: The Holland Press, 1986.

Pearson, Michael. *Those Damned Rebels: The American Revolution Seen Through British Eyes*, New York: G. P. Putnam's Sons, 1972.

Perrin, Noel. *Giving Up the Gun: Japan's Reversion to the Sword, 1545–1879*, Boston: Godine, 1979.

Peterson, Harold L. *Arms and Armor in Colonial America, 1526–1783*, New York: Bramhall House, 1956.

————. *American Knives*, New York: Charles Scribner's Sons, 1958.

————. *The Treasury of the Gun*, New York: Ridge Press, 1962.

————. *The Book of the Continental Soldier*, Harrisburg, PA: Promontory Press, 1968.

————. *Round Shot and Rammers*. New York: Bonanza, 1969.

Prothrow-Stith, Deborah, M.D. *Deadly Consequences: How Violence Is Destroying Our Teenage Population and a Plan to Begin Solving the Problem*, New York: HarperCollins, 1991.

Ransford, Oliver. *The Battle of Majuba Hill*, New York: Thomas Y. Crowell, 1967.

Reavis, Dick J. *The Ashes of Waco*, New York: Simon & Shuster, 1995.

Regan, Geoffrey. *SNAFU: Great American Military Disasters*, New York: Avon, 1993.

Reid, William. *Weapons Through the Ages*, New York: Crescent, 1986.

Reitz, Deneys. *Commando: A Boer Journal of the Boer War*, London: Faber & Faber, 1968.

Roberts, Kenneth. *Rabble in Arms*, Garden City, NY: Doubleday, 1947.

Saxon, Kurt. *The Poor Man's James Bond*, Eureka, CA: Atlan Formularies, 1972.

Sharpe, Philip B. *Complete Guide to Handloading*, 3d ed., New York: Funk & Wagnalls, 1953.

Sheehan, Neil. *A Bright Shining Lie: John Paul Vann and America in Vietnam*, New York: Random House, 1988.

Sherrill, Robert. *The Saturday Night Special*, New York: Charterhouse, 1973.

Shields, Nelson "Pete." *Guns Don't Die—People Do*, New York: Arbor House, 1981.

Simpkins, Michael. *Warriors of Rome*, London: Blandford, 1988.

Smith, Joseph E., and Smith, W.H.B. *Small Arms of the World: A Basic Manual of Military Small Arms*, 10th rev. ed., Harrisburg, PA: Stackpole, 1973.

Smith, W.H.B. *The NRA Book of Small Arms, Vol. I, Pistols and Revolvers*, Harrisburg, PA: Stackpole, 1946.

Smith, W H.B. *Small Arms of the World: A Basic Manual of Military Small Arms*, 6th rev. ed., Harrisburg, PA: Stackpole, 1960.

Snodgrass, A.M. *Arms and Armour of the Greeks*, Ithaca, NY: Cornell University Press, 1967.

Stoeger, A.F. *Shooter's Bible*, reproduction of 1939 Stoeger Arms Co. catalogue, Hackensack, NJ: 1983.

Sugarmann, Josh. *National Rifle Association: Money, Firepower and Fear*, Washington: National Press, 1992.

Sugarmann, Josh, and Rand, Kristen. *Cease Fire*, Washington: Violence Policy Center, 1994.

Taber, Robert. *The War of the Flea: A Study of Guerrilla Warfare Theory and Practice*, New York: Citadel, 1970.

Tabor, James D., and Gallagher, Eugene V. *Why Waco? Cults and the Battle for Religious Freedom in America*, Berkeley, CA: University of California Press, 1995.

Tarassuk, Leonid, and Blair, Claude. *The Complete Encyclopedia of Arms and Weapons*, New York: Bonanza Books, 1986.

Thayer, Charles W. *Guerrilla*, New York: Harper & Row, 1963.

Toynbee, Arnold J. *War and Civilization*, New York: Oxford University Press, 1950.

————. *A Study of History*, vol. I–III, New York: Oxford University Press, 1962.

United States Congress. *United States Code, U.S. Code Service*, lawyer's edition, Rochester, NY: Lawyer's Cooperative Publishing Company, 1985

Warner, Ken, ed. *1993 Gun Digest*, Northbrook, IL: DBI, 1992.

Warner, Ken, ed. *1992 Gun Digest*, Northbrook, IL: DBI, 1991.

Webster's Encyclopedic Uabridged Dictionary of the English Language, Avenel, NJ: dilithium Press, Ltd. 1989.

Weeks, John. *Infantry Weapons*, New York: Ballantine, 1979.

————. *World War II Small Arms*, New York: Galahad Books, 1979.

Weir, William. *Written With Lead: Legendary American Gunfights and Gunfighters*, Hamden, CT: Archon, 1992.

————. *Fatal Victories*, Hamden, CT: Archon, 1993.

————. *In the Shadow of the Dope Fiend: America's War on Drugs*, North Haven, CT: Archon, 1995.

Westhorp, Chris, ed. *The World's Armies*, New York: Military Press, 1991.

Wilkinson, Frederick. *Edged Weapons*, Garden City, NY: Doubleday, 1970.

Wright, Benjamin Fletcher, ed. *The Federalist by James Madison, Alexander Hamilton and John Jay*, Cambridge, MA: Harvard University Press, 1961.

Wright, James D., and Rossi, Peter H. *Armed and Considered Dangerous: A Survey of Felons and their Firearms*, Hawthorne, NY: Aldine de Gryter, 1986.

Wright, James D.; Rossi, Peter H.; and Daly, Kathleen. *Under the Gun: Weapons, Crime and Violence in America*, Hawthorne, NY: Aldine, 1983.

Wright, Stuart A., ed. *Armageddon in Waco: Critical Perspectives on the Branch Davidian Conflict*, Chicago, University of Chicago Press, 1995.

PERIODICALS

American Rifleman, Sept. 1957, "Almost a National Affair," by Nils Kvale.

————, Jul., 1986, "Gun Laws in Scandinavia," by Nils Kvale.

————, Feb. 1988, "The Warsaw Ghetto: 10 Handguns Against Tyranny," by David I. Caplan.

————, Mar. 1991, "Madison and the Bill of Rights," by Michael T. McCabe.

————, Nov. 1993, "The Randy Weaver Case," by Jim Oliver.

————, Aug. 1994, letter.

————, Nov./Dec., 1994, "ILA Report."

Arms and the Man, May 1911, editorial.

Atlanta Constitution, Nov. 10, 1993, "It's Not the People—It's the Guns," by Arthur L. Kellermann.

Atlantic Monthly, Mar. 19, 1993, "The False Promise of Gun Control," by Daniel B. Polsby.

Chicago Tribune, Jun. 9, 1992, "More Handguns No Answer to Crime," by Jeffrey Y. Muchnick, legislative director, Coalition to Stop Gun Violence.

————, July 2, 1993, "Tax My Sins, but Tax Guns, Too," by Matthew Reese, political advisor to the Coalition to Stop Gun Violence.

ConnPIRG, the newsletter of the Connecticut Public Interest Research Group Citizen Lobby, Fall 1994, "Special Interest PACs Thwart Clean Water."

Denver Post, Mar. 15, 1992, "Firepower, Firepower Everywhere; When Will Politicians Think?" by Molly Ivins.

Hartford Courant, Apr. 8, 1993, "Parents Must Respond to TV Violence," by George F. Will.

———, Oct. 26, 1993, "Weicker Favors Ban on Handguns," by Mark Pazniokas.

———, Oct. 27, 1993, "Wider Gun Ban Weighed," by Mark Pazniokas.

———, Nov. 21, 1993, "A Corner Where Crack Is King," by Edmund Mahony.

———, Dec. 7, 1993, "The Historic Right to Bear Arms," by Don B. Kates and Alan J. Lizotte.

———, Dec. 9, 1993, "President Says Time Has Come to Consider Strengthening Gun Controls," by *Los Angeles Times* syndicate.

———, Dec. 10, 1993, "Clinton Seeks 'Action Plan' to Stop Crime," by Robert A. Rankin, Knight-Ridder Newspapers.

———, Dec. 12, 1993, "Courts Haven't Supported Right of Individuals to Own Firearms," by Laurie Asseo, Associated Press.

———, Dec. 17, 1993, "Gun Laws Penalize Honest People, Not Criminals," by Bill Clede, technical editor of *Law and Order* magazine; "The Solution to Crime Is to Arm the People," letters by John Robert Burgoyne and Scott Cooper.

———, Dec. 19, 1993, "A Resounding Clash of Cultures Over the Right to Bear Arms," by Mark Pazniokas.

———, Dec. 20, 1993, "One Gun's Journey into a Crime," by Mark Pazniokas; "GOP Anti-Crime Package Targets Gangs, Gun Use," by Larry Williams.

———, Dec. 22, 1993, "Handgun Ban Has Support in State," by Mark Pazniokas.

———, Dec. 28, 1993, "Fight Crime by Replacing Paper Money with Debit Cards," by Michael Tierney.

———, Dec. 30, 1993, "Develop Ways to Detect Concealed Weapons," by Lloyd Cutler.

———, Jan. 5, 1994, Editorial: "License Gun Owners as We Do Drivers."

———, Jan. 17, 1994, Editorial: "A Cancer in the Streets . . . . . . Continues to Take Its Toll."

———, Jan. 18, 1994, "Compromise Is Essential on Gun Control," by Donald D. Hook.

———, Jan. 23, 1994, "Controlling the Right to Bear Arms," letters by Martin T. Connors, John Kunsey, and Candace Drimmer; Editorial: "Bipartisan Pistol Denial."

———, Jan. 26, 1994, "Challenge to State's Gun Law Begins," by Mark Pazniokas; "Assault-Weapon Fears Unfounded, Expert Says," by Mark Pazniokas.

———, Jan. 27, 1994, "Gun Maker in Court Makes No Apologies," by Mark Pazniokas.

———, Jan. 29, 1994, "Banned Weapons Not Needed for Self-Defense, Witness Says," by Mark Pazniokas.

———, Mar. 10, 1994, Editorial: "No Guns, but No Metal Detectors"; Editorial: "A Barbaric Message, A Repulsive Act."

———, Mar. 11, 1994, "Bill to Keep Guns Off Black Market Approved by Key Legislative Panel," by Hilary Waldman.

———, March 30, 1994, "Gun Lobby Distorts Brady Bill," by Deborah Mathis.

———, Mar. 31, 1994, "1,605 Denied Guns in Brady Law's First Month," by *Washington Post* syndicate.

———, Apr. 3, 1994, Editorial: "Trouble in the 'Gun Society.'

———, Apr. 30, 1994, "Woman's Death Spurs Hartford Police to Form Gun Squad," by Maxine Bernstein.

———, May 2, 1994, "Keeping Gun Dealers in Sights," by Alan Levin and Maxine Bernstein.

————, May 6, 1994, "Major Legislation Awaits New Session," by Larry Williams; "House Grapples with Issues of Constitutional Guarantees," by David Lightman; "Taxpayers to Pick Up Slack on Guns for Goods Plan," by Matthew Kauffman.

————, May 16, 1994, "House Passes Weapons Ban in Close Vote," by Kenneth J. Cooper, *Washington Post* syndicate.

————, May 18, 1994, "House Kills Bill to Restrict Handgun Sales," by Christopher Keating.

————, May 19, 1994, "Failure of Gun Control Bill in House Leaves Many Puzzled," by Christopher Keating; "Trooper Found Not Guilty in Assault," by Associated Press; Editorial: "Legislature: From Dud to Worse."

————, June 1, 1994, "The Unintended Consequences of the Brady Law," by David S. Broder.

————, June 2, 1994, "Prisons Hold Nearly a Million, Report Says," by *Washington Post* syndicate.

————, June 30, 1994, "Weicker Puts on the Pressure for Gun Control Vote," by Christopher Keating.

————, July 1, 1994, "Gun Restrictions Skirt the Real Problem," by Bill Clede; "Judge Upholds State Ban on Assault Weapons," by Mark Pazniokas.

————, Jul. 8, 1994, "Stricter Gun Control Law Signed by Weicker," by Christopher Keating; "Law Penalizes Legitimate Gun Owners," letters signed by Joseph J. Birchall, Jr., Russell Turner, and Thomas C. Graboski; Editorial: "Now, Pass the Crime Bill."

————, Aug. 5, 1994, Editorial: "Don't Give in to Gun Bullies;" "A Law to Stop Peddling Guns Like Fish," by Don Noel.

————, Aug. 11, 1994, Editorial: "Don't Sabotage the Anti-Crime Bill."

————, Aug. 13, 1994, "Clinton Vows to Fight for Crime Bill: Democrats Divided on Strategy," by Ann Devroy and Kenneth J. Cooper, *Washington Post* syndicate; "Clinton Vows to Fight for Crime Bill: Deal Might Add Police in State," by David Lightman.

————, Aug. 16, 1994, editorial: "Don't Give Up on the Anti-Crime Bill; Compromise May Be Tried on Crime Bill," by combined wire services; "Johnson and Shays Await Clinton Move," by David Lightman; "Franks Defends His Vote," by Fran Silverman.

————, Aug. 17, 1994, "Crime Bill Delay Hurts Incumbents," by David Lightman; "Crime Bill: Fads in Search of Funding," by George F. Will; "The Summer the Democrats Lost Their Grip on Congress," by David S. Broder.

————, Aug. 18, 1994, "Crime Bill Engulfed by Uncertainty," by Michael Ross, *Los Angeles Times* syndicate.

————, Aug. 19, 1994, "Key Lawmakers on Crime Bill Got NRA Cash," by Associated Press; "House Considers Cuts in Crime Bill," by Associated Press.

————, Aug. 26, 1994, "Senate Approves $30 Billion Crime Bill," by Combined Wire Services.

————, Sept. 11, 1994, "Stories on Crime Bill Misled Readers," by Henry McNulty.

————, Oct. 10, 1994, "Gun Activists Organizing Independent Militias," by Associated Press.

————, Oct. 15, 1994, "Major Retailers Target Toy Guns," by Donna Larcen.

————, Oct. 20, 1994, "Tough Stands on Crime May Ignore Reality," by Mark Pazniokas.

————, Oct. 31, 1994, Editorial: "The Disease of the Century;" "Survey: Violent Crimes Rose 5.6% in 1993," by Associated Press.

————, Dec. 9, 1994, "Police Gun Swap Could Help Dealers Through Legal Loophole," by John Springer.

————, Dec. 27, 1994, "Deadly Bullets for Handguns to Go on Sale," by Robert Dvorchak, Associated Press.

————, Dec. 28, 1994, "Tulisano to Introduce Legislation Prohibiting Rhino-Ammo in State."

————, Dec. 29, 1994, "Production of New Bullet Put on Hold," by combined wire services.

————, Feb. 18, 1995, "Sovereign Citizens Throw Off Government-Forged Chains," by Kenton Robinson.

Journal of the Medical Association of Georgia, Mar., 1994, "Guns in Medical Literature—a Failure of Peer Review," by Edgar A. Suter, M.D.; "Health Care and Firearms," by Larry Pratt; "The Allure of Foreign Gun Laws," by David B. Kopel, J.D.; "Guns: Health Destroyer or Protector?" by W.W. Caruth III.

Los Angeles Times, Washington Edition, May 19, 1992, "Still Time to Cancel Your Order," by Michael K. Beard, president, Coalition to Stop Gun Violence.

Military History, April, 1985, "Hand Launched Missiles," by William Weir.

Minneapolis Star Tribune, July 13, 1993, "State Must Act to Halt Gun Violence," by Douglas D. Brunette.

The Nation, Apr. 5, 1971, "Detention Camps."

————, Jul. 1, 1978, "Internment Camps for Citizens: The FBI's Forty-year Plot," by Robert Justin Goldstein.

New Haven Register, March 22–29, 1992, "The Young Guns," an eight-part series on juvenile gun violence.

————, April 6, 1993, "Hints of Conspiracy Demand Opening of Files on King's Death," by Robert Andrews.

————, April 17, 1994, Editorial: "Connecticut Needs Assault Rifle Ban;" "Waco Tragedy Caused by Gun-Control Laws," by Paul Craig Roberts, Scripps Howard News Service.

————, June 4, 1993, "Poll Finds Gun Ban Supported," by Associated Press.

————, Dec. 8, 1993, "U.S. Admits to Radiation Testing," by Associated Press.

————, Dec. 10, 1993, "Clinton: Violence Tearing Us Apart," by Associated Press.

————, December 12, 1993, "Courts Leaning Toward Gun-Control View," by Associated Press; "Property Owners and Hunters Battle as Trespassing Becomes Big Problem," by Associated Press; "Clinton Urges All to Replace Violence with Values in Kids," by Associated Press; "Lawmakers Take Aim at Bullets that Expand in Body," by Allan Drury; "National Deathclock to Keep Tabs on Gun Total and Related Deaths," by *Chicago Tribune* syndicate.

————, Dec. 19, 1993, "Guns and Gore: Who's Next and Where? by Robert Dvorchak; "State's Waiting Period Effective—to a Point," by Alvin Powell; "Bam! State Gun Crazy With Legal, Illegal Weapons," by Associated Press.

————, Dec. 21, 1993, "Clinton Wants to Boost Fees for Gun Sellers, by Associated Press.

————, Dec. 27, 1993, "Americans Demand Return of Order," by Associated Press.

————, Dec. 28, 1993, "Gun-Toting People Could End Shootings," by John W. White; "Gun Shows Provide Loophole to Brady Bill," by Associated Press; "Washington Passes 1992 Murder Rate," by Associated Press; "New Laws Home in on Safety, Security," by Associated Press.

————, Dec. 29, 1993, "Brady Bill's Provisions Worry Lawmen," by Associated Press.

————, Jan. 5, 1994, "Firearms Licensing System Is Praiseworthy Objective," by Tas Papathanasis; "Self-Defense Stands High on List of Basic Civil Rights," by Robert C. Wilcox.

————, Jan. 6, 1994, "Gun Buybacks Effective: Who Knows?" by Associated Press.

————, Jan. 27, 1994, "Assault Weapon Ban Debated in State Court," by Associated Press; "Postal Carriers Keep an Eye Out for Local Crime," by Associated Press.

————, Jan. 30, 1994, "Congress Eyes Weapons Ban," by Associated Press.

————, Feb. 21, 1994, "Gun Fees Could Raise Millions," by Gregory B. Hladky.

————, Mar. 2, 1994, "Law Profs Tout Armed Inner-City Militia," by Patrick Dilger; "For a Price, NRA Lists Ex-Members' Names," by Associated Press.

————, Mar. 11, 1994, "Panel Snubs Weicker on Gun Plan," by Alvin Powell; "Blacks Have Good Cause to Oppose Gun Control", by Wayne Howard; "Gun Control is Really People Control," by Robert C. Wilcox.

————, Mar. 24, 1994, "Elders Calls for Multifaceted Gun Policy," by Associated Press.

————, Mar. 30, 1994, "Guns Don't Kill People: Welfare Does," by Frank Whelan.

————, Mar. 31, 1994, "Police Gun Sweeps Debated," by Associated Press; "Meaning of 'In Custody' Argued," by Associated Press.

————, May 6, 1994, "State Grant Resurrects Gun Effort," by Gregory B. Hladky; "Assault Guns Banned," by Tamara Lytle.

————, May 16, 1994, "Data Show Dramatic Rise in Handgun Crimes," by Associated Press.

————, May 18, 1994, "Gun Bill Dies in House," by Gregory B. Hladky and Alvin Powell.

————, May 19, 1994, "Lawmakers, Weicker Meet on Gun Control," by Gregory B. Hladky.

————, May 22, 1994, "Does Connecticut Need a Tough, New Handgun-Control Law? Yes," by Michael P. Lawlor; "No," by Sam Stewart; Editorial: "House Shirks Duty on Handgun Bill."

————, June 1, 1994, "Mobsters Ruining Russian Economy," by Associated Press.

————, June 2, 1994, "Federal Inmate Population Nears 1 Million," by Associated Press; "Few in Japan Know a Lawyer: Field Is Carefully Controlled," by *Chicago Tribune* syndicate.

————, June 20, 1994, "Ban Won't Wipe Out Weapons," by Alvin Powell.

————, June 23, 1994, "Koop Says Pediatricians Should Warn About Guns," by Associated Press.

————, June 30, 1994, "Weicker Vows to Force Legislation on Guns," by Alvin Powell; "Study to Assess TV Violence," by Knight-Ridder syndicate.

————, Jul. 1, 1994, "State Ban on Assault Weapons Ruled Legal," by Associated Press.

————, Jul. 13, 1994, " 'Club' Can't Stop Car Thieves, Experts Say," by Warren Brown of the *Washington Post*.

————, Aug. 3, 1994, "Black Market in Plutonium a Cause for Worry," by Lance Gray.

————, Aug. 4, 1994, "Incarceration Rate Highest in the Nation," by Associated Press.

————, Aug. 12, 1994, "House Shoots Down Crime Bill," by Knight-Ridder syndicate.

————, Aug. 13, 1994, "Local Officials, Activists Decry Crime Bill Death," by Karla Schuster; "Is Midnight Basketball: Pork or Crime Prevention?" by Associated Press.

————, Aug. 19, 1994, "Crime Bill Opposers Got NRA Donations," by Associated Press.

————, Aug. 26, 1994, "Crime Bill Passes," by Scripps Howard News Service.

————, Aug. 29, 1994, "America Needs a Jobs Bill, Not a Crime Bill," by Steve Lopez, *Philadelphia Inquirer* columnist.

————, Sept. 21, 1994, "Shoes in Capitol Symbolize Footsteps Lost to Gunfire," by Tamara Lytle.

————, Oct. 16, 1994, "State Prisons Bursting at Seams, Despite Opening of New Facilities," by Associated Press.

————, Nov. 1, 1994, "Candidates Find They Can Make Points On Crime," by Gregory B. Hladky.

————, Nov. 2, 1994, "Rumor of Foreign Takeover Finds Believers in America," by George de Lama, *Chicago Tribune*.

———, Nov. 4, 1994, "City Man Indicted on Weapons Charge."

———, Nov. 14, 1994, "Smith Knew Where to Find a Scapegoat," by Derrick Z. Jackson.

———, Dec. 4, 1994, "Overall Crime Rate in Country Decreases," by Associated Press.

———, Dec. 7, 1994, "New Law Strips Man of Four Guns," by John Ferraro.

———, Dec. 28, 1994, "Ban on Rhino Pursued," by David Ross.

———, Feb. 2, 1995, "Murder Rate Same as It Was 60 Years Ago," by Knight-Ridder news service.

New York Times, Mar. 8–12, 1993, series on gun ownership and gun crime.

———, April 25, 1993, "The Battle Over Gun Control," letter by John T. Wilson, Jr., to the Connecticut Editor.

———, Dec. 19, 1993, "Pow! It Skinned Me," by Bob Herbert; "As Boot Camps for Criminals Multiply, Skepticism Grows," by Adam Nossiter.

———, Jan. 2, 1994, "Add Gun Buybacks to the Public Wish List," by Erik Eckholm.

———, Jan. 27, 1994, Editorial: "Tough and Smart on Crime?"

———, Jan. 30, 1994, "Does Anybody Here Know What Time It Is?" by James Barron.

———, Feb. 6, 1994, "Los Angeles Police Refuse to Aid in Inquiry," by Associated Press; "Firearms Agency Bans Armor-Piercing Bullets," by Associated Press.

———, Feb. 13, 1994, "U.S. and East European Weapons Dealers Clash," by Raymond Bonner; "Furious Debate on Carrying Guns in Colorado," by Associated Press.

———, Feb. 27, 1994, "Giuliani Plans Initiative to Curb Gun Violence," by Clifford Krauss; "Guns, Laws and Giuliani, by Alison Mitchell.

———, Mar. 12, 1994, "Gun Tracked in Shooting of 4 Students," by Clifford Krauss.

———, Apr. 2, 1994, "Crime Levels Fell in 1993, Report Says," by Clifford Krauss.

New York Times Magazine, June 12, 1994, "The Crime Funnel," by David C. Anderson.

New York Times, June 12, 1994, "Of Proms and Prisons," by Bob Herbert.

———, July 24, 1994, "Hidden Arsenal: Gun Owners, Their Weapons and Their Reasons," by Librado Romero.

———, Aug. 13, 1994, "Clinton Fights Back: 'This Crime Bill Cannot Die,' " by Douglas Jehl; "Democratic Leaders Promise to Try Again on Crime Bill," by David E. Rosenbaum; "On Crime Bill, Giuliani Is a Clinton Ally," by Steven Lee Myers.

———, Aug. 27, 1994, "The President Foresees Safer U.S.," by Neil A. Lewis.

———, Aug. 28, 1994, " 'Victory' Over Crime, at Least Politically," by Gwen Ifill.

———, Sept. 18, 1994, "The Perils of Police Hiring," by Clifford Krauss.

———, Sept. 19, 1994, letter: "Brady Bill 2 Would Overhaul Gun Business," by Sarah Brady.

———, Oct. 14, 1994, "Teen-Age Homicide Rate Has Soared," by Fox Butterfield.

———, Oct. 15, 1994, "Shootings Lead Chain to Ban Toy Guns," by Stephanie Strom.

———, Oct. 16, 1994, "New Tactics Urged in Fight Against Crime," by Fox Butterfield.

———, Oct. 17, 1994, "State-of-the-Art U.S. Prison Awaits Hard-Core 400."

———, Oct. 28, 1994, "Ranks of Inmates Reach One Million in 2-Decade Rise," by Steven A. Holmes.

———, Nov. 8, 1994, "Urban Crime Rates Falling this Year," by Clifford Krauss.

———, Nov. 14, 1994, "Fearing Conspiracy, Some Heed a Call to Arms," by Keith Schneider.

———, Nov. 19, 1994, "The High Cost of Death," by Anna Quindlen.

New York Times Magazine, Dec. 4, 1994, "The Black Man in America," a symposium chaired by Bob Herbert.

New York Times, Dec. 4, 1994, "Killings, Legal and Otherwise, Around the U.S.," by Tom Kuntz; "Targeting Women for Guns," by Bob Herbert.

————, Dec. 5, 1994, "Serious Crime Is Still Declining, but Fears Remain, FBI Reports," by Keith Bradsher.

————, Dec. 7, 1994, "The Ride Over, Demons Remain," by N. R. Kleinfield.

————, Dec. 11, 1994, "The Long Shadow of Russia's Mob," by Stephen Kinzer.

————, Dec. 12, 1994, "When the Family Heirloom Is Homicide," by Don Terry.

————, Dec. 13, 1994, "Idaho Siege Report Says FBI Agents Violated Procedure," by David Johnson; "Crack's Legacy of Guns and Death Lives On," by Isabel Wilkerson.

————, Dec. 14, 1994, "Televison Gets a Closer Look as a Factor in Real Violence," by Elizabeth Kolbert.

————, Dec. 28, 1994, editorial: "High Tech Death from Alabama"; "Congressman Wants to Ban Ammunition," by Associated Press.

————, Dec. 29, 1994, "Company Puts a Hold on Plastic Bullet," by Fox Butterfield.

————, Jan. 4, 1995, "Russian War: Corpses and Wild Dogs," by Michael Spector.

————, Jan. 30, 1995, editorial, "Stand Up Again to the NRA."

————, Jan. 31, 1995, "What Americans Want," by A. M. Rosenthal.

————, Feb. 18, 1995, "Police Officials Are Said to Be Rethinking Rapid-Fire Guns," by Garry Pierre-Pierre.

————, Feb. 19, 1995, "Registration of All Guns Proposed in Canada," by Clyde H. Farnsworth; "Lawyers for Shooting Victims Seek to Sue a Gun Manufacturer," by Associated Press.

————, Mar. 3, 1995, "Celebrity's Killing Stirs Talk of Intrigue in Russia," by Alessandra Stanley.

————, Mar. 6, 1995, "States Seek to Let Citizens Carry Concealed Weapons," by Sam Howe Verhovek.

————, Mar. 18, 1995, "Dole, in a 2nd Nod to Right, Pledges to Fight Gun Ban," by Jerry Gray.

————, May 23, 1996, "China Arms Aides are Sought by U.S. in Smuggling Plot," by David E. Sanger.

————, May 24, 1996, "Chinese Arms Seized in Undercover Inquiry," by David E. Sanger.

————, May 29, 1996, "Revisting the Issue of Crime, Dole Offers List of Remedies," by Katharine Q. Seelye.

The New Yorker, Jul. 26, 1976, "A Reporter at Large: Handguns," by Richard Harris.

————, Apr. 22, 1991, "Letter from Medellín," by Alma Guillermoprieto.

————, Feb. 20 and 27, 1995, "The Tycoon and the Kremlin," by David Remnick.

————, Nov. 13, 1995, "The Stranger," by Mary Anne Weaver.

————, Jan. 8, 1996, "How Nazis Are Made," by Ingo Hasselback with Tom Reiss.

Notre Dame Magazine, Summer, 1994, "Prophecy Unheeded," by John H. Yoder.

Philadelphia Inquirer, May 17, 1981, "Gun Rules . . . or Worldwide Gun Control," by Garry Wills.

The Poor Man's Armorer, Volume I, Number 9, "Improvised Munitions Handbook," reprinted from U.S. Army Training Manual Number 31–210.

The Progressive, May 1985, "The Take Charge Gang," by Keenen Peck.

The Public Interest, Fall, 1993, "A Nation of Cowards," by Jeffrey R. Snyder.

Rolling Stone, September 30, 1993, "A Pistol-Whipped Nation: Pass the Brady Bill—Then Ban Handguns," by William Greider.

Telephone Bulletin, Nov. 1966, "The Last Gallant War," by William Weir.

Time, Jul. 17, 1989, "Death by Gun."

———, Nov. 14, 1994, "Going Soft on Crime," by Jill Smolowe, Jon D. Hull, Sylvester Monroe, and David Seidman.

USA Today, December 29, 1993, "Better Yet, Ban All Handguns," by Jeff Muchnick, legislative director, Coalition to Stop Handgun Violence.

USA Today, May 26, 1994, "Baton Rouge: A Letter to My Boy's Killer," by Richard Haymaker.

Wall Street Journal, "Want to Play Safe? It Might Be Sensible to Stay Out of Brazil," by Everett G. Martin.

Yale Law Journal 99 (1989), "The Embarrassing Second Amendment," by Sanford Levinson.

PAMPHLETS

Author unknown (it may or may not be a forgery attributed to HCI). *HCI's 5-Year Master Plan*, obtained from the National Rifle Association.

Coalition to Stop Gun Violence. *Who, What, How* and *Participating Organizations*.

———. *Handguns and Health Care*.

———. *Handguns and Education*.

———. *Public Health Studies on Gun Control*.

———. press release: *FBI Uniform Crime Report: Handgun Murders Up; Overall Murder Rate Declines*.

———. *Legislative Update, May 9, 1994*.

Common Cause. *Campaign Money Chase Turns Off Quality Challengers, Incumbents, Too*, by Ann McBride.

Educational Fund to End Handgun Violence. *Kids & Guns Fact Sheet*.

———. *Kids and Guns: A National Disgrace*, Washington: 1993.

Federal Election Commission, news release, Apr. 4, 1996.

Libertarian Party. *Responsible Gun Ownership*.

Rand, Kristen. *No Right to Keep and Bear Arms*, Violence Policy Center, Washington: 1992.

Sugarmann, Josh. *Assault Weapons and Accessories in America*, Violence Policy Center, Washington: 1988.

Sugarmann, Josh, and Rand, Kristen. *Assault Weapons: Analysis, New Research and Legislation*, Violence Policy Center, Washington: 1989.

———. *Cease Fire: A Comprehensive Strategy to Reduce Firearms Violence*, Violence Policy Center, Washington: 1994.

Violence Policy Center. *Phantom Ammo: The Advent of Caseless Ammunition*, Washington: 1993.

REPORTS

U.S. Department of Justice, Bureau of Justice Statistics *Sourcebook of Criminal Justice Statistics—1994*, Washington: U.S. Government Printing Office, 1995.

———, Selected Findings: *Weapons Offenses and Offenders*, Washington: U.S. Government Printing Office, 1995.

———, Executive Summary: *Spouse Murder Defendants in Large Urban Counties*, Washington: U.S. Government Printing Office, 1995.

———, Bulletin: *Prisoners in 1994*, Washington: U.S. Government Printing Office, 1995.

———, Selected Findings: *Guns Used in Crime*, Washington: U.S. Government Printing Office, 1995.

———, Bulletin: *Criminal Victimization 1993*, Washington: U.S. Government Printing Office, 1995.

———, Special Report: *Tort Cases in Large Counties*, Washington: U.S. Government Printing Office, 1995.

———, Bulletin: *Jails and Jail Inmates 1993–94*, Washington: U.S. Government Printing Office, 1995.

———, *Selected Findings: Guns Used in Crime*, Washington: U.S. Government Printing Office, 1995.

———, *Bulletin: National Crime Victimization Survey, Criminal Victimization 1993*, Washington: U.S. Government Printing Office, 1995.

———, *National Crime Victimization Survey: Questions and Answers About the Redesign*, Washington: U.S. Government Printing Office, 1995.

———, *Sourcebook of Criminal Justice Statistics—1993*, Washington: U.S. Government Printing Office, 1994.

———, *Drugs and Crime Facts, 1993*, Washington: U.S. Government Printing Office, 1994.

———, Special Report: *Women in Prison*, Washington: U.S. Government Printing Office, 1994.

———, Special Report: *Murder in Families*, Washington: U.S. Government Printing Office, 1994.

———, Special Report: *Pretrial Release of Federal Felony Defendants*, Washington: U.S. Government Printing Office, 1994.

———, Bulletin: *Prisoners in 1993*, Washington: U.S. Government Printing Office, 1994.

———, Bulletin: *Felony Sentences in the United States*, 1990, Washington: U.S. Government Printing Office, 1994.

———, *State Drug Resources: 1994 National Directory*, Washington: U.S. Government Printing Office, 1994.

———, *Criminal Victimization in the United States, 1992*, Washington: U.S. Government Printing Office, 1994.

———, Special Report: *Prosecuting Criminal Enterprises*, Washington: U.S. Government Printing Office, 1993.

U.S. Department of Justice, Federal Bureau of Investigation *Law Enforcement Officers Killed and Assaulted, 1992*, Washington: U.S. Government Printing Office, 1993.

U.S. Department of Justice, Federal Bureau of Investigation *Killed in the Line of Duty: A Study of Selected Felonious Killings of Law Enforcement Officers*, Washington: U.S. Government Printing Office, 1992.

U.S. Department of Justice International Criminal Police Organization (Interpol), U.S. National Central Bureau *Statistics for Argentina, Canada, Norway, Sweden, Switzerland, Germany, Russia, Czechoslovakia, France, Italy, and Myanmar for 1990*.

U.S. Department of Justice *United States Department of Justice Report to the Deputy Attorney General on the Events at Waco, Texas, February 28 to April 19, 1993*, Redacted Version, Washington, U.S. Government Printing Office, 1993.

U.S. Department of the Treasury, *Report of the Department of the Treasury on the BATF Investigation of Vernon Howell also Known as David Koresh*, Washington: U.S. Government Printing Office, 1993.

MISCELLANEOUS

103d Congress, 2d Session, S. 1882, *A Bill to Amend Title 18, United States Code, to Promote the Safe Use of Guns and to Reduce Gun Violence.*

Help Stop the Real Cop Killers, a "Dear Colleague" letter from Rep. Fortney Pete Stark of California dated May 4, 1994.

INDEX